D0982690

Equilibrium and Macroeconomics

Equilibrium and Macroeconomics

Frank Hahn

The MIT Press
Cambridge, Massachusetts

First MIT Press edition, 1984

First published 1984
Basil Blackwell Publisher Ltd
108 Cowley Road, Oxford OX4 1JF, UK

© Frank Hahn 1984

Library of Congress Cataloging in Publication Data

Hahn, Frank.
Equilibrium and macroeconomics.

Bibliography: p.
Includes index.
1. Economics. 2. Equilibrium (Economics)
3. Macroeconomics. I. Title.
HB171.H23 1984   339.5   84–14418
ISBN 0–262–08149–0

Printed in Great Britain

Contents

PART IV

Acknowledgements

The publishers acknowledge with gratitude permission to reproduce the following texts:
'Expectations and Equilibrium' from the *Economic Journal* (December 1952) 62: 802–19; 'On the Notion of Equilibrium in Economics' (1974) inaugural lecture, Cambridge University, © Cambridge University Press; 'General Equilibrium Theory' in D. Bell and I. Kristol (eds) *The Crisis in Economic Theory'* (1981), © Basic Books, Inc.; 'Some Adjustment Problems' from *Econometrica* (January 1970) 38: 1–17, © The University of Chicago Press; 'Reflections on the Invisible Hand' from *Lloyds Bank Review* (April 1982) 1–21, © the Fred Hirsch Memorial Trust; 'The Winter of our Discontent' from *Economica* (August 1973) 40: 322–30; 'On Some Problems of Proving the Existence of Equilibrium in a Monetary Economy' in F. H. Hahn and F. P. R. Brechling (eds) *The Theory of Interest Rates*, (1965) 126–35, © Macmillan; 'On the Foundations of Monetary Theory' in M. Parkin and A. R. Nobay (eds), *Essays in Modern Economics* (1973) 230–42, published by Longman Group Ltd for the Association of University Teachers of Economics, University of Manchester. 'Keynesian Economics and General Equilibrium Theory: Reflections on Some Current Debates' in G. C. Harcourt (ed.) *The Microeconomic Foundations of Macroeconomics* (1977), © Macmillan; 'On Money and Growth' from the *Journal of Money, Credit and Banking* (May 1969) 1: 175–84, © the Ohio State University Press; 'The Balance of Payments in a Monetary Economy' from the *Review of Economic Studies* (1959) 26: 110–25; 'The Monetary Approach to the Balance of Payments' from the *Journal of International Economics* (1977) 7: 231–49, © North-Holland Publishing Co.; 'Professor Friedman's Views on Money' from

Economica (February 1971) 38: 61–80; 'Monetarism and Economic Theory' from *Economica* (February 1980) 47: 1–17; 'Why I am not a Monetarist' (1982) Political Economy Lecture at Harvard University, 'Economic Theory and Policy' (1982) Shell Lecture delivered at City University, London; 'The neo-Ricardians' from the *Cambridge Journal of Economics* (1982) 6: 353–74 © Academic Press Inc. (London) Ltd.

Introduction

This, with one or two exceptions, is a selection from my less technical papers.[1] A number of them were written for delivery as public lectures and a number of them are polemical. Nevertheless, all the papers are concerned with economic theory. This has sometimes required me to translate mathematics into English. Marshall advised economists to follow this course on all occasions. I am not convinced that this is sound advice. But sound or not as it may be, I find on rereading that I am not outstandingly good at following it. I could have attempted to make changes for this occasion but soon convinced myself that I was at least as likely to make matters worse as I was to improve them. Accordingly some difficulties of certain passages remain as they were but they should all yield up whatever mystery there may be on second reading.

I shall use this introduction to comment on some of the papers with hindsight and I shall allow myself the indulgence of some remarks on my theorising in economics.

I have frequently, and especially in my university, been classified as a neo-classical economist. Since I myself label others (e.g. as 'monetarists') I must not complain, but it is perhaps useful to say in which sense I accept the label. There are three elements in my thinking which may justify it:

(1) I am a reductionist in that I attempt to locate explanations in the actions of individual agents.
(2) In theorising about the agent I look for some axioms of rationality.

[1] In writing this introduction I have had valuable comments from R. Solow, M. Hollis, T. Lawson and J. Thomas. I am also much indebted to T. O'Shaughnessy for comments on the papers, proofreading and preparing the index.

(3) 1 hold that some notion of equilibrium is required and that the study of equilibrium states is useful.

If a historian of thought considers these to be sufficient elements in the making of a neo-classical economist then that is what I am. But I am not sure that this qualifies me on Lord Kaldor's characterisation or that of Marxists and neo-Ricardians.

I am not equally comfortable in my commitment to these three elements. My conviction that (1) is the right approach is pretty strong. For instance, although I have no difficulty with the idea of class I have not been able to give meaning to 'class interest' or the actions of a class until these interests and actions have been located in the individual member. Again I am quite prepared to accept that 'the whole may differ from the sum' but it seems only comprehensible when one starts at the level of the individual. Then, for instance, the theory of externalities can make for comprehension. I know too little of the philosophical literature on 'holistic' explanation to discuss them conclusively. But what I have read and what I have heard argued leaves me faithful to (1).

Element (2) is rather harder. A part of my acceptance of it is its theoretical fruitfulness. Another is the ease in which regular behaviour can be viewed in its light; for instance, by considering the time costs of computation and information gathering, Simon's satisficer does not contradict rationality. By far the largest part is that I know of no satisfactory alternative.

But I am aware of its weakness and of its dangers. In practice an axiom of rationality postulates a complete preordering of alternatives and a choice which is not dominated (in preference) by another available one. but the space of alternatives could be very general indeed and the perceived set of alternatives may not coincide with the actual one. The result is that the theoretical fruitfulness I spoke of requires considerable narrowing of the meaning. For instance, in a great deal of the literature, preferences are only between bundles of goods consumed by the agent and the set of available choices between them is also the perceived one. The danger of the latter is easily seen when one distinguishes goods by date as well as other characteristics and there are not enough futures markets. The danger of the former is that it may leave many actions unexplained; for instance, benevolent actions or envious ones. It also seems as well established as any empirical proposition in economics that the valuation a person places on some goods depends on the actions (and valuations) of others. But the real danger is this: one is tempted to confuse the narrowed formulation with the axiom of rationality itself. For instance, Keynes argued that workers care about relative wages. In the present context this amounts to the claim that the wages of others are arguments of one particular worker's utility function. This however has been condemned as an *ad hoc* procedure. Certainly it is not often considered in the current literature. But it is no more (or less) *ad hoc* than any other postulate one employs to make (2) usable, e.g. that the workers are only interested in their own wage.

So when I accept (2) I mean this: I want the superior 'advantage' of an action to serve as its explanation. As I have argued this cannot be accomplished without an empirically motivated specification of the domain of preferences and of the agent's perception of possibilities. This, of course, is hard because firm empirical knowledge on these matters is lacking. But in many applications it certainly seems straightforward. For instance, whatever the domain it seems safe to say that people will want to buy the cheaper of two identical goods which they regard as identical and that then leads to a theory of the equalisation of their prices. But even here information has to be specified from 'outside'. It is the concrete specification we give to preference theory which may also make it empirically interesting. To revert to the example: if two identical goods continue to sell at a different price then I for one consider that there is something for the theorist to explain. That is because I consider it plausible that people prefer more goods to fewer. In this I can be wrong. I can also be wrong in the acceptance of (2) and as I have already said I hold to it because I can see no other alternative of comparable power and appeal.

On element (3) I shall be brief because two of the papers which follow are concerned with equilibrium. I once again, as in the case of (1), feel rather secure with (3).

The notion of equilibrium is often misused and misunderstood. For instance, in parts of America it is restricted to denote market clearing everywhere under competitive conditions. Thus narrowly used it loses much of its usefulness. The latter, as I say in paper 2, seems to me to be its character as a critical point of an implicit or explicit dynamics. For instance, the competitive equilibrium gains its interest from the postulate that prices must change in all other states of the economy. But there are many other plausible dynamics and the competitive one suffers from having no theory of agents who change prices. But in any event if economic theory has anything to offer on the interaction of market signals and agents' actions then it will need to formulate an equilibrium concept.

But there are also dangers. One of these is that one considers nothing but equilibrium. Professor Lucas (in conversation with Oliver Hart) has in fact argued in favour of proceeding in just this manner but I have not been able to make any kind of sense of his argument. What is plain is that by narrowing our viewpoint in this manner we shall remove a great deal of interest and importance from scrutiny. For instance, imposing the axiom that the economy is at every instant in competitive equilibrium simply removes the actual operation of the invisible hand from the analysis. By postulating that all perceived Pareto-improving moves are instantly carried out all problems of co-ordination between agents are ruled out. Economic theory thus narrowly constructed makes many important discussions impossible.

However, there are also purely theoretical objections. It is only very rarely the case that one has any reason to claim that equilibrium is unique. This robs the axiom of instantaneous market clearing of its power either in comparisons or in the tracing of the evolution of an economy. The multiplicity of equilibria also means that determinateness requires a theory of the economy out of equilibrium. Many of these matters are more fully discussed in some of the papers which follow and in particular in paper 2. In any case my acceptance of (3) does not entail anything as foolish as the claim that all theory should be equilibrium theory.

Besides sketching the three principles that underlie all of my work, I also ought to say briefly how I view theorising in economics.

The short answer is that I view it as an ongoing attempt to bring some order into our thinking about economic phenomena and as the creation of a language in which these attempts can be discussed. I do not expect this activity to reach very many definitive conclusions. I shall call the attempt at orderly thinking the attempt to understand.

It is plain that we can claim understanding of an event without claiming that we can predict it. Geophysicists, for instance, believe that they understand earthquakes but cannot predict them; biologists claim to understand the process of speciation but in general cannot predict the next occurrence. Economists probably agree in their explanation of the recent rise of the dollar but it is doubtful that it could have been predicted with confidence. In all these cases there are very many elements which enter into the explanation of an event. This in turn hinders prediction and so also falsification. In economics it is certainly hard to think of any theory which has been conclusively falsified.

It would, of course, be nice if matters were as Professor Friedman (1953) once thought; I am referring to his 'as if' positivist methodology. But it does not correspond to what economists do or could do. For instance, econometric investigations have been much more useful in providing descriptions of the world which we seek to understand than they have been in confirming or falsifying theories. A striking example of the difficulty of refutation is this. It is now known (Debreu 1974) that any set of continuous homogeneous aggregate demand functions which satisfies Walras' Law can be generated by the behaviour of some rational consumers. Hence consumer theory cannot be falsified by studying such functions. One would have to study the individual consumer (to whom the theory is in any case not meant to apply in practice) or to find evidence of the characteristics of consumers which can then be shown to be not capable of rationalising the excess demand functions. Or one could resort to experiment. It will be agreed that these are tall orders and it is neither surprising nor scandalous that a very old theory has no very firm empirical basis. Yet it would be odd to claim that it does not aid understanding.

This, or course, is at a high level of generality and there are indeed various levels of theorising. Thus, there are theories in which important elements are given quite particular forms. Their justification rests on much more specific empirical hypotheses than that of rationality and it is thus easier to make empirical tests. These special theories are of obvious importance to practical economics and they also aid understanding. But I do not accept that all theory should be special nor do I accept that more general theories are bound to be vacuous tautologies.

If we have only special theories then we do not know where to look next if they are not confirmed. For instance, there is nothing in our understanding of the behaviour of agents which leads us to expect log-linearity in the equations which describe it. Or take a more purely theoretical specialisation. It has been suggested (Kaldor and Mirrlees 1962) that firms are guided in their investment by specifying a 'pay-back period' which any project must meet. This can be consistent with a quite general theory of maximising behaviour. But where do you go next when this special hypothesis is not confirmed, or when it contradicts some other specialisation? Moreover, the more general theory helps in establishing what else would have to be true if the specialisation were true.

One cannot object to bold hypotheses or to empirical hypotheses in economics; indeed, one welcomes them. But the regularities in human behaviour, if such there are, will almost certainly be found at a deeper level than, say, that of the pay-back theory of investment. Such behaviour itself needs to be further understood.

Now the objection to more general theorising is that 'anything can happen' and so the 'axiomatic deductive method' cannot yield empirical insights. This objection is false on two counts. It is true that often many things can be the case in a general theory but not that everything can be. Everyone who knows the textbooks can confirm that; for instance, you cannot get a Pareto improvement in an Arrow–Debreu equilbrium, nor can you observe firms producing under increasing returns. The point is, of course, that although theories like those of Arrow–Debreu are far more general in application than, say, recent three equation models of rational expectations equilibrium, they too are a long way from vacuous generality. For instance, there is perfect competition, a law of property and of contract etc. etc.

The second reason why the objection is false is that it does not understand either axioms or the axiomatic method. Axioms, like special hypotheses, are there to specialise. It is not that they are divorced from experience or observation but rather that they mark the stage beyond which one does not seek to explain. The axiom that firms maximise some function of profits is stated as such because the theorist is not proposing to answer the question why firms should so so. But it is not plucked out of the air or from dreams. It encapsulates an empirical phenomenon which many practical people and economists believe to be the nature of the capitalist. It does so at a more general level than, say, the pay-back theory but it is every bit as empirically motivated.

One of the more astonishing objections sometimes heard against the axiomatic method is that since it proceeds by logical steps from axioms to outcomes it cannot reach empirically relevant conclusions. This is like arguing that the manner in which calculus is derived (from axioms or number systems etc.) makes it impossible to apply to real problems. It seems of things which are logically true that they are also true. Of course, in economics there are contingent truths — contingent on the truth of axioms. But that is precisely why good theorists devote much care and attention to the formulation of these axioms.

Lastly, I want to argue that it is one of the virtues of theories derived from axioms more 'fundamental' than those used in special theory, that they usually do not yield single valued restrictions on the world. Although I have already maintained that it is false that 'anything can be true' it is the case that a number of different things could usually be true. This is a virtue because the economist is thereby restricted from claiming more than he has reasons for claiming. The axioms have summed up what one regards as pretty secure empirical knowledge. The set of outcomes which are possible is simply the reflection of our lack of knowledge. A special theory can usefully narrow them down. But our confidence in the special hypothesis is smaller than in the axioms. A claim of only one outcome should always include the proviso that given our state of knowledge there are also other possibilities.

The most strongly held of my views I have left to the last of these general reflections. It is that neither is there a single best way for understanding in economics nor is it possible to hold any conclusions, other than purely logical deductions, with certainty. I have since my earliest days in the subject been astonished that this view is not widely shared. Indeed, we are encompassed by passionately held beliefs. There are those with burning convictions in the virtues of 'small' models and in the absolute need for 'full' models; in the uselessness of mathematics in economics and in its absolute necessity; in the need to postulate 'market clearing' and in the meaninglessness of this postulate; in rational expectations models and in the madness of such models; in the absolute need for historical and institutional elements and in a purely analytical approach; in short run analysis and in long run analysis; in the uselessness of all theorising and in the uselessness of econometrics and fact collection; in short, in almost anything that has ever been tried. In fact all these 'certainties' and all the 'schools' which they spawn are a sure sign of our ignorance. Perhaps something like this is needed to spur us on but I regard it simply as *trahison des clercs*. For it is obvious to me that we do not possess much certain knowledge about the economic world and that our best chance of gaining more is to try in all sorts of directions and by all sorts of means. This will not be furthered by strident commitments of faith.

Of course, it is not difficult to propose a theory for this state of affairs. But I shall not do so except to note one of its possible elements. Economics like dentistry is expected to be 'useful' (although I have never seen why understanding is not its own reward). In particular it should be a source of advice to those with power to act. Such advice, it is held, must be given with conviction if it is to be sought, leave alone taken. Economists who seek to influence people in power soon come to resemble their patrons. Moreover, they come to feel an urgent need to defend what they proposed through thick and thin. Add this to political beliefs and one is well on the way to explaining some of the zealotry. My own position is that economists are at their most useful when they give an account of the alternative scenarios which the present state of our knowledge allows. (More on all of this will be found in paper 16).

I now turn more directly to the papers in this volume. It can be said of all of them that they exemplify a general equilibrium approach. By this I mean that they do not much utilise Marshallian partial equilibrium theory, and not that I am only concerned with equilibrium leave alone that I always postulate an economy in perfectly competitive equilibrium. No doubt partial analysis can also be very fruitful; I just do not happen to have employed it much.

The first two papers are concerned with a usable and interesting notion of equilibrium. One of these was written long ago (paper 1) whereas the other is more recent. When I was writing the latter I had not reread the former and I am now somewhat gratified to find that they do not contradict each other; indeed, the reader will I hope excuse a certain amount of repetition. I am also more convinced now than I have ever been that it is of high importance that economists should get this matter straight. For not only is there increasing evidence of sloppy thinking brought about by a sloppy equilibrium concept but this failing seems also to have become of some practical importance.

There are, of course, those who believe that definitions and language do not much matter as long as they are consistently employed. This seems to me quite false. Definitions used have an immediate and potent influence on the analysis which follows, and language has enormous potential for good or ill. One need only think of the use of and definition of 'exploitation' to see this. More pertinently the recent meaning given to equilibrium (and disequilibrium) has had quite disastrous effects. Equilibrium is defined as Walrasian competitive equilibrium or a rational expectation Walrasian competitive equilibrium. All other states are said to be in disequilibrium. But, as I have already noted (and argue at length in paper 2), the motivation of the definition is largely that disequilibrium states cannot last (the implicit dynamics of the definition). Hence it is concluded that only Walrasian rational expectations equilibria can have any permanence which I hope will be recognised as a substantial claim coming purely from the definition. The further step that is then taken is to claim that the equilibria are stable. But that in the literature is pure assertion and I am at a loss to understand why it should have been so widely adopted as an axiom.

A consequence of all of this has been, for instance, to designate all economic states with Keynesian features (e.g. involuntary unemployment) as disequilibria with the further implication that they will, if they can exist at all, also soon disappear. Those who have been somewhat more sympathetic to Keynes and who have been attempting to give his theory more modern expression have none the less quite supinely agreed to having their endeavours called 'disequilibrium economics'. They have also much to their cost gone along with the vacuous proposition that there could be no Keynesian problems if prices and wages were 'flexible' when this in turn is translated to mean 'if prices and wages at all times cleared all Walrasian markets'.Tautologies are here given instrumental interpretations. These are all examples which show that definitions and language matter profoundly. They are rather fully discussed in papers 14 and 15.

My own approach discussed in the two equilibrium papers is to take the use which we shall want to make of the equilibrium concept into account when formulating it. That use is to make a distinction between economic states which cannot last and those for which there is no theoretical reason to expect a change. I therefore think of equilibrium states as those in which agents learn nothing new. They therefore have a lasting policy which gives their actions as a map from relevant variables. Sometimes I refer to this policy as routine behaviour, an idea which I must have got from Schumpeter. The claim I make for this conceptualisation is based not on its generality but rather on the fact that it accurately captures the use we all want to make of equilibrium and so avoids some of the nonsense I have already described. For instance, there could be an equilibrium with rigid money wages and unemployment if none of the designated agents find it, in their perceived circumstances, advantageous to make any change. To clinch this should have nothing to do with any Walrasian axioms and everything to do with a theory of rational agents, their information and their learning.

There is one matter which the two equilibrium papers do not treat in any detail. That is the axiom of continuous 'market clearing'. No one had seriously proposed it at the time. I am not sure that it is worth much discussion even now especially in its perfectly competitive form. It has been much confused with another axiom to the effect that at any moment agents do what they prefer to do. To use that axiom for present purposes one needs to specify also what agents can do. For instance, if an unemployed worker cannot accept a lower wage without union agreement or without social action, and if an employer cannot lower the offered wage without courting a costly strike then everybody may be doing what they prefer and yet the offers to work at the current wage can exceed the demand for such work. There are many far less drastic examples of the same phenomenon. The most superficial acquaintance with game theory is enough to convince one that competitive instantaneous market clearing is not an axiom one wants to adopt. That, of course, does *not* mean that it may not be interesting to study the consequences of imposing such clearing as an assumption. What one must, however, not do is to claim that it comes from a deep 'universals' of economics or that there are profound philosophical reasons for its employment.

Indeed, the next two papers (3 and 4) are concerned with a discussion of theory when that assumption is made. Of course, I consider its realism and relevance but on the whole I am largely concerned with difficulties internal to the theory. Some of these are technical: for instance, those arising from multiple equilibria, or from the idea of a firm when assumptions exclude set-up costs. Others are concerned with the fact that certain important phenomena seem to escape the theory. On the whole my attitude is this: if we did not have the Arrow–Debreu machinery there would be an urgent need to invent it because it gives us the best base camp for sallies into new territory. On the other hand it *is* only a base camp. The rational expectations perfectly competitive economy is indeed a camp higher up but not much. It is, I argue, difficult to take it seriously, for instance as a basis for policy conclusions. (I return to all of this in paper 5.)

In paper 4 I consider some of the difficulties with the implicit dynamics which underlies the Walrasian equilibrium notion. It is somewhat technical in parts. The main conclusion is rather pessimistic: we have no good reason to suppose that there are forces which lead the economy to equilibrium. By that I mean that we have no good theory. I examine two examples in some detail. In retrospect I think I should have paid more attention to the 'practical' argument that we seem to live in an economy which on the whole is orderly. It will be recalled that Keynes argued that violently unstable models are for that reason bad models. No doubt there is some force in this view although it is so imprecise as to make it unclear what exactly is supposed to be the case. I should now want to say that I am agnostic on the general tenor of the practical claim although I lean in the direction of accepting it in some formulation. However, this does not at all affect the position I took; if indeed there is order we do not now understand how it is brought about. What we know is that in some circumstances orderly states (equilibria) are possible. But is it a mistake to believe that this provides an answer to the question of how order is imposed.

The last paper on this general topic (paper 6) is a review of Kornai's *Anti-Equilibrium*. I am not sure that I adequately conveyed my view that this is an interesting and stimulating book and I may well have been too eager to defend what Kornai attacked. I am now also somewhat more ready to grant that equilibrium may be the wrong, or at least a dangerous, benchmark. Certainly Kornai's 'systems' approach cannot be dismissed. But I confess that it still strikes me as both too difficult and too ineffable. Of course, it is descriptively superior to equilibrium but that I still hold need not be a decisive consideration when building theory. Moreover, I also continue to believe that Kornai greatly underestimated the theoretical richness of the orthodox approach and that he was wrong in his strictures on the axiomatic method. But there is something here to think and argue about and I hope that the paper will not give the impression that I regard matters as settled.

The next four papers are concerned with monetary theory and they are somewhat more academic than the preceding ones. A great deal of work continues in this field (for instance, recently there were published three important books by Grandmont 1983 and Gale 1982, 1983), and some of my puzzles have been resolved and others have arisen. My own starting point was deeply traditional: the difficulty of making Arrow–Debreu serve as a model of a monetary economy. I examined some minimal changes which seemed required in the Arrow–Debreu approach. Paper 8 is a summary and discussion of these.

Patinkin's work (1956) was the most important theoretical formulation of monetary theory when paper 7 was written. It had not, in its formal account, given a formulation of the economy which gave money 'something to do'. Hence it was easy for me to show that if there existed an equilibrium in which money had a positive exchange value then there are also existed one in which it was worthless. The exercise confirmed my long standing view that quite abstract existence theorems can teach us a lot of economics or at least a lot about the models which we use. For instance, in this instance it clearly demonstrated the mistake of regarding a competitive model of the usual kind but without money as a 'barter' model. For the useful functions money performs have simply been assumed performed without it. It alerts one to what I admit should have been obvious and shows that the institution of money can only be 'neutral' if the institution itself has no explanation. There has been much subsequent work on this matter (Grandmont 1983, Gale 1982, 1983 etc.). But problems remain: for instance, a precise formulation of the notion of liquidity and of transaction technologies.

Paper 10 is an exercise in the methodology of the previous papers in the context of simple one sector growth models. It is also concerned with Tobin's view that money in these models was not 'neutral'. I argue that his result depended partly on the manner in which money injections ensured that agents earned more than they produced. But I also discuss the splendid work of Diamond (1965) and Cass and Yaari (1966) which in turn have their origin in Samuelson (1958). The idea is to use money to satisfy asset hunger when otherwise it would lead to an excess of real capital (i.e. more than warranted by the 'golden rule'). In this work money's sole role is that of another asset and this seems to vitiate the usefulness of this line of argument when monetary theory is at issue. I have not found anything in this particular paper which I should change now.

Paper 9 was written for a conference and that too recent for me to wish to make alterations. If I had to highlight anything in it I should wish to do so for my remarks on wages and on Say's Law. Keynes, as far as I read him, never assumed 'fixed' money wages or 'downwardly rigid' money wages. After all that was offered as the explanation of unemployment by the 'classics'. What Keynes argued was that policy could establish more directly and more certainly what it was claimed 'flexible' money wages could do. Indeed, flexibile money wages by bringing uncertainty to the real value of debt and money could have very bad consequences indeed. I have already noted above that nowadays these Keynesian arguments are not demonstrated as wrong; they are simply assumed away. Of course, money wages may in fact be downwardly rigid or slow to change. Both the facts and theory of money wage behaviour are unsettled.

On Say's Law, Keynes and Keynesians were sometimes confused as indeed some people now are about Walras' Law. The latter is an accounting identity directly derivable from budget constraints. It is an identity in plans. Say's Law is a special form of this identity when there are no non-produced goods (including money). It is not true in an economy with non-produced goods that an excess supply of labour corresponds to an excess demand for goods produced with labour. In fact one would do well to forget about Say's Law and to concentrate on the real issue: how excess supplies and demands which are in people's heads are communicated to others. Clower (1965) took the first important step here. But as I have already argued this has not prevented much current economic theorising from neglecting this matter altogether. In a real sense Keynesian economics is about co-ordination failure which leads to outcomes which can be Pareto improved. These failures may be intrinsic to the economy as they are intrinsic to the prisoners' dilemma. It is all of this that needs urgent attention and not accounting identities.

The next four papers are polemical and concerned with 'monetarism' and the new macroeconomics. I have to confess that I have been scandalised by this development of our subject. That is because it ignores the richness of its own basic theoretical structure and so the variety of conclusions it can yield, because it is dogmatic and vastly overblown and lastly because it has propounded a crude and unconvincing empiricism to cut short theoretical argument. I do not hold the view that all the new macroeconomic propositions are false but I consider them as largely unargued and unproven. There are, of course, people with great intuitive gifts. Keynes probably would have claimed them – but the fruits of that gift must stand the test of normal argument and enquiry if they are to be accepted. It is vastly premature to regard the new macroeconomists as having passed such a test successfully.

Of course, a good deal of empirical work is undertaken. There are now many three equation log-linear models of the economy which have gone through a number of statistical hoops. There is also the massive work or Friedman and Schwartz (1982). All this empirical work is under debate by empirical workers and highly controversial. Put at its lowest, it would be unwise to accept it as at all conclusive. Equally important is the difficulty of accepting such evidence without understanding it. This is one of the reasons why many do not accept that rather massive evidence of miracles. In any event although it may be a failing in the papers that they do not explicitly discuss this empirical work I am convinced that on this issue it does not rule what I have to say out of court.

Paper 13 was written as a review article of Professor Friedman's book *The Optimum Quantity of Money*. On one matter my discussion there can be somewhat updated. That concerns my criticism of Friedman,s application of traditional Pareto-efficiency arguments to an economy (a monetary one) for which they are not self-evidently appropriate. I have already remarked that a monetary economy needs to have certain special features such as transaction costs and/or missing markets – features which do not appear in the classical theorems of welfare economics. These questions have since been further investigated by Grandmont (1983) and Bewley (1980). The former explicitly introduced a 'Clower constraint' into the formal model, and the latter gave proper attention to the possibility of self-insurance afforded by money balances. The Grandmont work lends some support to Friedman's theory which is not surprising since the monetary transactions constraint is the only feature distinguishing the monetary from classical economics. Bewley's results rather reinforce the line which I took in my review. Clearly when contingent markets are missing we cannot in the first instance expect more than constrained Pareto efficiency and the desirability of interest paying money is in doubt. Bewley shows that infinitely lived agents can to a certain extent use money balances to substitute for the missing contingent markets. If this could be done perfectly then Friedman's results would again be of interest. But that it appears may be impossible with a finite money stock. It would seem that I was right in arguing that traditional welfare theorems cannot just be used without further analysis in a monetary economy.

But I must confess that important as this new work is, it does not seem to me to go far enough in dealing with the special features of a monetary economy. For instance, borrowing and lending involve transaction costs (Baumol 1952) in the form of brokerage. The optimum quantity of money argument leads one to conclude that all the resources represented by these costs could be saved by satiating agents in money balances. That would then yield an economy without borrowing or lending. But such an economy would lose a signal — the price of loans — and this signal may be required for a fully revealing equilibrium in a world of asymmetric information. Or again there is the much neglected role of inventories. Satiation in money balances would imply that agents feel themselves to be adequately insured against collective (correlated) risks. This in turn has implications for the volume of inventories and so there may be real costs of satiation. Lastly, there is an important question quite undiscussed in the literature. Money balances are liquid in the sense that agents can respond more rapidly to circumstances when they hold relatively more money. Hence money balances are likely to be important for the lag structure of any dynamic theory and hence for stability analysis. The welfare economics of stability does not exist but it seems required here.

All of this illustrates my general contention that there is more to economic theory than meets the eye of the simple modeller. None the less on the optimum quantity of money Friedman and his successors have theorised clearly and seriously. The same cannot be said when it comes to the quantity equation and money in macroeconomics generally. Papers 14 and 15 are concerned with these perhaps more important matters.

I do not wish to repeat the arguments here except to lend emphasis to the importance which I attach to multiple equilibria.

Even in a world where all relevant economic signals are prices, multiple equilibria seem endemic once the economy is recognised as sequential. Brock and Scheinkman (1980) and Hahn (1982) have all drawn attention to the existence of a continuum of rational expectations equilibria in a perfectly competitive economy with overlapping generations. In models of infinitely lived agents it is also not the case that equilibrium is unique and again a continuum of equilibria is quite usual. Quite recently, once again in the context of an overlapping generations model, Grandmont (1983) has demonstrated the existence of infinitely many rational expectations equilibrium cycles without any stochastic elements. All this must surely be sufficient to cause a theoretical economist to take breath before he deduces, from the axiom of 'no money illusion', that a k-fold change in the money stock if fully anticipated will be accompanied by a k-fold rise in money wages and prices.

But matters are even more interesting than these results when one allows oneself the luxury of some realism. The evidence that important parts of the economy are not perfectly competitive is stronger than any econometric result ever proposed. Think of competitive advertising, cartels, price wars – or indeed of any stock exchange report. The device of ignoring this on 'as if' grounds has nothing to recommend it. Now, economies which are not perfectly competitive have many more economic signals of relevance; agents know too little when they only know prices. Equally importantly such economies exhibit intrinsic externalities (Makowski 1980). The actions of any one agent affect others (which is not the case in a non-atomic economy, which is the main foundation of perfect competition). Externalities are not only traditionally the occasion for policy but they also greatly strengthen the argument that multiple equilibria are endemic.

Some of these arguments will be found more fully in papers 14 and 15. Here I am only concerned with their significance. One best sees that by analogy with game theory. In that we are all familiar with the possibility of many Nash equilibria and of some of them being Pareto inefficient. The concept of such equilibria displays the externality I mentioned: agents have chosen their best strategy given the strategies of others. Keynes at least partly was after such situations when he talked of 'boot-strap' equilibria. But had he written twenty years later he would surely have accepted the summary of one of his main contentions, namely that there were co-operative equilibria which Pareto dominate the non-co-operative outcome of a market economy. The theory that the latter can have bad or unsatisfactory equi-libria is at the centre of Keynes. Government policy can here be considered as a kind of surrogate for co-operation – for internalising the intrinsic externalities. It can also be considered as a device to induce the economy to pick one equilibrium rather than another. All this can be properly studied and needs further study. The general argument will be further strengthened if we admit at least that element of increasing returns connected with set-up costs (Weitzman 1982). Diamond (1984) has given a nice example of the role of externalities in Keynesian theory by considering the effect of the search decision of the agents on the trade op-portunities of others.

Such intemperance of language as will be found in my papers on these matters is caused by the literature I discuss assuming all these problems away and reaching the triumphant conclusion that Keynesian economics is dead. I have to admit that even in retrospect I do not regret the expressions of my dismay.

Paper 12 is a review article of *The Monetary Approach to the Balance of Payments* (Frenkel and Johnson 1976). Its main contribution, as I say there, is that it insists on a proper stock—flow analysis. Indeed, that is one of the main contributions of the new macroeconomics in general. A non-zero balance of payments has its counterpart in changes in asset stocks, and theory had neglected this far too long. In the companion paper (paper 11) I had taken the first steps in that direction but I do not now think that they were big enough. Both my paper and the essays in the book lack a proper model of a monetary economy and both ignore far too much. What I now find particularly objectionable is that the stories all start from economies in Walrasian equilibrium. I was surprised to find that in the book it was felt worth while to subject these primitive theories to empirical tests. Once again I objected and still object to theories in which there is a tight link between the money stock and the price level. (To treat money wages as one would the price of fish struck me as particularly bizarre.) In short the paper is an example of my general critique of monetarist models.

The last paper, on the neo-Ricardians, is concerned with altogether different matters. My impression is that the whole sorry episode is all but over, although only the other day I found an eminent colleague holding the view that 'double switching disproves marginal productivity theory'. I reprint it because it may still do some good and as an illustration that I am as prepared to defend pure neo-classical theory from false attack as I am to argue for its inadequacy for Keynes. Moreover the case of the neo-Ricardians is a warning to all of us how piety (to Marx and Ricardo) and other 'non-scientific' motives can cause havoc.

As I say in the paper, I do not consider Sraffa to be mainly responsible for the ensuing mess. His book was both careful and completely honest. He was wrong to link the general impossibility of perfect capital aggregation with marginal productivity theory but he had aggregate 'parables' in mind. In all other respects the book (whose publication was very much delayed) contained little that was new or objectionable to practitioners of linear economic models. What followed I cannot explain. Sraffa was hailed as showing that neo-classical economics lacked a logical foundation, indeed was illogical. He had, so it was announced, shown distribution to be 'logically prior' to the determination of prices and (by the factor—price frontier) demonstrated the importance of class conflict. And so on. I confess that one of my motives for doing battle was that all of this was called 'Cambridge economics'.

And this is the point where I shall end on a personal note. In showing that neo-classical economics has nothing to fear from the neo-Ricardians I became in their eyes a dyed-in-the-wood neo-classical who considered Arrow—Debreu adequate for all of economics. I fear that, in just the same way, my dissatisfaction with the new macroeconomics will be regarded as a sign that I am an old Keynesian. In truth I am none of these things: 'any school of thought which would accept me I should not care to join.' On the final truths of economics I am completely agnostic. Until such final truth is unequivocably revealed I hold all coherent theorising as worthy of attention and respect.

There is one last matter which belongs to this introduction. Looking through the papers it is clear that in the more popular ones the reader will encounter a certain amount of repetition. For instance, he will find that I have explained the Arrow—Debreu economy on several occasions. This could have been avoided in this reprinting but only at the cost of losing the coherence of some of the essays. I have, therefore, allowed it to remain and I hope the reader will just skip such repetition when he comes across it without blaming me.

REFERENCES

Baumol, W. 1952. The transaction demand for cash: an inventory theoretic approach, *Quarterly Journal of Economics*, November
Bewley, R. 1980. The optimum quantity of money in J. Kareken and N. Wallace (eds) *Models of Monetary Economics*, Federal Reserve Bank of Minneapolis, Minneapolis
Brock, W. and Scheinkman, J. 1980. 'Some Remarks on Monetary Policy in an Overlapping Generations Model', in J. Kareken and N. Wallace (eds) *Models of Monetary Economics*, Federal Reserve Banks of Minneapolis, Minneapolis
Cass, D. and Yaari, M. 1966. A re-examination of the pure consumption loan model, *Journal of Political Economy*
Clower, R. 1965. The Keynesian counterrevolution: a theoretical appraisal

in F. H. Hahn and F. Brechling (eds) *The Theory of Interest Rates*, Macmillan

Debreu, G. 1974. Excess demand functions, *Journal of Mathematical Economics*, March

Diamond, P. A. 1965. National debt in a neo-classical model, *American Economic Review*, December

Diamond, P. A. 1984. Money in search equilibirum, *Econometrica*, January

Frenkel, J. A. and Johnson, H. G. (eds) 1976. *The Monetary Approach to the Balance of Payments*, University of Toronto Press

Friedman, M. 1953. The methodology of positive economics in *Essays in Positive Economics*, Chicago

Friedman, M. and Schwartz, A. 1982. *Monetary Trends in the United States and the United Kingdom: Their relation to incomes, prices and interest rates 1867–1975*, University of Chicago Press, Chicago

Gale, D. 1982. *Money in Equilibrium*, Nisbet and Cambridge University Press

Gale, D. 1983. *Money in Disequilibrium*, Nisbet and Cambridge University Press

Grandmont, J. M. 1983. *Money and Value*, Nisbet and Cambridge University Press

Grandmont, J. M. 1983. On endogenous competitive business cycles, mimeo CEPREMAP

Hahn, F. H. 1982. *Money and Inflation*, Basil Blackwell, Oxford

Kaldor, N. and Mirrlees, J. A. 1962. A new model of economic growth, *Review of Economic Studies*, June

Makowski, L. 1980. A characterisation of perfectly competitive economies with production, *Journal of Economic Theory*, April

Patinkin, D. 1956. *Money, Interest and Prices*, Row, Peterson and Co., Evanston, Illinois

Samuelson, P. A. 1958. An exact consumption-loan model of interest with and without the social contrivance of money, *Journal of Political Economy*

Weitzman, M. 1982. Increasing returns and the foundations of unemployment theory, *Economic Journal*, December

Part I

1

Expectations and Equilibrium

One of the most important developments in economic theory in recent times has been the growth of economic dynamics, that is, to quote Samuelson, the construction of economic models in which 'variables at different points in time' are involved in an 'essential' way (Samuelson 1947, p. 314). Rudimentary though these models still are and unsatisfactory as some of the assumptions dictated by the available techniques must be judged to be, there is no doubt that considerable progress has been made and new insights gained. For various reasons, however, recent dynamic theories, especially in the field of macroeconomics, have been characterised by a great deal of formal mathematics and relatively little economics, and nowhere is this more true than in the discussion of dynamic equilibrium and dynamic stability conditions.

Thus, while a great deal has been written on the conditions a dynamic system must fulfil in order that it should exhibit some form of regular motion or that it should approach equilibrium, hardly anything has been said about the particular economic assumptions which must be made to allow us to set up any particular dynamic system. Especially the role of expectations in such models, once the hallmark of dynamic theory, has been almost entirely neglected. It is the purpose of this paper to examine the type of expectations which must be postulated in order for dynamic equilibrium (of which static equilibrium is the special case) to be possible.

Since, however, recent writings on this topic seem to have been based on definitions of equilibrium other than the one customary in economic analysis for the last seventy years, the question of definition must first be examined. Much of what we have to say is as old as, say, the oldest living Swede and must go by the name of old wine in slightly new bottles. Nevertheless, recent writings on the topic of dynamic equilibrium, as we hope to show, appear to have been written without the help of a draught of that old wine, and that must be the justification for the rather lengthy discourse that follows.

The plan of the paper is as follows. In the first section we discuss what we believe to be the distinguishing features of an equilibrium situation. Next we turn to a formal discussion of the conditions of general dynamic equilibrium. The third section is devoted to a criticism in the light of what has gone before of some multiplier models, Harrod's recent writings on the warranted rate of growth, the concept of dynamic stability of Samuelson and Metzler and lastly Professor Samuelson's dislike of 'initial conditions.' The last section is a brief restatement of the results when the simplifying assumption of single valued expectations is discarded.

I

It is assumed that a producer must commit resources, in advance of the sale of output attributable to these commitments. The amount and form of the resources committed at any one moment of time will then depend on the producer's expectations of future demand and prices. We now also assume that the outputs and prices of all other producers remain constant throughout.

Making the above assumption, we can say that a producer's expectations as to future sales and prices will depend on his past sales and prices, since these are the only (variable) data available on which to base estimates concerning future events. We will call the function relating expected events to past events the expectation function of the producer. We also assume that expectations are single valued and that expected sales and prices are equal to actual production and actual prices charged.

Now when we speak of the long run equilibrium of a producer, what we have in mind is a situation such that the producer's behaviour through time will remain the same. It is the invariance of behaviour over a certain period which gives significance to the concept of equilibrium. We wish to generalise this concept of invariance to include the case of moving equilibrium. Suppose that as in the Swedish 'disequilibrium method' the producer always announces his price in advance and then sticks to it. Suppose, further, that the demand curve for the producer's output (at any given price) varies not in a random but in a systematic way over time. Then there exists an expectation function such that supply forthcoming at any announced price in any period is exactly taken off the market at that price. The invariance of equilibrium is not now to be found in a constant output and constant prices as in the stationary case, nor yet again in a constant rate of change of output and/or prices, but in the constancy of the form of the expectation function. Constant output or a constant rate of growth of output appear as special cases.

What the constancy of the expectation function indicates is that the method of arriving at expected (planned) sales and output, on the basis of past sales etc., remains unchanged. As long as the variations in demand are systematic and not random it is possible (it should be noted that we do *not* maintain that this actually happens) to learn by experience and thus to evolve a 'rule of thumb' or a mode of routine behaviour which will ensure that the output forthcoming at the planned price is exactly sold. If variations in demand are random, then there is no way for the producer of acquiring a method of forecasting which will ensure coincidence of expected and actual sales at every moment of time.

The existence of equilibrium through time therefore presupposes the existence of an expectation function of constant form or, what comes to the same thing, a form of routine behaviour on the part of the entrepreneur (for an excellent discussion of the distinction between routine behaviour and decisions proper see Katona, 1951). It is interesting to note that this implies that the recent writings of Shackle (1949, especially chapter VI), according to which each event experienced by the entrepreneur is in some sense unique, seems to apply to situations of disequilibrium only. Equilibrium always entails the repetition of some particular experiences, although these experiences need not be simple; for instance, the time path of any given variable need not be simple!

We have said that the significance of equilibrium lies in the invariance of behaviour when the latter is defined in a particular way. But in our definition of equilibrium we have required the expectation function to be not only of constant but also of particular form, namely such that planned sales and actual sales coincide at the planned price. It might now be argued that if individuals react to disappointed expectations in a given constant way, we would have invariant behaviour without requiring the fulfilment of expectations. If that were so, then the question of what process to label an equilibrium process would indeed, as Professor Samuelson suggests, be a purely verbal one (Samuelson 1947, p. 330). For if a definite behaviour pattern can be established for all situations, nothing is gained by labelling any particular situation an equilibrium situation.

The question then is: how does routine behaviour differ from decisions proper, and is routine behaviour compatible with a situation in which expectations are continuously being disappointed? Let us imagine a situation where the producer's expected sales fell short of actual sales by X units, and let us suppose that this caused him to plan to double his sales in the next period. It will, I think, be agreed that if in the next period he again experiences an excess demand of X units there is not reason to suppose that he will again plan to double his sales – the fact that this mode of behaviour has already been tried and found wanting will have an effect on his decisions today. Therefore the disappointment of expectations – the excess demand of any one period – will enter into his expectation function in a different way from the disappointment of any other period, which is only another way of saying that the producer is accumulating new experiences.

As long as behaviour is not routine behaviour and decisions have to be taken, all past experiences of the producer from the commencement of his career are relevant to his decisions. (Who, for instance, could deny that the experiences of the 1930s still exert some influence on producer's expectations, and that this influence would be very great at the danger of a falling off in demand?) That means that the order of, say, the difference equation representing the expectation function will be continuously increasing as new experiences are accumulated. It is *not* legitimate to assume that as experiences recede into the past their influence can be neglected, for it may well be that a relatively recent experience exerts relatively little influence, whereas one in the more distant past exerts a strong influence because it was particularly vivid. When expectations are being disappointed there is no way of defining behaviour by saying that a producer will act in the same given way in the same situation, for the simple reason that the same situation can never occur twice, since the experience of the first situation must always enter as a new parameter into the second situation. Only when behaviour is routine behaviour is it sensible to talk of a 'behaviour pattern' or of 'consistent behaviour'.

There is therefore a difference in kind between equilibrium processes where behaviour is routine and non-equilbrium processes where it is not. This has some bearing on the setting up of dynamic models, which are not equilibrium models in the sense that expectations are being fulfilled. Given available mathematical techniques, all these models must be relatively simple, and in fact all of them at present assume what we have called routine behaviour. Now it may be sensible to imagine producers as changing routine behaviour at discrete time intervals rather than as continuously taking new decisions. A routine is tried for a certain period of time and if found inappropriate replaced by another one. In that sense, then, non-equilibrium dynamic models of the type known to us must be short period models, that is the equations must be taken to hold for certain discrete periods of time only. From this, it follows that it is not legitimate to use such models to define long period moving equilibria, for unless expectations are being fulfilled, a new model will have to be set up. The truth of this is illustrated in a later section, where reference is made to some recent writings on this topic.

II

We now turn to a discussion of some of the conditions a general dynamic equilibrium model must fulfil.[1]

To do this we shall introduce a 'notional' system which is constructed on the assumption that all expectations are fulfilled. (The procedure which we adopt here is, as will be seen, similar to Ragnar Frisch's 'barring process', 1936.) The advantage of such a system, as will be seen, is that all its coefficients are determined by either technical conditions or 'tastes' and are independent of any expectational elements.

If we assume that all expectations have been fulfilled in the past so that no 'backlogs' have to be made good, current demand for inputs by 'firms' will depend on: (1) their economic horizon, (2) the length of various production lags, (3) their expected future sales, and (4) the coefficients of production. We can regard (1), (2) and (4) as given. Current demand for inputs is thus a function of expected future sales. (We assume throughout that this function is linear.) Consumers' demand may be regarded as a function of the income they expect to earn in the current period. If, now, in this model all expectations are fulfilled, expected sales equal actual

---

[1] In the writing of this section I have greatly benefited from discussions with W. M. Gorman, who in fact suggested the use of the 'notional system' as an alternative to an earlier, clumsier construction of my own.

sales, and supply is equal to demand in each sector. The path of income through time is thus fully determined by the 'lag structure' and the technical coefficients. What the system of equations tells us is how incomes must evolve through time if all expectations are to be fulfilled. We can then deduce from this what the form of the expectation functions must be if equilibrium is to be possible.

In the next section such a system is discussed in detail; here we may give a simple and familiar example. Let us assume that expectations have been fulfilled in the past, and that the desired stock of capital is equal to the actual stock. Let the production lag be one period and the economic horizon also one period. Then current demand for investment depends on the expected increase in sales in the next period. The demand for consumption goods depends on the income expected in the current period by consumers. We have:

$$D_t = v(S_{t+1}{}^e - S_t^e) + cY_t^e \qquad (1.1)$$

where D_t is agregate total demand in period t, S_{t+1}^e, S_t^e are expected sales in period $(t + 1)$ and t, Y_t^e is expected consumer income, and v and c are coefficients relating expected changes in sales to current investment demand and expected income to current demand for consumption goods. If all expectations are fulfilled, then there is no distinction between demand, supply and income (Y_t). We can then, on this assumption, rewrite equation (1.1) as

$$Y_t = v(Y_{t+1} - Y_t) + cY_t \qquad (1.2)$$

to yield the well known solution

$$Y_t = \left(1 + \frac{1-c}{v}\right)^t Y_0 \qquad (1.3)$$

Equation (1.3) then tells us at what rate incomes must expand if all expectations are to be fulfilled continuously. Equation (1.3) is a notional system, since it can be set up only on the assumption that expectations are fulfilled. If the expectation functions do not conform with equation(1.3), then incomes will not expand at the rate shown by the equation. It is in this sense that the writer has interpreted Harrod's warranted rate of growth (see later).

But let us extend the analysis a little farther. Decisions are taken by a multitude of individuals. The first requirement for the existence of expectation functions compatible with the notional system is that expectations should be consistent in the sense that there are conceivable actual events which would allow all expectations to be fulfilled simultaneously.

Consider a system of expectation equations in matrix notation:

$$Y_t^e = EY_{t-1} \tag{1.4}$$

where Y_t^e is a column matrix of n elements such as $_i y_t^e$, which is the income expected for period t by the ith sector in period $(t-1)$. Y_{t-1} is a column matrix of n elements such as $_i y_{t-1}$, which is the actual income of sector i in period $(t-1)$. E may be a diagonal matrix if the expected income of any one sector depends only on its own past income, or it may be a square matrix with no zero elements if the expected income of any one sector depends on the past incomes of all sectors, or it may have any other desired form. Its typical element e_{ij} is the coefficient relating the past income of sector j to the income expected by sector i.

If now expectations are to be consistent in the sense defined above, then by a well known theorem the rank of E must be the same as the rank of the augmented matrix

$$F = [E \mid Y_t^e] \tag{1.5}$$

This condition will always be fulfilled if the rank of E is n, that is if all the expectation equations are linearly independent. But suppose we had a situation such that the expectations of the first $(n-1)$ sectors were independent of the past income of the nth sector, whereas the latter's expectations depended only on the past incomes of the first $(n-1)$ sectors. Then equation (1.4) would be over-determined unless it is possible to eliminate one equation. If that is not possible, then the rank of E is $(n-1)$, whereas that of F is n, and expectations would be inconsistent. In order that expectations of this sort be consistent, it is necessary that the value of past incomes is such as to enable us to eliminate one of the equations. There are a number of other ways in which inconsistent expectations (in the sense defined) may arise. It is clear that such inconsistency excludes the possibility of equilibrium, quite independently of the form of the notional system.

But let us now assume that such inconsistency is absent. The second question now to be answered is, what conditions must be fulfilled if actual events and expected events are to coincide continuously?

If they do coincide continuously, then equation (1.4) can be treated as an ordinary system of difference equations, since expected and actual events are by assumption always the same and every past event was an expected event. But if that is to be possible, then the evolution of the system (1.4) must be the same as that of the notional system which does not involve any expectation coefficients but only technical and 'taste' coefficients. Let this notional system be represented by:[2]

$$\overline{Y}_t = N\overline{Y}_{t-1} \tag{1.6}$$

It will be clear that if the expectation system (1.4) is to be compatible with the continuous fulfilment of expectations, the matrices E and N will have to be related in a certain way. Given that the initial conditions in equations (1.6) and (1.4) are the same, we require that first

$$\overline{Y}_t - Y_t^e = [N - E] \, Y_0 = 0$$

$$\therefore \ |N - E| = 0 \text{ for some } {}_iy_0 \neq 0 \tag{1.7}$$

But the notional and expected values must coincide throughout; hence secondly,

$$\overline{Y}_{t+1} - Y_{t+1}{}^e = [N^2 - E^2] \, Y_0$$

$$= [N + E] \, [N - E] \, Y_0 - [NE - EN] \, Y_0 = 0 \tag{1.8}$$

By equation (1.7)

$$[EN - NE] \, Y_0 = 0$$

$$\therefore \ |EN - NE| = 0 \tag{1.9}$$

When equations (1.7) and (1.9) hold then the reader can easily satisfy himself that the notional and expectational values will

---

[2] It should be noted that it is normally possible to transform a matrix equation involving n lags into one involving one lag only. This, however, would affect our analysis under equation (1.7) and (1.9). See Samuelson 1947, pp. 419 *et seq.*

coincide throughout, since any expression such as $[N^n - E^n]$ can be factorised in terms of equations (1.7) and 1.9).

To make the implications of the above clearer and to demonstrate to what use the analysis can be put, let us assume that E is diagonal and that N is a square matrix with all off-diagonal elements not equal to zero. It will be clear that condition (1.9) can be fulfilled only if all the elements in E are the same ($e_{ii} = e_{jj} = \ldots = e_{nn}$). Moreover, equation (1.7) tells us that e_{ii} must be one of the latent roots of N. When these two conditions are fulfilled (and the initial conditions coincide), then expected and notional values will coincide. We can thus lay down the proposition that if expectations of all sectors depend only on their own past income, then all the expectation coefficients must be the same if equilibrium is to be possible, and these coefficients must equal one of the latent roots of the national matrix.

It should now be noted that the expectational equations in no way determine the equilibrium path of the system. The latter is fully determined by the technical coefficients and lags. Our analysis tells us what type of expectation systems are compatible and what type are not, with equilibrium through time.

These are some of the basic requirements for dynamic equilibrium to be possible. Clearly the technical coefficients of the notional system may be changing, and this would have to be taken into account in any moderately sophisticated model. But once we know how these coefficients are changing, the equilibrium paths of incomes could again be found. All this is, of course, very formal indeed, and yet the analysis may be of some interest, not only because a number of economists have written on the topic of dynamic equilibrium without once writing the word 'expectations', but also because the approach outlined may enable us to say which of the conditions of dynamic equilibrium are likely to be fulfilled in the real world. In other words, an equilibrium model may be useful if for no other reason than that it can possibly tell us why equilibrium is unlikely.

There is also another use to which the analysis can be put. It is clear that our equilibrium path places no restrictions as such on the equilibrium rates of growth — for instance, they need not be constant. If, then, the system yields oscillatory growth of output, we would have a model of fluctuations from which the element of 'wrong' expectations has been excluded. It would, in other words, have isolated the purely technical elements (coefficients of production, production lags, tastes) making for oscillations, from any expectational elements. In that sense it would be a 'pure' model of the cycle, for it would show how oscillations occur even when it is assumed that everyone anticipates the future correctly.

On the other hand, it may be argued that individuals are only able to assimilate simple experiences, e.g. constant demands or constant rates of growth, so that expectations are always of constant outputs or at best constant rates of growth of output. If that sort of intuitive assumption is justified, then if the notional model yields oscillating outputs expectations are bound to be disappointed, and the actual rates of growth of outputs are unlikely to be constant (because of changing reactions to disappointed expectations). If, on the other hand, the notional model yields constant rates of growth and if expectations are everywhere fulfilled, then an explanation of the trade cycle must concentrate on showing (1) how the notional and expectational systems come to be out of step and (2) how the consequently disappointed expectations lead to the oscillations it is desired to explain. The explanation of the cycle would then be mainly in terms of disappointed expectations.

III

This section is mainly critical. It is hoped to show how the neglect of some of the problems raised in the previous section has led some writers to some curious conclusions.

The Multiplier

Let us first set up a simple 'notional' model of the economy. We assume that the current demand for inputs by producers and consumers depends on the output (income) expected in the next period.[3] If D_i^t is the demand for the output of the ith sector in period t, we write:

$$D_i^t = \sum_{j=1}^{n} a_{ij} \, {}_j y^{t+1} \qquad (i = 1 \ . \ . \ . \ n) \qquad (1.10)$$

where ${}_j y^{t+1}$ $(j = 1 \ldots n)$ is the output producer j plans to produce

---

[3] Our conclusions would be in no way affected if we made consumer outlay a (linear) function of income expected in the current period. In that case one of the equations could be eliminated from our system.

in period $(t + 1)$ and $_n y^{t+1}$ is the income expected by households in that period. The a_{ij} are input coefficients, here assumed technically fixed, and they measure the proportion of j's expected output spent on the output of industry i in the current period.

If all expectations are continuously fulfilled, then actual and expected output, and demand and supply coincide. Equation (1.10) can then be rewritten:

$$_i Y^t = {}_i y^t = D_i^t = \sum_j a_{ij\, j} Y^{t+1} \quad (i = 1 \ldots n) \tag{1.11}$$

where the capital letters denote actual output produced. Let us now also suppose that there is a component in the demand for the output of each sector which is independent of income, and write:

$$_i Y^t = \sum_j a_{ij\, j} Y^{t+1} + K_i \tag{1.12}$$

or in matrix notation:

$$Y^t = A Y^{t+1} + K \tag{1.13}$$

Then by a well known procedure we can find the constant component y in the solution of equation (1.13) to be:

$$y = [I - A]^{-1} K \tag{1.14}$$

and letting Z_j^t be the divergence of j's output in t from $_j y$ we write the matrix equation in the divergences from y as:

$$Z^t = A Z^{t+1} \quad \text{or} \quad Z^{t+1} = A^{-1} Z^t \tag{1.15}$$

If now, as is usual in multiplier analysis, we assume that the matrix A obeys the condition that

$$A^t \longrightarrow 0 \quad \text{as} \quad t \longrightarrow \infty \tag{1.16}$$

it is immediately clear that the difference equation system (1.15) must be explosive. We thus reach the interesting conclusion that if it is assumed that expectations are continuously fulfilled and at the same time that the marginal propensities (i.e. the column sums in A) are less than unity, then no constant income levels will be reached by the ordinary multiplier process.

One of the essential assumptions therefore of the well known multiplier models which lead to convergence to y is that individuals do not anticipate future events correctly. Unfortunately these assumptions are rarely stated explicitly. But let us examine some of the conventional models in greater detail and see what sort of expectation functions they imply. The conventional model is usually written as

$$Y^{t+1} = A Y^t + K \tag{1.17}$$

A normal way of interpreting this model is as follows. Let us first assume that there is no consumption lag. Incomes are spent immediately they are received. But there is a production lag – increases in demand are not anticipated – of one period. Hence supply lags behind demand by one period. Thus if we assume: (1) that planned supply is always equal to actual supply (no factor shortage); (2) that planned supply in period t is equal to demand in period $(t - 1)$; (3) that receipts from decumulated stocks are not treated as income, whereas the current value of accumulated stocks is treated as income; and hence (4) that planned supply for period t is income of period t; and finally (5) that demand in period t is a function of income in period t; then we have the simple system;

$$\begin{aligned} D^t &= A S^t \\ S^t &= D^{t-1} \end{aligned} \Bigg\} \quad \therefore \ S^t = A S^{t-1} \tag{1.18}$$

where D^t is the demand matrix and S^t supply matrix. In this manner equation (1.17) can be treated as a system of supply equations.

It is now also seen that the introduction of a consumption lag does not materially affect the system beyond raising the order of the difference equations. But the question must now be asked: is it possible to interpret equation (1.17) on the assumption that there are only consumption lags, but no production lags? It will be clear that a consumption lag on the part of firms must imply, if there is to be no production lag, that the coefficients relating their past income to current demand for input must contain an expectational element. But this is normally ruled out by the conventional model, and hence we have to assume that the consumption lag applies to households only.

The absence of a production lag would mean that in our notional model, as well as in equation (1.17), we could eliminate all equations except the household one. This, then, is a case exactly analogous to the one to which Goodwin (1949) has drawn attention, in a static analysis, namely the case where only households save, and where it is therefore possible to eliminate all other equations from the system. But this is not an interesting case, and we shall henceforth assume that a production lag is present.

If, then, we interpret equation (1.17) as in equation (1.18), then as long as demand is changing, it will not equal supply in any one period. To simplify matters let us suppose the initial conditions in equation (1.17) to be such that no fluctuations in output occur, and where the expansion path of any sector i is given by the equation:*

$$_i y^t = - \lambda^t M_i + _i y \tag{1.19}$$

where M_i is a constant derived from the initial conditions and λ is a root of the system (1.17) which is real and numerically smaller than unity. A solution of the form (1.19) is highly unlikely, but it will do well enough for simple illustrative purposes. The output of each sector will therefore be increasing at a decreasing rate, and this must mean that demand is also increasing (at a decreasing rate). But by assumption increases in demand are not anticipated; hence each sector will experience excess demand during the 'adjustment' process. Since it is assumed that producers in any period t always produce what was demanded in period $(t - 1)$, it is clear that they will do no more than attempt to keep their stocks intact; that is, the increase in supply in any period is always exactly equal to the stocks decumulated in the previous period. But each period more stocks are decumulated until demand ceases to expand. After that a constant amount of stocks are accumulated and decumulated each period.

It is seen that the assumptions of the model imply that producers regard a certain demand, say $_i y' < _i y$, as normal, and any divergences from it as purely temporary. But their expectations will be continuously disappointed, for their action leads to a stabilisation of demand at $_i y$. Sooner or later the new situation will be regarded as normal. When that happens, producers' total

---

* Goodwin's conclusion that a system such as the one under consideration 'not only may . . . exhibit oscillatory behaviour – it must do so' is not correct, since it is not a sufficient condition for oscillations to occur to prove that some of the latent roots cannot be real and positive. In addition, it is necessary to show that the system is excited along the relevant co-ordinates, i.e. oscillations are not (in a linear model) independent of initial conditions.

orders will increase by $_iy - _iy'$. Demand everywhere will now increase above the previously constant level, but provided the old level of demand is now regarded as normal, this increase in demand will be temporary, and a genuine equilibrium with expectations fulfilled will be achieved.

The above example was simple, but it draws attention to an important point − we must not neglect the fact that in the transition from one stationary equilibrium to another expectations must change. This change itself will produce certain disturbances, which in the present example were only temporary, but must nevertheless be taken into account.

We have no serious quarrel with the type of multiplier model just discussed. But owing to the neglect of some of the expectational problems we have pointed out, certain curious results were achieved by some writers who have extended the model to deal with a situation where injections were not constant through time but growing at (say) a constant geometric rate.

It is easy to show that if in equation (1.7) K is replaced by $H(1 + g)^t$, where H is a column matrix with typical element h_i, then the output of each sector will, after a time, expand at a constant rate g. The assumption that supply in period t is equal to demand in period $(t - 1)$ is now quite untenable, since that would mean that the producer would soon have no stocks left to decumulate! On the other hand, if we assumed that expectations are continuously fulfilled, then, as we have already seen, no sector would expand at a constant rate. It is therefore crucial to postulate at what juncture in the process expectations change and become correct and 'normal'. If this occurs only when demand has been increasing at a constant rate for some time, and *if* individuals now come to expect this increase in the future and *if* the divergence from that rate due to this change in expectations does not cause them to change their expectations again, then a genuine equilibrium at a constant rate of growth will be established. It is seen that the assumption that all 'marginal propensities' are less than unity is quite insufficient to establish a constant rate of growth in output. In fact, this assumption deals only with the simplest of all problems, namely, where a system of difference or differential equations will converge on a certain path. Any reasonable elementary textbook in mathematics will supply the answer. The answer the economist must supply is the sort of economic behaviour that can be reasonably assumed to enable us to set up a structurally stable equation system. This, surely the most important aspect of the economists's contribution, has been too long ignored.

In fact, it is most unlikely that a constant equilibrium rate of growth will be established even when all questions of 'induced' investment are ignored, as in our model. For one thing the assumption that all injections are growing at the same rate is highly unrealistic. For another the transition between one set of expectations and another involves disturbances just at a time when expectations are most fluid, so that these may never become 'normal' and the system may remain in more or less permanent disequilibrium.

To sum up. Most conventional multiplier models are of a form such that convergence of income to some definite time path takes place. To establish that we have shown it must be assumed that expectations are being disappointed, during the 'adjustment' process. This we have argued is inconsistent with a constant expectation and behaviour function for any length of time. To prove therefore that some permanent equilibrium will be established, we must show how and at what stage expectations change and become 'correct'. In the static model that is relatively easily done on fairly realistic assumptions. In the case of changing injections this is not so. The really important point of principle is that models of type (1.17) cannot be used by themselves to prove convergence; some outside assumptions as to how expectations change must be introduced.

Harrod's Moving Equilibrium

In a recent article Alexander (1950) pointed out that Harrod's 'warranted rate of growth' assumed that expectations would be continuously fulfilled in that it was derived from what we have called a 'notional' model. In a later article, Harrod (1951) attempted to extend the concept of a warranted rate of growth to include the case where producers chronically find themselves short of stock and capital.

To do this, Harrod assumes that producers will maintain a certain type of routine behaviour in spite of the continual shortage of stocks, etc. The precise behaviour equation he suggests is that any producer will increase his demand for inputs in any one period by an amount by which his stocks currently fall short of the optimum amount. If orders are to increase at a constant rate g, then the desired stock and the actual stock must grow at the same rate, or what comes to the same thing, the absolute difference between these two must grow at the rate g. If the 'success' of this form of routine behaviour depends on the ratio of actual to desired stock, then the degree of success remains constant throughout. If however, success depends on the absolute difference between the two, then the degree of success will be decreasing. It is a moot point whether the former or the latter relation between stocks and success is the appropriate one.

But this is not the only objection to Harrod's new formulation. The fact that entrepreneurs never anticipate increases in demand, he maintains, 'betokens a more cautious temperament'. In Harrod's world producers perform the same experiment over and over again with the same result, and yet unlike other mortals they never learn from experience. Harrod therefore never allows for what Shackle has called 'clarifying' expectations, and that seems unrealistic to a high degree.

Moreover, if again in Shackle's terminology, the potential surprise attached to an increase in demand is high, then it may be more cautious to act as if no increase in demand were anticipated at all. But if it is found repeatedly that demand has in fact increased – and, what is more, in a regular manner – then such increases must before long be regarded with zero potential surprise, and a constant demand with ever-increasing potential surprise. The constancy of the behaviour of a Harrodian producer in such circumstances betokens not so much a more 'cautious temperament' as sheer perversity.

A similar criticism can be applied to Professor Hicks's (1950) equilibrium rate of growth. Here producers are continuously losing stocks and soon will have none left to lose, and they are assumed to persist in the type of routine behaviour postulated for them in spite of this.

Dynamic Stability Conditions

It will be clear from our foregoing discussion that the equilibrium behaviour equations cannot be utilised to assess the stability of a system, for any outside 'shock' will constitute a new experience in the face of which 'decisions' must be made and which cannot properly be treated by the established routine behaviour.

This is fully realised by the authors to whom we are indebted for an analysis of the dynamic stability of a Hicksian pure exchange system. (Metzler 1945, Samuelson 1944. See also Samuelson 1947 pp. 269–71.) They postulate a new set of behavioural equations, i.e. that the rate of change of the ith price is a function of the excess demand for the *i*th commodity, to examine whether a given disturbance will set up forces to restore equilibrium.

Yet this treatment of the problem is open to several objections. First they postulate the existence of a definite supply function, which relates current supply to current prices. Such a function, however, means that a given price at all times implies a given supply, irrespective of whether that price is the 'equilibrium' or 'normal' price or not. Thus expectations are assumed to be perfectly 'plastic' — any price that is established is regarded by producers as permanent. This assumption seems to me entirely unwarranted, and incidentally precludes the action of what economists have for long regarded as one of the main stabilising forces in the system — namely 'normal' expectations.

But there is worse to come. Suppose that the reaction equations postulated lead to ever-increasing excess demands, i.e. that the system is unstable. What then? In what sense has the final instability of equilibrium been proved? The routine behaviour postulated for the producer is clearly not a success from his point of view — he is continuously making lower profits than he could have made. It seems altogether fanciful to suppose that producers' behaviour will not change. The question to be answered is, what will happen when producers have, so to speak, started out on the wrong foot and have chosen an inappropriate form of routine behaviour. Will there be any forces at work leading to redress the balance? This is a question for economists —the exact mathematical conditions on which so much effort has been expended are secondary.

Let us for the moment look at a single industry model, with supply and demand functions as postulated by the stability theorists. Equilibrium for the moment is unstable, there has been a disturbance, and prices and outputs are fluctuating in the familiar cobweb manner. The producers find that each time they have increased supply in response to an increase in price, they have produced too much, and each time they have reduced supply in response to a fall in price they have produced too little. Whether the industry is monopolistic or not, this is the experience of the average producer. Is it really supposed that modern businessmen or even farmers[4] will not learn from this? Surely before long, when prices rise, the repeated experience of overproduction will

---

[4] It is interesting to note that it seems generally agreed that if farmers are to be induced to produce more of a particular product, higher prices are normally insufficient — they must also be guaranteed for a certain period at least.

induce the individual producers to increase their supply by less than they would otherwise have done, and reduce their supply by less when prices fall. If we like, the supply curve will become flatter, and that will eventually lead to the re-establishment of equilibrium.

The above example does not seem over-fanciful. It is not, however, intended to imply that all systems are ultimately stable. The case which is here pleaded is the importance of a distinction between short run and long run stability. A system possessing short run stability, provided its parameters remain the same, is also likely to possess long run stability. But the reverse is not true – short run instability does not necessarily imply long run instability. In the context of the models normally examined, namely the effect of a once-over distrubance on the system, it seems to me that it is long run stability conditions which are of importance and that the present treatment can leave the system happily oscillating or exploding without anyone caring a further rap about what will become of it.

Equilibrium and 'Initial Conditions'

In his discussion of the concept of moving equilibrium, Professor Samuelson (1947, chapter XI) is eager to find a definition such that the equilibrium path is independent of 'initial conditions'. (In, say, a difference equation of order n the solution depends on the roots of the equation and the n given past values of the variable. The latter are called the initial conditions.) Equilibrium in Professor Samuelson's work occurs if all the possible expansion paths of the system converge one on the other.

Professor Samuelson draws many of his examples from physics, and this perhaps explains why he has not made clear why independence of equilibrium from initial conditions is a sensible requirement in the realm of economics. The initial conditions, i.e. past values of variables, constitute the sum total of relevant experience of the economic units of decision. It would be very curious if their behaviour were to be quite independent of the form of that experience. In fact, of course, it is more sensible to assume that there will be different behavioural equations for different past experiences.

While therefore everyone, of course, is at liberty to define anything in any way desired, it does not seem useful to use concepts in economic analysis to which it is known in advance that there are no counterparts in the real world.

IV

Up to now we have proceeded on the assumption that all expectations were single valued and have insisted in our definition of equilibrium that all expectations would have to be fulfilled. It is, however, well known that expectations are not single valued, and it may therefore be argued that no sensible meaning can be given to the statement that all expectations are fulfilled. It is the purpose of this section to summarise very briefly some of the problems raised by these objections.

As I hope we have made clear, our main preoccupation in the analysis of equilibrium was to find a situation for which the behavioural equation could be regarded as remaining of constant form. We cannot observe expectation – only behaviour. Let us repeat what we mean by constant or routine behaviour. The latter is said to occur if the behaviour of the economic unit is the same whenever certain variables on which this behaviour is said to depend take on any same given values. Now without begging the question of single versus multivalued expectations, we have argued in this paper that the behaviour function will remain of constant form if, and only if (over a period of time), the routine behaviour it describes is successful. Thus, for instance, a permanent decumulation of stocks can hardly be described as 'successful'. If, then, we take as a criterion of success that demand is always equal to the supply for the commodity at the given prices, then we can use the model of the previous section without modification. In the notional model instead of 'expected' output we put planned output (and some ouput must be planned whatever the expectations). Instead of an expectation model we put a planning model. It is not now directly relevant to ask how planned outputs are related to multivalued expectations. Some decision must be taken and some output planned; if at given prices this is exactly taken off the market, we would say that the routine behaviour implied by the planning function has proved successful.

It may, of course, be that even partial success will be sufficient to ensure the constancy of the behaviour function. Our main point here is that if the actual achievement differs (over time) from a successful achievement in a systematic way, then this constitutes new 'experience' and attempts will be made to change behaviour.

We can thus bypass the problem of multivalued expectations

without invalidating our previous analysis. This does not mean that this is not an important problem, for it clearly is essential to know something of the relationships between expectations and the routine adopted.

REFERENCES

Alexander, S. S. 1950. Mr Harrod's dynamic model, *Economic Journal*, December

Frisch, R. 1936. On the notion of equilibrium and disequilibrium, *Review of Economic Studies*, February

Goodwin, R. M. 1949. The multiplier as a matrix, *Economic Journal*, 59, December

Harrod, R. F. 1951. Notes on trade cycle theory, *Economic Journal*, June

Hicks, J. R. 1950. *A Contribution to the Theory of the Trade Cycle*, Clarendon Press, Oxford

Katona, G. 1951. *Psychological Analysis of Economic Behaviour*, McGraw-Hill, New York

Metzler, L. A. 1945. Stability of multiple markets: the Hicks conditions, *Econometrica*, 13, October

Samuelson, P. A. 1944. The relation between Hicksian stability and true dynamic stability, *Econometrica*, July–October

Samuelson, P. A. 1947. *Foundations of Economic Analysis*, Harvard University Press, Cambridge, Mass.

Shackle, G. L. S. 1949. *Expectation in Economics*, Cambridge University Press, Cambridge

2

On the Notion of Equilibrium in Economics

Wherever economics is used or thought about, equilibrium is a central organising idea. Chancellors devise budgets to establish some desirable equilibrium and alter exchange rates to correct 'fundamental disequilibria'. Sometimes they allow rates to 'find their equilibrium level'. For theorists the pervasiveness of the equilibrium notion hardly needs documenting. In Cambridge the predominant recent preoccupation and controversy concerned the question of which techniques would be observed in different economics in long run equilibrium at different profit rates. The Marxian analysis of value and prices, in so far as it is comprehensible to me, seems to be describing an economy in equilibrium. The 'crises' which Marx predicts and studies gain their precise significance in comparison with the equilibrium which they disrupt. In what is, alas, called 'neo-classical' economics the last twenty years have seen the definitive investigation of the logical coherence of an equilibrium by Arrow and Debreu, the beautiful bringing together of the core – an equilibrium concept of game theory – with the traditional competitive equilibrium, and also numerous studies of mechanisms which might form the causal chain by which equilibrium is attained. The 'golden', 'silver' and 'leaden' ages of growth are too familiar to require comment. In Keynesian economics recent discussions have centred on the question whether Keynes' main insights are misunderstood when they are translated into the equilibrium framework of Hicks and of what Professor Joan Robinson calls the 'bastard Keynesians'. All this is familiar and some of it I shall return to. What is abundantly clear is that the claim which I started with, namely that an equilibrium notion is an all-pervasive one in economics, is easily substantiated.

It is of course not the case that there is a unique specification of the states of an economy which we want to describe as an equilibrium. The distinction between 'short run' and 'long run', for instance, is an ancient one and there are others less well discussed to which I shall return. But a central theme runs through many of these usages, namely the singling out of those states in which the intended actions of rational economic agents are mutually consistent and can therefore be implemented. This is as true of, for instance, neo-Ricardian economics as it is of Walrasian. In the former we search simultaneously for a set of relative prices and a rate of profit which if they ruled would cause rational producers to choose just those techniques which would allow them to earn that rate of profit at which the intended savings also equal intended investment. The Walrasian story, although of course much more general, is similar.

It is precisely this exacting correspondence of rational plans and feasible actions which has been causing concern to practical men and some unease to theorists. To the first of these, the world which he sees does not seem to be the world described by an equilibrium and so he is inclined to think that the notion is not of much use to him, although typically he continues to use it in a loose way. For the theorist the difficulty is that for important cases the notion is illdefined or not defined at all. This point will presently become clear.

For it is my intention in what follows to examine the theoretical and conceptual difficulties which arise with the Arrow—Debreu paradigm when it is modified to serve descriptive purposes. I shall also sketch a tentative proposal for dealing with these difficulties.

I have chosen to start with Arrow—Debreu for the following reasons:

(1) It is precise, complete, and unambiguous.
(2) It has been much maltreated by both friend and foe who know it only from hearsay.
(3) In the paradigm it is possible to pinpoint with great accuracy where a change is required if a change is made in the economic circumstances it is asked to illuminate.
(4) Because it so happens that all serious work which is now proceeding to recast the equilibrium notion is being undertaken

by those who have been most active in building the paradigm in the first place and who consequently understand it.

I fear that some of what I have to say may turn out to be a little hard to understand at first reading. I apologise for this but the difficulty seems to be inherent in the topic. I do not however apologise for the fact that an abstract line of thought is being pursued, although I understand the risks. Here is what Russell (1931) has to say:

> Many people have a passionate hatred of abstraction, chiefly, I think, because of its intellectual difficulty; but as they do not wish to give this reason they invent all sorts of others that sound grand. They say that all reality is concrete, and that in making abstractions we are leaving out the essential. They say that all abstraction of falisfication, and that as soon as you have left out any aspect of something actual you have exposed yourself to the risk of fallacy in arguing from its remaining aspects alone. Those who argue in this way are in fact concerned with matters quite other than those that concern science.

And he maintains that 'it is the characteristic of the advance of science that less and less if found to be datum and more and more is found to be inference'. I quote Russell here not because I want to maintain that economics is a science – whatever that claim would mean – but because I happen to believe that what he is here saying applies to our subject.

Before I start there is a tiresome matter to get out of the way. It is well known that on certain assumptions an Arrow–Debreu equilibrium of an economy can be shown to be Pareto efficient. Everyone who has understood this latter concept and the assumptions required to prove the result also understands that to claim this efficiency for any actual economy would be a singularly weak claim in an argument designed to persuade us that the economy is also in some sense morally to be approved.

The evidence that the theory has not been understood is readily available. Dobb (1973) claimed that Samuelson, who has done more than most to combat this mistake, had maintained that a competitive equilibrium 'gives the unique social optimum'. Again, the great fervour that is put into special models of the economy where equilibrium prices are independent of demand has its origin in the quite absurdly mistaken belief that in the more general case one would be led to conclude that the equilibrium was good, or just, or even optimal. Only rudimentary scholarly care is required to show what nonsense all this is. I do not see how a similar misreading by, say, Chicago excuses such lapses. Nor do I find the cause of reason and honesty served when Ellman (1972) declares that the theory is so vicious that it should be banned from University syllabuses.

But this unattractively illiberal view and others like it are connected with a rather more serious and all-embracing claim, namely that social science in general and economics in particular must be 'political'. By this it is claimed that the practitioners in these fields are bound consciously or otherwise to seek propositions which support or damage some section of society or support or damage existing social arrangements. One can, of course, ask straight away whether this proposition is not itself politically motivated. But in any case, at this level, the whole thing amounts to no more than the observation that a person's actions, intellectual or otherwise, will hardly be independent of his biography or of the society he lives in and that we are often engaged in the activity of persuading and of influencing others. Certainly also it is of interest to the historian of ideas to locate theories in these contexts in a precise way. I am also willing to concede that in certain instances the meaning of even non-normative sentences may not be understood without knowing the intention of the speaker. Yet when all this has been agreed to it is surely cant to maintain that we have no criteria of true and false in these fields. For instance there may be an adequate social and biographical account of why Marx wrote what he did write. But this does not help me to decide whether or not to accept any or all of his propositions. In particular this account is irrelevant to my observation that his version of the 'transformation problem' is logically at fault or that his prediction of falling real wages has so far been falsified.

'The faintest of all human passions', A. E. Housman remarks somewhere, 'is the love of truth.' The observation seems a just one. But it seems to me sad that to this general handicap under which economists, like others, labour, some should wish to add the further one of a belief that nothing in economics is either ture or false, or if you like, empirically or logically falsifiable. I do not know what activity those who hold this view believe themselves engaged in when they earn their living as economists. Nor do I want to enter into further epistemological speculation, at which economists have shown themselves to be conspicuously bad. I happen to believe that the view lacks all merit and accordingly in what follows will not be inquiring into the motives or biographies of those I agree or disagee with.

One final preliminary ramark remains to be made. Professor Kaldor on hearing what I proposed to discuss on this occasion urged me to take notice of his latest paper in the *Economic Journal* (Kaldor 1972). This I have done and it accounts for the fact that in certain sections, references to this paper are so numerous.

II

I begin with reminding you of the main features of the Arrow—Debreu equilibrium. Goods are distinguished one from the other by their physical property, by their location in space and in time and by the state of the world. A price is defined for each good. There are two kinds of agents — households and firms. Given any non-negative price vector each household chooses an action which defines a point in the space of all goods. It has the property that there is no other action available to the household under its budget constraint which it prefers. Again, given any non-negative price vector, firms choose an action represented by a point in the space of all goods such that there is no other action which is both tech-. nologically feasible and more profitable. An equilibrium is then a triple; a non-negative price vector, a vector of demand and a vector of supply, such that (a) the demand vector is the vector sum of household action at these prices, (b) the supply vector is the vector sum of firms' actions at these prices, and (c) for no good does demand exceed supply.

The first important point to understand about this construction is that it makes no formal or explicit causal claims at all. For instance it contains no presumption that a sequence of actual economic states will terminate in an equilibrium state. However it is motivated by a very weak causal proposition. This is that no plausible sequence of economic states will terminate, if it does so at all, in a state which is not an equilibrium. The argument is straightforward; agents will not continue in actions in states in which preferred or more profitable ones are available to them nor will mutually inconsistent actions allow given prices to persist. It will be seen that this is not a strong proposition in that no description of any particular process is involved. It is also clear that weak as this claim is, it may be false.

Professor Kaldor's theory of what it is that Debreu's (1959) book might be about is thus incorrect, as a perusal of its ninety-odd pages will quickly show. I do not here refer to his remarkable belief (Kaldor 1972) that Debreu or for that matter any of the general equilibrium theorists postulate 'linear-homogeneous and continuously differentiable production functions', nor to the even more surprising claim that the inventors of the beautiful theory of contingent markets postulate 'perfect foresight'. Nor again do I want to blame him for not reading the large literature on the 'removal of scaffolding', not even for not knowing that Arrow (Arrow and Hahn 1972) has provided a rigorous general equilibrium model with increasing returns and imperfect competition. What I want to note here is the incorrectness of the claim that Debreu was looking for the 'minimum basic assumptions for establishing the existence of an equilibrium set of prices which is (a) unique (b) stable'. Debreu did not concern himself with either (a) or (b). Here is one of those perennial misunderstandings which I have mentioned and I believe that, odd though it is that so clear a writer as Debreu should be misread, it can be explained by a genuine problem. For Professor Kaldor and others find it so natural to regard an equilibrium as the outcome of some particular process that they find it difficult to believe that any one should wish to use an equilibrium notion in a different way. And indeed it is a fair question whether it can ever be useful to have an equilibrium notion which does not describe the termination of actual processes.

For the purposes of this question uniqueness of an equilibrium is not an issue, for plainly what is to be discussed is the view that an equilibrium notion is only useful to economists in so far as it involves the falsifiable calim that all actual economic processes converge to *an* equilibrium state. Certainly this is the way, for instance, Marshall justified his interest in equilibrium. I want however to maintain that this view is not correct. I do so on two grounds. First, I shall much later argue that our need for equilibrium concepts is largely connected with ignorance of precisely those features of an actual economy which the view under discussion wishes us to be precise about. Secondly, I want to maintain now the related but weaker claim that even when equilibrium states connot be shown to be asymptotic outcomes of processes it is useful to have a concept of equilibrium states. As will however presently become clear, I do not believe the Arrow–Debreu notion to be the appropriate one.

It is the weak causal claim which I have already noticed that gives the clue. For it involves a perfectly good empirical statement which can be made of any given state, namely that it will not persist. Indeed with the aid of only the most general features of actual processes it is often possible to say something about the direction in which some variables will move next, without however being able to say what their final resting place, if they have one, will be. In an economy with unemployed resources an excess of intended investment over intended savings is used to predict that incomes will not persist at their present level and indeed they are very likely to rise. This we can do and usefully do, even if we have no means of knowing whether our observations are taken from a process which is oscillatory or from one which converges to some equilibrium. One could quote an endless number of examples with the same force. It is true that we should like to be able to describe and predict the course of economic processes in great detail, but it is not true that in our present stage of knowledge the notion of an equilibrium which may never be attained is not of very great help in doing the best we can.

But of course for all this to be possible we must be able to say of any given state whether it is an equilibrium or not and one must be satisfied that the weak causal claim is in fact correct. Here one encounters the first serious objection, for it is due to the work of general equilibrium theorists themselves that one is persuaded that the weak causal claim is false.

Let me recall that this claim is that any process purporting to describe an actual economy could terminate, if it terminates at all, only in an equilibrium. But returning to a line of study first pursued by Edgeworth, it was noticed that a feasible state of an economy in which no coalition of agents could improve themselves would certainly be one for which we would be prepared to say that it could be a resting place of an actual economic process. The same arguments as before would apply. This set of states is called the core of an economy. It is easy to show that every Arrow–Debreu equilibrium is in the core. But the converse is only true under an extremely restrictive postulate.

What this means is that one can describe states of the economy which if they obtained would leave us no plausible reason for supposing that these states would change; yet these states are defined without for instance prices entering into the description at all. Thus, except for the special case when the core and an Arrow–Debreu equilibrium coincide, there are already two differing equilibrium concepts of which the core is plainly the more general. I hope that this is sufficiently clear and that the plurality of equilibrium concepts is not confused with the possibility of there being many states which are Arrow–Debreu equilibria. In particular the method by which agents form coalitions and sustain a state in the core need have nothing to do with the paramenters of an Arrow–Debreu economy but may rest on rules of thumb, law etc. The core indeed has some claim to be regarded as a concept of a social equilibrium in the sense that for a core state we can think of no reason why self-seeking agents should wish to combine to upset the status quo.

The special circumstances for which the core and an Arrow–Debreu equilibrium coincide occur when the number of agents is very large – strictly when there is a continuum of agents. This is simply a formalisation of the notion that each agent is without power, which in turn is what Joan Robinson and others have always noted to be a requirement if prices are to be treated parametrically by economic agents. On the other hand when costs of coalition formation are zero it can be shown that when the number of agents is large enough (but less than infinite and of course not a continuum), any core state is 'near' an Arrow–Debreu equilibrium. Of course 'near' etc. must be properly defined. In any event, unless we are satisfied that the approximation is in practice a good one we must abandon the claim that all states which are not Arrow–Debreu equilibria cannot persist.

Now as far as households are concerned I have no great difficulties in accepting that a continuum or very large number of them is a satisfactory idealisation. But the same is not true of firms and indeed a consideration of these agents leads to great difficulties with the Arrow–Debreu equilibrium which are additional to those which arise from the core. For it now seems to me clear that there are logical difficulties in accounting for the existence of agents called firms at all unless we allow there to be increasing returns of some sort. But when there are increasing returns it may not be possible to show that there are any logically possible economic states which qualify as either Arrow–Debreu equilibria or as members of the core. It may also be wrong to think of a very large number of firms.

It is one of the great virtues of the way good economic theorising proceeds that it allows us to pinpoint difficulties precisely and to be precise about the difficulties. Thus while it is the case that I agree with Professor Kaldor that increasing returns are a telling objection to the perfect competition equilibrium notions I have so far discussed, it seems to me important not to let this observation be an occasion for the slackening of our intellectual muscles. So I shall first briefly explain what is known in the present context. Later, when I have made certain proposals I shall return to the problem.

The first point to emphasise is that an Arrow–Debreu equilibrium may exist when there are increasing returns. Not only is this so when these increasing returns are not internal to firms, but even if they are, provided they are not too large. I want to emphasise here the paradoxical position of some of the critics. They complain of the excessive generality of the construction but at the same time believe that the whole edifice must tumble if it ceases to be completely general. But if we have particular information about the relationships characterising the economy then it is perfectly possible for an Arrow–Debreu equilibrium to exist even though the axioms of the theory are violated.

But if it does exist then of course any particular equilibrium returns will not be increasing. This may be unacceptable to us on empirical grounds and we consider an alternative which turns on a second kind of approximation. This route was first explored by Lerner (1944), made much clearer in a spendid paper by Farrell (1967) and finally made general and rigorous by Ross Starr (1967). Here is the result. If in a precise sense increasing returns to scale are small relatively to the scale of the economy then there is an Arrow–Debreu equilibrium which is an approximate equilibrium for the increasing returns economy. This approximation improves with the scale of the economy.

If increasing returns are not to be important evidence against the equilibrium notions which I have been discussing then both approximations must be close enough. That is it must be the case both that increasing returns are small relative to the scale of the economy and that there are sufficiently many firms to allow us to deduce a close correspondence between the set of Arrow–Debreu equilibria and the core. I now want to say that although I think Professor Kaldor's belief in unbounded increasing returns to be false I do agree that we may not be able to maintain that they are small enough to allow the approximations here spoken of to be judged good enough.

I shall return to the whole matter later. Here I want to note that the rather uncontroversial view that increasing returns cause difficulties to perfect competition seems to me to bear no logical relationship to the claim that therefore equilibrium notions are not required or that they are sterile.

III

But let me now turn to other difficulties. The Arrow—Debreu equilibrium is very useful when for instance one comes to argue with someone who maintains that we need not worry about exhaustible resources because they will always have prices which ensure their 'proper' use. Of course there are many things wrong with this contention but a quick way of disposing of the claim is to note that an Arrow—Debreu equilibrium must be an assumption he is making for the economy and then to show why the economy cannot be in this state. The argument will here turn on the absence of futures markets and contingent futures markets and on the inadequate treatment of time and uncertainty by the construction. This negative role of Arrow—Debreu equilibrium I consider almost to be sufficient justification for it, since practical men and ill trained theorists everywhere in the world do not understand what they are claiming to be the case when they claim a beneficent and coherent role for the invisible hand. But for descriptive purposes of course this negative role is hardly a recommendation.

Once again I believe it important not to relax precision just when it is most required. It is difficult to think of words other than perhaps 'struggle' which are more of an incitement to idle chatter than is the word 'dynamic'. Samuelson (1967) noted this years ago, but it is still true that to claim your theory to be dynamic often allows you to get away with murder. So let me develop what I have to way with as much care as I can.

An Arrow—Debreu equilibrium can be interpreted as a state of affairs where (a) all actions are decided upon at only one instant of time and (b) actions always contain contingent elements. The latter follows from including the state of nature in a definition of goods and representing actions in the space of all goods. However this interpretation if it is to make sense requires there to be markets in all goods and so a large number of contingent futures markets. We have an empirical confrontation since we know that these markets are in fact very scarce. We also have a theoretical confrontation. Elsewhere (Hahn 1971) I have shown this by an appeal to transaction costs, and Roy Radner (1968) has shown that the state of the world formulation of contingencies is too narrow and that when it is supplemented by states which depend on the actions of agents, some contingent markets could logically not exist. So we are in the following position. We can use the Arrow–Debreu equilibrium in a very effective and empirical fashion. We can easily refute propositions such as those on exhaustible resources which I have already referred to. Moreover, one can locate precisely where the argument goes wrong. On the other hand we have now yet another reason why this equilibrium cannot be claimed to describe properties of all potential terminating points of any actual process.

We thus find it reasonable to require of our equilibrium notion that it should reflect the sequential character of actual economies. But I believe that we require more than that: we want it to be sequential in an *essential* way. By this I mean that it should not be possible without change in content to reformulate the notion non-sequentially. This in turn requires that information processes and costs, transactions and transaction costs and also expectations and uncertainty by explicity and essentially included in the equilibrium notion. That is what the Arrow–Debreu construction does not do. I do not at all believe that therefore it is quite useless. But certainly it is the case that it must relinquish the claim of providing necessary descriptions of terminal states of economic processes.

We have reached the point where a great deal of research and discussion is going on just now. We have also reached the point where the rather grandiose Arrow–Debreu notion gives way to the more 'feet on the ground' Keynesian one. I shall only be able to make passing reference to the many new ideas now being actively studied.

Certainly it is now widely agreed that it is undesirable to have an equilibrium notion in which information is as perfect and as costless as it is in Arrow–Debreu. This is so for the reasons which I have already discussed. Loosely speaking the information an agent gets can be thought of as a message from the environment to himself and the information he has can be thought of as a partitioning of the environment. The finer the partition the greater the information which one has. Radner (1968) has taken the first step in studying an equilibrium relative to the information available to agents. Hurwicz (1972) and others have been examining in a formal way the extent to which prices are adequate and, in a precise sense, efficient, informational signals. I and others have been studying equilibria relative to transaction possibilities which are costly and the resulting sequential character of the economy. Most importantly Radner (1972) has pioneered the study of stochastic equilibria in relation to the von Neumann growth and to Arrow–Debreu. In the latter he requires that agents do not differ in their expectations as to which price vector will be observed in each state of nature but that they assign different probabilities to the occurrence of each state. The economy is sequential, and the stationary distribution of prices at which in no state is any good in excess demand and which are the prices agents expect for each state, is the equilibrium. Green (1971) and Green and Majumdar (1972) as well as Hildenbrand (1971) have studied equilibrium notions for an economy in which preferences and endowments held by agents are random. There are theories for instance which give the precise circumstances in which the expected excess demands everywhere will be small and the market disappointments small on average with very high probability. Grandmont (1977) and others have studied short period equilibria with multivalued probabilistic expectations.

All of this work is in its infancy and one would be a very dull sort of chap if one could not think up objections. But the whole subject is plainly on a promising track. What I want to do now is to make a suggestion of how we may want to proceed.

IV

It will be useful to go back to the beginning. In particular one wants to re-examine the idea of the equilibrium actions of agents where the latter are taken as acting sequentially in real time. In what follows I do not assume perfect competition. I ask for your indulgence for a brief lapse into an abstract mode of proceeding.

At any date t there is a history of messages received by the agent. We divide these into those which the agent considers independent of his own actions, the *exogenous messages*, and the remainder. For instance observations on the weather, government policy and some prices will be exogenous. His own actions, such as the amount invested, are messages by the agent to himself and fall into the other category. But so does the amount of his output demanded at prices which he has set when competition is not perfect. Just as the brain must process the many complex messages received by the eye, so the agent must process the messages from the economy and nature. This processing at t I want to call the agent's theory at t.

To make this notion precise requires a careful description of the message space and I do not attempt this here. But by an agent's theory at t I want to mean the following:

(a) the agent has divided the messages into the two categories mentioned;

(b) for any sequence of exogenous messages from date t the agent has a probability distribution of the outcome of any proposed sequence of acts from t onwards;

(c) the agent has at t a probability which he will assign to receiving any exogenous message at any date in the future conditional on the messages received since the date t and that future.

Thus for instance if the agent is thought of as a Bayesian econometrician constructing a model of the economy in which he is an actor he would be said to have a theory.

I shall want to say that an agent is *learning* if his theory is not independent of the date t. It will be a condition of the agent being in equilibrium that he is not learning. There are at least two ways in which this requirement can be misunderstood, which I deal with now.

Suppose that at t the agent has assigned probabilities to the two events that it will and will not rain in Cambridge at $t + 1$. At $t + 1$ he will know which has been true. This increase in his knowledge is *not* what I mean by learning. An example of learning in my sense would occur if at $t + 1$ having observed rain, the probability he attaches to rain in Cambridge at $t + 2$ differs from that which he attached to that event at t conditional on rain at $t + 1$.

Secondly, the requirement that the agent should not learn does not imply that in the more customary sense his expectations must remain the same. For instance at t the agent may assign a probability of one to the price of some good at any subsequent date being equal to the exponentially weighted average of the prices for that good observed at all times up to that date. He may of course be wrong but as long as, roughly speaking, the method by which he makes his forecasts is the same at all dates he will not be learning in my sense.

I now return to the agrument. This is best conducted at the moment by thinking of the agent as a dynamic programmer. Given the agent's theory at t, the programme is solved if with every message array at any date from t onwards the agent can associate an act for that date. This mapping from messages to acts is called a policy. In general this policy will be independent of t only if (a) the agent does not learn in the sense I have used this term, and (b) his objectives do not change. So the reason why I want the absence of learning to characterise the equilibrium of the agent is that I want his policy to be independent of t.

Again there is a possible misunderstanding best dealt with now. The agent's policy being independent of t does not imply that it is independent of calendar time. For instance the agent's age can be an argument of his policy without that policy ceasing to be an equilibrium policy.

The concept of the equilibrium action of an agent here proposed is such that if it is in fact the action pursued by the agent an outside observer, say the econometrician, could describe it by structurally stable equations. When the agent is learning, however, then there is a change in regime so that one would require a 'higher level' theory of the learning process. Such a theory is not available at present. If it were then I still agree with what I wrote in 1952: 'If a definite behaviour pattern can be established for all situations then nothing is gained by labelling any particular behaviour as equilibrium behaviour.' In our present state of knowledge however it is routine behaviour and not behaviour which we can hope to describe. Indeed one of the reasons why an equilibrium notion is useful is that it serves to make precise the limits of economic analysis.

I have of course in my description made excessive demands on the rationality and computational ability of the agent. There are a number of ways in which one can depart from this. One way is via a route called 'bounded rationality' by Radner. As an example of this one can suppose that the agent peers only a short distance into the future, or that he has to ignore a class of messages which we can recognise as relevant to his objectives or again the objectives themselves can be drastically simplified, as say in the Robin Marris theory of managerial behaviour. But it will be clear that the particular description which I have used was chosen in order to lend precision to concepts and that these for a wide class of alternative routes will continue to serve. In particular the notion of the agent's theory, and of his actions conditional on that theory, as well as the rather general description of what one wants to mean by learning should continue to be appropriate in much less abstract formulation.

On the other hand this is the point to pause to take note of objections of practical men, of psychologists and of some economists, to the idea of the calculating rational agent. This notion of course is not peculiar to any school: it occurs in Marx and Ricardo as centrally as it does in the work of say Professor Hicks and it is used by Professor Robinson in her study of the choice of technique as much as by Professor Solow in his. Indeed, even hard-faced Treasury men are accustomed to assume such agents when they scrutinise new tax proposals both for their effects and for avoidance possibilities.

Now the objectors are by no means agreed in their objections. For instance Professor Kaldor (1972) believes that the received theory is vacuous by virtue of being unfalsifiable while Professor Kornai (1971) believes that the theory is false. Other critics point to the prevalence of habitual and conventional behaviour, and others emphasise the spontaneous and perhaps erratic element. Many simply dislike the formal apparatus which the doctrine has evolved and hold the views which Walras (1954) reports: 'such as "that human liberty will *never* allow itself to be cast into equations" or that "mathematics ignores frictions which is everything in social science" and other equally forceful and flowery phrases'. So the objectors are a mixed bunch and it is not at all clear what each of them proposes to do about the problem they raise. One proposal – to do without microtheory altogether – which is occasionally made I shall take up briefly later.

Some of the objections are of course easily met while others have more force. For instance it can be agreed that profit maximisation is not a falsifiable hypothesis until we have decided what the definition of profit in that proposition is to be. But of course we do decide on this when the theory is used. In my approach we would have to specify the theory which the agent holds as well. When this is done this falsifiability is obvious. What is more important in my present context is that it is precisely the empirical claim for the usefulness of the equilibrium notion that the theories and motives of agents are sufficiently stable and we are not allowed to invoke changing theories or motives to help us out of falsified predictions. That is the whole point of the distinction between the two kinds of actions which I have been making. It is worth noting here that even so abstract a hypothesis as the maximisation of Bernoulli utilities has been falsified by experiments carried out by Professor Raiffa at Harvard.

Another of the misconceptions arises simply from the difficulty the practical sound common sense man has in understanding what the theorist is doing. I have already noted before that he has difficulty in understanding that for empirical purposes it is not only possible but desirable to be far more particular and that this need not at all be damaging. For instance the assumption that individuals have a preference ordering over the whole commodity space is rather dotty – the postulate that they can order it in the vicinity of where they are is not. Moreover it has been known for a long time that theorising survives a certain randomness of preferences. The observation that preferences themselves are the result of complex social and biographical processes has of course noting to do with the issue.

The real objections are really quite different: they are that we know too little about motives and theories which are held by agents, and not that if we knew them it would be a bad hypothesis to suppose that agents do as well, in the light of motives and theories, for themselves as they can. For instance I have laid great stress on the difference between the perceived environment and the environment but very little seems to be known of how the two are related. There is also the very serious difficulty connected with the plausible requirement that the theory held by the agent must in some sense be simple enough to be intellectually and computationally feasible for him. Indeed I have no doubt that the simple textbook treatment of these matters is false, as are for instance many elaborate models of portfolio choice. But all these are indications that we have a lot to do in economics and they do not seem to bear on the basic methodological stance.

There is, however, an important link with my main argument which I wish to make. The reason why economists have for so long been interested in rational actions is because they claim that these have survival value. Schumpeter (1955), writing of what happened to people in the transition to capitalism, notes that 'they were rationalised, because the instability of economic position made their survival hinge on continual deliberately rationalistic decisions – a dependence which emerged with great sharpness'. One is here back to the weak causal claim which is to be made for an equilibrium and for equilibrium actions. But it is not only the way actions are determined but also the motives which determine them which may be selected. The low aspiration haberdasher may not survive Sir Isaac Wolfson's scouts. So it is one of the claims of this kind of theory that certain institutional environments only permit certain kinds of behaviour to qualify for equilibrium behaviour. In the institutional set-up of capitalism, as Marx noted, the biographical peculiarities of agents may be of little significance in describing equilibrium states. Objectors who focus on the failure of the theory to describe any given individual are thus wide of the mark.

Lastly, it is of course precisely my contention that equilibrium actions of agents will reveal themselves in habitual behaviour so that objections from that source I can ignore. But notice the difference between the man who says people choose goods out of habit and the one who says people have a habitual way of translating prices and incomes into choices. The former is not very helful.

I now turn to the most difficult of the remaining questions of how to characterise the equilibrium of the economy as a whole. The proposal which follows is not quite the proposal which I actually want to make. The latter would include a postulate on the distribution of agents by type. But I have found that in the present formative stage of my ideas the putting across of the full story would have been very complicated and so I shall concentrate on a kind of reduced form version.

The definition which I want to adopt is the following: an economy is in equilibrium when it generates messages which do not cause agents to change the theories which they hold or the policies which they pursue. This is not the usual definition and I return to the difference. The difficulty which arises is in specifying precisely the conditions which will cause an agent to abandon a given theory and change his policy. For the rather abstract formulation of the agent's theory and policy which I have adopted, even simple examples involve the language of statistical decision theory. I am at this stage not at all clear of what the precise formulation should be. So I content myself with the ill specified hypothesis that an agent abandons his theory when it is sufficiently and systematically falsified.

Here is an example. In a given economy an element of each agent's theory is that prices can be treated parametrically. In particular, firms believe they can sell what they wish at prevailing prices and households that they can buy what they wish. The theory of agents therefore predicts prices but not quantities. This theory would be falsified if sufficiently frequently firms found that they could not sell what they wished at prevailing prices or households that they could not buy what they wished. The amounts actually sold at any hypothetical price may have to become an element of the theory held by firms. So one of the conditions for the economy to be in perfectly competitive equilibrium is that agents almost always can sell and buy almost all they wish to at ruling prices. In this case the definition of equilibrium which I have suggested implies almost the missing traditional complement that markets are cleared.

It does not quite imply it for two reasons. First, when one makes the present ideas more precise the exact clearing of markets is not a reasonable necessary condition for the theory I spoke of to be persisted in. Secondly, short enough and rare enough episodes of uncleared markets would on my definition be consistent with equilibrium. These are to me agreeable implications. For instance I am not forced, as is tradition, to say that the economy is out of equilibrium if a housewife finds on a rare instance that the shop has sold out of butter or indeed if there is always some housewife who finds this to be the case in some shop.

It is of course not an implication of this formulation that in equilibrium any quantities and prices or rates of change of these are constant. What is required is a frequency distribution of prices conditional on exogenous events which in some precise sense corresponds closely enough with the prior conditional distributions held by agents. Here much depends on the precise description of the agent which we adopt and if we are much less abstract and demanding in this we shall also have simpler descriptions of equilibrium states. If we restrict ourselves to short intervals of time only the errors which we can permit in the theories held by agents became larger.

In a purely verbal exposition and at this level of generality I cannot really go very much further in describing the equilibrium which I intend. But I must note an important and interesting open question of a technical kind before I justify the approach. In order that any kind of equilibrium, even in simple cases, can be shown to exist I must show that there are theories which, if agents held them, would in that economy not be falsified. This is really what Radner (1972) did in the extremely simple case where the theory consisted in associating a given price vector with every state and having a probability distribution over states. In my case of course the complexity is far greater and it certainly will be a hard job to specify properly even a class of theories agents can hold which may be candidates for equilibrium theories. But it is not just a mathematical but a real problem. For what one is asking in the last resort is whether it is possible to have a decentralised economy in which agents have adapted themselves to their economic environment and where their expectations in the widest sense are in the proper meaning not falsified.

The traditional notion of an equilibrium which I described at the outset requires the equilibrium actions of agents to be consistent, whereas I have the weaker requirement that they not be systematically and persistently inconsistent. Again in the sequential formulation of the traditional notion, single valued expectations are exactly met while I very roughly require the convergence of prior probabilities to frequencies. In the traditional notion the environment to which agents are supposed to be adapted bears only a pale resemblance to a capitalist economy. In the notion which I am proposing adaptation is to fluctuating prices and to noise. If one lives in a capitalist society that is what one is likely to regard as 'normal' and that is what one will have adapted to.

V

It will not have escaped the notice of the professional that it will be a consequence of my approach that one can only discuss the stability in the small of an equilibrium. Disturbances which in a proper sense are small and short enough will allow us to suppose that agents continue in equilibrium actions. Stability will mean that for short enough periods and small enough disturbances the set of equilibria is large but that it shrinks. Some quite interesting arguments are possible here but cannot be pursued. What is to be emphasised is that the position which I have adopted makes it impossible to make any global stability claims.

Indeed it is part of the case that when 'regularity of behaviour' has been translated into the rather broad definition of 'equilibrium behaviour' which is here proposed, we have gone as far as an economist can in the present state of knowledge go. That is why the notion of equilibrium behaviour is of interest and importance. I take this up again in my concluding remarks.

I know return to increasing returns. It has long been a commonplace that in a sequential setting with uncertainty, internal economies to scale and perfect competition need not be incompatible. Moreover in the fuller version which I have refereed to we are permitted the waxing and waning of firms which Marshall had in mind. So there are good grounds for believing that in the formalisation of the ideas here put forward, and it is perhaps useful to stress that this has not yet been accomplished, increasing returns will not prove a great embarrassment.

But it would not be satisfactory to leave it at that when I have undertaken to take special note of Professor Kaldor. The first thing to notice is that Professor Kaldor is describing an equilibrium process where market coherence is ensured by the actions of merchants. These merchants endowed with suitable expecations are quite traditional maximising agents. The increasing returns which are being discussed are, except for the volume/circumference case, of the 'learning by doing' kind. We are not told whether firms in the process grow very large relative to the scale of the economy or not. Curiously enough the process continuing smoothly depends on expectations being more or less correct. Great stress is laid on the mutual interaction of economic forces, in particular that between the extent of the market and the division of labour.

At first sight there is nothing here to cause distress to a champion of the equilibrium notion in economics. Indeed even if learning by doing is internalised by firms and we allow for uncertainty everything is shipshape for traditional tools. Among these of course I include those provided by Professor Kaldor (1939) in a splendid paper on speculation which he wrote many years ago. It is also worth stressing that 'learning by doing' is perfectly consistent with the absence of learning in my sense. So even given the quite natural propensity for all of us to differentiate our produce and given also that there is intrinsic interest in the role assigned to merchants, one is puzzled by the extraordinarily revolutionary implications Professor Kaldor detects in his ideas.

The answer I think is partly provided by the textbook picture Professor Kaldor has of what his colleagues are saying. Roughly speaking the well behaved transformation and indifference curves in two dimensions fill his imagination. For instance the old neoclassical theorem that as we let time progress into the future the transformation surface gets flatter and flatter even without increasing returns is not a result he mentions. Nor I think is he familiar with the rather sophisticated intertemporal version of opportunity cost. The other part of the answer is that he is simply wrong.

In saying this I want to grant everything that is being claimed for the division of labour and its interaction with the extent of the market. I also want to accept the merchants and the importance given to financial matters. One then asks whether Professor Kaldor has any foundation for his claim that one can no longer speak of the efficient allocation of resources and of production or of an equilibrium.

Now we say that a given path taken by the economy is production inefficient if there is an alternative one which gives us more of some good at some time and not less of any good at any time. There is nothing in the economy here discussed which makes such an ordering impossible. If we take finite time horizons, as long as we like, and suppose the set of alternatives closed, then an efficient path also exists. It is simply a muddle to go from the difficulties increasing returns pose to perfect competitive decentralisation to the view that allocation does not matter. Indeed the truth is orthogonal to this view. For the more important increasing returns are, especially the dynamic variety, the greater the potential losses from misallocation. I recommend here Professor Landes' (1970) splendid analysis of why inventions in the textile industry became innovations in England and not for a long time on the continent. Also Professor Kornai (1971) on the consequences of misallocation for the Hungarian economy is very instructive.

I have already dealt with the second part of the question and do not repeat the argument. But I now want to say that not only do Professor Kaldor's critical thrusts go astray, but they are also far too mild. For at no stage does he notice that important increasing returns, not only in production but also in information in the widest sense, will in due course have profound consequences for the institutional arrangements of an economy. Indeed one answer is that it is precisely the difficulty of efficient decentralised acts, if you like the growing realisation of their potential wastefulness and irrationality, which will generate just these forces which may bring the whole system down. In addition of course there are the classical Marxian forces of increased concentration and of formation of coalitions. It is at this point, as I have already remarked before, when a large historical vision is at issue, that equilibrium economics, whether my kind or Professor Kaldor's, is inadequate to the task. I fear that in tilting at the windmill of some old fashioned textbook Professor Kaldor has missed the dragon.

VI

I have already noted that there are economists who wish to do without a microtheory altogether. I have only time to treat the matter slightly.

There are first of all those who believe that an analysis of the kind which I have been developing and which of course has firmly traditional roots, implies that the explanatory emphasis is put on the individual agent when it should be put on social institutions, such as property rights and the social relations which flow from them. I can deal with this very briefly because the view is simply based on a misunderstanding. As I noted right at the outset, traditional equilibrium theory does best when the individual has no importance – he is of measure zero. My theory also does best when all the given theoretical problems arising from the individual's mattering do not have to be taken into account. The social institutions of property and markets have the dominant role. Indeed as Arrow and I wrote in our book (1972) 'The notion that a social system moved by independent actions in pursuit of different values is consistent with a final coherent state of balance and one in which the outcomes may be quite different from that intended by the agents is surely the most important intellectual contribution that economic thought has made to the general understanding of social processes.' So the point is quite simple: to argue that one requires a theory of the action of agents is not at all to maintain that the economy is to be understood by what any one agent wants. For my money, general equilibrium theorists are much closer to Marx than many a Marxist!

It is of course true that it is part of my case that I do not believe there to be an adequate theory of learning in my sense or of routine formation. Certainly here I am at variance with the Marxists. But this fact does not bear on the issue of whether indeed these are important problems. I say that they are and I hope that to this all good Marxists will say amen.

Let me not turn to macroeconomics in its relation to the present issue.

About two thirds of the *General Theory* deals with the theory of the action of agents, their motives for saving and for holding money, their investment and speculative behaviour etc. It is a consequence of intellectual coarseness and not of Keynes that university syllabuses are so frequently divided into watertight macro- and microeconomics courses. Even if it is granted that in the manipulative, one might almost say arithmetical, stages of Keynesian economics, relative prices play a subordinate role, it is after all the case that Keynes argues that the actions of agents in markets would not result in the equilibrium posited by his predecessors. It is hard to see how this very important proposition is to be understood without microtheory. Moreover the fundamental postulate that agents will not persist in actions when more advantageous ones are open to them plays a central role in the Keynesian scheme.

But of course it is absolutely correct to maintain that every feature of an actual economy which Keynes regarded as important is missing in Debreu. Indeed a great deal of what I have said already was in the direction of remedying that deficiency. But it is also true that Debreu and others have made a significant contribution to the understanding of Keynesian economies just by describing so precisely what would have to be the case if there were to be no Keynesian problems.

In the context of the suggestion which I have been making it is for instance plain that for Keynesian reason the theories held by the sellers of labour must include forecasts about the amount they will be able to sell, and that in the description of an equilibrium the theory that there is a ruling wage, at which one can or cannot work, will not be an equilibrium theory. I have constructed a miniature and rather crude model of a simple economy in my kind of equilibrium and it has a satisfactory number of Keynesian characteristics. There seems no good reason to suppose that the careful study of the interaction of agents is an activity hostile to Keynes.

But there is another and more difficult point. Keynes deals essentially with a Marshallian 'representative or average' agent and that is reflected in the work of practical men when they speak of say 'the investment of manufacturing industry' or of 'the savings of the private sector'. This of course is a drastic short cut and it lends to macroeconomics that enviable air of sound common sense. But certainly one must ask when such a short cut is justified and in particular whether it will lead to significant errors. It is one of the oddities of the present scene that the very people who are most convinced that aggregation errors are decisive in rejecting a short cut in the theory of capital are also the most disinclined to enquire what it is claimed to be the case when say investment equals savings. The latter equality is certainly consistent with disequilibrium in every market. I cannot pursue this in any detail now but I should like to make the following point. A macroprocedure is likely to be most reliable and approximately valid when the economy is in the kind of equilibrium which I have described.

The argument here is pretty obvious. In any event it suggests that macrotheorists should not be disinterested in the study of such equilibria.

I do not deal with the view that macroeconomics is in some sense essentially different from other kinds of economics in dealing with relations which are not deducible from the actions of agents, since it is rather obviously false. Also I have already touched on a related view at the beginning of this section.

I have left to the last a quite different matter, which I believe to be best exemplified by Professor Champernowne's important study (1953) of the distribution of incomes between persons. As you know he described a stochastic process, the stationary distribution of which has the Pareto property over the relevant range of observed distributions. This stationary distribution has a claim to be called an equilibrium. Champernowne's work is to be distinguished from that of Green and Majumdar, which I have already referred to, in that the whole theory treats the agent, not as making choices or taking decisions but as a passive receptacle of the random forces to which his income is subject. Another example of this kind of approach is Maurice Kendall's (1953) well known work on the behaviour of share prices, which showed that it could be understood as a Brownian motion.

From the present point of view the importance of these examples and of others like them is that it appears that a successful equilibrium interpretation has been put on observations without the notion of equilibrium actions of agents. Moreover it is usually an equilibrium in a strong sense in that not only will it persist if once attained but that all paths converge on it. But important and interesting as this work is, I do not believe that it contributes evidence against the approach which I have adopted. For it seems to me the case that the argument which these models have in common can only be clinched by an appeal to considerations which are outside the model, among which the equilibrium action of agents is one.

For it is of course not only an open question whether having exhibited one process with a satisfactory asymptotic state there are not others which will do equally well. More importantly the theory must be made congruent with other things which we know, for instance the income chances of different social classes, the genetic distribution of the population and its economic relevance, choices and so on. In other words we shall want to distinguish the randomness generated over states of nature from the random prices generated by actions and choices. To take an extreme example, we may take the distribution of bulls and bears at any price as being random simply because the past has provided no evidence for agent's theories to converge. The quality of bullishness or bearishness acts like a state of nature which is assigned with certain probabilities over agents. But we must still know what it is that bulls will wish to do and what it is that bears will wish to do. Of course this is not a criticism of the very important work which I have referred to – it is an argument designed to show that this work does not lead one to want to do without a theory of equilibrium behaviour of agents. Indeed, as the literature testifies, the processes cannot be understood without such a theory.

VII

I have come to the end of what I can say in the allotted space and also to the end of what at the present stage of my thinking I can usefully say. It will be quite clear that this leaves me very much at the beginning of what could be called a theory. For instance I must draw your attention to the fact that although I used game theoretic considerations to criticise the Arrow–Debreu equilibrium I have hardly mentioned them again since. It is true that the notion here proposed is sufficiently general to accommodate such considerations but then also by the same token the level of generality is too high. Mathematical economists will have noted that the relevant spaces of action and of the environment for instance have been left rather undefined, and it is clear that in any concrete instance of the ideas here discussed they will have to be attended to and may eventually prove very hard. In particular will this be true of acts concerned with coalition formation and preservation. But my purpose has been not to construct a general model of the economy but to outline some of the conceptual operations which I believe now to be required. I have, as I have already reported, tried some extremely simple examples. But very many more will have to be tried before even a tentative judgement on what has been proposed is possible.

But it must be confessed that I have some confidence in some of the main features of the story.

Thus the view that we require an equilibrium notion to make precise the limits of economics and think accordingly, seems to me to be sound. The fact that our evidence is always from the past makes it important to be able to say in what sense and in what circumstances we expect the past to shed light on the future. Our task is both more analytic and far less profound and universal than that of a historian. Certainly we want to study quite specific relationships – say between wage changes and unemployment – which take history for granted and to make generalising claims for regularity. But this regularity which we are interested in is surely associated with the kind of adaptation to an economic environment which I have been discussing.

For instance when one looks at the interesting work by Godley and Nordhaus (1972) on the pricing behaviour of firms one notices that one is asked to accept evidence for a particular form of routine behaviour. In judging it one is naturally interested in the question of whether this behaviour can and will persist and under what circumstances it may do so. It is not only natural but important to think of the proposed regularity as a form of equilibrium behaviour. Certainly it sheds light on this work. But in any case Godley and Nordhaus have made claims not for how firms' behaviour in general is to be understood, but for how equilibrium behaviour should be understood. And that is as it should be.

This view of the arther limited possiblities of economic analysis is not one which will recommand itself to those who want economics to be a study of the 'laws of motion of a capitalist society'. I am not sure what sort of propositions would qualify as such laws nor what their status would be. But I am certain that in such an ambitious intellectual programme the expertise of the economist will only be a very small part of what is required. In the meantime there are many important problems in all societies which if they are not understood by economists will not be understood by anyone and it is here that our main obligation must lie.

I have also considerable confidence in my view that the main progress to be made now is to recognise quite explicitly the essentially sequential structure of the economies which we study and to wrestle with some of the very serious conceptual problems which this raises. In particular the distinction between the perceived environment and the environment and the consequential importance of the theories which are held by agents seems to me bound to become increasingly important in analysis, although it may come to be tackled rather differently than I have suggested here. Lastly I am rather convinced that the rational greedy economic agent will continue in a central role.

The kind of issues which I have been discussing have been concerned with the conceptual apparatus of economic theory. As such the analysis is almost bound to lack concreteness especially when some of the terrain is so speculative, and this fault causes me no feelings of guilt. But since some of what I have to say turned on the inadequacy of our present paradigms I fear that the impression may have been gained that I think the latter to be 'sterile' and 'useless'. Nothing could be further from the truth. Not only does the Arrow—Debreu equilibrium continue to be a special ideal type of the notion here proposed, but it is also of great use for many purposes, some of which have already been noted. But the paradigm itself is of course of ambitious generality and for very many important purposes a much more modest Marshallian apparatus will do very well. For instance no economists required the recent investigation into beef prices. Most economists can go a long way in analysing the consequences of successfully controlling both wages and prices with perfectly traditional tools. In particular they can successfully use traditional notions of equilibrium and disequilibrium.

Indeed given that any actual economy is at least as complex as say the human brain it is surprising of how many propositions concerning it we can say that they are false. One need only think of the amount of misery which has been averted by the demonstration that the arguments for balanced budgets are false to agree that economics can do good even when it does not predict. The many false and harmful views on the role of prices which Arrow—Debreu confine to oblivion are also a feather in our cap.

I have therefore been concerned with the task of extending the range of phenomena the theory can deal with and not at all with a demonstration that the theory at present cannot deal with anything at all. Indeed I attach the greatest importance to the continuity of intellectual enterprises and would consider it a sure signal of bad scholarship and reasoning if I have kicked away all the ladders which we have. Professor Kaldor (1972) has quoted Einstein evidently engaged in answering a Kaldorian critique of abstract and difficult theory. Einstein in effect says that of course the final arbiter of any theory will have to be the evidence and this Einsteinian aversion to sin I share. It is not at all clear that the views of a physicist of genius on matters of epistemology or economics should have a special claim on our attention. But it so happens that Einstein has also delivered a pronouncement on the matter (Sacks 1972) which I have been discussing in the last few minutes. Since I so much agree with it I conclude by giving it here:

Creating a new theory is not like destroying an old barn and erecting a skyscraper in its place. It is rather like climbing a mountain, gaining new and wider views, discovering new connections between our starting point and its rich environment. But the point from which we started still exists and can be seen, although it appears smaller and forms a tiny part of our broad view gained by the mastery of the obstacles on our adventurous way up.

REFERENCES

Arrow, K. J. and Hahn, F. H. 1972. *General Competitive Analysis*, Oliver & Boyd

Champernowne, D. G. 1953. A model of income distribution, *Economic Journal*

Debreu, G. 1959. *Theory of Value*, Wiley

Ddob, , M. 1973. Marshall Lecture, unpublished

Ellman, M. 1972. Review of Kornai: *Anti-Equilibrium, Economic Journal*, December

Farrell, M. J. 1967. The convexity assumption in the theory of competitive markets, *Journal of Political Economy*

Godley, W. A. H. and Nordhaus, W. D. 1972. Pricing in the trade cycle, *Economic Journal*

Grandmont, J. M. 1977. Temporary general Equilibrium, *Econometrica*

Green, J. R. 1971. Stochastic equilibrium: a stability theorem and application, Technical report no, 46, August, Stanford

Green, J. R. and Majundar, M. 1972. The nature and existence of stochastic equilibria, mimeo

Hahn, F. H. 1952. Expectation and equilibrium, *Economic Journal*, chapter 1 above

Hahn, F. H. 1971. Equilibrium with transaction cost, *Econometrica*

Hildenbrand, W. 1971. Random preferences and equilibrium analysis, *Journal of Economic Theory*

Hurwicz, L. 1972. On the dimensional requirements of informationally decentralized Pareto-satisfactory processes, mimeo

Kaldor, N. 1939. Speculation and economic stability, *Review of Economic Studies*

Kaldor, N. 1972. The irrelevance of equilibrium economics, *Economic Journal*

Kendall, M. 1953. The analysis of economic time series, *Journal of Royal Statistic Society*

Kornai J. 1971. *Anti-Equilibrium*, North Holland

Landes, David S. 1970. *The Unbound Prometheus*, Cambridge University Press
Lerner, A. P. 1944. *The Economics of Control*, Macmillan
Radner, R. 1968. Competitive equilibrium under uncertainty, *Econometrica*
Radner, R. 1972. Existence of equilibrium of plans, prices and price expectations in a sequence market, *Econometrica*
Russell, Bertrand 1931. *The Scientific Outlook*, Allen and Unwin
Sacks, O. 1972, *Listener*, 30 November
Samuelson, P. A. 1967. *Foundations of Economic Analysis*, Atheneum
Schumpeter, Joseph 1955. The sociology of imperialism, in *Social Classes, Imperialism*, Meridian
Starr, R. M. 1967. Quasi-equilibria in markets with non-convex preferences, *Econometrica*
Walras, L. 1954. *Elements of Pure Economics*, Allen and Unwin, London

3

General Equilibrium Theory

In decentralised economies a large number of individuals make economic decisions which, in the light of market and other information, they consider most advantageous. They are not guided by the social good, nor is there an overall plan in the unfolding of which they have preassigned roles. It was Adam Smith who first realised the need to explain why this kind of social arrangement does not lead to chaos. Millions of greedy, self-seeking individuals, in pursuit of their own ends and mainly uncontrolled in these pursuits by the state, seem to 'common sense' a sure recipe for anarchy. Smith not only posed an obviously important question, but also started us off on the road to answering it. General equilibrium theory as classically stated by Arrow and Debreu (1954) and Debreu (1959) is near the end of that road. Now that we have got there we find it less enlightening than we had expected. The reason is partly that the world has moved on and is no longer as decentralised as it used to be, and partly that the road we pursued was excessively straight and narrow and made — we now feel — with too little allowance for the wild and varied terrain it had to traverse. We have certainly arrived at an orderly destination, but it looks increasingly likely that we cannot rest there.

Here is a simple account of general equilibrium theory. The basic building block is the individual agent. Agents are divided into two types: households and firms. Start with the latter. A firm is an agent that transforms inputs into outputs. There may be many ways of doing this (there may be many *activities*), and the firm is assumed to know a book of blueprints or *production set* which gives the menu of activities from which it must choose. Given the prices of all inputs and outputs which the firm regards as beyond its own control, the firm will choose from the menu the activity which is most profitable, that is, which gives the maximum difference between the value of outputs and the value of inputs. The activity choice of each firm thus depends in principle on the prices of all goods.

At this stage, a crucial convention and a crucial assumption is introduced. The convention is this: goods are distinguished by their physical attributes, their location, the date of their delivery, and by the state of nature. (A state of nature is a complete description of the environment which is independent of the actions of agents.) The crucial assumption is that all goods thus defined have markets, that is, each of them has a price. Thus, for instance, there is a price quoted today for umbrellas to be delivered in Cambridge on Christmas Day 1980 if it rains. This is not a very realistic assumption and I return to it. Here we may note that at least some of the disorders of a capitalist society which Keynes considered can be traced to the absence of some of these Arrow - Debreu markets. With this crucial assumption, profit maximisation entails the choice of an activity which specifies inputs and outputs at each date and location and in each contingency. Since all goods as defined have current markets, the firm undertakes no uncertainty.

The household, when the story starts, is endowed with a basket of goods (which includes its stock of leisure of a certain type which it can supply as labour to firms), and with certain entitlements to shares in the profits of firms.[1]

The household takes prices as given. Its choice menu consists of all those bundles which it could physically consume and which it can also 'afford'. A bundle can be afforded if the cost of purchases does not exceed the receipts from sales. With our definition of goods and our assumption on markets, borrowing and lending and indeed all intertemporal transactions are included in this notion of affording. For instance, selling (or buying) a dollar for delivery next year is equivalent to borrowing (lending) a certain sum now. The household is now supposed to choose a bundle

---

[1] The taking of these initial endowments as exogenous has been criticised and much misunderstood, in particular by Marxist critics. For instance, it is often argued that this makes the distributions of income and of wealth exogenous. But to go from the distribution of physical endowments to the distribution of wealth, we need to know the value of the endowment and that depends on prices and these are fully endogenous. In any case, even Marxists have to start the clock sometime after Neanderthal man, and when they do they will find people equipped with axes, seed, and the like, and they will not attempt to explain these possessions further.

such that there is no other bundle in its choice menu which it prefers. The household choice will thus in general depend on all prices and on the household's endowment. (We do not have to include its entitlement to profit here separately, since we already know these themselves are, uniquely, given once prices are.)

An equilibrium of the economy is a state in which the independently taken decisions of households and firms are compatible. Thus it is a set of prices such that if they ruled there is a profit maximising choice of firms and a preference maximising choice of households *such that the total demand for any good is equal to the amount of it initially available, plus the amount of it produced*. The equilibrium prices impose order on potential chaos. To show that these equilibrium prices can indeed be found, one needs a number of further assumptions. The most important of these is the absence of significant economies of scale in production.

But the theory goes further than showing that order is a possibility in a decentralised economy. It shows that an equilibrium has this property: that there exists *no* reallocation of goods such that *every* household attains a position preferred by it to its equilibrium position – *at least one household must be made worse off by every such reallocation*. The equilibrium allocation is thus shown to be *Pareto efficient*. It is important to understand that this does not mean that the allocation is just. Indeed, there are many Pareto efficient allocations (in general a continuum). Under certain assumptions, in particular the absence of increasing returns to scale and non-convex preferences,[2] one can show that each of these allocations could be a competitive equilibrium for some distribution of endowments. That is, by varying the distribution of endowments we change the equilibrium allocation (and prices), but every equilibrium is Pareto efficient. Or put differently: every Pareto-efficient allocation can be decentralised into a competitive equilibrium. Hence the moral questions concern the distribution of endowments, and equilibrium as such is only of limited moral relevance. A bad nomenclature (Pareto optimum) in the literature, together with much carelessness in textbooks, often misleads people into thinking that there is some theorem which claims that a competitive equilibrium is socially optimal. There is no such claim.

---

[2] Suppose a household is indifferent between a and b, two points in commodity space (one axis each good). Preferences are non-convex if some point c, with $c = \alpha a + (1-\alpha)b$, $0 < \alpha < 1$, is inferior to both a and b.

It is convenient to break off the account here and to take stock. It is clear from what has already been said that in part at least general equilibrium theory is an abstract answer to an abstract and important question: can a decentralised economy relying only on price signals for market information be orderly? The answer of general equilibrium theory is clear and definitive: one can describe such an economy with these properties. But this of course does not mean that any actual economy has been described. An important and interesting theoretical question has been answered and in the first instance that is all that has been done. This is a considerable intellectual achievement, but it is clear that for praxis a great deal more argument is required.

FRIENDS AND CRITICS

The theory itself has often suffered a good deal from its friends. Some friends – in what might be called roughly, and a bit unfairly, 'Chicago' economics – have taken the theory in practical applications a good deal more seriously than at present there is any justification for doing. Paradoxically they are rather hostile to its abstract foundations, yet are happy to put a great deal of weight on them. For instance, Milton Friedman's definition of the natural level of unemployment is a good example of application outrunning applicability. I return to these friends again briefly below. Other dangerous friends are certain textbook writers. Enemies find their books an endless mine of careless language and slipshod claims. Whole books have been written to refute some textbook scribblers, whose besetting sin is that they use the theory mechanically and apparently without understanding. For instance, there are many accounts to be found of the proposition that a free-trade equilibrium is Pareto efficient for the world as a whole. Very rarely do these textbooks spell out completely and precisely what is required to reach this result, in particular, absence of increasing returns and a complete set of Arrow–Debreu markets. If these assumptions were stated and discussed, they might be less inclined to declare free trade 'optimal'. As it is, their concentration on the case of two goods, for 'expository reasons', leads them to forget that this device stops them from discussing intertemporal problems, that is, at least half the story. I often wonder whether other subjects suffer as much from textbook writers.

The enemies, on the other hand, have proved curiously ineffective and they have very often aimed their arrows at the wrong targets. Indeed if it is the case that today general equilibrium theory is in some disarray, this is largely due to the work of general equilibrium theorists, and not to any successful assault from outside. Before I discuss this disarray, I shall very briefly consider some recent critics.

One view frequently expressed is that the neo-classical theory is pre-eminently concerned with the allocation of given resources among alternative uses and that it is thus best considered as relevant to a theory of exchange, rather than to a theory of production and growth. For example, it is said that the theory begins, 'not with production but with exchange' and then 'adds on' production 'to make possible the indirect exchange of factor services for final commodities' (Walsh and Gram 1979). This is then contrasted with classical theory which apparently 'starts' with production. It is very hard to make anything of this argument. I do not see in what sense general equilibrium theory, except perhaps historically, 'starts' with exchange or, for that matter, with production. Both take place and are incorporated in the theory. Nor is it easy to see why so much fuss has been made about exogenously given endowments. No sensible theory would, as I have already noted, start with Neanderthal man. At whatever date we start, we had better take the available resources at that date, and their distribution, as exogenously given by history. Starting with these endowments, an economy has a large number of possible futures which, among other things, depend on technological 'knowhow' and the rate at which durable inputs are augmented. General equilibrium theory considers a very narrow subset of these futures, i.e. those which are Arrow–Debreu competitive equilibria. This is indeed restrictive, but that is not the issue here. These futures are characterised by accumulation, and the distribution of wealth is an outcome and not a given. Among other things which the theory accomplishes is an end to the nonsensical view that intertemporarily, or because there is production, the notion of opportunity cost loses its relevance either for explanation or planning.

It is possible that the outputs produced in an Arrow–Debreu economy in the far distant future are independent of its initial endowments. That would mean that in such an economy the relative scarcities prevailing now would have no influence on the relative prices and rentals in the distant future. This should be enough to persuade the critics that the theory is not committed to a relative scarcity theory of distribution, though they seem to believe it is and and that often motivates them in their attacks. General equilibrium theorists are aware that some inputs are reproductive and production is an integral part of the theory they study.

It is of course the question of distribution which is the most urgent for many of the critics. Many of them are after a theory which will explain the distribution of income between classes, specifically between workers and capitalists, and they wish to formulate the theory in such a way that class conflict and power become central explanatory variables. It is perfectly true that general equilibrium theory is not suitable for this project; the question is whether it is in direct conflict with it, or more modestly, whether it can be of use in the ambitious projects of the critics.

Suppose that it was claimed that a particular class-conflict theory can explain the prevailing level of wages. In looking at this claim, one might ask whether at those wages any one capitalist could increase his profits by hiring more labour than he does. If the answer is yes, and more labour is not hired, then there is something to explain. Or it may be a way of explaining something, such as a more or less explicit convention not to compete for labour. If, on the other hand, no capitalist is tempted to change his hiring, then each worker is worthy of his hire and the marginal productivity relations hold. *The point of the argument is this: the fundamental element of neo-classical theory, that agents will, if it is open to them, take actions they consider advantageous, cannot be ignored by any grand theory of power and conflict.* Indeed, if such theories ever mature, this feature of the situation may also be central for them. There may of course be more sociologically based definitions of 'advantageous' and a much broader class of actions than the neo-classical ones may have to be considered. But it is very hard to see how anything can be achieved without at some stage coming to grips with the agent and his interests. It is therefore not at all clear that from the vantage point of such an achieved theory, general equilibrium analysis will not be seen as a stepping stone rather than as a cul-de-sac.

There are two further points to make. The first one is this: there exists at present no alternative theory which explains what general equilibrium theory seeks to explain, and in particular none which does this by means of consideration of power and class conflict. Ask the Marxist economist why the composition of output is what it is and at best you will get a Leontief answer which is a linear general equilibrium answer. Ask him to explain relative prices and you get the 'transformation problem' which you surely do not want. Ask him to predict the 'subsistence' wage of Western industrial workers on the basis of power and conflict; ask him to study the impact of OPEC on techniques of production; indeed, ask him to explain recent trends in the distribution of income, and you will find that he has either nothing to say or that he gives answers which in no way conflict with an analysis starting from neo-classical premises. He may have deep things to say about the 'innate laws of history' but he is likely to offer stones in those areas whrere general equilibrium theory provides the basis for some answers. These answers, of course, may be wrong. But the point remains: there are no credible rivals in answering the particular questions which general equilibrium analysis has posed. (On the other hand, as I argue below, these questions may be too narrowly and academically based.)

Does not the classical revival led by Sraffa (1960) present a valid challenge and a well formulated alternative to general equilibrium theory? My second point is that the answer to this question is no. I have documented this answer at length elsewhere (Hahn, 1982) and it would be inappropriate to repeat it here. I accordingly simply assert that there are no logically coherent propositions of Sraffian analysis which are not also true propositions of general equilibrium analysis, and although the classical revivalists often speak of the importance of power and of conflict, these find no formal place in their theory. They do sometimes argue that the rate of profit is determined by these forces, but they leave the manner of it impenetrable.

BUTTRESSING THE DEFENCES

The ease with which so much current critique of general equilibrium analysis can be countered is potentially dangerous. For as I said at the outset, the citadel is not at all secure and the fact that it is safe from a bombardment of soap bubbles does not mean that it is safe. Fortunately, those 'inside' have begun to build new walls and to lay new foundations.

The first important need is to develop the theory so that it can deal with a larger range of questions than it now does. For instance, it is not possible to pose any monetary questions in the context of an Arrow–Debreu model since, according to that construction, money would have no role and hence would not be viable. Similarly, the theory cannot explain a market in shares, and it cannot take account of certain forms of uncertainty and certain forms of market expectations which are important in Keynesian theory and important for policy. Oligopoly and imperfect competition have also been abstracted from and the theory does not allow one to answer interesting questions which turn on the asymmetry of information among agents. For all of these purposes, the strict assumptions of the theory will have to be restyled — with possibly fateful consequences.

There is also a canker at the heart of the theory. This arises from the logical necessity that a theory based on rational self-seeking actions ensures that its equilibrium notion is indeed that of a state in which no agent can improve himself by any action. But all general equilibrium theory has done is ensure this *provided market prices are independent of these actions*. Moreover, we have not considered the possible actions of agents which consist in forming a coalition. When these matters are seriously considered, the set of economies for which general equilibrium could be the appropriate theory shrinks. In particular, it is generally true that the theory can apply only to 'large economies', i.e. economies with many (indeed perhaps a continuum) of agents.

Recent work by Ostroy (1976) and Makowski (1979) allow one to clarify part of this problem. Consider an equilibrium allocation for an economy with n agents. Suppose now that one agent withdraws from the economy. If in the equilibrium with $n-1$ agents all of these do as well as before when there were n, if indeed their allocations remain unchanged, then the withdrawing individual has no power in the economy — he cannot harm or indeed aid anyone. This is called by Ostroy the 'no surplus' condition. Each agent contributes exactly as much to the economy as he takes out. It can be shown that no surplus is a condition which must be satisfied if rational agents are to treat prices parametrically as general equilibrium theory supposes to be the case. For if the no surplus condition does *not* hold, an agent can by his actions affect the equilibrium prices of the economy. In general, this condition will only be satisfied in large economies, although there are some special small economy examples.

This line of analysis has close but not yet completely understood connections with the theory of the core. Consider any arbitrary allocation of goods in an economy without production. Ask whether any group of agents (which includes the group of all agents) could each feasibly improve themselves by reallocating the goods which they have among themselves. If such a group exists we say that it blocks the given allocation. An allocation is in the core if it cannot be blocked by any group (coalition). Notice that prices and markets do not enter into this definition and that the core could be considered a sort of social equilibrium.

Now it can be shown that for large economies the only allocations in the core are in fact the equilibrium allocations of general equilibrium analysis. On the other hand, for 'small' economies there are core allocations which are not equilibria of this kind. But such allocations have considerable claim to be called equilibrium allocations. Production causes further problems.

The outcome of all of this is that one must agree that the Arrow–Debreu theory will run into logical difficulties in small economies; that is, those in which the actions of a single agent can affect equilibrium outcomes. Yet as formulated, the theory stipulates a finite number of agents and takes these as given. Strictly speaking, then, the received theory is inconsistent. It is also incomplete. For though one can argue that it is reasonable to take the number of households as exogenous, this is not so when it comes to the number of firms. In fact we have here another difficulty with the theory which does not turn on its realism and relevance.

For the firm is a shadowy figure in general equilibrium analysis. It is simply an agent which converts inputs into outputs. But why is not every household its own firm when increasing returns have been ruled out? Why does not every firm produce all the goods there are? Why is the number of firms finite? It would seem that to make sense of firms at all we must at least stipulate the existence of set-up costs and so allow for some increasing returns. Once again, by excluding these the existing theory is dangerously close to being inconsistent. It certainly has not answered the question why the number of firms is what it is. Recent work by Novshek and Sonnenschein (1978) and by Hart (1979) has gone some way to rectifying this difficulty regarding economies which are large relative to the set-up costs of firms. But for economies which are not large in this sense, we .have no theory at present. (It should be added that the work referred to relies on a Cournot–Nash approach which itself is not free from objections.)

Thus, there are purely theoretical problems which general equilibrium theory has left unresolved, and it is only quite recently that logical holes have been plugged by an appeal to large economies. The latter in a loose sense are economies in which agents are without economic power. Therefore, as I have already argued, those who regard power as central to economic understanding must look beyond classical general equilibrium theory. I rather count myself among those, and my earlier strictures were directed at the unfortunate fact that no serious work in new directions is available.

If Arrow-Debreu economies take no heed of power, they are also cavalier in their treatment of time. *The assumption that all intertemporal and all contingent markets exist has the effect of collapsing the future into the present.* A man who wants to exchange labour today for orange juice tomorrow *if he has a cold*, can do so today by selling current labour and buying the contingent contract: orange juice tomorrow if I have a cold and nothing if I do not. Such a man must form expectations on the probability of getting a cold but not of any market variables. This scenario can be attacked on the grounds of realism and relevance. We know that many of the stipulated markets do not exist.

But it can also be questioned on more fundamental grounds. These are of two kinds. First, in the example it may not be possible for a second person to observe whether I have have a cold or not, and so the seller of the contingent orange juice would be in trouble. In general, when agents have different information, some of the required markets cannot exist (Radner 1971). Secondly, if exchange is costly (because agents must find one another and/or shops and advertising are required), then certain markets will not open because it does not pay to do so. Both these considerations suggest that the conditions for all Arrow — Debreu markets to exist are very restrictive indeed.

Once these markets are incomplete, rather terrible things happen to the theory. The economy will now have trading at every date – we are dealing with a sequence economy. Agents' actions at any date will now depend on their beliefs concerning *future* events (e.g. rain or shine, war or peace, cold or no cold) and on the prices which will rule *given these events*. But we have no theory of expectations comparable with our theory of household or firm choice; that is to say, we certainly have no axiomatic foundations for such a theory and scarcely have we a psychologically plausible account.

TWO STEPS

There are two steps one can take. One is to take expection formation as exogeneous and to restrict attention to short period equilibria; that is, to consider only those current prices which, given the expectation formation and given that agents have done their best for themselves with the expectations, will clear current markets (see Grandmont 1977 for a survey). In the next period, of course, expectations may be falsified and a new equilibrium in then current prices may be established. Taking this route means that the price mechanism will no longer ensure Pareto efficiency in the usual sense. On this account, then, the economy staggers from one short period equilibrium to another, and a good deal of this rests on unexplained expectations formation.

The other route is to invoke rational expectations. Price expectations are rational if each agent correctly predicts the equilibrium prices which are associated with every possible state of nature.[3] A rational expectation equilibrium obtains if the optimising actions of agents in the light of their rational expectations lead to the clearing of markets at all dates. Once again, such an equilibrium (if it exists) is not Pareto efficient in the usual sense, since the absence of some markets still prevents mutually advantageous exchanges between agents. Rational expectations themselves are justified by the argument that rational agents will learn what is the case. The argument at present is ill founded in theory for it must be shown that agents *could* learn. That, except for examples, has not been demonstrated. Just as classical general equilibrium theory has never been able to provide a definitive account of how equilibrium prices come to be established, so rational expectation theory has not shown how, starting from relative ignorance, everything that can be learned comes to be learned. The obvious route here is via Bayes' Theorem but there are formidable difficulties in general equilibrium application.

Put at its mildest, the sequence economy has presented problems of market expectations which are not yet resolved. Unfortunately, this is not all. In a sequence economy, it is not at all clear what it is that the firm should maximise; or, to put it differently, it is not clear what we mean by the best interest of shareholders. Once again, the villain is the absence of some markets. Suppose sharehold a wants the production plan of his firm to change by substituting some output of rainwear for summer frocks. He attaches a high probability to a rainy summer. Shareholder b wants the reverse change because his climatic beliefs are the reverse of those of a. In an Arrow-Debreu economy, this situation would lead to mutually beneficient exchange in contingent contracts between a and b. As it is, the two just disagree. A very large literature has grown up on this subject (most recently Grossman and Hart 1979). But although there are many suggestions, the issues are fundamentally unresolved. This is extremely serious for neo-classical theory since simple profit maximisation has been a cornerstone of the analysis. It may well be that the theoretical difficulties which we face when we have decided to take missing markets seriously will only be resolvable by a managerial theory of production.

As I have already noted, the lack of some Arrow–Debreu markets can be partly explained by the difference in information available to different agents. But the problems with information do not stop there. Classical general equilibrium theory assumes that every agent knows all prices and that every agent has all the information that is needed about every good. Think of a second hand motor car or the hiring of a new assistant professor to see that it would be interesting to relax the last assumption. Once again, it turns out that the received theory is less robust than one might wish.

All sorts of new problems arise, but also all sorts of new insights have been gained. One of these is this: sellers must find a way of signalling the quality of what they have to sell. In the labour market, this may be done by means of educational qualifications. These are costly to acquire but one may reasonably postulate that the better worker has a lower cost of doing so. One then studies a 'signalling equilibrium' which is a schedule of wages such that no worker has an incentive to change the qualifications he acquires and employers have no incentive to change the schedule relating wage to qualification. In a splendid early work, Spence (1974) showed that there are many such equilibria, so that there is no presumption that the resources used in acquiring qualifications are used efficiently. Recently certain weaknesses in this analysis have been corrected. But this is only one example and many other cases have been studied. In particular, much attention has recently been given to cases where

---

[3] There are other more econometrically based definitions which are more or less equivalent to the above.

information is market dependent. For instance, in accident insurance the choice of contract by the agent may reveal to the insurer his accident probability. In a most fruitful paper, Roths-child and Stiglitz (1976) have shown that these cases no equili-brium may exist. The reasons for this have been further investigated by Hahn (1977).

None of this has yet been properly integrated into general equilibrium analysis. At the first attempts, some unexpected problems were encountered. If agents have asymmetrical infor-mation before the market opens, it may be the case that when it does open the market price will reveal all the information there is to everyone. (Think of someone with special knowledge trying to cash in on the stock exchange.) But then special information is worthless to its possessor. On the other hand, if no one had the special information, then the equilibrium would be different and it would be worth while to acquire it. This paradox – crudely summarised here – has been much studied recently and with some success. It appears that the situation will arise rarely or not at all if the information mart is noisy (Radner 1979).

Lack of information concerning prices leads to a search for the best bargain. This has been much studied in the context of the labour market. One can, on certain hypotheses, calculate the optimum search strategy. There is interest now in the idea of a search equilibrium – that is, a state where there are always some agents engaged in search but there is no tendency for their number or the relative prices to change. This is at the bottom of Friedman's 'natural rate hypothesis', the proposition that there is an equilibrium account of unemployment of those engaged in search. This literature has led to the view that most of the unemployment which we observe is voluntary, and it leads me to the last topic that space permits.

No meaning can be given in classical general equilibrium theory to the notion of an equilibrium with involuntary unemployment. The neo-classical axiom, that wages will fall as long as not all those wishing to work can find a job, sees to that. In this world, there is no occasion for Keynesian policies. Indeed no very good sense can be made of the Keynesian opus, a circumstance re-inforced by the fact that Keynes and most of his followers never attempted to ground their theory rigorously. But certainly Key-nesian theory and policy cannot be reconciled with classical general equilibrium theory.

But general equilibrium theory has never justified its pricing axiom and certainly has not given any account of how wages are set when the economy is out of equilibrium. When, however, one looks for such a theory taking account of hiring costs, the divergence of interest between the employed and unemployed, the risk aspects of the labour contract and the possible formation of coalitions of workers, it becomes clear that there may be no inducement to change wages even when there is involuntary unemployment. There is as yet no definitive theory, but there are strong indications that the rational interests of the agents involved may result in some wage inflexibility. This line of research also reveals quite generally that if price changes are themselves the outcome of rational assessment of their consequence for the agent making the change, then we can no longer take the neo-classical axiom for granted. This in turn means that we must consider new equilibrium notions. At least this is so for economies which are not large in the appropriate sense.

In this new equilibrium we think of agents observing not only the prices at which they can trade, but also any limits there may be on the amount they can trade. Thus an unemployed worker notices that the likelihood of selling his labour at the going wage is less than certain and he adjusts his other actions, such as his consumption, accordingly. Agents must now consider whether they can affect the limitations on their trading by offering to trade at different prices. The farmer who cannot sell all his apples must consider the consequences of lowering his price. An employer who sees that workers have been constrained in their sale of labour must consider whether to lower the wage. If there are monopolistic elements in the economy and, more generally, if the economy is not large enough, there may now be states in which agents are constrained in their transactions and yet prices do not change. Such a state would have strong claims to be regarded as an equilibrium. It is clear that this could be consistent with involuntary unemployment.

THE CORRECT PATH

These new, non-Walrasian equilibrium concepts are in their infancy. No complete or fully convincing theory is available. But I consider them to be on the right lines for the following reason. There is overwhelming evidence to suggest that production and investment decisions are taken on the basis of calculations of expected demand. If you gave General Motors all the prices which will rule in 1981 and nothing else, they would not be able to formulate plans for 1981 simply because they know that they cannot sell (and buy) all they want at these prices. If you like, non-perfect competition must be invoked to account for this. General equilibrium theory as we now have it cannot deal with this situation. But it is a situation for which we should like to have a theory. When we have it, the present theoretical disillusionment with Keynes will, I conjecture, be reversed.

If we think of an economy in non-Walrasian equilibrium with involuntary unemployment, it would seem that Keynesian policies would once again come into their own. To this it has been objected that fully foreseen policies – as all systematic ones in principle can be – will be ineffective. For example, if, when there is X per cent unemployment, government spends Y per cent more, and this is anticipated, then it will be known that prices will be higher and agents will demand less and offset the government injection. These arguments seem false and are certainly unproven. Those which I have seen are based on unexplained linear macroequations, and essentially rely on the neo-classical axiom that prices must change as long as there is a constraint on transactions. I cannot here develop the full argument (for this see McCallum 1980 and Hahn 1980), but only dogmatically assert that there are good grounds for believing that we shall soon have satisfactory theories of non-Walrasian equilibria and that these are highly likely to leave scope for government macropolicy to be effective.

There is, of course, much more to say that is outside the confines of this paper. As I see it the situation can be summed up as follows. Classical general equilibrium theory is a major intellectual achievement. It describes a situation where private self-interest, governed only by market prices, can be consistent with a coherent and orderly economy. We now know that, generally speaking, the original postulates must be augmented by appealing to 'large' economies. This leaves an obvious lacuna – the 'small' economy. Similarly, we know now that the theory is very sensitive to the postulate that all goods have markets and that it has assumed away many interesting informational problems. The journals are full of papers addressed to these matters, and although we are still in the tunnel there are also chinks of light. If we successfully reach the end, I believe it will be found that the route has been straighter and cleaner than it would have been had we not started from general equilibrium theory. The theory itself, however, is likely to recede and be superseded. There seems absolutely no reason to believe that the new theory will have been anticipated by some defunct nineteenth century economist or that it will be in the form of linear identities. Nor, on the other hand, does it seem likely that it will give much support to those who are now teaching politicians from vulgarising neo-classical textbooks.

REFERENCES

Arrow, K. J. and Debreu G. 1954. Existence of an equilibrium for a competitive economy, *Econometrica*
Debreu, G. 1959. *Theory of Value*, Wiley
Friedman, M. 1959. *The Optimum Quantity of Money*, Macmillan
Grandmont, J. M. 1977. Temporary equilibrium, *Econometrica*
Grossman S. J. and Hart, O. 1979. A theory of competitive equilibrium in stock market economies, *Econometrica*
Hahn, F. H. 1977. On equilibrium with market-dependent information, in *Quantitative Wirtschaftsforschung Studien*, Mohr
Hahn, F. H. 1980. Comments on McCallum, *Economica*, August
Hahn, F. H. 1982. The neo-Ricardians, *Cambridge Journal of Economics*, chapter 17 below
Hart, O. 1970. Monopolistic competition in large economies with differential commodities, *Review of Economic Studies*
McCallum, B. T. 1980. Hahn's theoretical viewpoint on unemployment: a comment, *Economica*, August
Makowski, L. A. characterisation of perfectly competitive economics with production, economic theory discussion paper no. 25. Cambridge
Novshek, W. and Sonnenschein, H. 1978. Cournot and Walras equilibrium, *Econometrica*
Ostroy, J. 1976. The no-surplus condition as a characterisation of perfectly competitive equilibrium, mimeo
Radner, R. 1971. General equilibrium with uncertainty, *Econometrica*
Radner, R. 1979. Rational expectations equilibrium: generic existence and the information revealed by prices, *Econometrica*, May
Rothschild, M. and Stiglitz, J. 1976. Equilibrium in competitive insurance markets, *Quarterly Journal of Economics*
Spence, A. M. 1974. *Market Signalling*, Harvard University Press
Sraffa, P. 1960. *The Production of Commodities by Means of Commodities*, Cambridge University Press
Walsh, V. and Gram, H. 1979. *Classical and Neo-Classical Theories of General Equilibrium*, Oxford University Press

4

Some Adjustment Problems

I am concerned on this occasion with the preformance of the 'invisible hand' in a number of abstract economies which have been discussed in recent years. My findings are rather pessimistic in the sense that I see no support for the view that any of the traditional methods of response of various agents to changes in their economic environment makes the 'hand' perform as it is often taken to perform. One cannot exclude the possibility that the world behaves a good deal better than the models – but it is the models that lead people to view the economic system as they do. It certainly is hard to find a justification for the great preoccupation of both research and teaching with equilibrium economics unless one is also prepared to believe in, at least, a Marshallian tendency to equilibrium.

Of course one of the reasons why so much of our effort is devoted to the study of equilibria is that they are singularly well suited to study. We all know the endless variety of adjustment models, not uncongenial to common sense, that one is capable of constructing. No unifying principle, such as maximisation, seems available; no elegant separation theorems reduce the mass of ugly differential or difference equations to the splendid order of a chapter in Debreu. To discuss and analyse how the economy works it may be necessary to go and look.

The achievements of economic theory in the last two decades are both impressive and in many ways beautiful. But it cannot be denied that there is something scandalous in the spectacle of so many people refining the analyses of economic states which they give no reason to suppose will ever, or have ever, come about. It probably is also dangerous. Equilibrium economics, because of its well know welfare economics implication, is easily convertible into an apologia for existing economic arrangements and it is frequently so converted. On the other end of the scale, the recent, fairly elaborate analysis of the optimum plans for an economy which is always in equilibrium has, one suspects, misled people to believe that we actually know how an economy is to be controlled. When we talk of decentralising a plan we think of agents maximising at given shadow prices and not of the design of decentralised information systems and responses which have only recently begun to be discussed by such economists as Kornai and Malinvaud. It is an unsatisfactory and slightly dishonest state of affairs.

It cannot be claimed that in this paper I can escape the charge of *tu quoque*, or that I do more than shake a few skeletons in dusty cupboards. But I hope that it may perhaps cause someone here and there to consider the problem worthy of attention.

I THE WALRASIAN ECONOMY

It must now, I fear, be admitted that the study of the Walrasian 'groping' or tâtonnement process has not been very fruitful. It was hoped that, by considering a situation so drastically simplified by the supposition of 'recontract' or no exchange, it would be possible to lay bare the essentials of the law of 'supply and demand' and that once revealed they would be found to be 'good'. What has been achieved is a collection of sufficient conditions, one might almost say anecdotes, and a demonstration by Scarf that not much more could be hoped for. The villain of the piece, at least in the differential equation form of the process first suggested by Samuelson, was the income effects of households. If, for instance, all households are alike in the sense of Gorman, the process is convergent and the unique equilibrium stable. This is somewhat surprising since in other branches of the subject, say trade cycle theory, no one had ever thought that the Hicksian income terms should be regarded as of such paramount importance. It suggestes that the world one is here concerned with is somewhat odd. I will return to this later. But first, one should note that even in the best cases the exact form of the adjustment process is important. For instance, even that congenial circumstance when all goods are gross substitutes will not allow us to deduce that our artificial invisible had is doing well, should the process be described by a set of finite difference equations. The speed of adjustment now also plays a crucial role. Secondly, even when convergence can be demonstrated the speed of convergence may be very slow – a point which in a different context has received recent attention from Atkinson and Sato. The return on our heroic assumption appears to have been small.

It may also have been misleading. Consider a pure exchange economy. Let the pricing rule be Samuelsonian but allow exchange at all prices. Assume that two individuals exchange if and only if neither suffers a utility loss by so doing and one gains. With some further, rather innocuous technical assumptions, it can be shown that this process is always convergent on to a Pareto-optimal allocation. I will argue in a moment that this is not a process that can be readily defended as an appropriate picture. But I now wish to draw attention to some of the lessons it has to teach.

It is easily seen that matters have been so arranged as to make the economy follow a gradient process – the vector of utilities is never declining in any component and increasing in some. We have here one of the few constructions where the invisible hand can be analysed under the grand unifying principle of maximisation, and when that is possible then it is also a beneficient hand. If one can understand why this is not generally true then one is well on the way to seeing how little current modes of theorising can help in these problems. In particular, it is not hard to understand why we cannot allow production without sacrificing the theorem – for if production decisions are allowed to be actually carred out at all prices, and they may be the profit maximising ones at any set of prices, it clearly will not be true that, during the process, normalised profits behave in any regular fashion, either increasing or decreasing. If we were further to allow for the embodiment of production decisions in some durable concrete objects, the path of the system will at any time be strewn with the remnants of past mistakes, the maximsation possible at any moment will be constrained by these and we shall have a picture of the world, more faithful to what one suspects it looks like, but plainly not amenable to simple gradient analysis.

The pure exchange economy example also suggests that income effects of householders are not the real villains here. These have to be looked for on the production side: the tâtonnement analysis suggests the reverse. Understanding of the working of the system is therefore very sensitive to the assumption of whether exchange and production is or is not allowed at any set of prices. Since this is the case, and since we know full well that actual binding decisions are in fact made at all prices, it seems doubtful whether a tâtonnement is the appropriate simplification for an analysis of these problems. I shall have more to say on this, but first I should like to make a brief degression to another problem suggested by the pure exchange economy.

The economy that we have been considering, although one where the auctioneer regulates the terms at which goods shall exchange, is essentially one of barter. In the world we live in, however, most acts of exchange are of goods for money and money for goods. It cannot now be sensibly argued that every act of exchange increases the utility of at least one of the participants and diminishes it for neither. For if a household is constrained to use a medium of exchange, it may be willing to exchange one good for money on the supposition that the money so acquired will be used in exchange for some other good. But should the second leg of the transaction fail to materialise, the first transaction may be associated with a fall in utility. A speculative element is introduced and one can no longer be certain that a gradient process operates.

I have analysed this problem elsewhere and will sketch it here only in so far as it is relevant to my general story.

It was found convenient to distinguish between *target* utility and excess demand of a household and its *active* utility or excess demand. The target quantities are those which would prevail if the household were not restrained to use money in exchange; the active quantities take account of this constraint. This distinction also allows one to improve on the auctioneer's rule by allowing prices to respond to active and not to target excess demands. This is congenial to a Keynesian view of things; it permits for instance the existence of an active excess supply of some service without a corresponding active excess demand for some good. Lastly, I specify a process with the not unreasonable property that a household at any moment cannot complete its desired transactions in any market c if and only if active excess demand in that market is of the same sign as the total active excess demand of the economy. This in a different form was a postulate made by Negishi and myself in another context. I then find that this economy is always convergent provided that every household at every moment of time is in a position to effect some purchase if it so desires. If this is not so, one can construct examples of non-convergent economies.

What this extremely abstract construction suggests is that the invisible hand may encounter obstacles to its smooth operation owing to the difficulty that in a market economy agents may have to sell before they can signal their intention to buy. Introducing the possibility of borrowing modifies but does not radically alter the conclusion. As I have already noted, although no production is allowed, this is none the less a kind of Keynesian 'effective demand' problem in a pure form which both the tâtonnement and pure equilibrium analysis obscures. Clower has already drawn attention to this, and we must add it to the difficulties on the production side as one of the factors that will require careful attention on the analysis of the working of an economy.

But let me now return to the more conventional Walrasian analysis, for there are a number of further troubling features that require attention.

If one interprets the economy in a Debreuan fashion, so that one is concerned not only with current markets for current goods, but also with current markets for all future goods, the invisible hand – if it works successfully – must be taken as working once and for all. As the future unfolds, changing spot prices are not signals suggesting the correction of an 'error' but simply represent the terms agreed to in the past, at which transactions are taking place; they are without significance. In this world it is difficult to see how, at the primeval date when the infinite equilibrium, here supposed to exist, is to be established, anything but a tâtonnement can hope to establish it. For if one permits commitments to be undertaken at all prices, the errors of the first generation may reverberate to the ultimate descendants. Certainly, even if a final clearing of all markets were achieved, it would represent an equilibrium constrained by the debris of the actual groping process and it will in general be without agreeable welfare implications. To be committed to a veiw of the economy which contains all required future markets and which is brought to coherence by a tâtonnement is a far cry from Adam Smith, and I can see no way of building a bridge between this view and the workings of a capitalist economy or, for that matter, the process of planning in a controlled one. Moreover as I stressed before, to argue that such an economy can be efficiently decentralised does not mean that any information process containing messages between agents can be so decentralised.

The alternative view one may take of the Walrasian system is that it represents the forces of supply and demand in a small number of future markets only. This has the consequence that both the expectations of agents and the economic endowments of various goods must appear as arguments of the excess demand functions. Both of these one expects to be recursively linked to previous values of economic variables and one arrives at a picture of a sequence of markets, which is, of course, the stage at which the construction makes contact with modern descriptive growth theory.

What does one wish the invisible hand to do here? Clearly it should establish an equilibrium at every stage of the sequence, for if not, the economy will certainly perform inefficiently. But it has a further task. Suppose that in the Debreuan economy infinite present values are maximised and that it has a unique equilibrium. Then if the sequence of equilibria of the present construction does not generate the prices which would have been established by the Debreuan economy, it cannot be Pareto optimal. The Debreuan economy is thus an important benchmark and we are demanding that the imperfect information system, for which the lack of future markets is responsible, should none the less be no obstacle to the attainment of Nirvana. This is a steep demand and I will return to it. I now want to concern myself with the first of the tasks the invisible hand is to perform.

The expected prices that enter the excess demand functions may have to be indexed by the agent who entertains the expectations. If so (that is if expectations of agents differ), then one already implies that the second task will be ill performed. As a matter of plain fact, of course, expectations do differ between agents. But let us none the less neglect this and let us also neglect all questions of uncertainty which of course make the expectation problem more difficult to formalise. To neglect these matters is to neglect the very stuff of the economies we live in. Even so we are not out of the woods.

Suppose we rely on a tâtonnement and also make the assumption, introduced by Arrow and others, that agents expect constant prices for the indefinite future, although of course these may differ from current prices. This supposition once again, it should be noted, makes it generally impossible for the invisible hand to perform its second task efficiently. Even so, convergence of the process can only be generally established if at least one of the usual sufficient conditions for convergence holds and if the expectation formation process is a 'conservative' one. For instance, if all goods, including the future goods represented by expected prices, are gross substitutes and if expectations are formed extrapolatively, convergence can be established. The gross substitute assumption is of course pretty restrictive, but, so I feel, is the expectations formation hypothesis. Although it is true that in a properly formulated construction to which it can be applied, a Hicksian elasticity of expectations of less than one is neither necessary nor sufficient for convergence, it is none the less true that elastic expectations can always make the tâtonnement perform poorly. There are, moreover, very cogent reasons for wanting the expected rate of change in prices rather than the expected level of prices represented in the excess demand function; and that destroys such convergence results as we have.

There is now also the rather pressing problem of convergence time. If the time in the tâtonnement serves as a proxy for the number of computer steps, that is if the process is fictitious, this is of no great importance. But if one is to take the process as somehow representing real events, the possibility of slow convergence in the docile cases, when it can be established, is awkward for the simple reason that the no transaction requirement becomes very strained, and one is concerned to establish convergence to a momentary or short run equilibrium. If, on the other hand, production and consumption decisions are allowed at all prices, then once again there are no results, optimistic or pessimistic, available.

In recent years all these problems have been avoided by simply supposing the economy to be in equilibrium at every moment of time and concentrating on the second task of the invisible hand, inducement of a coherent sequence of such equilibria. To that extent then we seem to be prepared to live on faith. But let us not flinch from examining matters on these terms, which I shall now do. For this purpose I find it convenient to give a more definite structure to the Walrasian construction, which I do by examining a multisectoral neo-classical model of growth. This in turn will allow me not only to consider the general points with which I am here concerned, but also to draw attention to certain problems peculiar to this view of the economy.

II MULTISECTORAL GROWTH

We now consider an economy with a unique balanced growth ray which, together with the associated prices, would be a Debreuan equilibrium if the economy started on the ray. Capital goods are malleable and transferable and the production set is in every way 'well behaved'! The question asked in the literature is whether, from an arbitrary starting point, a sequence of monetary equilibria seeks the steady state. To put this into the context of our primary concern here we may agree to consider only economies with the following properties. For any starting point, the associated Debreuan equilibrium would be unique, infinite present value maximising and would asymptotically generate the balanced ray and its associated prices. By the latter I mean that for large enough T, the interest factor for prices as viewed by T would be arbitrarily close to that of the balanced ray. This would also hold for successive quantities of goods produced and consumed. If these things are so, then one is justified, for reasons already discussed, in one's concern that the invisible hand should guide the system to the steady state.

I have shown elsewhere – then Samuelson and Kurz have further analysed – the following proposition. If agents' myopic expectations of the development of prices at the starting point are arbitrarily given and if the system develops in a manner (at least for as long as this is feasible) that leads to the fulfilment of these expectations, then, in general, it will not approach the steady state. I do not propose to discuss the proposition further here, except to emphasise two points. If the system developed in a way in which expectations were not fulfilled, it would also not be efficient. If one considers a world of only one capital good where consumer expenditure depended on current receipts only (and not at all on expected prices), none of the problems would arise because no expectations need be, or are, formulated. Now to suppose that the trajectory of monetary equilibria is always expectation fulfilling is of course very stringent, and since it appears in any case to have unfortunate consequences, it has been suggested that the invisible hand would perform better if one allowed for mistaken expectations, and in particular for static expectations. Before I attempt to show that this is not generally true, I should again emphasise that even if it were a correct view it would not be very flattering to the invisible hand. Atkinson has drawn attention to the rather long time span involved in these kind of adjustments, and for as long as the economy is an appreciable distance from the values of the corresponding Debreuan economy, for so long it is also inefficient.

I now examine the case of static expectations in a fairly general model and in the Appendix to this paper I give two examples.

Let there be a single consumption good indexed 0 and let it be consumed by wage earners only who do not save. Let y_i stand for output of good i per head and k_i for the amount of the ith capital good per head. The labour force grows at an autonomous rate n, and it is the only non-produced input. I may write $y_i = \overset{*}{k_i} + nk_i$, $i > 0$. There is a strictly concave twice differentiable efficiency frontier

$$y_0 = F(y_1, \ldots, y_m, k_1, \ldots, k_m) \tag{4.1}$$

Let

$$R = -\frac{F_{m+i}}{F_i} \quad \text{where} \quad F_i = \frac{\partial F}{\partial y_i}, \quad F_{m+i} = \frac{\partial F}{\partial k_i} \tag{4.2}$$

which is the common rate of profit in terms of consumption goods that the momentary equilibrium establishes when all prices are expected to remain unchanged. From the saving assumption one has

$$\Sigma \, F_i \overset{*}{k_i} + (n - R) \, \Sigma \, F_i k_i = 0 \tag{4.3}$$

It is quite trivial to establish that this system possesses a unique balance state, which here happens to be the golden rule.

To examine the behaviour of the economy I expand equations (4.2) and (4.3) about their steady state values. Let κ be the vector whose components are $k_i - k_i^*$ where k_i^* is the steady state value of i. The system can be represented by the matrix equation

$$A\kappa + B\overset{*}{\kappa} = 0 \tag{4.4}$$

where A and B are $m \times m$ and

$$a_{ij} = n^2 F_{ij} + nF_{im+j} + nF_{m+ij} + F_{m+im+j} = a_{ji}$$

$$b_{ij} = nF_{ij} + F_i \hat{F}_j + F_{m+ij}, \qquad F_j = \frac{F_j}{\Sigma \, F_i k_i}$$

Indeed from the assumptions on equation (4.1) it is easy to see that A is the matrix of a negative definite form. B, however, is not symmetric. It seems quite clear that from the information given to us we cannot deduce that equation (4.4) will converge.

It is instructive to consider a case where convergence can be demonstrated. Suppose that B is quasi negative definite. Then if one writes $V(k) = -(1/2)\kappa'B\kappa$, we find from equation (4.4) that $\dot{V}(k) = \kappa'A\kappa < 0$ for $\kappa \neq 0$, and since $V(k)$ is positive definite, the local convergence of the system is assured.

It is worth while to examine the economics of B quasi negative definite. Let $P_i^* = -F_i(nk^*, k^*)$ be the steady state price of i in terms of consumption good and choose units so that $P_i^* = 1$ for all i. I shall be concerned with 'neighbouring' steady states which would be feasible with some non-negative consumption. I take the neighbourhood:

$$N(k^*) = \{ k \,|\, \|\kappa\| \leqslant \epsilon \}$$

where ϵ is positive and small. If $P_j = -F_j(nk, k)$, $k \in N(k^*)$, I write $\widehat{dP}$ as the vector with components $P_j - P_j^*$ and $\widehat{dR} = R - n$. Lastly $b_{ij}^* = b_{ij} - F_i\hat{F_j}$, and $B^* = [b_{ij}^*]$. (All partials are taken at k^*.)

Since $\Sigma_{ij}F_i\hat{F_j}\kappa_i\kappa_j = -(\Sigma_j\kappa_j)^2/\Sigma_j k_j^*$, one wants $\kappa'B^*\kappa < 0$ for $k \in N(k^*)$. But $\kappa'\widehat{dP} = -\kappa'B^*\kappa$ and so the sufficient condition for convergence will certainly hold if

$$\kappa'\widehat{dP} > 0 \tag{4.5}$$

This condition says that the change in the price index of capital with weights k should exceed that with weights k^*.

Be expanding equation (4.2) about k^* with $\dot{k} = 0$ one finds

$$\widehat{dR} \; \Sigma \; \kappa_i = \kappa'A\kappa < 0, \qquad \Sigma \; \kappa_i \neq 0 \tag{4.6}$$

But $\Sigma \kappa_i$ is the change in the value of the capital stock at constant prices, and equation (4.6) says that this is inversely related to the change in the interest rate.

To fix ideas, suppose there to be only one capital good. Then equations (4.6) and (4.5) together are similar to the Uzawa 'intensity condition'. That is, if $\Sigma \kappa_i > 0$ then $\widehat{dR} < 0$, so if the 'consumption sector is the more capital intensive', $\widehat{dP} > 0$ and so equation (4.6) holds. A similar argument applies to $\Sigma \kappa_i < 0$. When there are many capital goods the interpretation is similar. If the index of capital with steady state prices as weights increases ($\Sigma \kappa_i > 0$), one wants the index of capital with present prices as weights to increase by more ($\Sigma P_i\kappa_i > \Sigma \kappa_i$). That is, the associated fall in R should raise the prices of capital goods. In particular this is to hold for $k \in N(k^*)$ and so we want $dP_i/dR < 0$, all i. If the economy is organised into sectors producing single goods, then one may derive the sufficient condition for this to be the case that the consumption sector should be more intensive in every capital good than is any capital good sector, and that *is* pretty stringent.

It is a conjecture that should it be possible to write $y_0 = F(Y$ $(y_1 \ldots y_m)$, $k(k_1 \ldots k_m))$, that is if Leontief aggregates exist and if the intensity condition is satisfied, stability will be assured.

One notices that quite old fashioned capital theoretic issues are at stake. I fear that it is true that the heterogeneity of capital goods not only causes problems because properly one should allow for expected capital gains, but also because in general we cannot make proper capital intensity comparisons between different situations.

The conditions I have discussed are, of course, only sufficient for a convergence of the sequence of momentary equilibria. The saving assumption also is rather special. I have accordingly thought it proper to produce two examples (given in the Appendix) where the actual phase diagrams can be derived and in one of which a proportional savings assumption is employed. These examples, based on the assumption of two capital goods and Cobb Douglas production functions, show that quite reasonable technological assumptions can make the invisible hand in its present restricted role misbehave even when there are static expectations. As an aside, I should like to notice here that the reasons why these difficulties are not encountered in one sector putty—clay or clay—clay models with static expectations is that old capital goods are never newly produced so that some of the above mentioned capital theoretic problems are not found.

Properly speaking, I should now investigate the apparently much more favourable situation, where agents always expect prices to return to their steady state values. One conjectures that while the behaviour of this world will depend on the rate at which such a return is expected to be accomplished, it will give a rather more pleasant picture. But the assumption itself is extremely limiting and in any case still leaves plenty of scope for misbehaviour.

I conclude from all this that there is no theoretical evidence to suggest that the invisible hand performs better 'asymptotically' than it does 'momentarily', at least in the role in which it has been cast by the recent literature. Moreover the simplifications of one or two sector models which lead to happier conclusions are seen also to be vastly misleading.

Before leaving this example I should like to make a brief comment on the casual empirical evidence. I do not believe that the sequence of momentary equilibria construction is a very persuasive one. But even so it must again be borne in mind, when one is concerned with 'errant' paths, that they have 'catenary' features which may cause them to be near the steady state for long intervals and that it may take a very long time indeed before their errant nature can become manifest to the naked eye. When one adds to this the undoubted fact that the appropriate balanced ray is changing through innovations and other forces, it will be agreed that it is singularly hard for the evidence to be taken to point in any particular direction. But, as I have noted, the whole construction is suspect, first because of the rather cavalier way in which momentary equilibrium is taken for granted and secondly, because it really pays quite insufficient attention to the problems associated with the decision to purchase durable producer goods in the absence of requisite futures markets. I am now inclined to regard my own earlier work on heterogeneous capital goods models as more relevant to the study of the stock exchange than to investment behaviour. In the absence of satisfactory markets for second hand capital goods – and this absence is a fact – the expectations relevant to investment decisions are unlikely to be myopic (Arrow and Kurz have done some interesting work on this). If, in addition, certain clay elements are present, the difficulties become very great. All I can say is that no marriage has as yet been effected between the econometric study of investment and the study of the invisible hand, although one should not, I fancy, be equally keen to try all the ones on offer. Lastly there is the difficulty caused by perfect competition should there be constant returns to scale. Not only does the ordinary tâtonnement run into difficulties, but so does our attempt to fix the investment scale of producers. This, of course, is no problem in the study of equilibria; it is, however, quite serious in the study of adjustments. Lastly of course there is the question whether perfect competition is the appropriate idealisation anyway.

Of all these difficulties, I have time only for noticing a few connected with constant returns to scale.

III CONSTANT RETURNS TO SCALE

It is of some interest to examine a manner in which a tâtonnement process can be constructed for a constant returns economy. I examine a case here where convergence can be established.

Consider an economy in which there are as many non-produced inputs as there are outputs. There is no joint production, constant returns, and the minimum unit cost functions are strictly concave. Then if p is the vector of output prices, w the vector of input prices, $c(w)$ the vector of minimum unit cost functions, it is easy to show that $p = c(w)$ has a unique solution for w. At $c(w)$, producers are willing to supply whatever is demanded. Of course they may not be able to do so.

Let the auctioneer, for any w, always fix $c(w)$ as the supply price vector. Let him further change w_i in proportion to the excess demand for input i. Let all inputs be supplied by households. Then if x is the demand vector of household and is taken as strictly positive for all (p, w), and y is their supply vector of inputs, one writes the budget constraints $B = c(w)x - wy = 0$. Differentiating B partially with respect to w_j, keeping x and y constant, and denoting this by an asterisk, one has

$$\frac{\partial B^*}{\partial w_j} = \Sigma \, c_{ij}(w)x_i - y_j = z_j$$

where z_j is the excess demand for. input j. (The last equality follows from the well known fact that $c_{ij}(w)$ is the amount of input j per unit of output i, and the assumption that what is demanded, producers stand ready to supply.) But then one has from

$$\dot{B} = \Sigma \, z_j \dot{w}_j + c(w)\dot{x} - w\dot{y} = 0$$

and the auctioneer rules $z_j \dot{w}_j \geqslant 0$ so that $c(w)\dot{x} - w\dot{y} \leqslant 0$. But if all households have parallel linear Engel curves we may deduce from this that the utility of all households is now increasing during the process. Since one may take these utilities as bounded from below and since it is easy to show that the path of $w(t)$ is bounded also, convergence is easy to establish.

The reason for working this example is not because it has anything to recommend it on the grounds of realism but because it shows that constant returns do not inhibit the formulation of a satisfactory tâtonnement (which is sometimes questioned), and it brings out the further point that it is in the market for inputs that this particular invisible hand will have to work. Of course variations in the assumption concerning household behaviour will have the usual dubious consequences.

But all this is really of academic interest only, and in any case we are concerned with economies in which goods are produced by capital goods and labour. Constant returns, however, offers an opportunity for considering what may be a rather more acceptable hypothesis than I have examined so far.

It may be argued that economic theory, in dealing with adjustment problems, has with rare exceptions fluctuated between two extremes. There are the trade cycle models of the 1950s, which are quite unconcerned with prices, and there are the price flexible models which we have been discussing. There have been some attempts to effect a combination but none can be judged very persuasive and they are all highly macroeconomic.

Now if one is willing to abandon the perfect competition assumption — at least for sectors where constant returns prevail — then it is easy to argue that the mechanism of price change is through effects on the cost side rather than directly through excess demand. One blade of the scissors is here enough for market price analysis. As an example of this I sketch a hypothesis which I have more fully analysed elsewhere.

Let us suppose that the rate of profit R that producers expect to be able to earn in normal times is given. Let $Q(i)$ be the vector of prices, other than his own, which the ith producer expects to prevail in the long run. Let the components of $Q(i)$ be formed by extrapolative expectations. Write P_i^* as the solution of $P_i^* = c_i(Q(i), P_i^*, R)$ where $c_i(\ )$ is minimum unit cost, in terms of labour. Lastly suppose $\dot{P}_i = a_i(P_i^* - P_i)$, $a_i > 0$ which can be given an obvious justification. Then it is not hard to show that prices will converge on P_i^{**}, where $P_i^{**} = c_i(P_i^{**}, R)$. It should be noted that these are prices in terms of labour, so that this result would be consistent with always rising or falling money prices.

In the spirit of the substitution theorem the behaviour of prices has been made independent of the forces of demand. This is, of course, rather stronger than realism suggests. It is partly due to regarding R as uniform over producers and fixed, and partly to the fact that producers pricing responses follow a rule of thumb in which long run considerations predominate. But I believe that the above construction is one which may eventually be an element of a satisfactory picture.

But of course the cost of the view here taken is that other signals are required to indicate disequilibrium in the market for goods. Of these, unintended inventory changes, as well as queuing customers, are the obvious candidates. But now we are faced with the necessity of specifying precisely the forces which shape the producers' demand for goods, and in particular how this demand reacts to these signs. These are familiar problems. The striking point is that they have been avoided by neo-classical theory, which, I have argued, is none the better for that. In any event we all know that there is no theoretical reason to suppose that these 'quantity' signals will lead the economy to a convergent path.

I cannot pursue these matters further on this occasion. I apologise for the mixture of rather negative criticism and small theorems that I have produced. But I fear that I, like the Victorian parson of old, am assailed by 'doubts', and this seemed the appropriate moment for expressing them.

Twenty years ago Samuelson expounded the correspondence principle. Although on closer analysis it did not turn out to be a principle at all, what I take to be its basic content is surely correct. The study of equilibria alone is of no help in positive economic analysis. Yet it is no exaggeration to say that the technically best work in the last twenty years has been precisely that. It is good to have it, but perhaps the time has now come to see whether it can serve in an analysis of how economies behave. The most intellectually exciting question of our subject remains: is it true that the pursuit of private interest produces not chaos but coherence, and if so, how is it done?

APPENDIX

I consider an economy of one consumption good with the label 0 and two capital goods. The notation is as follows: P is the vector of capital goods prices in terms of labour, K is the vector of capital goods per head of population, K_{ij} represents the jth capital–labour ratio in industry i, Y_i is output per man employed in i, L_i is the proportion of the labour force employed in i, and R is the common rate of profit. Labour, like consumption good, is given the label 0. Lower case letters denote the log (to the base e) of capital letters. Further notation will be introduced as required.

Production conditions are given by

$$y_i = \sum_{j=1} \alpha_{ij} k_{ij}, \qquad i = 0 \ldots 2, \qquad \sum_{j=0} \alpha_{ij} = 1, \qquad \alpha_{ij} \geqslant 0, \qquad \alpha_{io} > 0$$

$$(4.7)$$

The equilibrium prices of capital goods may be calculated from the usual dual formulation as

$$p = (I - A)^{-1} a + (I - A)^{-1} A e r \tag{4.8}$$

where a is a two vector, $a_i = -\sum \alpha_{ij} \log \alpha_{ij}$, A is the matrix of coefficients α_{ij}, and e is the unit vector. From this we can calculate the equilibrium rental wage ratio (μ_i) in sector i as

$$RP_i = \mu_i = e^{\beta_i} R^{\alpha_i}, \qquad i = 1, 2 \tag{4.9}$$

where

$$\begin{pmatrix} \alpha_1 - 1 \\ \alpha_2 - 1 \end{pmatrix} = (I - A)^{-1} A e$$

and

$$\begin{pmatrix} \beta_1 \\ \beta_2 \end{pmatrix} = (I - A)^{-1} a$$

Since k_{ij} is uniquely determined by μ_j, we may use equation (4.9) to find

$$Y_i = m_i R^{1 - \alpha_i}, \qquad i = 1, 2 \tag{4.10}$$

where

$$m_i = \prod^{j} ((C_{ij})^{\alpha_{ij}}) e^{-\sum \beta_j \alpha_{ij}}$$

$$C_{ij} = \alpha_{ij}/\alpha_{io}$$

All these nasty expressions can be checked by routine calculations.
I first consider

Assumption A: Workers do not save, only workers consume.

Then in equilibrium it must be that $L_0 = \alpha_{00}$; but also

$$\sum_{i=0} L_i = 1 \tag{4.11}$$

and

$$\sum_{j=0} K_{ji}L_j = K_i, \qquad i = 1, 2$$

From equation (4.11) I find

$$L_i = g_i K_i R^{\alpha_i} - h_i, \qquad i = 1, 2 \tag{4.12}$$

where

$$g_i = e^{\beta_i}/C_i, \qquad C_i = C_{ii} - C_{ji}, \qquad h_i = \frac{\lambda C_{ji} + \alpha_{00} C_{0i}}{C_i}, \qquad \lambda = 1 - \alpha_{00}$$

Lemma 1: If $C_i < 0$ for all i, or $C_i > 0$ for all i, then the momentary equilibrium of the economy is unique.

Proof: Sum equation (4.12) over $i = 1, 2$ and rearrange to

$$\sum g_i K_i R^{\alpha_i} = \lambda + \sum h_i \tag{4.13}$$

Take the case $C_i < 0$, $i = 1, 2$. From the definitions one finds $h_i < 0, i = 1, 2$ and $\lambda + h_i \leqslant C_{11}(1 - \alpha_{00})/C_1 < 0$, so the left side of equation (4.13) is negative. But $g_i < 0, i = 1, 2$ and $\alpha_i > 0, i = 1, 2$ so the left hand side is monotone in R and negative. The case $C_i > 0$ is proved similarly.

In equilibrium,

$$\dot{K}_i + nK_i = L_i Y_i, \qquad i = 1, 2$$

Using equations (4.10) and (4.12) I may write this as

$$\dot{K}_i = Rm_i[g_i K_i - h_i R^{-\alpha_i}] - nK_i, \qquad i = 1, 2 \tag{4.14}$$

With assumption A, the steady state occurs where $R = n$ and so we can calculate the steady state K^*:

$$K_i^* = \frac{m_i h_i R^{1-\alpha_i}}{N_i}; \qquad N_i = n[m_i g_i - 1] \tag{4.15}$$

If $C_i < 0$, $i = 1, 2$ equation (4.15) gives a unique solution $K^* > 0$. If $C_i > 0$, $i = 1, 2$, then one wants g_i large enough to give $N_i > 0$, i.e. (C_i) small. This once again, is simply the requirement that the system be productive.

I examine the behaviour of equation (4.15) in the vicinity of the steady state. Let

$$S_i = \left(\frac{dk_2}{dk_1} \right)_{\dot{K}_{i=0}}, \qquad i = 1, 2$$

calculated by linear expansion about K^*. Let

$$R_i = \frac{\partial R}{\partial K_i} \frac{K_i^*}{R}, \qquad i = 1, 2$$

Then one can calculate, by differentiating equation (4.13) partially with respect to K_i^*, at K^*:

$$\begin{cases} \alpha_1 R_1 = (Z - 1)^{-1} \\ \alpha_2 R_2 = (Z^{-1} - 1)^{-1} \end{cases} \qquad (4.16)$$

where

$$-Z = \frac{\alpha_2}{\alpha_1} \frac{g_2}{g_1} n^{\alpha_2 - \alpha_1} \frac{K_2^*}{K_1^*}$$

Now expanding equation (4.15) and using (4.16) one finds

$$S_1 = -\{B_1 Z + (1 - B_1)\} \frac{R_1}{R_2} ; \qquad S_2 = -\{B_2 Z^{-1} + (1 - B_2)\}^{-1} \frac{R_1}{R_2}$$

$$(4.17)$$

where

$$B_i = \frac{N_i \alpha_i}{n + \alpha_i N_i}$$

I now examine two cases.

Proposition 1: If $C_i < 0$, $i = 1, 2$, that is, if each sector uses the output of the other sector relatively more intensively than it does its own, the steady state is stable.

Proof: (a) Certainly $B_i > 0$, $i = 1, 2$, since $N_i \alpha_i < 0$, and $n + \alpha_i N_i = n[1 + \alpha_i(m_i g_i - 1)] < 0$, since $1 - \alpha_i < 0$, $g_i < 0$. But then $B_i > 1$, $i = 1, 2$.

Some Adjustment Problems

(b) Using equation (4.17) one finds

$$S_1/S_2 = B_1B_2 + B_2(1 - B_1)Z^{-1} + B_1(1 - B_2)Z + (1 - B_1)(1 - B_2)$$

But every term on the right hand side is positive (recall $Z < 0$) and $B_1B_2 > 1$, so $S_1/S_2 > 1$. The phase diagram is shown in Figure 1. The singular point is stable.

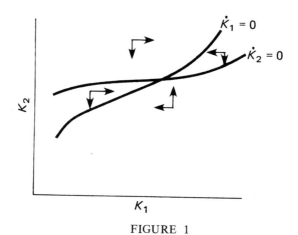

FIGURE 1

Proposition 2: If $C_1 > 0$, $i = 1, 2$ and

$$0 < \frac{1}{\alpha_i(m_1g_1 - 1)} < \frac{\alpha_2g_2m_2h_2N_1}{\alpha_1g_1m_1h_1N_2} > \alpha_2(m_2g_2 - 1) > 0$$

the singular point is a saddle point.

Proof: The inequality is equivalent to

$$\frac{1 - B_1}{B_1} < -Z > \frac{B_2}{1 - B_2}$$

So $S_1 > 0, S_2 < 0$. The phase diagram is given in Figure 2.

Remark 1: One needs to check, by example, that the inequalities of proposition are possible. I sketch a way of doing so. Take $h_1/h_2 = C_2/C_1$.

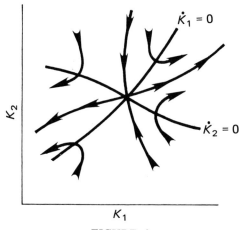

FIGURE 2

Then one may verify that

$$-Z = \frac{\alpha_{10}}{\alpha_{20}} \frac{g_2 m_2 N_1}{g_1 m_1 N_2}$$

We know that $\alpha_i > 1$ always. One verifies that $N_1/g_1 m_1$ can be made infinitely large by taking C_1 small enough.

Remark 2: The condition $C_i > 0$, $i = 1, 2$ is not as restrictive as it may appear. In a two capital goods model one expects a high degree of aggregation.

I now consider a second assumption.

Assumption B: Savings are a constant fraction of total income.

I write c as the propensity to consume, $s = 1 - c$, and $\gamma = c/s$;

$$v_i = \frac{\alpha_{i0} - \alpha_{00}}{\alpha_{00}}$$

In equilibrium

$$c \sum_{i=0} P_i Y_i L_i = L_0 P_0 Y_0 \qquad (4.18)$$

But $P_i Y_i = 1/\alpha_{i0}$, $i = 0$,   2, so using equation (4.11) one has

$$L_i = \hat{g}_i K_i R^{\alpha_i} - \hat{h}_i, \qquad i = 1, 2 \qquad (4.19)$$

where

$$\hat{g}_i = e^{\beta_i}/\hat{C}_i$$

$$\hat{C}_i = \left[\left(C_{ii} - \frac{v_i}{v_j} C_{ji} \right) + C_{0i}\left(\frac{v_i}{v_j} - 1 \right) \right]$$

and

$$\hat{h}_i = \frac{C_{0i} + \dfrac{1}{v_j}(C_{ji} - C_{0i})}{\hat{C}_i}$$

The rest of the analysis can proceed as before with these new parameters provided one can show that there is unique steady state and a unique momentary equilibrium.

Proposition 3: If $\hat{C}_i < 0, i = 1, 2$, the steady state is unique.

Proof: Let $V_i = P_i K_i$, $V = \Sigma\ V_i$, $u = n/s$. In steady state $s[1 + VR] = nV$ or $R = (u - 1/V) = T$ say. Corresponding to equation (4.15) one now has

$$K_i^* = \frac{m_i \hat{h}_i R^{1-\alpha_i}}{\hat{N}_i}; \qquad \hat{N}_i = [m_i \hat{g}_i R - n] \tag{4.15'}$$

Evaluating the differential of V always at K^* one find using equation (4.8)

$$\frac{\partial V_i}{\partial R} = \frac{m_i \hat{g}_i V_i}{n - m_i \hat{g}_i R} < 0, \qquad i = 1, 2$$

so $\partial T/\partial R < 0$. Hence in Figure 3 one has a unique steady state.

Proposition 4: If $\hat{C}_i > 0$, $i = 1, 2$ and $R > \bar{R} = \max_i(n/m_i \hat{g}_i)$, then the steady state is unique.

Proof: For $R > \bar{R}$

$$\frac{\partial V_i}{\partial R} = -\frac{m_i \hat{g}_i V_i}{m_i \hat{g}_i R - n} < 0$$

The uniqueness of the momentary equilibria can be established on the lines of lemma 1.

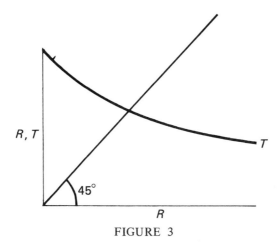

FIGURE 3

Remark 3: The condition $\hat{C}_i > 0$, $i = 1, 2$ does not now even require $C_i > 0$, $i = 1, 2$.

REFERENCES

Arrow, K. J. and M. Kurz 1967, Optimal growth with irreversible investment in a Ramsey model, technical report no. 1, March 15, Serra House, Stanford

Arrow, K. J. and M. Nerlove (1958). A note on expectation and stability, *Econometrica*, 26 (2), April

Atkinson, A. B. 1969. The time scale of economic models – how long is the long run, *Review of Economic Studies*, Spring

Clower, R. 1965. The Keynesian counterrevolution: a theoretical appraisal, in F. H. Hahn and F. P. R. Brechling (eds) *The Theory of Interest Rates*

Hahn, F. H. 1968. On warranted growth paths, *Review of Economic Studies*, 353 (2) (162)

Hahn, F. H. 1963. On the disequilibrium behaviour of a multisectoral growth model, *Economic Journal*, 73

Kurz, M. 1968. The general instability of a class of competitive growth processes, *Review of Economic Studies*, 35 (2) (162)

Samuelson, P. A. 1967. Indeterminacy of development in a heterogeneous capital model with constant saving propensity, in Ed. Karl Shell, *Essays on the Theory of Optimal Economic Growth*, MIT

Sato, R. 1963. Fiscal policy in a neo-classical growth model – an analysis of time required for equilibrating adjustment, *Review of Economic Studies*, 30 (1) (82)

Scarf, H. 1960. Some examples of global instability of the competitive equilibrium, *International Economic Review*, 1 (3)

Shell, K. and J. Stiglitz (1967) The allocation of investment in a dynamic economy, *Quarterly Journal of Economics*

5

Reflections on the Invisible Hand

INTRODUCTION

That a society of greedy and self-seeking people constrained only
by the criminal law and the law of property and contract should
be capable of an orderly and coherent disposition of its economic
resources is very surprising. Marx called such a society anarchic
and so it is. Yet, ever since Adam Smith, economists have been
concerned to show that such anarchy is consistent with order and
indeed with certain desirable outcomes. Smith proposed that the
market system acted like a guiding – an invisible – hand. It was
invisible since, in fact, there was not actual hand on the rudder.
The metaphor which he chose was exactly apposite.

Two hundred years on the basic theory has been much refined
and we know a good deal more about those instances where the
hand trembles or fails. Yet there is not agreement on some of the
fundamental ingredients of the story and there is also much which
we simply do not understand. In this lecture, I shall give my evalu-
ation of our present theoretical state in this matter and draw a
number of lessons of a somewhat practical kind.

Although I shall be concerned with theory, the practical significance of the subject is self-evident. It certainly is at the centre
of a great ideological divide. It matters a good deal whether Mrs
Thatcher or Mr Benn, or for that matter President Reagan, are
appealing to coherent and grammatical arguments when they
espouse the market or the planned economy. Certainly non-econ-
omic considerations, for instance the fate of liberty under either
system, are involved. But even these cannot be evaluated and
argued about until we can describe and understand the economic
stage on which the scenarios develop. In any case, it would be a
pity if, for instance, we embarked on large and portentous changes

in our society on the basis of arguments as flawed and incomplete as those recently presented by six of Mr Benn's supporters. It is also undesirable that we should allow Mrs Thatcher to engineer large reductions in employment and national income on the basis of an unsubstantiated belief that this is required for the invisible hand to do its job. All these people take it for granted that somewhere there is a theory, that is, a body of logically connected propositions based on postulates not wildly at variance with what is the case, which support their policies. It must be of some significance to enquire whether this is in fact so.

To do this, I shall have to give some account of the pure theory of the invisible hand as formulated now. I shall need this as a benchmark but I shall keept it short since its main outline is probably familiar. I shall then take up what seem to me to be important objections to this theory or significant lacunae. I shall lastly try to support the view that, on our present state of knowledge, it would be prudent not to place all our eggs into one or the other of the ideological baskets on offer. To some, this conclusion will appear wishy-washy and unpalatable; I shall want to argue that it is reasonable.

THE PURE THEORY OF THE INVISIBLE HAND

We think of a society where private property and contracts are adequately supported by law. The economic environment of any one person is fully specified once the prices of all tradeable objects are given. These prices give the terms at which one good can be exchanged for another and it is a basic assumption that all individuals can trade to any extent they wish at these prices. One notices that the economic information is conveyed very economically — the individual knows everything that he needs to know once he knows prices.

However, for the pure theory which I am now considering one has to make the unpalatable assumption that there are terms of exchange given for every pair of goods which an individual might wish to exchange. In the textbooks this assumption is formulated to read: markets are complete. It is a very important postulate and Keynes, for instance, placed great emphasis on the fact that he did not invoke it.

To understand the significance of the postulate of complete markets, one has to understand the economic classification of goods. It is obvious that butter today in Warwick is, from any trader's point of view, not interchangeable one for one for butter today in Cambridge. So, certainly we want to distinguish goods not only by their physical characteristics but also by their location. But butter today in Warwick is not, from any trader's point of view, the same as butter tomorrow in Warwick. So we must also distinguish goods by the date at which they are available. However, we are not yet through. Butter today in Warwick when the weather is hot will be valued differently by individuals from butter today in Warwick when it is cold. So we must also distinguish goods by what we call the state of nature. The latter is a description of the environment which is independent of anyone's action.

So, we have finished up with a collection of goods each of which is distinguished from the other by any one of the four attributes: physical description, location, date of delivery and state of nature obtaining. The postulate of complete markets now implies, for instance, that there is given to the individual terms on which he can trade butter in Warwick tomorrow if cold, for bread in Warwick today when it is hot. That is, every good, as defined, has a price and so a market on which it is traded. The postulate is wildly at variance with the facts and we have some theory to explain why this should be so. But the postulate is quite crucial for some of the claims made on behalf of the invisible hand and its rejection has far-reaching consequences.

The decision units — agents as we, alas, call them — are now divided into two groups: households and firms. The latter are owned by households and, in the pure theory, the managers of firms, in making decisions of what and how much to produce with what inputs, will act to maximise profits at prevailing prices, which is exactly what shareholders will want them to do. This again is a consequence of the complete market hypothesis, which ensures that uncertainty has been eliminated from the production decision, since markets permit complete insurance. This quite counterfactual implication I shall take up again later. I now add that each firm is supposed to have available to it a 'book of blueprints', that is, a list of input–output activities which are technologically feasible.

Households decide on trades including the trade in the leisure they are endowed with. They are assumed to have a preference ranking over all possible trades, that is, they can decide which of two trading activities they prefer or which they are indifferent between. This ranking if consistent so that it never happens that trade a is preferred to trade b, and trade b to trade c, and trade c to trade a. Given all prices and the households' ownership of goods, leisure and shares of firms, we can deduce the set of trades which is market feasible for the household. Any trade in that set has the property that expenditure on purchases does not exceed earnings from sales. Notice that borrowing and lending are included in this description. For instance, one borrows by selling a good (or money) for future delivery and one lends by buying a good (or money) for future delivery. Insurance is also included by the hypothesis that there are contingent future markets. Thus it is possible to make a contract for the delivery of goods in the future if the state of the world is that one is sick, and no delivery if one is well. It is now assumed that the household will choose a trade such that there is no other market feasible trade which it prefers to the chosen one.

Given the ownership of goods and shares and the available books of blueprints, each agent will make a decision which is best for it on the basis of existing prices — the decision thus depends on prices only. We now come to the first question concerning the invisible hand. There clearly is no reason why, for an arbitrary set of prices, the multitude of decisions, taken by each agent in the light of his own motives only, should be consistent. By this I mean that there is not reason why, at arbitrary prices, trades should balance so that the amount of anything offered for sale is equal to what is demanded for purchase. However, it was proved in the 1950s that under certain conditions there always exists at least one set of economically meaningful non-negative prices at which the decisions arrived at individually will just mesh — that is, are consistent.

Whatever criticism I shall level at the theory later, I should like to record that it is a major intellectual achievement. One must be far gone in philistine turpitude not to appreciate the quite surprising nature of this result, or to be unmoved by the elegant means by which it is proved. It establishes the astonishing claim that it is logically possible to describe an economy in which millions of agents, looking no further than their own interests and responding to the sparse information system of prices only, can still attain a coherent economic disposition of resources. Having made that clear, let me none the less emphasise the phrase 'logically possible'. Nothing whatever has been said of whether it is possible to describe any actual economy in these terms.

However, there is more to come. It can be shown under certain conditions that the allocation of goods achieved at the prices which lead to consistent choices – let us call them equilibrium prices – is such that there is no reallocation of goods between households possible which they all prefer to the allocation they have in equilibrium. Any reallocation must lead at least one household to a bundle to which the equilibrium bundle is preferred. We say that the equilibrium allocation is *Pareto efficient*. But we can also establish a deeper and potentially much more useful result. Suppose the Cabinet decides on some Pareto-efficient allocation. If it is fully informed it would be rather foolish of it to decide on some allocation which is not Pareto efficient, since it would gratuitously miss the opportunity of allowing all its citizens to reach a position which they prefer. Then it can be shown (again under certain conditions) that, provided it can impose any desired distribution of the ownership of goods among its citizens, there is one such distribution which, if it obtained in the unplanned economy, would lead the latter to reach an equilibrium allocation which coincides with the allocation the Cabinet had chosen. That is, every Pareto-efficient allocation can be decentralised – handed over to the invisible hand. These two results are known as the fundamental theorems of welfare economics. They have led many to claim that the invisiable hand is not only smart but also beneficent. However, we notice at once that the benificence is somewhat limited. For there are many Pareto-efficient allocations and each one of them will have a different distribution of welfare. Mrs Thatcher's choice of a Pareto-efficient allocation, for instance, seems unlikely to correspond to any acceptable notion of distributive justice. Mr Benn's choice on the other hand may not even be Pareto efficient. In any case, the sloppy habit in the literature in speaking of a Pareto *optimum* has misled many people into believing that their duty of serious moral argument has been fulfilled when they can show that some policy outcome is Pareto efficient. As a matter of fact, this is just the beginning of such an argument.

We can now look at some (but by no means all) of the limitations on the basic results which I have so far encapsulated in the phrase 'under certain conditions'. These limitations are separate from, and additional to, those which I shall discuss when I turn to the descriptive power of the pure theory. To make this clear I shall now speak of logical limitations.

LOGICAL LIMITATIONS OF THE PURE THEORY

The whole theory is at risk if there are increasing returns which are 'large relative to the size of the economy'. This last phrase can be made precise but I shall not do so here. This risk is not only due to the circumstances that large increasing returns are usually associated with large firms and hence monopoly power, which is excluded by the hypothesis that agents take prices as beyond their control. It arises from the fact that, even if firms continued to act as price takers, there may exist no equilibrium prices. Again I shall not document this. But it is clear that this logical limitation may, itself, rule out an appeal to the theory in concrete instances. If, however, an equilibrium exists it will again be Pareto efficient whereas it is no longer true that every Pareto-efficient allocation can be decentralised. So, even in the world of the pure theory, the invisible hand may falter and such market outcomes as appear may be unsatisfactory, since they may have to involve monopolistic elements.

But this remark leads to a deeper problem. The theory has a lively sense of original sin – all people act entirely in their self-interest quite narrowly defined. But, if that is so, will not individuals or groups of individuals seek to find ways to exert market power? By market power I mean a situation in which an individual's action can influence equilibrium prices. How can we be sure that the hypothesis that individuals act as if prices were given is not in conflict with the postulate that they are rational self-seeking agents? The answer is that we can only be sure if there is no market power for individuals to exploit. This can be shown to entail the condition that everyone in the economy, other than a given agent, can do as well when that agent trades as when he does not; this must be so whoever the given agent is. In general, this 'no surplus' condition will only be satisfied in 'large' economies. Large economies are those in which, in counting agents, we reckon any one individual as we would a single point in a collection of points on a continuous line – that is not at all. Of course, one can rest satisfied if this is approximately true. But once again the purely logical limitations of the theory will restrict its range of applicability.

When market power is present the Smithian vision of the invisible hand is lost. Instead of the machine-like responses of agents to prices, the agents will find themselves engaged in a game. That is, it will be necessary for them to take account of the decisions of other agents and, in particular, they may have to consider how these decisions are affected by their own. Their choices will now be among strategies. Here, economists are not agreed even what the appropriate notion of an equilibrium should be. But it becomes easy to show that plausible equilibria are not longer Pareto efficient. Moreover, it has not been established that all plausible notions are non-vacuous, that is, that they are logically possible. In short, there is no accepted theory of the invisible hand when the no surplus condition is not satisfied.

One must conclude that one cannot invoke the classical theory of the invisible hand in dealing with economies in which agents have market power. If such an economy attains some coherent state to be called equilibrium, all market information will not be summarised by prices. The signals to which agents respond will be much richer and the kind of things they would like to know, in order to arrive at decisions, much more varied. One can, however, assert that the outcome will, in general, not be Pareto efficient.

I have already noted that the complete market hypothesis is crucial and also counterfactual. Here, I want to draw attention to a purely logical difficulty which on reflection has rather wide implications. Two agents cannot enter into a contract in which delivery is contingent on an event which they cannot both observe. For, certainly, our greedy agents do not trust each other. Hence, if information differs between agents, certain contingent markets cannot exist as a matter of logic. This was first noticed by Radner (1968).

Now that we have considered the possibility of differences in information all sorts of other problems arise. Recall that we distinguished goods by, among other things, their physical description. What exactly is the physical description of a second hand motor car or, for that matter, any of the multitudinous objects which we use and whose properties we know nothing about? Similar problems arise in the market for labour and in insurance markets. In all these cases, agents on one side of the market have information which is superior to that possessed by agents on the other. The role of prices now becomes much more complex. In particular, prices will induce 'sorting' or 'selection' and they may also serve to transfer some of the information of the informed to the uninformed. For instance, in certain cases, not yet fully explored, the prices of a class of goods may be correlated positively with their quality and so serve as a signal of quality.

There are many difficult and interesting problems here which, at the level of the whole economy, have only been partially resolved. One thing is clear: in such situations the set of signals is again likely to be larger than that consisting only of prices. Thus, for instance, educational qualifications will be used to signal one's quality to prospective employers. Once again the fundamental theorems of welfare economics will fail. This brings me to the last two of the logical limitations of the pure theory which I shall take up.

Information can be acquired by expending resources but, once one has it, it is not diminished if someone else has it as well. It is an example of a public good. For quite obvious reasons the fundamental welfare theorems cannot hold when there are public goods. Indeed, the market economy will perform disastrously in such cases. No one will invest in the production of information if its market price is necessarily zero. That is why we have patent and copyright laws. Such devices are forced on us by the logic of the invisible hand. Of course, there are many other examples of public goods.

In the example of the education signal of my quality it will be clear that the effectiveness of my signal will depend on the signals used by others. There is here what we call an externality — that is, an effect of one agent's action on the welfare of another. There are many cases of externalities, both positive and negative. But this is so well known, and the failure of the invisible hand in such situations so widely understood, that I will not dwell on them. I only want to make one observation which is inspired by some recent work by Makowski, (1980). If the no surplus condition is not met there must be an externality, almost by definition; this means that externalities are implicit in any departure from perfect competition. This seems to imply that one cannot ascribe failures of the invisible hand in the face of externalities exclusively to defective property rights. In any case, ever since Marshall and Pigou it has been agreed that externalities constitute a *prima facie* case for government intervention in a market economy. Hence, economies which significantly depart from perfect competition — that is, in general, actual economies — would be candidates for the deployment of a visible hand.

This brings me to Fred Hirsch's famous book *The Social Limits of Growth*, where he considers the obstacles in the way of the invisible hand occasioned by non-augmentable 'social' or 'positional' goods. A simple and old example is the case of a common pasture where what your cow eats reduces what is available for mine. Another example is congestion on a motorway or in a beauty spot. In general, these are cases of externalities.

For many such cases corrections can be achieved without essential damage to the price mechanism. This can be done by a levying of suitable taxes and subsidies and by the creation of appropriate property rights. In some cases one may have to impose direct controls. But, even here, the price system can be utilised, for instance, a licensing arrangement with tradeable licences. On the other hand there are externalities, and these are the ones which preoccupied Hirsch, where the only remedy appears to lie in changing what people want. For instance, as Gilbert and Sullivan remind us, there may be no way to satisfy everyone's desire to be 'somebody'. If we all desire to dine in exclusive restaurants this cannot be met by giving us all equal access. The externality of envy is perhaps also only correctible when there is nothing to envy.

Hirsch considers these matters to be a source of what Marx would have called a 'contradiction'. In the early stages of a market economy most people are concerned with eminently reproducible necessities of life. The invisible hand works in harmony with expectations and leads to the growth in the output of goods which people desire. At a later and more materially opulent stage people develop wants for goods which are intrinsically non-augmentable and thus become increasingly concerned with positional goods. Their expectations are then bound to be disappointed and disappointment will lead to disaffection. The invisible hand cannot provide what people desire. The sum total of human happiness can now only continue to increase by a change in what makes people happy. In particular, greed and the desire for self-advancement must give way to the gentler social virtues of affection and co-operation. But these virtues are not consistent with the motives which provide power to the invisible hand. The intrinsic limitations in the supply of those things which capitalist economies come to desire most must essentially herald the end of that particular social arrangement.

Clearly, here is an important and interesting point. But I must confess to some discomfort with theorising on such a grand and ominous scale. For instance, it is not clear beyond doubt that the limits which Hirsch has in mind are absolute. To put it differently. Hirsch may have underestimated the availability of substitutes.

For example, although we cannot all enjoy comparative solitude in the same beauty spot, we may be able to do so in our garden. Athough we cannot all be equally esteemed as musicians or mathematicians, we can multiply almost endlessly the activities which provide opportunities to be esteemed. Moreover, one of the fruits of growth is the increase in leisure and I am unconvinced that there are intrinsic limitations to its beneficence. Lastly, the purely physical inventiveness of the system sees to it that we continue to have a healthy appetite for augmentable goods. What self-respecting person does not now desire a video tape recorder? In short, I think that Hirsch has undoubtedly shown that externalities in the most general sense are more pervasive and sometimes more intractable than had often been supposed. To that extent, he has diminished the scope of the invisible hand and enlarged that of collective action. It remains to be seen whether he has discovered a poison that will kill the hand altogether.

Adam Smith and John Stuart Mill, to name only two classical exponents of the invisible hand theory, were certainly aware of some of the limitations on the efficacy of the market. Indeed, they used these to formulate a theory of the legitimate, or at least appropriate, sphere of action of governments. But they and many of their modern successors undoubtedly underestimate the extent of the ground that has to be yielded. Moreover, their line of argument runs into another danger. To demonstrate the logical possibility of market failure, indeed to demonstrate that such failure actually occurs on a large scale, is not in itself a demonstration of the desirability of government intervention. For market failure is not a necessary ground for intervention – the market outcome may be associated with great injustice even when there is no failure. Nor is such failure sufficient grouns for intervention, since it remains to be demonstrated that 'government failure' is less damaging than market failure. Hence although there may be a prima facie ground for intervention when the invisible hand fails, and no such grounds when it does not, there is some arguing and thinking to be done before a case for intervention has been clinched.

But before I do some of this arguing I now want to consider – however briefly and superficially – some of the descriptive limitations of the pure theory.

THE DESCRIPTIVE LIMITATIONS OF THE PURE THEORY

I have already mentioned the logical grounds which arise from the circumstance that markets may be incomplete. I now notice that, as a matter of plain fact, they *are* incomplete. The proof is readily at hand: we observe that there is trading at every date which would not be the case in a complete market world. In fact, the complete market hypothesis is convincingly falsified.

But economists and particularly theoretical economists do not give up easily. Granted that markets are incomplete, is it possible that (a) the theory has made unnecessarily strong assumptions in asking for complete markets and (b) there are considerations not depending on all markets existing which allow the pure theory to look the facts in the face and continue serenely on its way?

As an example, suppose there are only two physically distinct goods and only one date and location to consider. Let there be five possible states of the world. Then the complete market hypothesis suggests that we need two times five, that is, ten markets. But Arrow (1963) noted that whatever allocation might be achieved by ten markets could also be achieved by seven. That is, two markets for the two goods and five markets for securities, each one of which would pay something positive in one of the states and nothing in the other four. An individual can always find a trade in these seven markets which allows him to do as well as by trading in ten. So the pure theory does make stronger assumption than it needs. But one can assert with confidence that even the reduced number of markets suggested by Arrow is much larger than the number of markets which we observe. This is clear when we think of many future dates and states.

Bewley (1980) has suggested that the holding of money balances can, in certain circumstances, provide almost all the insurance possibilities afforded by complete markets. His analysis is very impressive but I believe he would agree that it is impossible to claim that it applies to actual economies.

The second line of defence involves the invocation of 'rational expectations', a move widely favoured at present. By rational expectations one means that individuals who, because of incomplete markets, now have to form market expectations do so by using all the information available to them and do so consistently. The notion of an equilibrium is enlarged: not only must markets clear and individuals do as well for themselves as they can, but also there must be no systematic falsification of rationally formed expectations. The new concept has been christened rational expectations equilibrium. It has been vastly influential, especially with people who would not find it easy to really understand the idea.

For instance, the view that inflation can have no permanent effect on employment or that monetary policy has no real consequences even in the short term, if rationally anticipated, is based on the rational expectations equilibrium hypothesis. As empirical evidence one can point to the result that prices of securities traded on the stock exchange perform a random walk, which is consistent with the theory that the price of any security reflects all the information which can be rationally comprehanded plus a random error term which cannot.

The first point to make now is that this move does not re-establish the beneficence of the invisible hand: rational expectations equilibria need not be Pareto efficient. Indeed, there seem in general to be many rational expectations equilibria and it is possible that some of these can be Pareto ranked. Secondly, although the theory points in at least one right direction — namely that systematic errors in expectations will lead to the revision of those expectations — it is hard to consider this new equilibrium as descriptively satisfactory. For instance, to make it consistent with our observation of fluctuations in real magnitudes like employment and output, its proponents have had to resort to *ad hoc* postulates of mistakes rationally made. They often argue that it is government policy which induces people to make such mistakes. For example, unknowable or unobservable changes in the money supply will cause people to confuse price changes caused by 'real' events and those which are purely nominal.

But introspection and observation suggest that we are quite capable of making mistakes unaided. More importantly, most people do not have sufficiently well formulated forecasts to allow them to be mistaken in the first place. Thus, we all make some sort of guess at the inflation rate but few are sufficiently coherent and patient to form a probability distribution over such rates, nor are we clever enough to use correctly all the information at our disposal. If we lived in an essentially stationary environment and if we lived long enough, or knew history well enough, we might none the less come close to satisfying the postulates of the theory. But we do not.

The rational expectations approach has its theoretical uses. It allows us to examine economies free from expectational disturbances and perhaps isolate other sources of ill behaviour. It permits us to show that even in such a world the invisible hand may cease to guide before it has made citizens as well off as, in the given circumstances, they could be. It also allows us to sidestep an issue which is enveloped in ignorance, namely how expectations are actually formed. But people who base policies for real economies on the belief that citizens form their expectations rationally and that the invisible hand, if left to its own devices, will guide us to a rational expectations equilibrium with not much delay cannot, I think, be taken seriously. By this I mean that I consider the direct evidence overwhelmingly against this view, and I regard the 'as if' evidence from such econometric models as there are as I do evidence for miracles: the story is simply too much at variance with experience.

However, we should notice a spin-off from this approach which is at once obvious and important. In the formation of expectations, in whatever manner and however imperfectly people do form them, account will be taken of expected government policy. An act of policy which has been more or less foreseen will, in general, have different consequences from one which has not. This not very deep observation has often been neglected in discussions of economic policy. In analysis it can give rise to some tricky and interesting problems. Rational expectations theorists, although they have characteristically embraced rather extreme models, have none the less made an important contribution in making everyone aware of this consideration.

In so far as rational expectations are descriptively unsatisfactory, we would expect the invisible hand to falter and, perhaps to mislead in its actual intertemporal operations. For instance, speculative bubbles which eventually burst are possible. That such bubbles have been observed can be shown to be evidence against rational expectations. Quite generally, there is no logical obstacle to an economy pursuing a path which runs into feasibility constraints and so experiences discontinuous dislocation. It is not unimportant that this should be more widely understood than seems, at present, to be the case. I shall, therefore, make the same point again in a slightly different form.

If the invisible hand is to operate there must be sufficient opportunities for intertemporal and contingent intertemporal trade. In fact there are not enough of these opportunities. The lack of contingent markets means that the market economy is associated with more uncertainty than pure theory allows. The lack of intertemporal markets means that great weight must rest on market expectations. The rational expectations hypothesis substitutes an internal and psychic hand for the market. Each individual somehow has learned how the invisible would have performed if it had been given markets in which to perform. If it is agreed that this is not of high descriptive merit, there is, in fact, no obvious mechanism by which intertemporal decisions can be co-ordinated. This was Keynes' view. I have yet to see it refuted. The French drew the conclusion that they at least required indicative planning. The Japanese have for a long time employed non-market institutions to supplement private investment decisions. In Germany, the banks seem to act as market substitutes. In Britain, where politicians now follow gurus rather than arguments we are all set to rely on the invisible hand doing a job which, in practice, it will not and cannot do.

The other large misfit between the pure theory and the world which I have already noted under the heading of logical limitations is, of course, the postulate of perfect competition – that is, the assumption that economic agents know all they need to know when they know prices. That this is false many observations confirm. Advertising and market research, trade unions and market sharing arrangements, expensive business investigations to forecast demand are just a few of the falsifiers. The theoretical consequence of this misfit is that even when a coherent disposition of resources is achieved, one will not be able to claim that it is Pareto efficient. That is, in general, one can describe some form of collective or co-operative action which would improve the lot of everyone. But I will not now pursue further this quite important scent, for there are still many more central issues to be discussed.

THE INVISIBLE HAND IN MOTION

So far I have considered only situations in which the invisible hand has already accomplished its task. That is, I have been concerned with equilibrium states. But that must be no more than half the story. Suppose, for instance, it is possible for an egg to stay standing on its tip until it is disturbed. We should not attach great practical significance to this equilibrium of the egg until we were told some causal story of how it comes to be in that state. In exactly the same way, the proposition that, in certain circumstances, there is a set of prices which ensures equality between demand and supply in all markets tells us nothing of whether these prices will indeed be established by a market economy. On this central question neither economic theory nor evidence is at all satisfactory.

Before I enlarge on this I want to stress what a significant lacuna this represents and how dangerously it can be ignored by policy advocates. Seeing our ignorance, a number of Chicago and other economists have decided that the best way to proceed is to pretend that it isn't really there. This they do with the aid of some pseudo-philosophical remarks concerning the meaning of equilibrium and the autonomy of human action. In any case, they simply assume that the invisible hand performs its task instantaneously and, as it were, superinvisibly. Thus, for these economists, wages at any moment of time have just those values which, given other prices, ensures that everyone willing to work finds a willing employer. This is not a theory, or a deduction from a theory, but an axiom. Fluctuations in employment are then explained by the expectational errors which I have already discussed. For instance, Britain's unemployed workers are without a job because, at the going wage, they do not want one. They do not want one because either they prefer subsidised idleness or they expect real wages to rise and are thus trading present for future leisure. On the basis of this specious nonsense Keynes has been pronounced dead and Mrs Thatcher advised.

Although I am sure this is nonsense as descriptive economics I am, as a theorist, more concerned with the intellectual move which axiomatically ensures that the invisible hand is never observed in reconciling inconsistent plans and so provides no account of how it might actually do this. It seems clear that this leaves the theory essentially incomplete. It also seems obvious that it cannot be usefully confronted with other theories, for it is no answer to the Keynesian proposition that there may be states in which willing workers cannot find a job at the going wage to announce it as an axiom that this can never happen.

Less extreme theories have recognised that some story must be told and to the non-economist the chosen one is known as the 'law of supply and demand'. Here the invisible hand is actually set in motion. When demand for anything exceeds its supply the price will go up, and vice versa when supply exceeds demand. In taking this account seriously, one finds oneself studying a rather complex dynamic system. It is a fact that this study has not led to the conclusion that this behaviour of prices must guide the economy to its tranquil equilibrium. Indeed, almost the converse is true: only very special assumptions seem to ensure this happy outcome.

But this may be so because we have not told a correct story. Great difficulties are encountered in this undertaking when one insists on retaining the perfect competition hypothesis. For strictly speaking, there is no one agent who can actually be taken to do the price changing. Largely for this reason the analysis has followed Walras in postulating a fictional auctioneer whose task it is to adjust prices in accordance with the 'law of demand'. But while there are auction markets in actual economies they are pretty rare and it is not at all clear what real process the fictional auctioneer represents. If, however, we recognise that actual agents are involved in changing prices because they have transitory or permanent market power we shall also start to get a grip on the theory, by exploiting the really basic axiom that agents are out to improve themselves. This kind of analysis is in its infancy and there are no general results to report.

But certain rather important implications of this unsatisfactory approach can be observed. During the process individuals will encounter not only prices but also trading experiences which will influence their subsequent actions. If you find that the baker is frequently out of bread you may buy crackers instead. If the baker, in turn, is slow to notice that he has unsatisfied customers he may never notice it, because in the meantime they have gone to the cracker shop. If there are workers who cannot find a job, this will affect what they can buy and so the job prospects and actions of others. Employers noticing the unemployed willing workers may find it profitable to lower wages. On the other hand, they may not since this might lead existing trained workers to leave or to strike, or the firm may fear for its reputation as a good employer. It may also not be possible, for reasons to be explained by a theory of implicit labour contracts, to pay new workers less than existing ones. But, in spite of all this, money wages may indeed fall. However, since the demand signals were unfavourable, it is not at all certain that employment will rise. The analysis of the process is hazardous even in ruthlessly simplified models and not at all always favourable to the invisible hand.

In particular, there is now a possibility that the invisible hand may cease to move before its task is accomplished — I have elsewhere referred to this as the hand getting stuck. For if price changes are the outcome of the calculations of actual participants in the economy, they may certainly be miscalculated. That is, the participants may judge the price change not to be to their advantage when it really is. But even when they calculate correctly this may happen. For the consequences to you of your price change depend on the calculations of others as to the consequences to be expected from their price change in turn. Keynesians refer to such situations as bootstrap situations. A given employer's willingness to lower wages and a potential employee's willingness to accept the job on these terms will not be independent of whether other employers have calculated it to be to their advantage to lower the wage or, as Negishi (1978) has noted, a worker who would be willing to work at a wage below that ruling may none the less correctly calculate that the effect of lowering his wage on the probability of finding a job is too small to make it worth while.

Although I want to re-emphasise that these are all possibilities in particular constructions rather than general propositions, I feel confident enough to conjecture that very shortly a very large and rigorous collection of models with these possibilities will be available. In game theory we are quite familiar with the notion of multiple equilibria and with the insight that co-operative solutions may dominate non-co-operative ones. The paths which I am now indicating are much more familiar to game theorists than they are to orthodox pure theorists.

Of course, there is a great deal more to say on this matter but I can allow myself only one more observation. The pure market proponents sometimes argue against the possibilities which I have just described by noting that they would result in there being unexploited gains to trade. This they regard as inconsistent with a world of rational agents. In this last view I consider them to be profoundly mistaken. Opportunities for mutually advantageous trade must be recognised and hence signalled. We can imagine a world where groups of individuals bump into each other at random and proceed to explore the possibility of trade. It is not our world and it is not the world under discussion. In that world, trade opportunities are supposed to be signalled by prices which are public and anonymous – they do not depend on the persons engaged in the trade. Of course, there are exceptions to this but the theory under review does not consider these. In such a world, it is false to propose that, because there are unexploited gains from trade, it will always be rational to signal this by price changes. The manner in which potential traders can communicate is of basic significance. One should have thought that, in an age where the prisoners' dilemma (see any text on game theory) is known far and wide, this point hardly needed making.

SOME GENERAL REMARKS AND SOME TENTATIVE CONCLUSIONS

I have for much of the time been arguing that the emperor's clothes are not quite as fine as is often supposed. Although I have not been as precise and detailed as a more leisurely account would have permitted, I none the less hope to have shown that, both on purely logical considerations as well as on the basis of quite simple observations, the invisible hand is likely to be unsure in its operations and occasionally downright arthritic. However, as I have already warned, it is an unwarranted inference from this that there is some social device which will perform more satisfactorily or that we should cut off the hand altogether.

One of the reasons for the failings of the invisible hand, at least in theory, is that the task assigned to it is extremely complex. This task will not go away when, for instance, we propose to replace the market by the planner. In this connection Professor Hayek, whose doctrines on many economic matters I do not consider sound, made a very important point. He argued that economically relevant information was highly decentralised. A professional cook, for instance, will know more about the dishes he could prepare from a chicken and be better informed of his customer's tastes than would be a plumber or an economist. Indeed, it is quite clear that such specialised knowledge and information is commonplace. Now one of the claims made for the price system by Hayek was that it successfully aggregates this information so that the economy behaves as if there had been no specialised knowledge in the first place. Hayek did not prove this to be so and it is only very recently that we have understood the circumstances in which the claim made is correct.

I will not now discuss this particular issue in that particular way if for no other reason than that the matter is quite technical. However, we do not need to do that in order to see the force of Hayek's point that any planner must find means to utilise and to aggregate the private information of citizens. Even when the invisible hand performs the task imperfectly it does perform it after some fashion. It is not at all clear in what fashion it could be performed without the price system altogether. This may be the reason why so many socialist economies have progressively allowed the invisiable hand to regain some of its old importance.

The economising of information and the utilisation of widely dispersed information is one feature of a market economy which has only recently been studied with the seriousness it deserves. It is already evident that the outcome will not always be as good as it could have been if an all-knowing agent were in control. It also seems possible that a more limited agent could nudge the system to prevent it settling on unsatisfactory or downright bad outcomes. But no discussion of a planned economy begins to tackle the issues seriously when it ignores these informational tasks. Certainly, the literature on economic planning has for a good time been aware of this and, also, of other potential virtues of the price system. Indeed, sometimes the pure theory which I have outlined is not taken descriptively but prescriptively. That is, the task of the planners is to make the invisible hand work as the textbook says it does: for instance, by instructing functionaries to follow marginal cost pricing rules or to attain some prescribed rate of return in their investment plans.

But this leads naturally to another problem which I have already touched upon in my discussion of Hirsch. In so far as the invisible hand moves it is moved by greed. To buy in the cheapest and sell in the dearest market, to change job to earn a higher wage, to raise prices to tap some of the surplus from unsatisfied buyers, these are all virtues for the market system. If business managers were to take decisions in the light of what they perceive to be their 'social responsibility' or if, in general, agents were to value the welfare of others outside their family at all seriously, the invisible hand might still do this and that, but it would cease to do what Adam Smith claimed for it. This to many people is an unattractive feature of the hand, although I myself incline to the Johnsonian view that a man is, in normal times, rather innocently engaged when he is making money. But that is evidently contentious. What I believe is not so is the insight that the market system operates on relatively simple motivational precepts which, in principle, leave agents open to manipulation by authority, whereas substitute systems are partly unfathomable because they leave the motives of the actors nebulous. Once again, the history of socialist countries suggests that the dislike of bourgeois greed has frequently had to give way to the necessity of providing coherent and appealing motives for people to do what is wanted. Kornai (1971) has given an interesting account of how greed can be replaced by apathy and lassitude when greed has nothing to bite on, and of how unsatisfactory this proved to be in Hungary. In any case, to ask individuals or groups of individuals to act 'in the common interest' is, except in well defined and exceptional cases, not to ask anything comprehensible of them at all.

Of course the market system not only allocates resources, it also powerfully influences the distribution of the enjoyment of resources between individuals. The fundamental theorems of welfare economics suggest that to some extent one should be able to divorce these two sides of the same coin. In fact we know that, even in our most simplified models, this cannot in general be perfectly done: one may have to make trades between equity and efficiency. Pigou noted this over fifty years ago, and his arguments have since been refined without being altered in their essentials. The actual terms of such a trade are not really known. Greed may take many forms. For instance, it may be satisfied by rewards which, although they exceed one's neighbour's reward, do so only slightly. This is what Keynes believed, and he thought that the greed game could be played successfully for much smaller stakes. No one knows whether he was right. But this question will arise whatever the mode of economic organisation − if one wants people to act in a certain way one must give them a reason for doing so.

At this stage, it is proper to note an objection to the manner in which I have dealt with the market economy. Many people will argue that the allocative role of a market economy is not by any means the most important role. Rather it is the opportunities which it affords for innovation and ingenuity and for the risk taking entrepreneur and thus for growth in welfare. It was Schumpeter, rather than Walras, who saw down to the essence of things and it was Keynes on animal spirits, rather than Arrow−Debreu on general equilibrium, who understood the motor in the capitalist machine. On this view, obstacles placed in the path of greed and self-advancement, such as result from an egalitarian public finance, are liable to have much more serious consequences than 'just a misallocation of resources.' Such obstacles may lead to stagnation or continuous decline. Moreover, proponents of this view will argue that there is no substitute for the hero of the market. Civil servants are not readily cast in the mould of captains of industry or that of Schumpeterian innovators.

My first comment on this view is defensive. The critics are not right when they suggest that the market theory is not relevant to the story of growth. In fact, that theory is just as much concerned with the intertemporal, as it is with the intratemporal, allocation of resources. For instance, it is highly relevant to the understanding of the investment−consumption choice, which in turn is very near the centre of an understanding of processes of growth. It is simply a mistake to believe that the equilibrium which I have discussed is bound to be stationary or even quasi-stationary.

My second comment is that none the less the critics have a point. Certainly, economic theory does not provide an answer to Weber's famous question why Britain rather than China should have been the first to have an industrial revolution. Nor, indeed, has economic theory much helped in accounting for the Japanese post-war sprint or for the relative British decline. Plainly there are here crucial elements which go beyond market signals and market behaviour. On these grand matters economics is comparatively silent.

But it is not entirely mute either. To take one example, recent studies, based on the traditional view of market choice, have much illuminated the relation between market structure and R and D expenditure. Such expenditures are undertaken with peculiarly uncertain outcomes; they are part and parcel of competitive battles and they are likely, because of the operation of the law of large numbers, to be subject to significant increasing returns. Oligopolistic industries will, in this area, take decisions which differ from those of monopolistic or competitive ones and we can actually pin down that difference. Similar insights have been gained on the question of what are the main determinants of the adoption of inventions, once made. In all of this the invisible hand plays a part in guiding the direction of innovative activity. I need only remind you of the effects of the rise in the real price of oil on motorcar design to make the point obvious. Moreover, there are good reasons to suppose that the invisible hand will work imperfectly. This is partly due to the increasing returns and to the public good aspect of invention and discovery. The theory also suggests some ways in which these failures can at least be rendered smaller with market-using policies.

However, many people have a liking for grand questions and some of them have been arguing that economics should give way to political economy. Sometimes that is a disguised invitation to enter the claustrophobic world of Marx, often it is a plea for 'universal social science'. The latter is not a self-evidently plausible project. If it is, then it will certainly require a genius which makes such advice unhelpful. At its best, the invitation is to look circumspectly and in a precise manner a little beyond traditional boundaries. Hirsch has shown that this can be fruitful.

But we should not, I think, be surprised by our large areas of ignorance. Indeed, I would find it more surprising if there were available or possible a total theory of history and society. Such theories as have been proposed are pretty clearly bogus. The questions of the theory which I have been propounding are more modest and more useful. In the first instance, it is a powerful test for organising one's thought and for detecting unsound arguments. For example, the insight that the pursuit of self-interest need not have undesirable social consequences, as well as a precise account of the case where it does do so, is of great utility. Should fisheries be left to the market? Do we need an energy policy? Should the poor be aided by rent control? In these and hundreds of other instances the theory is not only the most powerful but the only available means by which we can attain coherence of argument. Robertson thought that benevolence was one of the scarcest of goods and that it should therefore be demanded only sparingly. Many politicians propose programs which suppose that it is a free good. It is a great virtue of the theory that it suggests ways in which institutions and policies might be devised, which harness self-interest and render it socially acceptable. It thus allows one to proceed while humanity is what it seems to be.

At the end of all this there is no crisp and clear final reckoning. The limitations on the applicability of pure market theory are numerous and some of them are quite serious. The exceptions to the benificence of the invisible hand have been piling up since Adam Smith and, much later, Pigou considered them. Our knowledge of the actual movements of the hand is rudimentary and vastly incomplete. The increase of market power of all kinds has produced formidable conceputal problems in the construction of theories. The Smithian vision still provides a reference point but an increasingly remote one. It can also be dangerously misleading when this limited role is not recognised. This, as I have argued, is illustrated by some recent American writings on the relation of wages and employment and is further exemplified by the exponents of supply economics. All these advocates say much more than even the pure theory allows them to say, and infinitely more than the applicability of that theory permits. Although Mrs Thatcher has recently denied vehemently that her policies are based on any economic theory – that is, that the policies have coherent origins – this must not be taken at its face value! She has after all diagnosed unique cures for our ills, and in her pronouncements the Smithian hand is quite visible.

The predominant conclusion must be that we are quite uncertain of what really is the case. The pretence that it is otherwise comes under the heading of religion or magic. Once the uncertainty is recognised it will greatly affect the set of rational or reasonable actions. Traditional theory is quite powerful on the question of the control of systems which are imperfectly understood. It suggests that, exceptional and near catastrophic circumstances apart, it will not in general be wise to put all your eggs in one basket or to give harsh pulls on levers, unless you are what economists call a risk lover — that is, unless you are willing to pay much more than the actuarial value of a bet. But risk loving itself is unreasonable. In any case, these are the reasons why as I said at the outset, the wishy-washy, step by step, case by case approach seems to me to be the only reasonable one in economic policy.

But many people, to my surprise, prefer to go out with a bang rather than a whimper. Very few people can live with a shadowy and ill defined picture of our world. So I place no bets on the reasonable approach winning through. In this country it is very likely that the non-fulfilment of the vastly exaggerated claims for the invisible hand will lead to a reaction in which the hand, to our great loss, will be amputated forever. The age of prophets and of witches is upon us and such an age is not friendly to reason.

REFERENCES

Arrow, K. J. 1963. The role of securities in the optimal allocation of risk-bearing, *Review of Economic Studies*, 31
Bewley, T. 1980. The optimum quantity of money in J. Kareken and N. Wallace, (eds) *Federal Reserve Bank of Minnosota*
Kornai, J. 1971. *Anti-Equilibrium*, North Holland
Makowski, L. 1980. The characterization of perfect competition, *Journal of Economic Theory*
Negishi, T. 1978. Existence of an underemployment equilibrium, in Schwödiauer, G. (ed), *Equilibrium and Disequilibrium in Equilibrium Theory*, Reidel
Radner, R. 1968. Competitive equilibrium under uncertainty, *Econometrica*, 38

6

The Winter of our Discontent

Anyone wishing to understand the operation of the market, be it that of a capitalist or socialist country, is bound to become acquainted with the work of the GE school. (Kornai 1971, p. 27)

Economists do not grow bitter gracefully. Many of them came to the subject hoping to do good and to be useful and find that they can do far less than they had expected. Many others with a theoretical bent find that they cannot now understand what the best minds in their subject are saying. Others again came to paint a great canvas and find themselves in the studio of miniaturists. Looking at, but not often studying, the pages of some learned journals or Debreu's work, they all agree: 'This is not what I meant, this is not what I meant at all.' If they are of the right age they then write a presidential address or a lament. What I think disturbing about so much of this literature is that it is so bad — because it is so bad and because some of the authors are so distinguished, I invoke the psychological explanation I started with.

But of course something is wrong. A good theory has powerful antibodies which soon destroy the carping which comes from incomprehension and hostility. But in our case the objectors are getting more strident and probably more numerous. It is therefore a welcome event when a critic appears of the calibre of Kornai. Although I shall argue that he has succeeded only partially and that in a number of important instances he has missed the point, there is little doubt that, amid all the present noise, his is one of the few grammatical voices. It is for this reason that I want to consider what he has to say in some detail. For who can doubt that there are already many, quite innocent of his book, *Anti-Equilibrium*, who are invoking Kornai to aid them in some foolish pronouncement? And who can doubt that others, having spotted one of his mistakes, have already dismissed the whole enterprise? It would be a pity if the opportunity to proceed with a coherent discussion should be so sadly missed.

Before we start there are a number of general things to get out of the way:

(1) Kornai is not concerned with the dreary question of whether we should or should not use mathematics. Nor, although he is strongly empirically oriented, does he share the astonishing view of Professor Phelps Brown (1972) that the gathering of data and the thinking about data should be a sequential process.

(2) Many people like quoting Keynes' dictum that economics should be like dentistry. Few of them note the singular lack of dentists who have written 'general theories'. Keynes did not take his own advice and there is no reason why we should. Kornai has not written a manual for economic dentists. Although he wants economics to be useful, he understands the need for much detailed theorising.

(3) Although Kornai is a Hungarian economist writing in Hungary, his work owes nothing to Marx. Indeed he claims (p. 356) a close affinity between the Marxian theory of competition and the market and the general equilibrium theory which is under attack.

(4) The book does not deal with some of the more recent sallies against neo-classical economics which turn on the use of aggregates or the meaning of marginal productivity theory. He understands the theory sufficiently well to realise that it is free of logical error and quite unconcerned with the possibility of aggregation. By 'the theory' he means the Arrow–Debreu general equilibrium theory.

(5) Kornai is extremely modest and does not claim to have discovered a new theory. The 'book wishes to outline a *programme for work*' (p. 375).

I

The first point to make is that methodology and epistemology are serious subjects in their own right and that few economists are equipped to do them justice. Kornai is no exception, and

what he does at the start of his book to distinguish between
'real science' and other activities never rises above the banal and
never looks the most obvious difficulties in the face. All he wants
to say is that the construction of a deductive logical system based
on axiomatic foundations is somehow a different activity from an
attempt to discover whether the moon is really made of green
cheese. By meddling with philosophy and by a certain predilection
for 'real science' he gains nothing and he loses the sharp focus he
requires in order to decide whether Arrow—Debreu general equilibrium theory (henceforth GE) is dead end or not.

Now Kornai speaking of the founders of GE remarks: 'They
themselves know best that increasing returns, uncertainty etc.
do exist.' (p. 359) He then proceeds to give a sociopsychological
account of the persistence of a concern with GE. It does not
occur to him that the most obvious explanation why one studies
this theory, which is known to conflict with the facts, is that
one is not engaged in description at all. Nor does he see that
even though it 'is merely on intellectual experiment', it can be
of very great practical importance.

Someone proposes an explanation of the origin of the earth,
say that it was sucked out of the sun. There is not way in which
the event itself can now be observed. A theoretical physicist
calculates the angular momentum of the earth if the explanation
were true. In doing so he provides a way in which the theory
can be falsified. When the claim is made — and the claim is as
old as Adam Smith — that a myriad of selfseeking agents left to
themselves will lead to a coherent and efficient disposition of
economic resources, Arrow and Debreu show what the world
would have to look like if the claim is to be true. In doing this
they provide the most potent avenue of falsification of the claims.
Consider the role of futures and contingent futures markets in GE,
and you will see what I mean. Such work is of great practical
significance simply because it is of the greatest relevance to action
in the present state of economic debate. When it is claimed that
foreign aid is unnecessary *because* only investment profitable to
private investors can be beneficial, we know at once that the
speaker or writer does not know the findings of GE. Anyone who
has this knowledge will have no difficulty in pointing to those
features of the actual situation which are at variance with what
would have to be true if such a claim were to be true. Or take the
discussions on floating exchange rates and concentrate only on the
claim that the rate will tend to the equilibrium level. Quite apart

from all the dynamic problems, the student of GE would note at once not only that there may be no equilibrium level, but also that if there is one such level there may be very many. It may for instance be to the advantage of a country to support an otherwise unstable equilibrium. And so it goes on. GE, by making precise an economic tradition which is two hundred years old and deeply ingrained in the thinking of many (including non-economists), has also greatly contributed to practical argument. Indeed, Korani is using that theory to great effect in arguing that much of reality is at variance with it. Before Arrow and Debreu there would have been nothing sufficiently precisely claimed to be the case to enable one to falsify the claim.

But of course this is only one part of the story. The student of GE believes that he has a starting point from which it is possible to advance towards a descriptive theory. In recent years, for instance, there have been successful investigations into the consequences of replacing given tastes by stochastic tastes, perfect by imperfect competition, anonymity by coalitions, tâtonnement, and so on. The theories and concepts are of course different, but the method of attack is firmly rooted in the tradition. However, Kornai writes: 'A synthesis of the careful attempts to improve the equilibrium theory may turn the "reform" into a "revolution"' (p. 367); and he notes that the difficulties with convexity and uncertainty alone point to revolution. His book is a prolegomenon for the revolt, and to this issue I now turn.

But before I do so I want to re-emphasise the first point. Kornai regards GE 'as useless as a real science theory' (P. 359). Since throughout he adduces empirical evidence to refute this theory, I take it that he really means that it is *false* as a theory of what the world is like. But then it cannot but be a 'real science' achievement to have formulated a two-hundred-year-old tradition so sharply as to enable such an unambiguous verdict to be reached.

II

There are great difficulties in coming to grips with the positive things Kornai has to say. This is so because he considers the first stage of the revolution to require a Linnaean classificatory approach. He takes a hard, common sense and often penetrating look at a feature of an economic problem and then invents a name for it. There must be at least fifty new terms which are being proposed as the language of the new theory. Most of them are empty boxes and Korani with characteristic candour admits this. But until someone has used this new conceptual paraphernalia, how is one to judge whether it can indeed be used? Yet Kornai has interesting and perceptive things to say, and it would be unhelpful to allow his predilection for coining new terms to irritate.

He views an economic system as an engineer views a system, and the aim is to make contact with cybernetics and systems theory. The book itself is to be taken as a description, which is regarded as minimally realistic, of organisations and units and the flows between them. It is argued at each stage that GE cannot encompass these crucial features of an actual economy. Thus a long discussion is devoted to the complexity of information flows and types. GE theory in general takes information to be exclusively transmitted by prices and effortlessly acquired by all agents. This, rather justly, strikes Kornai as being totally at variance with what is in fact the case when inventories, government announcements and newspaper articles and a host of other 'signals' are used by agents to map their environment. Similarly he argues that organisation is a complex system of authority and domains of authority, that this complexity is reflected in the decision process, and that GE quite neglects the study of these matters which are however a vital part of actual decisions. Not unnaturally this line of attack – call it very high level common sense – also leads him to criticise very sharply the use of the optimising agent in GE. Not only may there be no single such agent, for example, in business, but the informational complexities and the learning which takes place 'by deciding' make optimisation rather meaningless. In addition, he is persuaded by a Simon-like aspiration-level approach which is here much embellished by both useless and useful ideas. Here is a pretty useless statement: 'Certain activities of economic organisations and the efficiency of those activities depend on two major factors: the extensive level of aspirations of the organisation (the level to be attained) and the intensity of aspiration (its subjective importance).' (p. 172) Well yes, and . . . ? On the other hand when he later comes to distinguish between 'autonomous' (roughly, routinised) functions and those which he calls 'higher' functions, he puts the hammer right on the centre of an interesting and potentially fruitful nail.

All these ideas have as a common feature that they refer to an economy moving through real time. The organisations change and develop, information arrives, and decisions are taken, sequentially.

No present moment is like any past moment and the organisations and units adapt and readapt. They never attain that state of tranquility which we call an equilibrium in GE. Certainly one wants to agree with this vision since it is so nearly a description of what we see about us. But the question turns on how it can usefully be tamed to serve the analyst and practitioner.

Recall that GE is frequently taken to task for being (say in comparison with Marshallian tradition) too complicated and general to be useful. Kornai's point is that it is not nearly complicated enough. Over and over again he stresses the *complexity* of the phenomena and shows how GE has abstracted from it. But he has nothing to offer to that vital stage of understanding when description is superseded by a generalising insight which imposes coherence without being precisely descriptive of any element of the situation. This is his great weakness and he knows it to be so. But he also greatly underestimates the power of the stance taken by GE. By this I mean that he is too insensitive to the distinction between those matters which he describes which are a crucial challenge to the methodology of GE and those which may not be so at all. So he has far too much on his plate to allow one to see what it is that he is eating.

Here is an example. Unlike Professor Joan Robinson (1962), Kornai understands that the empirical content of preference theory is that preferences are relatively stable. He claims this to be false for all sorts of reasons such as the invention of new commodities, advertising and so on. He also notes that people seem to like variety and try things which they have not tried before. But when a good theorist thinks about preferences he is careful to describe the space over which they are taken to be defined. It is by now rather well known that we can think as easily of a 'quality space' as we can of a 'commodity space'. Indeed, much later in the book Kornai himself notes this point. Certainly this approach has been found useful in empirical demand studies. Now here is a simple exercise: reformulate GE with preferences defined over qualities. When you have done it, the essential GE vision is preserved. How do we now view the great mutability of tastes? It is an empirical generalisation that there is a positive association between people claiming that 'human nature is always the same' and 'we consume what advertisers tell us to consume'. There is an obvious way in which thinking in qualities rather than in goods can to some extent reconcile these two views.

Similar remarks apply to 'deterministic tastes'. The problems of how to specify stochastic tastes and how then to modify the main propositions of GE have all been tackled. The same applies to non-convex preferences. Rather precise statements are available as to the 'damage' these can inflict on the theory, and a measure of the damage and its dependence on the number of participants is available.

These remarks are not offered in a spirit of defence. They are meant to demonstrate that a critic of a so well studied a theory as GE would be wise to ask himself: how would I counter this argument if I were Arrow or Debreu? There are too many instances where Kornai fails to take this precaution and so weakens his case.

But of course this leaves a good many thrusts which do go home. GE is strong on equilibrium and very weak on how it comes about. It is a fair generalisation to say that the theory has proved so far less helpful in studying processes whether of decisions or of information or of organisation. If one takes the view, and it certainly is a reasonable one, that these processes must be understood if any actual economy is to be understood, then without denying the great merit of GE in settling a particular intellectual debate one may well wish to argue that the time has come to start from scratch. Kornai holds, I believe, exactly this position. But he has only made a small start in making his case, not because, as he recognises, he has so little to offer towards 'starting from scratch' – he may well be too modest here – but because the critical argument does not come to grips with essentials and is often misdirected.

This criticism may be illustrated by an example. Sidney Winter and others have taken seriously the Darwinian, adaptive and selection features which many have claimed to characterise an actual economy. Kornai very frequently uses the language of this idea. But, unlike say Winter, he has not studied it in any depth and that is what it deserves. In particular, there is a very old claim that the adaptive and non-optimising responses of agents will be weeded out by the competitive selection process to leave only the optimising survivors. If that claim were to be correct, then while at any moment we should expect to be observing agents in the process of adapting and of being eliminated, the asymptotic states would certainly be of great interest. I am not maintaining that this Darwinian scenario is the correct one; indeed, I rather doubt it. But plainly it has to be investigated and studied if a serious critique of a world of optimising agents is to be mounted.

This leads quite naturally to another example. Let us grant that the actions of agents are to be understood by using Kornai's aspiration levels and tensions. The question remains: can this view be usefully translated into an extremum problem? This has nothing to do with a sense of piety to our traditions; it is simply that such translations in all sorts of subjects have been found rather powerful aids to understanding (Samuelson 1972). Kornai does not even ask the question.

One could continue to give many more instances of Kornai stopping short at the crucial point where he is required to show that GE is 'a mathematical crystal, (which) cannot be improved' (p. 267). In fact I am not sure that I have been able to understand his view on this. For instance, when GE theorists turn, as they are now turning to a study of sequence economies, of stochastic equilibria and of equilibria relatively to information, and when they do these things by modifying some of the axioms of GE appropriately while retaining others, are they 'polishing the mathematical crystal' or are they engaged in the natural process of theoretical development? Put differently, why does Kornai object to a sequence of 'reforms' which a good many people are now engaged in and why does he think it a good strategy to introduce them all simultaneously? The taunt that GE has done no more than codify nineteenth-century economics has both some truth and a lesson. Economics deals (as Kornai continually notes) with enormously complex material and it takes a very long time to sort out even the simplest propositions. Is it really likely that by keeping one foot firmly in what we know while the other explores a segment of the unknown we shall do worse than we would by taking a running leap? I have found no argument of Kornai's which would incline me to answer in the affirmative.

III

I turn briefly to Part III of the book, 'Pressure and suction in the market', which is Kornai's way of characterising excess supply and excess demand. As usual he has some very shrewd things to say — for instance, his discussion of how pressure and suction will have different consequences for the innovatory activities of producers. However the whole of this part of the book is marred by some rather bad mistakes and misunderstandings.

On p. 230 he claims that in GE the concept of supply is unclear. He also claims that the theory does not distinguish between actual and intended actions on the market, and that markets are never cleared because a 'properly functioning market is always full of goods in the morning as well as in the evening' (p. 229). This is only one of a number of related mistakes. It is difficult to see how the set of vectors Debreu calls the supply correspondence can be 'unclear'. Everyone knows that it contains contingent elements and certainly storage elements, so that the observations in the above quotation seem quite beside the point. The theory distinguishes most sharply between 'actual' and 'intended' quantities since that is what it is about, namely to study the subset of a large number of possible situations for which the two kinds of quantities coincide. It is perhaps no accident that Kornai uses his most vehement language to criticise what he has not properly understood.

But nothing is gained by going through further instances, although it is a good exercise for readers (for example, p. 260 provides rich material). Let me instead attempt to excogitate what Kornai seems to be saying. It is (a) that an economy can only be understood when the sequential nature of learning and decision taking is understood, (b) that there is no reason why the economy should ever attain an equilibrium (zero suction and zero pressure); and (c) that it would not be desirable for it to be in equilibrium because, for example, pressure releases forces such as innovations and competition which are desirable. All of these points evidently have merit, but they are obscured by the unfortunate new terminology and harmed by being made in a spirit of confrontation.

The issue is not at all whether Kornai is correct when he points at important problems: it is how they should be tackled.

Let us consider the 'anti-equilibrium' remarks of Kornai. It was, I believe, always understood that the equilibrium of Arrow—Debreu is not a description of an actual economy, and I have already given reasons why the concept should none the less be important and interesting. However one certainly does want a conceptual apparatus which is much more nearly descriptive. It is, of course, for some of the reasons Kornai gives that Radner (1971) has studied statistical equilibria, and that there is at present great activity in this and other attempts at reformulation. All of these attempts have their roots firmly in GE. When Kornai says 'disequilibrium is beneficial' he has a point, but he fails to consider the important consequential question whether we should not find it useful to reconsider what we want to designate as equilibrium. Many years ago Samuelson made all the relevant remarks on these matters in the *Foundations*. To make just the simplest point, if one lives in a world in which one's relevant environment is changing, then one might argue that one will eventually have adapted one's responses to a world with changing environment. But equilibrium is precisely about such an adaptation, and Arrow—Debreu equilibrium is a special case of this general type.

The point I am making therefore is that although Kornai is pointing his finger at the right things, his call for anti-GE 'synthesis' is excessively vague and misdirected. Perhaps this can be understood as follows. Consider the claim that GE is a correct and complete theory of a decentralised economy. This surely entails that there is nothing more to learn and that all relevant events can be explained by the theory. It is Kornai's besetting sin that he writes as if such a lunatic claim had ever been entertained. His related sin is that he confuses theorems in Debreu with general equilibrium theory. The latter attempts to study rigorously the interactions of many economic agents. In this it is different from much of Marxian, Marshallian and 'practical' economics. Kornai really gives no reason why the next edition of Debreu should not contain theories on sequence economies, stochastic equilibria and equilibria relative to information structures, and why all these should not appear as quite natural developments from the first edition.

All this should not be taken as denying that what we call disequilibrium at present is ill understood. One is only too sadly aware of it. But I have found it hard to understand what it is that Kornai wants to be done. For he is not against formal reasoning; indeed he laments the lack of new von Neumanns, and he is not against studying 'the whole' by learning about the parts. He seems to be saying Hungary in 1972 and the United States in 1972, and so on, are not in the equilibrium the existence of which Arrow and Debreu have established. Who on earth ever thought that they were?

IV

I attempt a summing up. Kornai's work is valuable in mapping our areas of ignorance. There is no doubt that this is salutary if for not other reason than that the vulgarisations of GE which are the substance of most textbooks of economics are both scientifically and politically harmful. His insight into processes of economic decisions and adjustments will surely stimulate research. In

particular his sections dealing with information are extremely valuable. His insistence that prices constitute only a fraction of the
information bundle economic agents must digest seems to me to
be correct and to be one of the most important areas of further
study. The same is true of his remarks on learning and adapting,
routinised response and decisions. All this, if one firmly skips the
new terminologies and definitions, is most stimulating to read.

What the book suffers from is its title and so its adversary. He
writes about 'A god that failed', and good scholars do not have
gods. Whenever it comes to the section headed 'Comparison', where
Kornai shows that GE cannot account for the phenomena he has
been discussing, there is a sharp slackening of the intellectual
muscles. His incapacity to distinguish between the activity of
enunciating Debreuean theorems and the activity of 'doing' GE
is extremely trying, and it hinders his own progress. This is particularly so when he discusses economic policy.

But I would much rather have this book than not have it. Kornai
is so patently honest and so clearly a scholar of integrity that one
is always drawn away from the bad to the good things he has to
say. And among the good things some are very good indeed.

REFERENCES

Kornai, Janos 1976. *Anti-Equilibrium: On Economic Systems Theory and the
Tasks of Research*, North-Holland
Phelps Brown, E. H. 1972. The underdevelopment of economics, *Economic
Journal*, March
Radner, R. 1972. Existence of equilibrium of plans, prices and price expec-
tations in a sequence of markets, *Econometrica*
Robinson, J. 1962. *Economic Philosophy*
Samuelson, P. A. 1972. Maxiumum principles in analytical economics, *The
Collective Scientific Papers of Paul A. Samuelson*, vol. 3, M.I.T. Press,
Cambridge, Mass.
Winter, S. 1971. 'Satisfying, selection and the innovating remnant, *Quarterly
Journal of Economics*, May

Part II

7

On Some Problems of Proving the Existence of Equilibrium in a Monetary Economy

I THE PROBLEM

Recent work on the existence of an equilibrium has been concerned with a world without money whereas all work in monetary theory has ignored the 'existence' question. In this paper I propose to investigate some of the problems of rectifying this omission. Before doing so let us ask ourselves whether the task is worth undertaking.

Most theories in economics involve the equilibrium solutions of certain models. These solutions are used as benchmarks, or as states to which an economic system is believed to tend or as means for making long term predictions. Implicitly or explicitly most economists, whether 'practical' or 'airy fairy', use the notion of an equilibrium. It will also be agreed that very few of our models have as yet been exposed to exhaustive empirical tests. It therefore does not seem unreasonable or useless to expose them to some logical tests in the meantime.

Suppose we found that a given model has no equilibrium solution. This in itself need not mean that we should reject it, but it would surely mean that we should not continue to use it to describe equilibrium states. Take the well known example of an economy with strongly increasing returns to scale. It is agreed that in this case the assumption that all units of decision take prices as given may mean that no equilibrium solution exists. This, it seems to me, is valuable information to have. It means that if we judge increasing returns to scale to be prevalent and if we also wish to discuss the working of the price mechanism by comparing equilibrium states, or given situations with equilibrium situations, then the perfect competition model will not be of much use. This is textbook stuff, but it is also the kind of question existence proofs are concerned with and which has been illuminated by them.

To take an example nearer home, consider Patinkin's model of general equilibrium. Suppose it were shown that it possessed no equilibrium solution. Can it be argued that Patinkin and economists in general could reasonably be indifferent to this result? What would become of the various exercises in comparative statics which are the flesh and bones of Patinkin's argument? As it turns out, the problem is particularly interesting in this case since we must show not only that a solution exists but also that it is one in which money has positive exchange value. It is no good saying, 'We know from everyday experience that we live in a world described by Patinkin's model.' Indeed that is precisely the point at issue. We wish to enquire whether the model satisfied the minimal requirements of eveyday experience. If economists are willing to count equations they should also be willing to investigate the existence of a solution to their equations.

After these rather self-evident remarks, let us get down to work.

II EQUILIBRIUM IN A MONETARY ECONOMY

Let us first formulate the problem in the abstract. Let $P = \{P_0 \ldots P_n\}$, $X = \{X_0 \ldots X_n\}$ be two vectors. Suppose that we have $X_i = X_i(P)$ $(i = 0 \ldots n)$ or more compactly $X = X(P)$. The following assumptions[1] are made (I given them their economic names):

Assumptions A.1: Homogeneity H: $X(P) = X(kP)$ $k > 0, P \geqslant 0$
Walras' Law   W: $P'X(P) = 0$ $P \geqslant 0$
Continuity   C: $X(P)$ is continuous over $P \geqslant 0$
Boundedness B: $X(P)$ is bounded from below
Scarcity   S: $X(0) > 0$

Given A.1 it can then be shown that there exists $P^* \geqslant 0$ such that

---

[1] The notation $\geqslant$ denotes a weak vector inequality, e.g. $X_i \geqslant 0$ means $X_i \geqslant 0$ all i, $X_i > 0$ some i.

$X(P^*) \leqslant 0$. The following obvious points should be noted:

(1) By W, if $P_i^* > 0$, $X_i(P^*) = 0$, whereas only if $P_i^* = 0$ can we have $X_i(P^*) < 0$.

(2) By H, if P^* gives $X_i(P^*) \leqslant 0$ then so does kP^*, $k > 0$.

We refer to P^* as a solution of the system $X(P) \leqslant 0$.

Suppose we wished to ensure that some particular component of any solution P^* is strictly positive. Let us write $P(i)$ as the vector P with its ith component identically equal to zero. If it were true that $X_i(P(i)) > 0$ all $P(i) \geqslant 0$ then evidently $P_i^* > 0$ and our task would have been accomplished.

But now let us suppose that the 0th component of X has the property

$$X_0(P(0)) \leqslant 0 \text{ all } P(0) \geqslant 0 \tag{7.1}$$

then it can easily be shown that there exists some $P^*(0) \geqslant 0$ such that $X(P^*(0)) \leqslant 0$.

For let us set $P_0 \equiv 0$ and concentrate on the vector $P(0)$. By H we may confine ourselves to only those $P(0)$ contained within an n dimensional simplex. Also by W, $\sum_{i \neq 0} P_i X_i = 0$ all $P(0) \geqslant 0$. Also if we write $\hat{P} = \{P_1 \dots P_n\}$ we may substitute $X'_i(\hat{P})$ for $X_i(P(0))$ all i. A.1 will therefore hold for the problem $X' = \{X'_1 \dots X'_n\}$, $X'(\hat{P}) = X'$ and this has a solution $\hat{P}^* \geqslant 0$. But then evidently our original problem must have a solution $P^*(0)$ where this vector has the same components as $\hat{P}^*$ and an additional zero component.

We may now consider an economic interpretation of the argument so far. Let all economic agents have a two period horizon and let the expected price of goods be always identically equal to their current price. Let there be no price uncertainty and let the initial endowments of all the agents be given. Let one of the goods have a futures market and interpret P_n as the present price for the future delivery of that good and P_{n-1} as its current price. Let all prices be expressed in fictional units of account. Assume that households maximise continuous quasi-concave utility functions and that they are not satiated at any $P \geqslant 0$ and that they have positive initial endowments of every good. Suppose that the economy's production set is compact and that production without inputs is impossible. All profits are distributed to households and production agents maximise profits. They always have the choice of not producing at all and of costless disposal. We may then interpret P as a price vector and X as an excess demand vector for the current period and A.1 will hold. Note that the future market defines an interest rate $P_{n-1}/P_n - 1$. The solution P^* gives the equilibrium prices for the current period.

The model just given is in all respects similar to Patinkin's except that it as yet contains no money. Let us designate the good with the label 0 as fiat money. We are told that the demand for fiat money depends on its exchange value (absence of 'money illusion'). It follows that no money will be demanded if its exchange value is zero. But that means that X_0 has the property (7.1). We therefore reach the rather displeasing conclusion (based on the earlier argument) that the Patinkin model always contains a 'non-monetary' solution. Moreover it is not at once clear how we could establish that it also contains a solution with $P_0^* > 0$. For evidently we cannot make use of the device discussed for ensuring this. Something has gone wrong.

Now Patinkin – and others – assume that money always has positive exchange value and it can be argued that his model is not defined for the case where it has not. For if there were no money we would have to specify more closely the activities connected with exchange. That is we are asked to replace A.1 by

Assumption A.1': (H), (W), (C) and (B) hold for all $P \geqslant 0$, $P_0 > 0$

The question is: can we prove that an equilibrium exists when A.1 is replaced by A.1'? Curiously enough Patinkin introduces two further assumptions which make the answer to this question affirmative. I say curiously enough, because at least one of these assumptions was introduced with a quite different end in view. Let us examine this in a little more detail.

We write $\bar{x}_{0\alpha}$ as the initial endowment of cash of individual α and $X_{i\alpha}$ as this individual's excess demand for the ith good. Given the absence of 'money illusion' it is well known that we may write, using the notation introduced earlier,

$$X_{i\alpha} = X_{i\alpha}(\hat{P}, P_0 \bar{x}_{0\alpha}) \text{ all } i$$

Moreover, $X_{i\alpha}$ possess H in the given arguments. Write $\bar{x}_0 = \sum_\alpha \bar{x}_{0\alpha}$.

Patinkin's two further assumptions are:

Assumption A.2: We may write $X_i \equiv \sum_\alpha X_{i\alpha} = X_i(\hat{P}, P_0\overline{x}_0)$ all i

Assumption A.3: $X_0(\hat{P}, P_0\overline{x}_0) > 0$ for all $\hat{P} \geqslant 0, P_0 > 0, \overline{x}_0 = 0$.

A.2 states that all individuals are exactly alike so that the total excess demand for any good is independent of the distribution of initial cash balances between them. By 'exactly alike' we here mean that they all have parallel linear Engel curves going through the origin. A.3 states that the demand for money is always strictly positive for all prices admissible by A.1'.

Now using A.1', A.2, and A.3 the existence of an equilibrium can be established. Here I shall only sketch a proof. Set $P_0 \equiv 1$ and consider the simplex

$$S = \{P, \overline{x}_0 | P_i \geqslant 0 \text{ all } i, \overline{x}_0 \geqslant 0, \sum P_i + \overline{x}_0 = 1\}$$

A.1' holds over S. We may now use a slightly modified mapping of S into itself first proposed by Uzawa:

$$P_j = \frac{1}{k} \max [0, P_j + hX_j] \text{ all } j \neq 0$$

$$\overline{x}_0 = \frac{1}{k} \max [0, \overline{x}_0 + hX_0] \tag{7.2}$$

$$k = \sum_{j=0} \max [0, P_j + hX_j] + \max [0, \overline{x}_0 + HX_0]$$

where h is taken sufficiently small to ensure $k > 0$, (Recall B of A.1'.) The mapping (7.2) can be shown to have at least one fixed point $\hat{P}^*, \overline{x}_0^*$. Using W we easily find

$$(k - 1)[\sum_{i \neq 0} (P_i^*)^2 + \overline{x}_0^*] = h[\sum P_j^* X_i(P^* \overline{x}_0^*) + X_0(P^* \overline{x}_0^*)] = 0$$

So that at the fixed point $k = 1$. It is now easy to see that, using A.3, $X_i(\hat{P}^* \overline{x}_0^*) \leqslant 0$ and $P_i^* X_i = 0$ all $i \neq 0$ and $X_0(\hat{P}^*\overline{x}_0^*) = 0$.

Since by A.3, $\overline{x}_0^* > 0$ and by A.2 its redistribution between individuals leaves all excess demand functions unaffected, we may redistribute it between individuals in the ratio of their actual initial endowments. A simple scale change (of $\hat{P}^*$ and $\bar{x}_0^*$) will then give us the money stocks for each individual which he started out with and the problem is solved.

It is evident that a proof of the existence of equilibrium which turns crucially on a supposition such as A.2 is hardly acceptable. Indeed the role of this assumption is simply to enable us to employ a technical trick to ensure that we can use a fixed point theorem, and one cannot believe that it has any fundamental significance to the whole problem. The trick of course was to keep the exchange value of money strictly positive throughout so that money was always 'desirable' and to obtain the desired continuity by varying initial total stocks knowing that once an equilibrium was found the actual initial stock distribution could be restored without upsetting the equilibrium. But quite apart from A.2, A.3 too will repay further scrutiny.

The supposition that the demand for money will always be positive when $P_0 > 0$ is justified by Patinkin by an appeal to the alleged uncertainty of the exact instant of sales and purchases within a given time period. We are also asked to imagine there to be a 'penalty' for being out of cash when a given purchase comes due. Tobin and Baumol justify the same assumption by the existence of transaction costs (brokerage fees). All assume that no transactions are possible without the intermediate use of money. It is, I think evident that none of these rationalisations can be taken as a explanation of the positive exchange value of money since that is already assumed.

Now explanations which turn on 'brokerage' fees and the 'inconvenience' of indirect transactions are not easy to accommodate in a model such as Patinkin's. These are all 'imperfections' which find no place in the model. Indeed the notion of 'liquidity' would be hard to accommodate in Patinkin's world for that, as Marschak has pointed out, turns rather crucially on the imperfection of markets. But even Patinkin's own preferred account is not easy to understand. We are told that there exist claims to debt. A unit of these is the promise to pay one unit of account in perpetuity. Let us suppose that they are (or have been) issued by the government which otherwise plays no role in the economy other than financing its interest payments by lump sum taxes. There is no price uncertainty. Why should transactions not be carried out by means of these claims to debt? But even if that is not granted it is not clear why when I come to make a purchase, being out of cash (having miscalculated the timing of my receipts), I could not offer to pay a little later (after I have cashed my claim) a little more (offer interest). In Patinkin's world such an offer should always be acceptable, and if trade credits cause no social embarrassment in the world we live in why should it in the abstract world of the textbook?

All this suggests that while Patinkin has rendered signal services he has failed to provide a model which can serve as an adequate foundation for a monetary theory. Such a model, it seems to me, must have two essential features beside price uncertainty. It must distinguish between abstract exchange opportunities at some notionally called prices and actual transaction opportunities. The latter requires a precise statement of the methods of transactions open to an individual with their attendant costs. Secondly it must specify rather precisely the conditions in which futures markets for various commodities would arise. For if there were future markets in all goods and services and no price uncertainty there would, as in Debreu's world, be only need for one single set of transactions over an individual's lifetime and there would be no problem of the non-coincidence of payments and receipts. This involves questions of costs of storage etc. But it also involves questions of the 'standardisation' of commodities. It forces one to recognise that there is no commodity called 'a second hand car' and makes the unsuitability of 'perfect competition models' to monetary theory rather obvious.

The reason why I do not propose to attempt the construction of such a model here is as follows: in the usual existence problem the 'initial' position of the participants can be described independently of prices, i.e. in terms of the initial endowment of goods, technological knowledge etc. The interesting point of a monetary economy is that we cannot do so. For it is one of the features of such an economy that contracts, as Keynes noted, are made in terms of money. In particular, debt obligations are of this kind. By postulating the possibility of 'recontract' etc. this difficulty could be overcome — but it would then, it seems to me, turn out to be a somewhat arid exercise. In any case it is on this aspect of the problem that I wish to dwell in the remainder of this paper.

Before doing so, however, it might just be worth while to sketch a procedure which could be used to establish the existence of an equilibrium in Patinkin's world if his basic assumptions are granted, but A.2 is not used.

We imagine a world without money. Each individual attaches certain probabilities to being able to effect a given exchange at the exchange rates 'called'. However, he may, if he wishes, take out insurance. A unit of insurance is the guarantee of being able to carry out a transaction worth one unit of account at a given moment of time. One may suppose that as long as exchange is desired at all and as long as the price per unit of insurance is not equal to unity, some insurance is demanded. Insurance is supplied by some outside agency, say the government. The price charged per unit of insurance per unit time is $(P_{n-1}/P_n) - 1$, the rate of interest. At any price the amount of insurance supplied is just equal to what is demanded. The government redistributes the proceeds from its activity to households. It can then be shown with the aid of a number of purely technical assumptions that an equilibrium exists. It can then further be shown that corresponding to this fictional economy there would exist an actual one in which individuals 'brought' the same amount of insurance as in the fictional equilibrium by holding certain stocks of cash. Notice that this procedure begs the question: is the government service the only way by means of which economic agents could insure their transactions?

III ARE THERE SOLUTIONS OF REALISTIC MONETARY MODELS?

So far I have been concerned with the question of whether it is possible to construct an abstract model of economic exchange and activity in which money is used and whether the existence of an equilibrium can be proved for such a model. I hope to have shown that even for this task the difficulties are fairly formidable and that they have not yet been faced. I now wish to concern myself with the more interesting question of the existence of a solution to monetary models which are to be taken not as idealised but as in some sense as representing actual relationships. The most famous of these is of course the Keynesian short period flow equilibrium model.

It will be recalled that Keynes argued that if we set up a model which included the requirement that everyone willing to work at the going money wage should be able to do so, then whatever the money wage specified, no equilibrium solution may exist. Keynes further maintained that it was the existence of money in the economy, or more precisely that fact that wage bargains were made in terms of money and that money was always the preferred asset at a rate of interest 'low enough' which was responsible for that conclusion.

This has been widely rationalised in a way best given by a quotation taken from Modigliani (1944):

> Since securities are inferior to money as a form of holding assets, there must be some positive level of the rate of interest (previously denoted by r) at which the demand for money becomes infinitely elastic or practically so. We have the Keynesian case when 'the full employment rate of interest is less than r'' . . . From the analytical point of view the situation is characterised by the fact that we must add to our system a new equation, namely $r = r''$. The system is therefore over-determined.

That this way of putting the case is wrong seems quite clear. The hypothesis that the equilibrium rate of interest cannot fall below a certain minimum is not an additional restriction on our system and provides no new independent relation between any of the unknowns. It is simply a hypothesis concerning the form of one or more of the excess demand functions of the system. Provided these satisfied A.1 and there were as many excess demand functions as unknowns the 'liquidity trap' would not prevent the existence of an equilibrium.

This has been recognised by a large number of writers although the objection is not usually put in this way. Instead it is argued that Keynes ignored the connection between real cash balances and consumption. It is now widely believed that there always exists a level of money wages low enough to ensure the existence of a 'full employment' solution. The argument is as follows: we are concerned with the technical problem of the existence of a solution. Thus while the 'Pigou effect' may be small in practice, by making money prices and wages low enough we can always make the Pigou effect 'large enough'. Indeed since at zero money wages and prices there will always be excess demand (non-satiation and scarcity) for goods and labour, there will be some positive set of prices at which the excess demand for goods and labour is zero. I now wish to give reasons why this argument rests on some rather shaky foundations.

One of the main problems faced in establishing the existence of an equilibrium is to find acceptable assumptions which will ensure that the excess demand functions are continuous over the relevant domain. Among these the one that has caused most difficulty is the necessity of ensuring that at all admissible prices every individual can, if he wishes, participate in some exchange. Consider an individual who owns positive stocks of one good only: say x_1. Let there be only two goods. Suppose that as long as he is able, our individual always prefers to have whatever quantities of the second good he can get, to the good he has. Then for all $1 > P_1 > 0$, he will demand nothing of the first good ($P_1 + P_2 = 1$). But at $P_1 = 0$ he has no choice but to hold the good he has. There will be a discontinuity in his demand function. To exclude this possibility we can either postulate that he has strictly positive stocks of every good or that, loosely speaking, he is always capable of supplying a service which can be transformed into a good with positive price. One might equally well suppose that there is some suitable social redistribution mechanism at work which allows every individual to participate in exchange.

But now let us suppose that our individual has initial endowments which include debt fixed in terms of money at a rate of interest also so fixed. Then as the price of goods in terms of money is made lower and lower (i.e. in our earlier notation as $P_0 \rightarrow 1$) our individual will be unable to meet his obligations: he will go bankrupt. At that stage the creditors find that – even if they get all the debtor's assets, and even if debtors and creditors are similar as in A.2 – the value of these assets may be less that the money value of the debt. For the debtor being capable of rendering services will go 'bankrupt' when he can no longer meet his interest payments. At that stage his assets may already be negative. The possibility of 'bankruptcy' is therefore also a possibility for the occurrence of some rather sharp discontinuities. In a society where contracts are made in terms of money and recontract is not possible, an equilibrium solution may not exist. Of course in the 'long run' all contracts are escapable but that is another story.

The point just made is perhaps of more than purely academic interest since it focuses attention on what is probably one of the most important features of a monetary economy: namely that contracts are made in terms of money. The fact that money is the actual numéraire is of some significance. If the route from unemployment to high levels of demand is strewn with bankruptcies then the smooth curves of the textbooks will be harder to justify. No doubt some sort of story could be invented to get over this difficulty, but it would be a curious one. Let me emphasise again that the difficulty cannot be overcome by supposing creditors and debtors to be exactly alike. For as long as any debtor is not bankrupt the real value of his debt to me increases with lower money prices. When he goes bankrupt and I take over his assets their money value will be less that the value of the debt and so there is a discontinuous change in the real value of money assets. I conclude from all this that the assertion that the 'Pigou effect' ensures the existence of an equilibrium is unproven.

REFERENCES

Modigliani, F. 1944. Liquidity preference and the theory of interest and money, *Econometrica*, 12, pp. 45–88

Patinkin, D. 1965. *Money, Interest and Prices*, 2nd edn, Harper and Row

8

On the Foundations of Monetary Theory

I

I am interested in an economy where money is of no intrinsic worth and is universally accepted in exchange. An agent who holds money now contemplates its exchange for money in the future. If not, then a mild non-satiation postulates ensures that no money would now be held. It follows that a minimum requirement of a representation of a monetary economy is that there should be transactions at varying dates. An economy which has transactions at every date I shall call a *sequence economy*.

A good of given physical characteristics available at a given place at a given date may be the subject of transactions at all dates not later than its date of availability. Let us say that transaction dates are *inessential* if the set of equilibria attainable by an economy is independent of these dates. If transaction dates are inessential then the description of the economy is not altered by concentrating all transactions at the first date. Accordingly in such an economy money is *inessential* in the sense that no monetary variable need enter into the description, or determination, of that economy's equilibrium. It is important to distinguish the property 'money is inessential' from the quite different property 'money is *neutral*'. By the latter, as usual, I want to characterise the claim that the set of equilibria of an economy is independent of the quantity of money (provided that the latter is always positive).

To fix ideas let us consider an Arrow–Debreu economy with all transactions concentrated at the first date. Since it does not matter in what follows I suppose there to be a unique equilibrium with price vector p^*. Let us see whether there is an equivalent sequence economy which can be derived from this one.

First, let us allow transactions at every date in every good with availability date not preceding the transaction date. There is a full vector of Arrow–Debreu prices at every date and I call it q_t. If in this enlarged economy equilibrium is attained when each q_t is proportional to p^* as viewed from t, then nothing will have been altered by allowing transactions at every date. A condition for this to be the case is that the sequence of markets and the extra prices should not make possible more information on the environment than was available when transactions were concentrated in the first period. This point has been splendidly discussed by Radner (1968) and we may refer to this requirement as the *absence of sequential learning*.

But let us go further and permit only spot transactions at every date. Intertemporal transfers would now require the storage of some good or goods which may be costly and there are difficulties with the replacement of contingent markets. Let us therefore introduce money (which can be costlessly stored). At the initial date give money the accounting price of one. Its subsequent account prices depend on the state. In particular the accounting price at date t in state s is such as to preserve proportionality between the spot prices in terms of money at date t and state s and the Arrow–Debreu prices p^* in terms of money between agents and a terminal obligation to hold money such that the economy's equilibrium would be the same as it was when all transactions were concentrated at the first date. (The terminal conditions arise from the artificiality of considering a finite economy.)

If the derivation of this equivalent sequence economy is possible then money is inessential as are the transaction dates. To obtain such an inessential economy (a) there must be absence of sequential learning and (b) the prices at all dates must be known to all agents at any date. In addition, as I shall later argue, certain assumptions are required about transaction costs. I find it difficult to persuade myself that an economy satisfying these requirements is a promising foundation for the study of money.

If one looks back at the steps just taken one sees that money was introduced to sustain the intertemporal connectedness of an equivalent sequence economy of spot markets. It will be clear that the same result could have been achieved by creating a contingent futures market, one for each state, in unit of account and for each pair of adjacent dates. This leads one to the following formulation.

Under classical conditions every Pareto-efficient allocation of an inessential economy must be independent of transaction dates. The manner of its decentralisation however does not have this independence. But every decentralisation must leave agents with the identical opportunities as they have in the decentralisation associated with transactions which are all concentrated at the first date. In particular, if money is part of the decentralisation then money yields a return, contingent on states. Since every equilibrium is Pareto efficient this conclusion applies to all equilibria.

The main content of the monetary theory of an inessential economy is implicit in its construction: there is nothing we can say about the equilibrium of an economy with money which we cannot also say about the equilibrium of a non-monetary economy. But the money of this construction is only a contingent store of value and has no other role. Moreover its existence is fortuitous since there is nothing which demands the sequential structure which will necessitate the introduction of such a store. Lastly the assumptions which I have already discussed and which seem required for an inessential economy are rather unacceptable.

It may help the understanding of these ideas if I relate what I have just said to a very interesting paper by Grandmont and Younès (1973), a paper which is itself related to the ancient dichotomy controversy.

Grandmont and Younès start with a sequential structure which is unexplained. Indeed in their economy the only means of transferring wealth from one date to another is by means of storing money. There is no uncertainty. Money is also given the role of a medium of exchange by the following device: all purchases require the exchange of money and only a part of the money receipts from sales can be used for purchases of the same date as the sales. (A similar rather arbitrary scheme is to be found in the work of Ross Starr 1971, and Kurz 1972a, b). The model, and in particular the role of money, is a good deal different than it was in the economy I discussed earlier.

But let us see whether in certain circumstances the construction is isomorphic to an inessential economy. Consider an inessential economy with all transactions concentrated in the first date so that it has no money. Suppose it has an equilibrium of the kind that in its equivalent sequence form no household would be transferring wealth between dates and that there is no pure time preference. So one might just as well call this a stationary equilibrium. But the stationary equilibrium of this fictional economy must also be an equilibrium of the Grandmont—Younès economy. For all we need to do is to fix the accounting price of money and give each agent a money stock which the Grandmont—Younès rule requires for the transactions indicated by the equivalent fictional sequence economy. All agents now have the same best choices as before since the money stocks simply take care of the extra constraint. One concludes that certainly money is inessential in all stationary equilibria of the Grandmont—Younès economy. This conclusion is of course related to the account of these matters by Archibald and Lipsey (1958).

Indeed one can verify that the isomorphism to an inessential economy need not be confined to stationary states. Certainly if money is the only means of storage the isomorphism must in general fail to hold. But money is not the only means of storage nor the only costless means (recall Keynes' remarks on land). If then some non-money costless storage is possible then one can adjoin to an inessential economy a stream of money going to each agent and a sequence of accounting prices of money, such that every inessential equilibrium is also a monetary equilibrium.

To sum up. One may introduce money into a model of the economy by introducing an *ad hoc* constraint of the Grandmont—Younès variety which ensures that agents hold money. Since this constraint can always be exactly met in a stationary equilibrium of the inessential economy by an appropriate distribution of money stocks and in general by an appropriate sequence of money stocks and prices of money, one can ensure that money is inessential. If there are equilibria of the inessential economy not realisable in the monetarily constrained economy it is because monetary management has not neutralised the transaction constraint, or because money is the only means of storage. Moreover it is easy to show that Pareto efficiency in this construction requires money to be inessential.

Lastly, in this connection, consider Patinkin's theory. I showed (Hahn 1965) that every equilibrium of the inessential economy is realisable in the Patinkin economy. This is because money is held only when it has a positive exchange value and Patinkin gives no reason why a zero accounting price of money should be inadmissible. Put slightly differently, Patinkin gives no reason why he can insist on an always positive accounting price of money in an economy which otherwise is inessential.

After all this I can state with some precision what it is that I have in mind when I claim, as I now want to claim, that the foundations of monetary theory have not yet been laid. The position of formal theory on this matter can be summed up as follows: the representations of the monetary economy used are either isomorphic to an inessential economy or, if not (as in the case of Patinkin), give no account of either the role of money or the sequential character of their construction. But the inessential economy does not need money and one must give reasons for grafting on to it monetary constraints. These reasons have not been given. In particular until recently no study has been undertaken to see whether the common sense advantages claimed for money can be shown to hold in the inessential economy. Until recently no rigorous studies have been made to discover (a) whether the postulated sequential structure is inherent in the process of exchange, the economies of information and the computational demands on agents, (b) whether if so the resulting intrinsic uncertainty concerning the terms at which future transactions can be undertaken allows one to formulate an interesting and coherent notion of short run equilibrium, and (c) whether there is a sequence of short run equilibria which it is useful to designate as an equilibrium. A good many people have now realised that it is questions such as these which require answers and that the real problems of monetary theory are connected with the task of obtaining representations of an economy in which money is essential. Much remains to be done. The literature on the optimum quantity of money suggests that it is not widely realised that the task needs doing.

Of course I have been speaking only of works of formal theory and not of macroeconomics in general or Keynesian economics in particular. Certainly no one working in the framework of the *General Theory* would be tempted to enunciate Pareto-efficient theorems for money. Let me quote from Professor Joan Robinson (1971, p. 90): 'The *General Theory* is a "monetary theory" only in the sense that relationships and institutions concerned with money, credit, and finance are necessary elements in the "real" economy with which it is concerned.' Precisely. But although there is here no one-to-one relation to an inessential economy, it is the case that the *General Theory* is notoriously deficient in its treatment of relative prices and sufficiently informal and evocative as to allow continuous controversy as to its content for almost forty years. But that Keynes was the first economist to notice the tension – I do not claim contradiction – between the paradigm of the inessential economy and monetary phenomena seems hard to dispute. His insistence on the fundamental importance of the intrinsic sequential structure of a monetary economy which allows the future to play a dangerous game with the present, is enough to support the claim I have made.

II

I now turn to some of the work that has been going on to lay the foundations. This work is in its infancy and it is likely that in retrospect it will be seen that some false steps have been taken, The intellectual debt everyone in this field owes to Roy Radner is very great.

The natural place to start is by taking the claim that money has something to do with activity of exchange, seriously. There are a number of ways of setting about this. Ostroy (1970), Starr (1970a, b, 1971) and others have studied exchange activities in an economy without money and production. Their aim is to show that the introduction of money allows Pareto-superior outcomes. These are achieved partly because it permits an economy in exchange effort and partly by the avoidance of the coincidence of wants. The last point bears expansion. It is of course not true that such double coincidence is required by a proper barter economy for there is no reason why one should not accept in exchange a good in one transaction which one proposes to exchange again in another. But this introduces both a speculative and a costly element into non-monetary transactions, some of which are avoidable when money is present. For it is one of the rather notable features of a monetary economy that it permits agents to unbalance their books in goods at any moment of time. This is a point to which I shall return.

But while this work makes precise some of the claims on behalf of money it has not led to a rigorous formulation of sequence economies using money. It also, so it seems to me, is open to a methodological objection.

When we consider a pure exchange economy we do so only in a contingent and preparatory way. Plainly we must build sufficiently robustly not to have to start all over again when production is allowed. But there is an important feature of a monetary economy, certainly familiar since Adam Smith, which makes the extension to production difficult. This is of course that a monetary economy allows specialisation and that specialisation will indeed be a feature of such an economy because, at least to the individual agent, there are increasing returns to specialisation. None of use are jacks of all trades. Accordingly the comparison of a given barter economy with a monetary one when the endowments of agents are the same in both misses an important feature of a monetary economy which one may loosely call the division of labour. No doubt a historical account of a transition between the two economies with due attention to this point is possible, but an analytical one is hard. It also seems to me unnecessary to take so historical a stance. My preference is to start with a fully fledged monetary economy and to study those features of it which make money essential in the sense in which I have been using that term.

Taking this position one is naturally led to a study of markets and in particular to an examination of those features of the situation which cause there to be markets at every date and hence to ensure the sequential structure which is required. It is not unimportant to stress that one is really looking for something stronger, namely an explanation of why the transaction date may be essential.

Foley (1970) and I (1971) independently decided to study these questions by adjoining a transaction technology to the traditional pure exchange economy. Foley did not formulate an explicit intertemporal structure and so our results differ a great deal. David Starrett (1972) has achieved an elegant simplification of what I had to say and has extended the story. I do not wish to go over the ground again in any detail, but after a bare summary start where Starrett left off.

The market technology is not independent of the available institutions and in particular it is not independent of the institution of money. If one considers the set of dated purchases and sales which is feasible, I simply assume that the set without money is wholly contained in the monetary set. Here I short cut the detailed comparison between barter and monetary exchange. In my first attempt at all this I had, however, to leave unresolved an explicit formalisation of the demand for money and I shall take this opportunity to report on some progress with this. In the terminology I then adopted I regarded money at t traded at t as both anonymous and named, that is such trade incurred no transaction costs, but the distinction between named and anonymous continued to apply to money at t traded before t. This is a point of some importance, to which I return.

A good deal of the initial effort was simply directed to the un-expectedly difficult task of showing that an equilibrium relatively to the transaction technology exists. I leave this to one side except to note (a) that the equilibrium is described by two price vectors, one for sales and one for purchases, and (b) that it is a feature of the equilibrium that many feasible transactions are not profitable, that is potential markets are inactive. I took the market technology to be convex but noted this was a bad assumption. Presently I shall consider how one might proceed when this assumption is relaxed. There was no uncertainty.

The interesting features which emerged were these:

(a) Agents were constrained by a sequence of budget constraints. In general no 'present value' calculations could be made which were independent of the agent or of his plans.
(b) The efficiency of the economy has to be defined not only relative to the transaction technology but also relative to the endowment matrix.
(c) In general the equilibrium of the economy attained when all prices are announced is not efficient in the sense in which I have just defined it. (Starrett has produced some very nice examples of this inefficiency.)
(d) Only quite peculiar transaction technologies allowed the economy to be inessential.
(e) I noted the difficulty of dealing with producer decisions when no present values were defined.
(f) I concluded that it was premature, to say the least, to formulate theorems of the optimum quantity of money.

Now Starrett has shown rigorously that the inefficiency results can be avoided, if the sequential budget constraints can be avoided. He avoids them in just the way in which I earlier constructed an equivalent sequence economy, that is he introduces a costless set of markets in unit of account. Kurz (1972b) has used the same device and rather more incautiously seems to believe it to be a route by which money can be shown to be efficiency enhancing. The Starrett result is beautifully proved, but I believe that it proves too much. For it seems to me implausible to require an intertem-poral transaction in apples to use resources without making the same demand on all intertemporal transactions including that in money or unit of account. Indeed one of the popular theories of the transactions demand for money relies rather heavily on the transactions costs in forward money. If this is admitted then the Starrett route out of the difficulty is not possible.

I should not add that I am also rather less impressed than I was at first inclined to be with my own inefficiency theorem. For although it is mildly surprising at first sight it also supererogatory. For one is after all concerned with an economy which is sequential and yet has announced prices and no uncertainty. When these stringent restrictions are dropped it will not be clear, as I argued earlier, how to characterise the equilibrium of an economy. To demand that all expectations be fulfilled at each date now strikes me as leading to uninteresting conceptualisations. All the real work remains to be done here, and the most promising route probably lies with Radner's idea (1970) of a statistical equilibrium. How to characterise efficiency in that context is still quite obscure.

But let me return more explicitly to money. The difficulty which is found is that one must not just show that a transaction equilibrium is possible but that in each such equilibrium money will be held. This is of course familiar but, if precision is required, not easy to accomplish. There is another difficulty. If the existence of this or that market is to be treated as an economic unknown of the problem then so must be the periodisation of the construction. That is reasons, if they are available, must be given why one should not deal in continuous time and so for instance perhaps lose the comforting 'non-coincidence of payments and receipts'. If one considers the problem it soon becomes apparent that one will want to do without the convexity of the transaction technology.

III

I now come to work which is not yet completed and can therefore only deal with such results as are now available.

There are a number of routes which one can take when non-convexities are present. One of these is to deal with a continuum of agents. Another is to study a fictional convex hull economy and to show that every equilibrium of the fictional economy will be 'close' to that of an actual economy if the number of agents is large enough. A young colleague Roger Whitcomb has pursued the first of these lines of attack for the present problem and Walter Heller (1971) has pursued the second. I have taken a different route largely because I do not seek those answers which can be obtained when the non-convexities have been suitably sterilised. I want them to be very much present in the final description. As it turns out this can be, at least partially, achieved.

Let us consider the case of pure set-up costs. Here every market at t requires an input vector of goods dated t, if it is to operate at a positive activity level. The set of net market vectors obtained by subtracting the vector of fixed input vectors is strictly convex. The periodisation of the economy is, for the moment, taken as given.

There is no theorem which states that competitive equilibrium is impossible in the presence of non-convexities. What is the case is that one can construct examples satisfying the axioms of agents' behaviour which do not permit a competitive equilibrium. One can ask whether the reverse procedure is possible. That is, can one for the present problem characterise a class of cases for which equilibrium does exist in spite of set-up costs? If so will this class be interesting? With a reservation to be mentioned shortly I want to answer both questions in the affirmative.

The economy which I consider has money and is of finite duration. We can calculate the maximum number of markets this economy could have. To each such market assign the number one if it is active and the number zero if it is not. This procedure gives rise to some difficulty because I shall want zero to designate the state when no exchanges in the good which this market represents are possible rather than a state of affairs when at the going prices no agent wishes to be active in this market. This causes a complication with the definition of equilibrium to which I return later.

One can now consider the set of economies which can be constructed by assigning zero or one to the various markets. For instance, one such economy arises when zeros are assigned to all markets and we call this the *trivial* economy. Another special case will be the economy in which zeros are given to all future markets and I call this the *spot* economy. In general one can associate a number with every combination of zeros and ones which is technically possible.[1] If that number is k, the resulting economy is called the k *economy*. It is important to remember that in many of these economies the optimising actions of agents are conditional on the impossibility of exchange in some markets.

The kind of result one is looking for is the demonstration that for some k economy with set-up costs an equilibrium exists when

---

[1] For example, if the technology of a given market requires as inputs the 'output' of some other market, then both will have to be permitted if the first one is.

k is not the trivial economy. Of course this may be possible for many k. But every equilibrium is relative to k and that of course is bound to leave a loose end.

The next step is to particularise. A household in the economy is described by its preferences, its endowments and its entitlement to the profits of marketeers. Debreu has provided a measure of 'distance' between households which I will not now use. But, intuitively, one is looking for cases where these distances are sufficiently large (given the market technology) to be associated with gains from trade which are sufficient to 'overcome' the set-up costs in at least some markets. It is not very easy to make this precise but it can be done.

The most interesting route is to suppose households to have identical preferences but very different endowments. There are a number of measures of this difference which one can use but what one is looking for is really a measure of 'specialisation'. For as I have argued earlier, the pure exchange theory is only a pre-paratory construction for the production economy. It is one of the features of the monetary economy that it leads to some specialisation of agents. The underlying, and yet to be formally articulated, story of specialised endowments is that they are the outcome of specialised production activities. We are not endowed with potatoes because we have specialised in teaching economics.

The technicalities of the appropriate measure and subsequent procedures are somewhat involved and I reserve them for another occasion. Here I will only give an intuitive sketch.

To fix ideas consider the simple case of no transaction costs first. The equilibrium of this economy will be Pareto efficient. Let x_h^* be a Pareto-efficient allocation to h. Consider the set of x_h which is no smaller (in the vector sense) than either the endowment of h or some vector on the indifference surface through h. This set is non-convex if the endowment does not lie on the indifference surface. A measure of its non-convexity is the inner radius.[2] Under certain regularity assumptions on preferences this radius is related to the gains from trade for this household. We can calculate the radius for each household and taking every Pareto-efficient allocation in turn find the smallest of the largest of the radii amongst households, say r^*. If all households have the same endowment, since they have the same preferences, r^* is zero. In general, given the preferences r^* depends on the endowment matrix. Moreover the length of the trade vector depends on r^*. Thus one can say that for a certain set of endowment matrices, the inner radius r^* is at least r^{**} and the length of the trade vector at least t^* in equilibrium (since every equilibrium is Pareto efficient).

When transaction costs are considered the argument is a good deal more complicated.

If for any k one takes the convex hull of the transaction technology, the resulting fictional economy has a k equilibrium. Every such equilibrium can be shown to have the property that there exist no transactions different from the equilibrium ones in any one period *given* each household's transactions in all other periods, which are both feasible in the convex hull and Pareto superior. I call this property *quasi-efficiency*.

Essentially one can now use quasi-efficient allocations as one used Pareto-efficient allocations, to calculate the appropriate inner radius. It is now rather more complicated to relate the latter to the endowment matrix since the transaction technology enters into the construction. But one can characterise, given the transaction technology, a set of endowment matrices such that every quasi-efficient allocation in some k economy has a trade vector of length greater than some number. Moreover if the actual endowment is in that set then the trade vector belongs to the transaction technology (and not just to its convex hull). Since every k equilibrium is quasi-efficient, one has then shown that there is a k equilibrium in the actual transaction technology.

But these are really all technicalities designed to formalise the idea that if agents are sufficiently 'specialised' and the economy's endowment of each good is large enough relatively to set-up costs, the gains from trade will overcome the latter in at least some markets. I now want to note some problems and conclusions which are of economic interest.

The first point I have alluded to already several times, namely that the equilibrium of a k economy is in one respect peculiar. This is so because it gives no conditions under which markets which have been excluded, essentially by prohibition, would in fact be excluded on economic grounds. This is specially serious when an equilibrium exists for different k. In fact we cannot leave matters there. For I must be able to show that at least one k equilibrium is a proper sequence equilibrium with spot markets at every

---

[2] For a definition and discussion see Arrow and Hahn (1971). Since this was written a technically simpler method not using this route has turned out to be available. But it is not very easily verbalised and I thought it best to stick rather closely to the paper as presented.

date. If not, then it will be hard to maintain the basic postulate that the exchange technology is defined for a monetary economy. In fact it would be highly desirable to be able to exclude all k which are not sequence k. This, if achievable, would of course not exclude future markets.

Consider the set of k for which an equilibrium exists. Under mild assumptions this includes at least one sequence k. Suppose that it also includes some k' with the characteristics that it has no markets after some date t which precedes the terminal date. The ideal resolution of our difficulties would be to show that every such k' equilibrium is Pareto inferior to some proper sequence equilibrium. One would then have grounds for considering only sequence equilibria, although I still would not know why one rather than another should hold.

Although I believe on general economic grounds that this route should be possible I have run into rather formidable difficulties in pursuing it. At the moment I have only a rather weaker result.

Let us say that a given k equilibrium is *complete* if there is no k' equilibrium in which all the markets in k have been assigned the number one. It is important to remember here that if a market has the number one trade is permitted on that market but need not take place. That is, one distinguishes between markets which simply do not exist and markets which are not active. With some extra assumptions one can show that only sequence equilibria are complete. The idea is that when a theory of the setting up of markets comes to be developed complete equilibria will be of special interest. For instance in considering whether an excluded market can profitably be set up one expects the calculating potential marketeer to suppose all presently existing markets to continue in existence. This is far from satisfactory but it is as far as I have got and I suppose that a full theory will in fact be only interested in complete equilibria.

If we agree to this resolution the next problem is to show that every sequence equilibrium will in fact use money. In thinking about this I shall not worry about the terminal date problem and simply patch it up by brute force. Even so reflection will show that the problem is not straightforward. Thus it is perfectly possible that the sequence equilibrium we are interested in is a stationary one for every household, and why should it then store money? It almost looks as if in spite of all the effort one will have to introduce some *ad hoc* and fortuitous constraint like that of Grandmont—Younès.

It is now that what I have called periodisation becomes of central importance. Sticking to discrete time we can yet make our fundamental intervals as short as we like. Since each market has a set-up cost it is then not too hard to show that there will be some intraperiod storage and that one can exclude full stationarity, fundamental interval by fundamental interval. Of course one must now specify a storage technology. One then takes advantage of the costlessness of money storage and the 'specialisation' of endowments which we needed in the first place, to arrive at the desired results.

This can probably be greatly improved upon by the following further modifications.

(a) One allows composite markets which have their activities specified by a row of outputs and inputs, the set-up costs being incurred at the date of contract. For instance the forward sale of labour for five days is such an example if payment were made at the contract date *or* if given other markets, the payment date were of no significance. In any case set-up costs will of course encourage such markets. The modification required in the technical procedure I have so far used is small.
(b) One allows for transactions costs incurred by households themselves. This of course requires more convexification etc. but I do not pursue this.

I now want to emphasise not only that the construction I have just given is in some ways incomplete — there are a good many properties still to be studied — but also that even if it were complete it would be quite inadequate. Certainly the economy and money are essential but it is all a pale shadow of the real thing. I have not allowed for uncertainty and my prices are announced. Rather worse, I have nothing to say about non-equilibrium situations. All these are serious defects and they will not be easily cured.

One is tempted, at least for the present, to try something rather less ambitious and in particular to study the short period only. Grandmont (1971) and Green (1971) have recently done this, as did Arrow and I (1971) in a somewhat simpler context. Surprisingly it turns out to be rather difficult to establish even some of the minimal results one would like. But Green has elegantly shown what is required for a short period equilibrium to exist when he allows in principle a full set of markets, spot and future, at the present and the next date. The expectations of agents of the prices in the next period are given by probability distributions. He paid no explicit attention to the question of money.

The next step is to rectify this and I also believe to introduce much simpler expectations and more rule of thumb behaviour by agents. There is also a further difficulty noted by Arrow and myself. Short period equilibrium runs into formidable difficulties if one allows agents to have had a prior history. That is if they start the period with commitments from the past, especially commitments specified in terms of money. This will have to be explored much more thoroughly and it is likely that this is where the abstract formulations make important contact with Keynesian economics.

After all this it will not come as a surprise that I believe that we are only at the beginning of a theory of the economy in which money is essential. In particular I think that we have for a good long time been on a quite unimportant and uninteresting track. The challenge of monetary theory is not the neutrality theorem or related results; it is the required reconstruction of our paradigm if we are to make sense of money.

IV

I should like to conclude on a defensive note. To many who would call themselves monetary economists the problems which I have been discussing must seem excessively abstract and unnecessary. They are accustomed to recognising the importance of expectations and uncertainty and liquidity and they are also predominantly macroeconomists. Will this preoccupation with foundations, they may argue, help one iota in formulating monetary policy or in predicting the consequences of parameter changes? Are not IS and LM sufficient unto the day? Or put in Friedman's recent terms, is it not more fruitful to be Marshallian and to put the Walrasian search for generality and rigour behind us?

I am surprisingly sympathetic to some of these hypothetical objections but I wish to maintain that they can be valid without casting doubt on what I regard to be one of the central reasons for the studies on which I have reported. This is to do away with a dichotomy which has nothing to do with Patinkin and the classicals. This dichotomy is best seen when the same economist's writings on IS and LM are compared with his writings on welfare economics, or when a 'long run' is involved which has great difficulty in living with any 'short run' – in short, the dichotomy which arises when we do monetary theory when money is essential and all other theory when money is inessential. It may well be that the approaches here utilised will not in the event improve our advice to the Bank of England; I am rather convinced that it will make a fundamental difference to the way in which we view a decentralised economy.

REFERENCES

Archibald, G. C. and Lipsey, R. G. 1958. Monetary and value theory: a critique of Lange and Patinkin, *Review of Economic Studies*

Arrow, K. J. and Hahn, F. H. 1971. *General Competitive Analysis*, Holden-Day

Foley, D. K. 1970. Economic equilibrium with costly marketing, *Journal of Economic Theory*

Grandmont, J. M. 1971. On the short-run equilibrium in a monetary economy, CEPREMAP discussion paper, February, Paris

Grandmont, J. M. and Younès, Y. 1973. On the role of money and the existence of a monetary equilibrium, *Review of Economic Studies*

Green, J. R. 1971. Temporary and general equilibrium in a sequential trading model with spot and futures transactions, unpublished

Hahn, F. H. 1965. On some problems of proving the existence of an equilibrium in a monetary economy, in *The Theory of Interest Rates*, ed. F. H. Hahn and F. P. R. Brechling, Macmillan, chapter 7 above.

Hahn, F. H. 1971. Equilibrium with transaction costs, *Econometrica*

Heller, W. P. 1971. Money and transactions with set-up costs, discussion paper, University of Pennsylvania (Dept. of Economics), June

Kurz, M. 1972a. *Equilibrium with Transaction Costs and Money in a Single Market Exchange Economy*, Institute for Mathematical Studies in the Social Sciences, Technical Report no. 51, January

Kurz, M. 1972b. *Equilibrium in a Finite Sequence of Markets with Transaction Costs*, Institute for Mathematical Studies in the Social Sciences, Technical Report no. 52, February

Ostroy, J. M. 1970. Exchange as an economic activity, PhD dissertation, Northwestern University

Radner, R. 1968. Competitive equilibrium under uncertainty, *Econometrica*, January

Radner, R. 1970. *Existence of Equilibrium Plans, Prices and Price Expectation in a Sequence of Markets*, I and II; Technical Report no. 5, Centre for Research in Management Science, University of California, Berkeley, June

Robinson, J. 1971. *Economic Heresies*, Macmillan

Starr, R. M. 1970a. Structure of exchange in barter and monetary economics, Cowles Foundation Discussion Paper no. 295, June

Starr, R. M. 1970b. Equilibrium and demand for media of exchange in a pure exchange economy with transaction costs, Cowles Foundation Discussion Paper no. 300, October

Starr, R. M. 1971. The price of money in a pure exchange economy with taxation, Cowles Foundation Discussion Paper no. 310, June

Starrett, D. 1972. Inefficiency and the demand for 'money' in a sequence economy, unpublished

9

Keynesian Economics and General Equilibrium Theory: Reflections on Some Current Debates

I INTRODUCTION

To many economists Keynesian economics deals with important relevant problems and general equilibrium theory deals with no relevant problems at all. This view is often the consequence of the ease of learning Keynesian macroarithmetic compared with reading Debreu. But it also has, alas an element of truth. This quite simply that general equilibrium theorists have been unable to deliver one half at least of the required story: how does general equilibrium come to be established? Closely related to this lacuna is the question of what signals are perceived and transmitted in a decentralised economy and how. The importance of Keynesian economics to the general equilibrium theorist is twofold. It seems to be addressed to just these kinds of questions and it is plainly in need of proper theoretical foundations.

Starting with Clower (1965) and Leijonhufvud (1968), there has been new work by economists who like and can do theory. The outcome is very encouraging although we are by no means out of the wood and in some instances seem to have got deeper into it. What follows discusses some, but by no means all, of these developments. I have chosen to discuss what I find most interesting. I shall repeatedly have to refer to Keynes and Keynesian economics. These are sloppy terms and certainly do not imply that I know what 'Keynes really meant'. But I do not know how to avoid this difficulty.

III EQUILIBRIUM

If Keynesian theory is about equilibrium, it must be short period equilibrium. That is, one is concerned with states of the economy which require the 'mutual compatibility' of the actions of rational agents only over a given interval. In particular, agents' plans over a more distant future are permitted to be incompatible. This then is certainly a world in which many markets for uncertain future deliveries do not exist or are inactive and there is trading and decision taking at each date. Such a world is speculative in the sense that agents must provide links between the present and the uncertain future by holding assets for the purpose of future exchange. The future is doubly uncertain for not only are future states of the world uncertain but so are the market possibilities which will be available in any given state.

It is only recently that the theory of a short period Walrasian equilibrium has been rigorously studied, although it has been in the literature for a very long time (see Hicks 1939, Green 1973 and Grandmont 1976). In its simplest form such a model makes the desired actions of agents depend on current prices and the single valued expectation of future prices. The latter are thought of as generated by past and present price experiences. A short period Walrasian equilibrium is then a set of current prices and associated expected prices such that the preferred action of every agent on current markets can be carried out. To show that such an equilibrium exists one needs, in addition to conventional postulates, certain assumptions concerning the nature of expectations. In particular, the price expectation hypothesis must be compatible with the possibility of different terms of trade between the present and the future which can move both against and in favour of present goods. In addition, one needs to suppose that the expectations of different agents are not sufficiently dissimilar to allow unbounded arbitrage (Green 1973 and Grandmont 1976). If there is money, one needs to make sure that in the short period equilibrium it has a positive exchange value. The above expectation assumptions accomplish that since, when properly stated, they ensure that money is always expected to have a positive exchange value in the future (Hahn 1965, Grandmont and Younès 1973 and Grandmont 1976). Lastly, if there are debts denominated in money, one must ensure that no discontinuities can occur at some admissible set of prices due to bankruptcy (Arrow and Hahn 1971). At the end of it all one has an existence theorem. Has it any relevance to Keynesian theory?

Until relatively recently the answer would have been in the affirmative. Indeed, the answer would often be that Keynes attempted to show that full employment short period equilibrium did not exist and that in this he was, under plausible assumptions, wrong. His mistake was attributed to his neglect of real cash balances in influencing the demand for current goods. Therefore, Keynesian theory is either not about equilibrium at all or it depends on certain price rigidities, particularly in money wages.

Before I look more closely at these claims, it is worth while noting that they were made in response to a number of mistakes made over and over again by authors who accepted the short period Walrasian equilibrium as decisive in the argument but claimed that it did not exist. These claims rested on the 'liquidity-trap' and/or on the alleged zero interest responsiveness of investment demand (Klein 1949). But in different contexts it had been discovered that 'existence' was at risk only from discontinuous and not from oddly shaped excess demand functions. The purported reasons for non-existence are worthless.

Now the most striking feature of the short period Walrasian equilibrium approach to Keynesian theory is that it leaves a vast part of the *General Theory* unaccounted for. In particular, it makes it impossible to make sense of the Keynesian dependence of agents' choices on quantities as well as on prices (e.g. the consumption function and the demand for money). So if the Walrasian short period model is the right one, then almost everything, and not just the unemployment theory, in Keynes is wrong. The counter-revolution is complete. The considerable progress of the last ten years is due to our recognition that the Walrasian short period model may not be the right one — indeed, almost surely is not. That this recognition was so long delayed is partly due to the increased difficulties there are in transcending a well developed and articulate tradition and partly due to Keynes himself whose attention to the reconciliation of his microtheory with his main theory was small and inexpert.

The easiest way of proceeding is, quite provisionally, to consider the case of a given money wage. The Walrasian short period model is now evidently over-determined. In what sense then can one speak of a short period equilibrium with a given money wage? The obvious answer seems to be to remove the condition (equation) that labour markets should clear, but it will not do, for Walras' law then implies that in this kind of equilibrium at least one market other than that for labour will not clear. But that is not what Keynes proposed. For instance, in the long used IS/LM version all non-labour markets clear. There seems no way in which a fixed money wage Walrasian model can make sense of Keynesian unemployment equilibrium. It is here of course that Clower makes his contribution. It is, as I shall argue, not free from faults and he had notable predecessors, particularly Robertson. But it was Clower who took on the Walrasian model on its own terms and made a decisive change.

The basic point is, of course, like much else that is good, very simple. If involuntary unemployment is to be an equilibrium phenomenon, then agents must have adjusted all their planned actions to the circumstance that they cannot sell as much labour as they would like. Put in more old fashioned language, we require the coincidence of *ex ante* and *ex post* in equilibrium states. But this coincidence is now only possible if agents treat their ration of labour as a signal on a par with price signals. That is, to their usual budget constraints we must add the further constraint that not more than a certain amount can be sold. It should be noted that this way of putting the matter is in the spirit of Drèze (1973), Grandmont and Laroque (1976) and Hahn (1976) and not in that of Clower (1965) or Benassy (1974). The latter makes a good deal of the need to use money in exchange when they tell this story. But as I shall argue later, money really has nothing intrinsically to do with the matter and indeed, when it is brought to the forefront, leads to muddles.

Even at the cost of some notation it seems convenient to write down the simplest model explicitly. For this purpose I consider an economy which can produce a single good by the aid of this good and labour. The good is perfectly durable if not consumed. The reader will know how to interpret this assumption to make it plausible and will realise that nothing depends on it. Firms issue one period shares to pay for the quantity of good which they need to produce. At the end of the period (beginning of the next), the share is repaid and all the profit distributed in proportion to share ownership. This rather crazy sounding postulate avoids complications and leaves everything of interest to us here intact.

Consider household a. The Walrasian budget constraint for the current period is written

$$pc_a + m_a + \frac{1}{r}b_a + s_a = w\ell_a + \pi_a + \bar{s}_a + \bar{m}_a + \bar{b}_a\left(1 + \frac{1}{r}\right) \qquad (9.1)$$

Here all prices are in terms of money, c_a is consumption demand and p is the price of output, m_a and $\bar{m}_a$ are desired and initial balances respectively, b_a is the number of perpetuities (yielding one unit of money) demanded ($b_a > 0$) and supplied ($b_a < 0$) by a. Also $\bar{b}_a$ is the endowment of debt ($\bar{b}_a \leq 0$) or credit ($\bar{b}_a > 0$), and r is the rate of interest on intra-household debt. One interprets s_a as the money value of the demand for shares by household a and $\bar{s}_a$ as the current value of shares bought previously and repaid currently. Lastly π_a is the profit entitlement of a, w the money wage and ℓ_a the desired labour supply.

There is also a budget constraint for 'the future'. The money balances, debt and shares demanded today constitute, properly priced, the endowment of the future. Prices for the future are in the mind of the agent and not in the marketplace. One must add the profit entitlement of household a at the beginning of the future. If π^e, for instance, is the expected profit, that entitlement is $(s_a / \Sigma s_a)\pi^e$ if in the current period the supply and demand for shares are equal. This can also be written in a different form by writing $s_a = q n_a$ where n_a is the number of shares and q their price. Then if d^e is the expected dividend per share, $d^e n_a$ is the expected profit entitlement. In order to avoid problems with portfolio choices I shall not assume point expectations (but distributions).

Suppose next that household a perceives that it cannot sell more than $\bar{\ell}_a$ units of labour in the current period and expects to perceive a similar constraint $\bar{\ell}_a^e$ in the future. Then its rational choices are not only constrained by the current and expected budget constraints but also by

$$\ell_a \leq \bar{\ell}_a \text{ and } \ell_a^f \leq \bar{\ell}_a^e \tag{9.2}$$

where ℓ_a^f is planned labour supply in the future. The rational choice of household a is taken to result from maximising the expectation of utility of current and future consumption and leisure. This, as everyone knows, will yield shadow prices for the constraints and in particular $\mu_a \geq 0$ for the constraint $\bar{\ell}_a \geq \ell_a$ such that if ℓ_a^0 is chosen

$$\mu_a (\bar{\ell}_a - \ell_a^0) = 0$$

Whence $\mu_a > 0$ implies $\bar{\ell}_a = \ell^0$.

Consider a situation where $\mu_a > 0$ all a. This of course implies a given rationing scheme of employment at given prices, etc. Denote

summation over a by the omission of the subscript a (e.g. $x = \sum_{a} x_a$).
Then summing equation (9.1) over a one has:

If $\mu_a > 0$ all a: $pc^0 + (m^0 - \bar{m}) + \frac{1}{r} b^0 + (s^0 - \bar{s}) = w\bar{\ell} + \pi$ (9.3)

(since perpetuities are bought and sold only by households $\bar{b} = 0$).

Now consider the firms. I shall treat them altogether under the orthodox neo-classical assumptions of the *General Theory*. In the current period output y depends on the stock of capital $\bar{k}$ (there is only one good) inherited from the past and the current employment of labour L. So the current demand for labour is the resultant of maximizing $py(\bar{k}, L) - wL$ and the profits which result are available to households owning shares to the value of $p\bar{k}$ in the current period. I assume that physical disinvestment is not possible, so that if pk is the value of shares issued currently then $pk \geqslant p\bar{k}$. So the new shares help to reduce the old and provide for investment. The choice of k is made by maximising the discounted expectation of $p^e y(k, L) + p^e k - wL - pk$ where $1 + r$ is the discount factor. I do not claim that this is the way the world looks but I claim that it is rather close to Keynes' world.

However, one must pause here to take explicit notice of a serious problem peculiar to sequence economies which despite the splendid labour of for example, Drèze (1974) and Hart (1974), is still quite unresolved. The firm is not a person. So what do we mean by the expectations of the firm? Clearly it must be the managers who are meant. But can managers take actions which are independent of those of shareholders? Someone after all hires the managers. I need not continue since the difficulty is well known. Until a satisfactory theory emerges all I can do is to look the problem in the face and pass on. But I venture the prediction that we shall have to consider credit rationing (as well as employment rationing), before we are very far on the road to a solution.

Returning to the present story we now suppose that

$$\mu_a > 0 \text{ all } a \Rightarrow \bar{\ell} = L^0$$

That is, firms can buy the labour they require if households are rationed in the labour market. So substituting for π in equation (9.3) we get

$$pc^0 + (m^0 - \bar{m}) + \frac{1}{r} b^0 + (s^0 - \bar{s}) = py^0$$

and substituting $\bar{s} = p\bar{k}$ we have

$$p[c^0 + (k^0 - \bar{k}) - y^0] + m^0 - \bar{m} + \frac{1}{r}b^0 + (s^0 - pk^0) = 0 \quad (9.4)$$

which may be written as

$$pX_g^0 + X_m^0 + \frac{1}{r}X_b^0 + qX_n^0 = 0 \qquad\qquad (9.5)$$

where X_g^0 is excess demand for goods, X_m^0 is excess demand for money, X_b^0 is excess demand for bonds and X_n^0 is excess demand for shares.

Now equation (9.5) is the appropriate Walras' law for all values of $(p, r, q, \bar{\ell})$ and given w and expectation functions for which $\mu_a > 0$ all a, i.e. for which there is involuntary unemployment. As Clower noted, the excess demand for labour will not appear in equation (9.5). Also, of course, the actions of households will depend on their ration of labour, i.e. on a quantity signal as well as on prices. It is, however, important to understand that I have only written down the half of the story which interests us here. There is another half which would arise at parameter values in which the constraint $L \leqslant \ell^0$ would be a quantity constrain on firms. Here $\mu_a = 0$ all a and firms are rationed in the amount of labour which they receive. (See Benassy 1976 and Drèze 1973.)

One can now proceed to look for a non-Walrasian unemployment equilibrium. This requires technicalities all similar to those in Grandmont (1976), and I confine myself to brief remarks. First, notice that by the neo-classical firm assumptions one may write

$$p = g(\bar{\ell}, w)$$

So given the money wage w, the unknowns are $(\bar{\ell}, r, q)$ and in view of equation (9.5) there are three independent excess demand relations for the range of household rationing. So solving for $X_i(\cdot) = 0$ $(i = g, m, b, n)$ which I suppose to be possible, we obtain $(\bar{\ell}^0, r^0, q^0)$. If this is to be a real solution we require it to be non-negative and we must see that $\mu_a(\bar{\ell}^0, r^0, q^0) \gtrless 0$ all a. When proper attention is paid to expectational assumptions etc. there will indeed be values of w for which a non-Walrasian unemployment equilibrium exists. It has all the familiar Keynesian features and, in particular, agents' choices depend on quantities as well as prices. But we have arrived at this point with a fixed money wage.

Before I return to that important matter it will be possible to lay a number of old and new ghosts.

The argument of the simple model, but in fact the general answer we seek, has nothing intrinsically to do with money or any axioms that 'only money buys goods' (Clower 1965). It is, of course, true that the model is not one of barter since nothing has been said about any transaction technology. But if a computer costlessly co-ordinated transactions we could replace money by, say, land and work with a fixed land wage.

But there is here so persistent a false train, first laid by Clower and followed more recently by Benassy (1974), that it is worth making the point in another way. It is argued that involuntarily unemployed labour can only signal its willingness to work but not, until it is employed, its willingness to buy, since an offer of work constitutes a demand for money and not for goods. That is because 'only money buys goods'. But it is a muddle to suppose that in the absence of this axiomatic restriction, things would be different. In reality there are many goods. In a barter world a man would not offer his labour in exchange for, say, some of the sulphuric acid he helps to produce, except on the speculative basis that he could exchange it again. One would expect 'market failure' to be far worse here than in an economy with a medium of exchange (Ostroy and Starr 1974). In the fable world of labour and corn this problem would not arise but there would also be no need for a medium of exchange.[1]

It is, of course, true that Keynes thought of effective demand as demand backed by purchasing power. Since we live in a monetary world, this is a convenient and not misleading shorthand for the proposition that in order to actually acquire anything (as distinct from planning to do so), one must have something else, desired by

---

[1] Robert Solow has pointed out to me that he considers it misleading to keep separate the difficulties which arise from barter and those which arise from a contract having to be made in terms of money. In other words, he considers it correct to assert that involuntary unemployment could not occur in a barter economy in which labour was paid in its own product. I am not persuaded that this is the case. Consider the producer of gumdrops in a situation where the marginal product of labour exceeds the gumdrop wage. If there are workers who, in spite of their horror of gumdrops, are willing to be paid in them, it must mean that they consider there to be sufficient demand for gumdrops in terms of other things which they like, if they are to work. That is, the problem of there being insufficient demand for gumdrops is now transferred from the employer to the worker.

the exchange partner, to give up. In general then, effective demand and demand differ whenever it is the case that the allocation an agent can reach is smaller than his budget set because of quantity restrictions which he perceives, and when his preferred allocation falls into the area where some of the constraints intersect.

However, there is another monetary ghost. Suppose that starting from the equilibrium of our simple model we attempted to have one more unit of employment. If the marginal propensity to save is positive this may be impossible at constant prices, and if the equilibrium is locally unique, the higher employment level will be incompatible with equilibrium. One of the reasons for this is that there are in this economy resting places for saving other than reproducible assets. In our model this is money. But land, as Keynes to his credit understood, would have just the same consequence and so would old masters. It is therefore not money which is required to do away with a Say's Law kind of proposition that the supply of labour is the demand for goods produced by labour. Any non-reproducible asset will do. When Say's Law is correctly formulated for an economy with non-reproducible goods, it does not yield the conclusions to be found in textbooks. As I have already noted, Keynes was fully aware of this and that is why he devoted so much space to the theory of choice among alternative stores of value.

Money, in economic theory, always brings out the worst in us. One may take it for granted that in the world exchange is mediated by money. It is one of a number of non-reproducible assets. All such assets must compete with each other as well as with reproducible ones to be held at a positive price. The equilibrium outcome in the labour market is, of course, not independent of the number of different assets there are and so the existence of money contributes to the outcome. But that, as far as the present story goes, is all. Keynes' view that the rate of return on money (psychic or otherwise) sets a lower bound to the rate of return on any other asset which will command a positive price in equilibrium does not endanger the existence of Walrasian equilibrium and, if the view is correct, it affects the amount of unemployment in any fixed money wage non-Walrasian equilibrium but does not affect the theory. There is nothing to suggest that in a world of costless mediation without money with, say, a fixed land wage, the story would be different.

So much for the ghosts. But it can not be argued that all that has been achieved is the formulation of a proper concept of short period unemployment equilibrium with a given money wage. Indeed, all one has done is to make explicit the microtheory which underlies the budget identities and behavioural postulates of generations of macroeconomists. It is easy to replace the postulate of a given money wage with the assumption that it is positively and arbitrarily bounded below, and one then is tempted to say that the sum total of Keynesian theory is in this 'price rigidity'. Many textbooks say just that. It is true that, until recently, it was not understood that the set of signals to which agents respond must now include quantities if a proper notion of equilibrium with some fixed prices is to be formulated. But once this is done there is not much left of the 'revolution'. For Keynes' contemporaries were all agreed that lack of 'price flexibility' was responsible for the trouble. I believe there is a good deal more to Keynesian economics than that.

Let us first return to the Walrasian short period equilibrium. I have already mentioned that there are certain technical requirements if it is to be shown as always possible. The first point to be made is that these requirements are by no means trivial or unimportant. If in the 1930s the computer had to search for the Walrasian equilibrium money wage, the search path would have been littered with bankrupt debtors[2] and one needs great heroism to assume that this would have left the computer with continuous behaviour functions. Keynes (1936, p. 264) explicitly refers to this. Next, the history of the economy is given and the conjectured future depends on it and on current events. As current observations depart increasingly from past experience, it is not at all clear that it is proper to think of conjectures as continuous in current observations. Moreover if, for instance, a much lower money wage than is customary is currently observed, the expectational requirement of 'uniform tightness' (Grandmont 1976) may well be vio-

---

[2] Since this was written there has been a proposal by Aumann and Kurz (1976) that bankruptcy need not cause difficulties if the lender at the time of the contract took the possibility into account when setting the terms on which the loan is granted. In an ingenious formulation they show that in very large economies with independent risks, lenders will have fully insured against the bankruptcy of the debtor. Moreover, they believe that there will then be no problem with 'existence'. For present purposes the following remarks suffice: (1) the assumptions of independence etc. are extremely strong; (2) the formulation, when there is more than one good, requires rational expectations so that all agents know the equilibrum prices for each state of the world. If there is anything uncontroversial about Keynes, it is his view that expectations are not rational. I consider this to be a correct view.

lated. Again, Keynes (1936, p. 269) refers to all these points. It is therefore not at all obvious that a short period Walrasian equilibrium exists for an economy in a given state.

But in thinking of this equilibrium the money stock was taken as fixed and there is no government. If this is rectified, one comes to what seems to me a central Keynesian point: a short period Walrasian equilibrium with fixed money wages but variable government net spending plausibly exists, whereas one in which government net spending is fixed but the money wage is the 'unknown' plausibly does not exist. (Later this is strengthened by saying it cannot be reached (Keynes 1936, p. 253) if it exists.) The reasons are that the Walrasian equilibrium will now have prices which are higher and not lower than in the non-Walrasian equilibrium so that bankruptcies of debtors are avoided. There is also some evidence that marginal productivity schedules are fairly flat. Because the past is given and the future expected to be not too dissimilar, speculative dishoarding will stop spectacularly higher interest rates. All in all no great strain is put on the expectation mechanism. Keynes' point then on this interpretation is not that money wages could not be lower but that it would be better if they stayed where they are. That is, if you are looking for a Walrasian equilibrium, you have a better chance of there being something to find if you treat government net spending as an unknown rather than the money wage. Notice that in the Walrasian equilibrium found this way, the given money wage becomes the neo-classical equilibrium money wage.

I now want to make a related point in another way. Consider Patinkin's (1965) short period Walrasian model. The unknowns can be listed as all prices in terms of labour, cash balances in terms of labour (m/w) and the rate of interest. It follows that one instructs the computer to search for an equilibrium among these unknowns. One may clearly fix m or w. But here it departs, so I want to maintain, from Keynesian economics. First, the result depends on the absence of effects from redistribution between debtors and creditors. This in turn depends not only on an implausible postulate on preferences but on the very un-Keynesian stipulation that agents have identical point expectations. Secondly, it is supposed that expectations do not at all depend on the history of prices before the present moment. If they do, Patinkin's homogeneity postulate is extremely dubious. Nor is attention paid to expectational disorders which are possible and with which Keynes was concerned. So if this familiar model is given some necessary improvements, it may easily sustain the conclusion that with a fixed money wage but unknown m an equilibrium can be found, whereas this is not the case when w is unknown.

Taking the money wage as given forces new equilibrium concepts to be adopted. Taking expectations seriously causes us to recognise that the short period depends on an unalterable past and a conjectured future and so also to recognise that short period Walrasian equilibrium gives rise to new difficulties. Green (1973) and Grandmont (1976) deserve much credit here.

First, notice that if households are rationed in their sale of labour they cannot, evidently, be taken to assume that they can sell what they wish to sell at the going wage. They do not face the world of perfect competition. Secondly, we notice that since in fact there is no auctioneer (a fact I think widely known by most economists but properly stressed by Iwai 1974 and Benassy 1976), the decision whether or not to change money wages must be that of some economic agent. If this is the firm then it too cannot be taken to behave like a perfect competitor. In any case as Arrow (1959) pointed out many years ago, perfect competition and prices changing by the decisions of actual agents cannot be reconciled.

Let us stick for the moment to the labour market and think of money wages as being quoted by the sellers of labour. One now needs to supplement the description of the household by a demand curve conjectured by it. This is just like the famous story told by Negishi (1961). The household must have some beliefs as to how its ration of labour would respond to a change in the wage it quotes. If there is an equilibrium, it is what I have called a conjectural equilibrium (Hahn 1978). That is, it is a state such that actions of agents are compatible and such that, given the conjectures, no price can be advantageously changed by an agent.

Now one can show (Hahn 1978) that for certain conjectures an economy can be in conjectural equilibrium which is not the Walrasian equilibrium even if the latter also qualifies as a conjectural equilibrium. More importantly, one can also show (Negishi 1964, Futia 1975) that there are certain examples where in a certain sense locally rational conjectures give non-Walrasian equilibria. Much of this is in its infancy. But sufficient work has been done to warrant the following conclusion. If an equilibrium is a state where rational actions are compatible and if among possible actions one includes changing of price, then there exist non-Walrasian unemployment equilibria. The wage is neither fixed nor arbitrary nor inflexible. It is what it is because no agent finds it advantageous to change it. The invisible hand has ceased before its job is accomplished.

In what sense is unemployment involuntary in such an equilibrium? In the following sense: at the going wage and prices the agents would wish to supply more labour. The wage is not reduced because the conjectured demand curve is not favourable to the agent doing this.

A great deal more work, of course, will have to be done here. The labour market is particularly difficult to study (1) because normally a man is either employed or unemployed, (2) because the interests of the employed conflict, and (3) because there are coalitions and probably a great deal of conventional behaviour. But there is no reason to suppose that the Walrasian equilibrium concept will turn out to be appropriate.

What has just been said of the labour market can be applied to almost all markets. If the economy is not in Walrasian equilibrium then agents must find the hypothesis that they can buy and sell what they like at going prices falsified. They will not persist in these beliefs. Moreover, it is up to them to take action, i.e. they can change the terms on which they offer to trade. This formally puts them into the position of monopolistic competition even if the intrinsic situation is not one of monopolistic competition. All this leads to important departures .from Walrasian modes and Iwai (1974) and Benassy (1976) have been in full cry for some time to the more stately accompaniment of Grandmont and Laroque (1976). In general, agents will be reacting to both price and quantity signals, their expectations will include expectations of quantity constraints, and they will need conjectures relating these constraints to the prices they quote.

One can thus argue that the short period Walrasian equilibrium is not the proper, or at least the only, benchmark. If that is agreed then even invisible hands which seek equilibria may seek equilibria that we do not like. For instance, they are not efficient. So the Keynesian spirit of the thing, namely that there is something for government to do, receives confirmaton even before any dynamic processes have been studied. But I think that is ail the Keynesian juice there is, and I do not think it useful to call Keynesian each and every departure from Walras. For instance, recently there has been investigation of the extreme case where no one ever wishes to change any price as an equilibrium is established purely by rationing.

Almost inevitably such equilibria have been called Keynesian (see Futia 1975, Grandmont and Laroque 1976 and Hahn 1976). But they have precious little to do with what Keynes actually wrote. He certainly did not posit fixed prices. Rather the reverse. Nor did he seem to argue that prices change more slowly than quantities as can be verified in the chapter which tells us why labour cannot control its real wage. It seems to be far less confusing to call such equilibria Drèzian or 'French'. We simply have to live with the fact that Keynes never managed to get his micro-theory to mesh properly with the rest of what he had to say.

This leads me to the last point in this section. A picture has emerged in which prices are set at 'the beginning of the period' and the length of the period is then the smallest interval before some price is changed (see Grandmont and Laroque 1976). This 'fixed price' model does not strike me as very useful but in any case the short period here is not Keynes' short period .

III OUT OF EQUILIBRIUM

In this section I want to talk mainly, and briefly, about false scents. I have no theory of 'out of equilibrium behaviour' on offer.

Since Leijonhufvud's (1968) stimulating book which followed on Clower's (1965) insight, it has become a commonplace to say that Keynesian economics is economics without the Walrasian auctioneer (see Barro and Grossman 1971). I do not, however, believe that the cited work logically entails this view, or that the view is very helpful.

In the 1960s a number of non-tâtonnement models of adjustment were studied. Trade took place at 'false' prices and the value at going prices of what was actually bought was always equal to the value of what was actually sold. These models, however, still used the auctioneer. Moreover, during the adjustment process, agents were quantity restrained just as they are in the papers which are so popular now. In later versions even Clower's axiom that only money buys goods was included and still the auctioneer appeared. He did so because no one had the faintest idea how prices are actually changed and because it seemed reasonable to suppose that when more was known, it would be found correct that prices rose when there were unsatisfied buyers and fell when there were unsatisfied sellers.

Now this last supposition may turn out to be far from correct (see the previous section). One the other hand, we can see that the present cliché is based on a muddle. When people think of an auctioneer, they think of tâtonnement. But the former does not imply the latter. One can agree that Keynesian economics is not about a tâtonnement, which is quite different from the claim that it cannot accommodate an auctioneer. As I have already remarked, Keynes was in no better shape to tell us how prices change in his perfectly competitive world than we are. This then leads to the second observation, that economics without the auctioneer requires non-perfect competition economics and not Keynesian economics. Thirdly, the Keynesian non-tâtonnement is not the one which is at present being studied. The assumption in the current non-tâtonnement theory is the rationing of the 'short side' at given prices. Thus, if the demand for shoes, before any quantity constraint is perceived, exceeds the supply of shoes then the demand side will be rationed (Barro and Grossman 1971, Benassy 1976). In Keynesian economics suppliers of shoes lose inventories and demands are satisfied. That is, shoemakers will supply more than they planned to do. Anyone who knows the discussion in the 1930s of the multiplier will recognise the story. Yet, for some unknown reasons, the short side rationing scheme has been christened as Keynesian (Benassy 1976, Grandmont and Laroque (1976).

Of course, the inventory story will only work if there are inventories – the economics of 'depression' was what Hicks called it. Equally clear, the short side rationing scheme will do for the labour market.

This mistaken interpretation of Keynesian economics goes with a methodology which takes prices as fixed during a short period and misses an important insight into Keynesian economics due to Kaldor (1939). He did not argue that prices were fixed because agents think about price only on Mondays but because 'normal' price expectations combined with inventories prevented prices from changing by much. The argument is straightforward. Anyone encountering an excess demand for what he has to sell could raise prices. But the price is expected to revert to its normal level, so either he or others will decumulate stocks. But this means that the current price cannot rise by much. This process Keynesians thought of special significance in the market for loans. Here the expectation of normal interest rates induced the dishoarding of cash which enabled an 'excess demand' for loans to be financed at more or less constant interest rates. No one dreamt of working with models in which the interest rate had already been fixed on Monday.

In a multiplier process the accumulation of inventories was a signal to producers to expand production. However, it is hard to give an interpretation to this under perfect competition unless one postulates constant returns. If that is done, producers at the 'right prices' simply produce whatever is demanded. Losing inventories is a signal that demand has not been correctly estimated. Many 'mark-up' theories of pricing can be formulated in this way. Indeed, even without constant returns, it is possible to use a mark-up mechanism to generate a reasonable theory. Alternatively one can tell a story based on 'perceived demand curves'. Speculative behaviour makes them pretty flat, inventory changes shift them. When there are no inventories to accumulate the story is radically different. In particular, since desired inventories are not in general zero, we are already in a situation with a histroy of buoyant demand. It is not the situation of the *General Theory*. The short side rationing scheme may here be the appropriate hypothesis.

Recent theorising, however, seems to have been on the right track in arguing that Keynesian dynamics is ill served by a perfect competition postulate. In particular, the Keynesian investment theory does not seem either helpful or correct. The possibility of bankruptcy is alone sufficient to make of every demand for loans a 'named' demand. That is, every debt differs by the actual borrower. This really is enough to kill perfect competition in the market for loans and leads to a theory of 'self-finance' (Wood 1976). The lack of perfect competition in the market for goods requires firms to estimate quantities at different prices. Investment decisions cease to depend on prices only. All this leads to complex models and only economic advisers to governments claim to have the answers. It will be a triumph of accountancy over economics if the simple arithmetic of the multiplier turns out to be correct.

One can certainly now see that the view, that with 'flexible' money wages there would be no unemployment, has no convincing argument to recommend it. (I am here interpreting this to be a view about dynamics and not 'existence' which I have already discussed.) Even in a pure tâtonnement in traditional models convergence to an equilibrium cannot be generally proved. In a more satisfactory model matters are more doubtful still. Suppose money wages fall in a situation of short run non-Walrasian unemployment equilibrium. The argument already discussed suggest that initially this will lead to a redistribution in favour of profit. The demand for labour, however, will only increase on the expectation of greater sales since substitution effects in the short run can be neglected. If recipients of profits regard the increase as transient (as they sensibly might), their demand for goods will not greatly increase. On the other hand, if wage earners have few assets, their demand will decrease. But that means that producers get a signal to reduce output. Wages continue to fall and prices begin to fall also. Real cash balances increase but expectations about future prices may give a positive rate of return to money. There may be many periods for which falling money wages go with falling employment. Where the system would end up in the 'long run' I do not know.

IV LOOKING BACK

The recent literature for the first time took seriously the importance of the past and the expected future in Keynesian economics. The first step was therefore a careful study of short period Walrasian equilibrium. This not unnaturally led to the discovery that certain restrictions are required on the way expectations are formed if existence results were to be possible. It is not clear that there are plausible restrictions. In addition, some way is required for a smooth transfer of ownership from a bankrupt debtor. It is not clear that such smooth transfers do take place. So even at this level there is cause for Walrasian anxiety.

But the most interesting development is undoubtedly the change in the requirement for short period equilibrium. In particular, the study of the given money wage case suggested an equilibrium notion as a snapshot of a non-tâtonnement. That is, one abandons the implausible view that agents consider that they can transact what they wish to at going prices when they in fact find that they cannot. This important line, starting with Clower, is now developing briskly. It has led some enthusiasts to go to the extreme of fixed price equilibrium and to call that Keynesian. But, of course, there is no good prior reason why agents should treat quantity constraints and prices parametrically. When that assumption is dropped things become more interesting and more difficult. Negishi conjectures appear. These so far have, except in very special models (see Negishi 1964, Futia 1975), not been treated as the outcome of rational learning. One thinks of them as the outcome of past experience. That may be the right route: the equilibrium of an economy is today what it is because the past was what it was. But much work is required here.

Keynes deserves the credit for forcing one to look sequence economics in the face. He deserves little credit for the rest since he insisted on a purely neo-classical microtheory. At least this is so at a highly theoretical level. On the other hand, if one looks at the sum total of his informal insights, one may conclude that all one is doing is to give them adequate theoretical form.

Money in all of this has been a disaster from beginning to end. For a long time it was held that monetary matters are somehow at the root of what is to be learned from Keynes. All sorts of dreadful pronouncements on Say's Law testify to that. The element of truth in this is only that monetary theory requires a sequence economy. But the idea that there would be no unemployment in a barter economy is grotesque. Keynes' own discussion of the consequences of the wage bargain being in money terms only makes sense as a discussion of 'homogeneity' and in any case it was not, as given in that chapter, correct. The 'classical' story being attacked is the corn economy, a 'paradigm' which should not detain one. On the other hand, Keynes fully understood that money was not the only non-reproducible store of value. He attempted to bring the demand for money into a proper theory of portfolio choice and clearly that was the right way of 'integrating' money into real theory. The special properties he claimed to find in the demand for money turn out to make no difference in kind to any theoretical proposition.

That money is of special significance to the non-tâtonnement view of short period equilibrium seems, as I have argued, simply false. The same conclusion holds for claims that it has this special significance for the multiplier. If we study an economy which is not a barter economy – say, a computer mediated economy – then any non-reproducible asset allows for a choice between employment inducing and non-employment inducing demand.

But, of course, in a monetary economy money is an important non-reproducible asset. It also has one special property among assets, namely that it has no uses other than exchange uses. This leads rational agents to care only about real balances. However, once again 'real balance effects' need not refer to money. As prices in terms of land approach zero, land holders become quite wealthy enough to do what is required of them.

These remarks refer only to the pure theory of monetary matters. Of course, in actual economies it makes sense to study, say, money wages and not land wages. Keynes, however, knew that for very purely theoretical purposes it made no difference.

Lastly, of course, there is the view that a certain behaviour of the money stock will ensure a 'natural equilibrium'. There seems to be no theoretical foundation for this.

This leaves at least one important matter undiscussed. That is, of course, macroeconomics, which we think of as an essentially Keynesian invention. The reason for not discussing it is that I have nothing to say. Certainly, macroeconomics serves as a good 'simple' model which many economists feel is what we need. It also no doubt helps in treasuries. But how one is to give it a theoretical foundation, I do not know. Whether, for instance, in discussing investment behaviour one is to think of some 'representative' investor or some particular statistical average seems unresolved. The law of large numbers is perhaps not as applicable to social as to physical phenomena. Think of expectation formation. In addition, macroeconomics seems to suppose that the invisible hand is working smoothly and quickly in allocating resources. It is pretty clear that usable economics will have to be of some sort of macro character. But what sort?

REFERENCES

Arrow, K. J. 1959. Towards a theory of price adjustment, in Abramovitz, A. (ed.), *The Allocations of Economic Resources*, Stanford University

Arrow, K. J. and F. H. Hahn 1971. *General Competitive Analysis*, Edinburgh: Oliver and Boyd; San Francisco: Holden-Day.

Aumann, R. J. and Kurz, M. 1976. Incomplete markets and bankruptcy: A Walrasian perspective, IMSSS Summer Session.

Barro, R. J. and Grossman, H. I. 1971. A general disequilibrium model of income and employment, *American Economic Reivew*

Benassy, J. P. 1974. Neo-Keynesian disequilibrium in a monetary economy, *Review of Economic Studies*

Benassy, J. P. 1976. The disequilibrium approach to monopolistic price setting and general monopolistic equilibrium, *Review of Economic Studies*

Clower, R. W. 1965. The Keynesian counterrevolution: a theoretical appraisal, in F. H. Hahn and F. P. R. Brechling (eds.), *The Theory of Interest Rates*, London: Macmillan; New York; St. Martin's Press.

Drèze, J. 1973. Existence of an equilibrium under price rigidities, CORE Discussion Paper No. 7326

Drèze, J. 1974. Investment under private ownership: optimality, equilibrium and stability, in J. Drèze (ed.), *Allocation under Uncertainty*, United Kingdom: The Macmillan Press Ltd

Futia, C. A. 1975. Excess supply equilibria, Bell Telephone Laboratories.

Grandmont, J. M. 1976. A temporary general equilibrium theory, CEPREMAP.

Grandmont, J. M. and Laroque, G. 1976. On temporary Keynesian equilibria, *Review of Economic Studies*

Grandmont, J. M. and Younès, Y. 1973. On the the role of money and the existence of a monetary equilibrium, *Review of Economic Studies*

Green, J. R. 1973. Temporary general equilibrium in a sequential trading economy with spot and future transactions, *Econometrica*

Hahn, F. H. 1965. On some problems of proving the existence of equilibrium in a monetary economy, in F. H. Hahn and F. P. R. Brechling (eds.), *The Theory of Interest Rates*, London: Macmillan, Chapter 7 above.

Hahn, F. H. 1978. On non-Walrasian equilibria. Review of Economic Studies.

Hahn, F. H. and Negishi, R. 1962. A theorem on non-tâtonnement stability, *Econometrica*

Hart, O. D. 1974. On the existence of equilibrium in a securities model, *Journal of Economic Theory*

Hicks, J. R. 1939. *Value and Capital*, Oxford: The Clarendon Press.

Iwai, K. 1974. The firm in uncertain markets and its price, wage and employment adjustments, *Review of Economic Studies*

Kaldor, N. 1939. Speculation and economic stability, *Review of Economic Studies*

Keynes, J. M. 1936. *The General Theory of Employment, Interest and Money*, New York: Harcourt, Brace and Company

Klein, L. R. 1949. *The Keynesian Revolution*, New York: Macmillan

Leijonhufvud, A. 1968. *On Keynesian Economics and the Economics of Keynes*, New York: Oxford University Press

Negishi, T. 1961. Monopolistic competition and general equilibrium, *Review of Economic Studies*, June

Negishi, T. 1964. Existence of an under-employment equilibrium, mimeo, London School of Economics

Ostroy, J. M. and Starr, R. M. 1974. The informational efficiency of monetary exchange, *Econometrica*

Patinkin, D. 1965. *Money, Interest and Prices*, 2nd Edition, New York: Harper and Row

Wood, A. 1976. *A Theory of Profits*, Cambridge University Press

10

On Money and Growth

Economic theory still lacks a 'monetary Debreu'. The study of some simple problems raised by considering the growth of a monetary economy which follows must therefore be regarded as tentative. At some future date the issues here raised may be found to be peripheral to a proper understanding of money.

I SIMPLE STEADY STATE THEORY

Present growth models which make no allowance for money are *not* barter models. No attention is paid to the economics of transactions and one must suppose that in this world the 'mediating' function of money is performed costlessly by some outside agency. To say that money is 'neutral' if the steady state values of the 'real' variables are what they would have been had we never introduced a monetary asset is, therefore, misleading. In order to compare the two economies we should have to provide a theory of transactions for the non-monetary economy, and no one has yet done so. Money can be found to be 'neutral' in the above sense only if it is given no function to perform.

After this warning, let us consider the arithmetic of a one sector neo-classical growth model with money. I write n for the rate of growth of the labour force, and y and k for output and capital per head. The single produced good is the numéraire and p is the price of one unit of money. The value of the money stock per person is m. I let g stand for the own rate of return of money; if money bears no interest $g = \dot{p}/p$. Also μ is the rate of growth in the nominal money stock. There is a 'well behaved' neo-classical production function $y = y(k)$.

There are two hypotheses we may make concerning the demand

for money: the *speculative* one and the *Keynesian* one. In the recent literature the former has received most attention. Let $g(k, m)$ be the rate of return required to induce the holding of m when $y = y(k)$ and $y'(k)$ is the rate of return on productive capital. On the speculative hypothesis, asset equilibrium requires:

$$g(k, m) = y'(k) \quad \text{all} \quad m \geqslant 0 \qquad (10.1)$$

Also $g(k, m) > y'(k)$ implies that no one wishes to hold capital and $g(k, m) < y'(k)$ that no one wishes to hold money. When hypothesis (10.1) holds no one cares either way. It is seen that on this hypothesis money has no role to perform.

On the Keynesian hypothesis, asset equilibrium in the absence of satiation requires:

$$g(k, m) < y'(k) \qquad (10.2)$$

Here some account is taken of the 'convenience yield' on money which is always positive. On traditional Keynesian grounds one will wish to suppose $\partial g/\partial k \leqslant 0$ and $\partial g/\partial m \geqslant 0$. Suppose one is interested in the set of pairs (k, m), which satisfy:

$$g(k, m) = \text{constant} < \infty$$

Then I shall assume that $(k, 0)$ belongs to this set with $k > 0$. The argument here is as follows: as $k \to 0$, $y'(k) \to \infty$ and $y(k) \to 0$. There is then a positive k small enough which, when the rate of return on money is fixed, would make agents prefer to resort to barter rather than incur the high opportunity cost of holding money. The Keynesian hypothesis does give money a role.

Next, one must consider how the nominal stock of money is changed. Johnson (1966, 1967) and Tobin (1965, 1967) examine only the case where either the stock is not changed at all or it is changed by means of government gifts to households. But the money stock can also be changed by government purchases of goods. I write μ_1 for that part of the rate of change in the nominal money stock attributable to gifts and μ_2 as that part attributable to government purchases:

$$\mu = \mu_1 + \mu_2$$

In a one sector model it is easiest to suppose that the government purchases part of the capital stock. In particular let the government always own a fraction α, $0 \leqslant \alpha \leqslant 1$, of the capital stock, Then

$$\mu_2 m = \alpha(\dot{k} + nk)$$

Let σ be government subsidies per head given in kind (e.g. health service), and d be disposable income per head. Then

$$d = y - \alpha y'(k)k + (\mu_1 + g)m + \sigma \qquad (10.3)$$

If there were income taxes as well, obvious modifications would be made in this expression. It is important to note that the rate of return on money is included in this definition of disposable income.

The simplest saving assumption one can make is to suppose that a constant fraction s of d is saved. For an economy in steady state this is not implausible but even then one might wish to take s as depending on some of the variables of the model, e.g. the wealth–income ratio. To the theorist the most appealing procedure for determining the savings of the economy is probably that of the lifetime savings hypothesis. There are, however, difficulties with this when the economy is not in steady state. First, one must suppose agents to form expectations as to the development of rates of return etc. over their lifetime. Secondly, if one wishes to investigate equilibrium paths, these expectations must always be correct. In general, this will mean that of all possible expectations a given generation can form there is a unique set which it must form if it, and all subsequent generations, are to make no 'mistakes'. There seems to be no mechanism, other than an infinite set of future markets, which could ensure this.

I propose therefore to stick to the simple 'rule of thumb' assumption that the savings at t are given by $sd(t)$. However, I shall on occasions notice the modifications introduced into the analysis by the following possibilities: s depends not on μ_1 and g but on $\bar{\mu}_1$ and $\bar{g}$ which are respectively the rate at which gifts of money are regarded as being made permanently and the rate of return on money which is thought to be permanently available. This last modification is designed to allow for the fact that a capital gain regarded as transitory will not be treated for consumption purposes in the same way as a rate of capital appreciation expected to recur indefinitely.

I shall take a steady state to be an equilibrium where, for con-

stant parameters α, σ, μ_1 and μ one has $\dot{k} = 0$. Certainly this requires:

$$sd = n(1 - \alpha)k + (\mu + g)m \qquad (10.4a)$$

$$g = g(k, m) \qquad (10.4b)$$

$$\mu_2 m = n\alpha k \qquad (10.4c)$$

If $m > 0$ then since $\partial g / \partial m \geqslant 0$ and $s < 1$, one easily verifies that
equation (10.4a) cannot hold independently of time with $\dot{k} = 0$
unless $\dot{m} = 0$, i.e.

$$(\mu + g)m = n \qquad (10.5)$$

On the speculative hypothesis, if $\alpha = \mu_2 = 0$, we may be able to
solve equations (10.4a) and (10.4b) for $m = 0$. I shall take the solution to be inadmissable.

Tobin and Johnson postulate $\alpha = \sigma = 0$ and $\mu_2 = 0$. Writing
$c = 1 - s$, and using equation (10.5), then gives

$$sy - cnm = nk$$

If this can be solved for $m > 0$, $k > 0$, it must be that $k/y < s/n$;
the steady state capital–output ratio must be less than its 'Harrod'
value. Tobin (1967) writes: 'If money is in any degree a substitute
for material wealth in satisfying the thrift propensities of the
population, then it is not "neutral".' That this is false can be seen
by putting $\sigma = y'(k)\alpha k$ and $\mu_1 = 0$. Then if k^* is the Harrod capital–
labour ratio it will also be the steady state value of k for the
monetary economy, provided only that $g(k^*, \alpha k^*) = 0$ has a solution
$0 < \alpha \leqslant 1$.

It is perhaps not unimportant to understand why Tobin's statement is not generally valid. The 'non-neutrality' which he claims
has nothing to do with money being 'in any degree a substitute
for material wealth'. It is due to the fact that matters have been
so arranged as to ensure that the disposable income of agents
exceeds what they produce. This need not inevitably be so in a
monetary economy. Nor is a monetary economy the only one
where this may occur. For instance, in a two sector growth model
without money and Hicks-neutral technical progress in the consumption sector, there will be a steady rise in the price of the capital good in terms of consumption good. However, on the purely

speculative hypothesis, Tobin's assertion is plainly correct – but that is just the case where money is given no role to perform.

II EXISTENCE OF STEADY STATE

I consider the Keynesian hypothesis first. Taking μ as given, one requires in steady state:

$$g(k, m) = n - \mu \tag{10.6}$$

Certainly one may take $n - \mu < 0$. But μ must be small enough not to make barter preferable for all finite k. Because of the monotonicity of $g(.)$ we may solve equation (10.6) for m in terms of k and write the solution: $m(k)$. Certainly $m'(k) \geqslant 0$ and by the assumptions made earlier, $m(k) = 0$, some $k > 0$. I shall now in fact suppose that $m(k)/k$ is increasing in k.

It will be clear that not all policy parameters can be taken as independently given. For equations (10.6) and (10.4c) are sufficient to determine k and m, and we still need to satisfy equation (10.4a). To make things simple I let $\sigma = y'(k)k\alpha$, all k, and treat μ and α as fixed. This makes μ_2 an unknown. All sorts of other cases may be investigated; I do not do so here.

From equations (10.3) and (10.4a),

$$sy + s(\mu_1 + g)m - (\mu + g)m + \alpha nk - nk = 0$$

Add and subtract $s\mu_2 m = sn\alpha k$, use equation (10.5) and divide by k to obtain:

$$\phi(k) = \frac{sy(k)}{k} + n(\alpha c - 1) - \frac{cnm(k)}{k} = 0 \tag{10.7}$$

It is easy to see that a 'monetary' solution exists if $\phi(\hat{k}) > 0$ when $\hat{k}$ solves $m(\hat{k}) = 0$. Certainly if this condition holds, since $\phi(k) \to -\infty$ as $k \to \infty$, a simple continuity argument ensures a solution for equation (10.7) with $m(k^*) > 0$. Then $k^* > \hat{k}$. But then $\phi(\hat{k}) > 0$. For suppose not. Since the production function is 'well behaved' and $m(k)/k$ increasing in k, it must be that $\phi'(k) < 0$ and so $\phi(k^*) < 0$, a contradiction. Hence $\phi(\hat{k}) > 0$ is a necessary and sufficient condition for the existence of a steady state with money.

The steady state value of μ_2 (and so of μ_1) is determined by equation (10.4c).

If one wishes to make s depend on the wealth–income ratio, then provided (a) this ratio is increasing in k, and (b) s is a diminishing function of the ratio, all the above arguments remain intact. Of these requirements (a) may be a little doubtful for low values of k, but it does not seem worth while exploring the possibilities which might arise.

In the purely speculative case one requires:

$$y'(k) = n - \mu$$

and this equation uniquely determines k^*. Evidently we may now only permit values of μ lower than n. A steady state with money exists provided that $sy(k^*) - nk^* > 0$. In particular, if this condition is satisfied when $\mu = 0$, the steady state is the golden rule. It is clear that to ensure the existence of a steady state with money in this case may require $\mu < 0$. The reason is obvious: in order that agents be induced to hold money its rate of return must be as high as that of capital and this may imply a rise in the value of money stock per person unless the nominal quantity is declining.

III OPTIMALITY: A DIGRESSION

Before proceeding with the descriptive story it may be worth while to consider how a government acquainted with recent writings in learned journals might wish to arrange its monetary policy. The exercise will allow us to discuss the desirability or otherwise of 'neutrality'. I treat only the Keynesian case.

As usual, the government has a strictly concave instantaneous valuation $U(C)$, where C is consumption per head. It seeks to maximise:

$$\int_0^\infty U(C(t)) \, dt \tag{10.8}$$

What are the constraints? Certainly one has:

$$C(t) = y(k(t)) - nk(t) - \dot{k}(t) \quad \text{and} \quad k(t) \geqslant 0 \text{ all } t \tag{10.9}$$

and, on the behavioural assumptions already made, if there is no government investment:

$$C(t) = c[y(k(t)) + \dot{m}(t) + mm(t)] \text{ and } m(t) \geq 0 \text{ all } t \qquad (10.10)$$

where

$$\dot{m}(t) = [g(k(t), m(t)) + \mu(t) - n]m(t) \qquad (10.11)$$

It is here supposed that the actual rate of return on money is at all times what is required for the given money stocks to be held. Thus if $\mu(t)$ as well as $k(t)$, $m(t)$ are all given, then these equations also determine the rate at which the return on money must be changing so as to ensure that the actual changes in the money stock are also the desired ones.

But on the grounds already argued, I do not wish to permit $m(t) = 0$, since I claim that we cannot pass from a world with a medium of exchange to one without, unless we have available a theory of barter economy. Instead, I put a lower bound on g or, what comes to the same thing, let $\underline{m}(k)$ be the minumum quantity of cash required at k. One has the constraint

$$m(t) \geq \underline{m}(k(t)) \quad \text{all } t, \underline{m}'(k) \geq 0 \qquad (10.12)$$

If $m(t) = \underline{m}(k)$ and (10.12) is binding in the interval $(t, t + \epsilon)$, then in this interval, from equations (10.9) and (10.10):

$$(1 + \underline{m}'c)\dot{k} = sy - nk - cn\underline{m}(k) \qquad (10.13)$$

whence, given $k(t)$, the values $k(t')$ and $C(t')$ are determined for $t \leq t' \leq t + \epsilon$. Also, since $g(k, \underline{m}(k)) = \hat{g}$ say, equation (10.11) tells us what the government choice of $\mu(t')$ must be in that interval.

Now take $m(0) > \underline{m}(k(0))$ and consider the maximisation of equation (10.8) subject to equation (10.9) only. The answer is well known: the economy should pick among the set of trajectories satisfying equation (10.9) and

$$\frac{d \log U'(C)}{dt} = y' - n \qquad (10.14)$$

the unique one leading to the golden rule value c^*, k^*, $y'(k^*) = n$. From equations (10.10) and (10.11) we can then determine the behaviour of $\mu(t)$ and so of $m(t)$ along this optimum path. If $m(t) \geqslant \underline{m}(k(t))$ all t, for this path, there is nothing further to be said. Asymptotically the government ensures a stock of money such that at k^*, and m constant, agents are induced to consume C^*. Evidently this is the Cass–Yaari result in another guise. On our assumptions this policy is only possible if $sy(k^*) - nk^* > 0$, that is, if a non-monetary economy (with costless mediation provided), would save more than the golden rule requirement, i.e. if the steady state of such a non-monetary economy were inefficient. It is clear that the policy just discussed may not always be feasible. It is convenient to rewrite the constraint (10.12). Evidently if the constraint operates it must be that even if the government wishes to, it cannot further reduce consumption by lowering the money supply. In fact using equations (10.9) and (10.10) we obtain a lower bound on consumption:

$$C(1 + cm') \geqslant c[y(k) + n\underline{m}(k) + cm'(y - nk)] \qquad (10.12')$$

(This expression follows from $m(0) \geqslant \underline{m}(k(0))$ or $m(t) + \dot{m}(t) \geqslant \underline{m}(k(t) + \underline{m}'\dot{k}(t))$.) If we now carry out our maximisation exercise in the usual way but incorporate constraint (10.12') we find among the necessary conditions:

$$U'(C) = \lambda - \beta(1 + cm') \qquad (10.15)$$
$$-\dot{\lambda} = \lambda(y' - n) + (U' - \lambda)cy'(1 + m') \qquad (10.16)$$

where λ is the Pontryagin 'auxiliary variable' and β the Lagrangean multiplier, which is positive only if (10.12') holds with equality and zero otherwise.

The easiest way to proceed is by diagram. We note that (10.13) is a stable equation converging on $\bar{k}$. I shall suppose $\bar{k} < k^*$ (see Figure 1).

In Figure 1 the trajectory CC is derived from equations (10.13) and (10.10). It gives the path of k and C if the constraint (10.12') is always satisfied with equality. No point below this trajectory is feasible. The dotted curves are examples of trajectories satisfying equations (10.14) and (10.9). Call these 'unconstrained' trajectories. All of these which lie wholly above CC lead the system to a point where all capital is exhausted and cannot be optimal. Consider an unconstrained trajectory which cuts CC twice, first from above and then from below. Certainly we cannot follow it below CC and

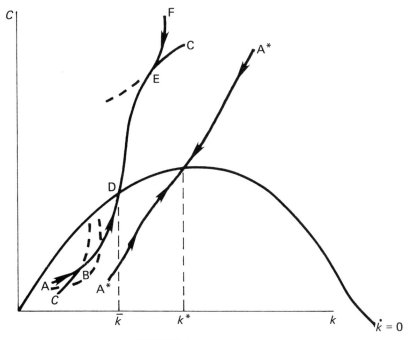

FIGURE 1 Optimum path

do not want to follow it after it has cut CC from below. If we follow it until it cuts CC from above, then at the cut the two trajectories have a different slope. But at the cut it must be that $\beta = 0$ in equation (10.15) and so in equation (10.16) we would violate the necessary conditions for an optimum. Hence we can only follow on an unconstrained trajectory which has only one point of contact with CC as long as it leads to CC. I conclude that the optimum path is ABDEF. (It is clear that we shall never wish to be on CC to the left of B or the right of E.)

The case just examined is one of several possibilities. Also it would have been possible to carry out the analysis in the (λ, k) plane, which would show perhaps more clearly that the described optimum path satisfies all requisite condtions. But nothing much can be learned from the details of the exercise; the question is whether anything can be gleaned from the outline just given.

If at no positive stocks of money agents can be induced to save enough for golden rule investment, the government will aim at the asymptote which is the steady state with the minimum quantity of money $\underline{m}(k)$. If one calls the cost of mediation the difference in social valuation achieved when the paths are unconstrained by (10.12) (or $m(t) > 0$), and the valuation when the paths are constrained, then certainly mediation in the present case is not costless. This is unsatisfactory since the medium can be costlessly produced. The reason of course is the 'wealth affect' of Tobin. In the case examined by Cass—Yaari this effect is welcome (society asymptotically is too thrifty); here it is not.

It is not difficult to see what the government should do: it should both tax and invest. In the policy I have investigated, taxes were imposed only in order to reduce the quantity of money and so, indirectly, consumption. If the authorities enter the market for capital, they can tax without reducing the quantity of money and so encountering the constraint. It is not hard to see that once this extra 'instrument' is provided, policy makers can follow the optimum unconstrained path A*A*, provided $m(0) \geqslant \underline{m}(k(0))$. Assuming $\underline{m}(k)$ independent of taxes, the government will, asymptotically, own a fraction $\alpha^* = m(k^*)/k^*$ of the capital stock. It will be investing $n\alpha^*/k^*$. It will be paying a rate of return on money of $g(k^*, \underline{m}(k^*))$, which may be negative and paying a subsidy in money of $\mu m(k^*)$ where $\mu = n - g$. This will lead to a disposable income $y(k^*) = y(k^*) - n\alpha^* k^* + nm(k^*)$. Part of the savings of agents at this income are directed to the acquisition of new money which is exactly equal to the investment of the government Thus, although the government may start by taxing, once it owns a sufficient amount of the capital stock it will start subsidising. In any event, there exists a policy which can make mediation 'costless'. It is worth noting that none of this would be changed if we allowed the private saving rate to be influenced by the wealth—income ratio.

Now of course our social valuation was rather arbitrarily specified. Had the government sought to maximise:

$$\int_0^\infty e^{-\delta t} U(C(t))\, dt \qquad \delta > 0$$

then the optimum asymptotic capital—labour ratio would have been less than k^*. Moreover, it is perfectly possible that the unconstrained optimum trajectory for this problem never lies below CC. In that case mediation can be made costless once again without the government entering the market for capital.

One concludes that either mediation is always costless or can be made so.[1] This seems to me to be the proper way to look at the neutrality question also. I have already argued that we have not at present a framework for comparing monetary with barter economies. What we can do is ask whether mediation by money must restrict the accumulation choices of an economy. The answer is no, and so in a proper sense, for a rational society, money is neutral.

IV EQUILIBRIUM DYNAMICS

This section is concerned with the behaviour of all equilibrium paths.

The Case of Pure Speculation

Suppose the government imposes no taxes and pays no subsidies so that the nominal stock of money is constant. From hypothesis (10.1) one has

$$\dot{m} = [y'(k) - n]m \tag{10.17}$$

and, as usual,

$$\dot{k} = sy(k) - cy'(k)m - nk \tag{10.18}$$

It is convenient to suppose here, not that the government pays a return on money but

$$v'(k) = \dot{p}/p$$

The equations (10.17) and (10.18) have two singularities (provided that for $m = 0$, savings exceed golden rule investment). I am only interested in that for which $m^* > 0$, which evidently is the golden

---

[1] I have not included money in the valuation to be maximised and thus the asymptotic optimum is consistent with a negative rate of return on money. Had money been included in $U(\cdot)$ then one would have to examine whether, asymptotically at least, 'satiation money' is optimal. The reason why this may cause difficulties is this: if households are to have satiation balances then it may not be easy to ensure that they also have the wealth which will ensure the 'right' saving rate.

rule. It is easy to show that 'almost all' equilibrium paths diverge from the steady state. (A local analysis leads to two roots which are of opposite sign but not equal). The case is analogous to that of growth with heterogeneous capital goods (Hahn 1966) and has been discussed in Shell and Stiglitz (1967).

It may be worth while to have a more or less verbal account of the behaviour of the system. Suppose $k > k^*$. Then $y'(k) < y'(k^*)$ and, by the rules of the game, $\dot{m} < 0$. It is possible that $\dot{k} > 0$ since $\dot{m} < 0$ means that there is a reduction of consumption out of capital gains. If so the system surely moves away from its steady state. Suppose however $\dot{k} < 0$. As long as $k > k^*$ one has $\dot{m} < 0$. If then $m(0) \leqslant m^*$, it must be, should k ever return to k^*, that the money stock is lower and so $\dot{k} > 0$. Hence by continuity $\dot{k}$ will change sign before it reaches k^*. Thereafter it will steadily increase and m will steadily fall. Evidently the same analysis shows that the system cannot converge except for a singular set of initial conditions. For if $m(0) > m^*$ when $k(0) < k^*$ and one has $\dot{k} < 0$ it must not be true that either $m(t)$ attains m^* or $k(t)$ attains k^*, 'first.' In the former case we should be back in the case already discussed. In the latter it must be true that $\dot{k} < 0$ at the point (k^*, m), $m > m^*$ and so $\dot{m} > 0$, and once again there is divergence.

Can the government stabilise this world by a suitable policy? Assuming it never enters the market for goods but is prepared to pay money subsidies and levy money taxes, I consider the following case:

$$\dot{\mu} = a(y'(k) - m) + b\mu \tag{10.19}$$

where of course now:

$$\dot{k} = sy(k) - c(y'(k) + \mu)m - nk \tag{10.18'}$$

$$\dot{m} = (y'(k) + \mu - n)m \tag{10.17'}$$

Considering 'small' disturbances about k^*, m^*, $\mu^* = 0$ shows that for stability one requires: (1) $a < 0$, $b < 0$ (2) $|b| > -(cn + \epsilon w)$, where $\epsilon = (y''/y')k^*$, $w = (sy/k) - n$ (3) $|a| > n$ (4) $|a| > |b|$. Not unexpectedly, a stabilising policy can be found. What is of interest is its perversity. For $a < 0$ implies that in times of 'excessive' inflation the government should be increasing the nominal stock of cash and the reverse in times of 'excessive' deflation. The responsibility for this result is to be laid at the door of the 'wealth' effects. The prescription shows that one is here concerned with a bogus world. It should be noted in particular that there is no explanation of why the price of money is changing – it is changing because we demand asset equilibrium.

The Keynesian Case

The two differential equations now are:

$$\dot{m} = [g(k, m) - n]m \qquad (10.17'')$$

$$\dot{k} = sy(k) - cg(k, m)m - nk \qquad (10.18'')$$

where once again there are no taxes or subsidies. I assume that the conditions for the existence of a steady state, discussed in section II, are satisfied. Local analysis, assuming $\partial g/\partial k < 0$, $\partial g/\partial m > 0$, once again reveals unstable roots. The phase diagram is given in Figure 2. The system behaves no better than in the speculative case, and that is just what one could expect since essentially the same mechanism is at work. The development shown in Figure 2 can be understood rather simply. Suppose $k(0)$ given but that we were at liberty to choose the initial quantity of money per person. Suppose the choice of $m(0)$ leads to (m^*, k^*) as $t \to \infty$. Is there

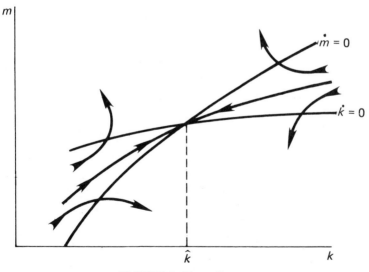

FIGURE 2 Phase diagram

any other choice with the same asymptotic outcome? Suppose one chose $m'(0) > m(0)$. Then $\dot{k}'(0) > \dot{k}(0)$ (where the prime denotes the path originating at $(k(0), m'(0))$. Also $\dot{m}'(0) > \dot{m}(0)$ and so it is easy to see, since two trajectories cannot cut, that the choice of $m'(0)$ cannot lead to (m^*, k^*). A similar result is easy to establish for $m'(0) < m(0)$. There is thus at most one choice of $m(0)$ which is consistent with convergence. It can be left to the reader to check that there is indeed one such choice.

The interest of both these stories in this section is this: they show that the supposition that the economy is at all times in asset and flow equilibrium imply, except for a singular instance, that all paths diverge from the steady state. Now the justification for considering these odd models is this: they represent paths of an economy in which some authority somehow or other ensures the desired equilibrium. This is, for instance, how Meade looked at it. What we have learned is that the government will have to do a good deal more − it cannot be indifferent between the monetary equilibria which it is open for it to establish. Shell and Stiglitz (1969) and I (Hahn 1966) have discussed this matter elsewhere in a different context and I do not do so again here.

V THE ECONOMY OUT OF EQUILIBRIUM: A PARTIAL CONSTRUCTION

It will be readily agreed that nothing that I have done so far would have been congenial to Keynes − and rightly so. It is indeed a feature of current growth theory that it pays no attention to the question of effective demand. Thus instead of asking 'what will the demand for investment be', it asks 'what must the demand for investment be to match savings?' For reasons at once obvious to an undergraduate the procedure is not entirely foolish in a world in which there is no money and there are no transaction costs. But when the concern is with a monetary economy one cannot leave matters there.

By stipulating that at all times the return on money was just that consistent with asset equilibrium, these difficulties were avoided in the previous section. But if the return on money is the rate of change in its price then, pure autonomous cost changes apart, one expects this to be a consequence of market disequilibrium. This makes equilibrium dynamics a doubtful procedure. In the foregoing the price of money was changing because this was required for asset equilibrium and not because any reason was adduced why in fact it should change.

Evidently it is not possible at this stage to develop and discuss a full disequilibrium model and I confine myself to some special points only (What follows is an extension of part of Hahn 1960.)

If desired and actual cash accumulation do not always coincide one has:

$$sy(k) - c(nm + \dot{m}) - nk - \dot{k}^* = \dot{m}^* - \dot{m} \qquad (10.20)$$

where the asterisk denotes a desired quantity. If one supposes the market for labour to be always cleared this equation is simply a form of Walras' Law. In what follows I shall examine those cases only for which, at full employment, $\dot{m}^* \leqslant \dot{m}$. That is, I consider only situations where the full employment output of goods does not exceed the demand for them. Of course this leaves the most interesting 'Keynesian' problems out of account. On the other hand the excise may help one to clarify how far the requirement of continuous equilibrium was responsible for instability already discussed. I introduce the following assumptions, writing E for the operator d log/dt:

(1) $\quad Ep = sy(k) - c(nm + \dot{m}) - nk - \dot{k}^*$ for $\dot{m}^* \leqslant \dot{m}$ $\quad$ (10.21)

where it will be recalled that p is the price of money in terms of goods. I am here assuming that money wages are always such as to preserve equality between the full employment marginal product of labour and the real wage. It would not be hard to incorporate an autonomous 'Phillips' term into the analysis.

(2) The monetary authorities at all times increase the nominal money stock at the rate n. It follows that $Ep = Em$. (If money wages were rising autonomously this assumption would have to be modified.)

(3) Let $h(k, m)$ be the rate of return on capital required by agents *at constant prices* if they are to be satisfied with the portfolio (k, m). Then I stipulate:

$$\dot{k}^* = a[y'(k) - h(k, m) - Ep], \ a > 0 \qquad (10.22)$$

and

$$h_m = \frac{\partial h}{\partial m} < 0, \ h_k = \frac{\partial h}{\partial k} < 0$$

The assumption has an obvious intuitive interpretation.

(4) Given that the adjustment speed in equation (10.21) has been normalised at one, I now suppose $a < 1$. There are some good reasons for liking this assumption but this of course does not make it 'correct'.

(5) Whenever there is an excess demand for goods it will be supposed that it is consumption demand which is satisfied.

(6) I assume that if $\hat{k}$ solves:

$$h\left(k, \frac{sy(k) - nk}{cn} \right) = y'(k)$$

that this is the only solution and $sy'(\hat{k}) - n < 0$. Evidently, $\hat{k}$ is the steady state capital–labour ratio. Existence of such a solution has already been discussed.

Using these assumptions one may write the rate of change in the value of money per person as

$$\mathrm{E}m = \frac{1}{1 + cm - a} \left[sy(k) - cnm - nk - a(y'(k) - h(k, m)) \right]$$
$$\tag{10.23}$$

and

$$\left. \frac{dm}{dk} \right|_{\dot{m}\,=\,0} = \frac{sy'(k) - n + a(h_k - y''(k))}{cn - ah_m} \tag{10.24}$$

Also for all $\mathrm{E}m \leqslant 0$ assumption (10.8) gives

$$\dot{k} = sy(k) - cm(n + \mathrm{E}p) - nk \tag{10.25}$$

The expression for

$$\left. \frac{dm}{dk} \right|_{\dot{k}\,=\,0}$$

is long and unlovely and of ambiguous sign almost everywhere. I return to this after considering the possible situation depicted in Figure 3.

We are interested only in points not below the curve $\dot{m} = 0$ since these are the points consistent with assumption (10.8) for

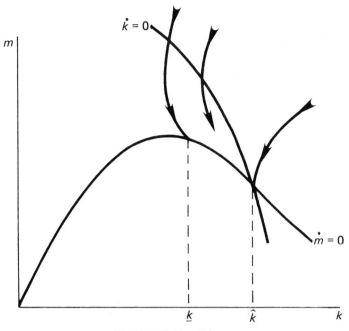

FIGURE 3 Possible curves

which all the behavioural rules are taken to hold. For all such
points $\dot{m} \leqslant 0$. For points above the curve $\dot{k} = 0$, the capital–labour
ratio is falling; for points below the curve, it is rising. It is seen
that for all $k(0)$ between $\underline{k}$ and k for which there is an excess
demand for goods, the system converges. For $k(0) < \underline{k}$, the trajectories starting with excess demand encounter the point of zero
excess demand at a point where deepening is taking place and such
deepening raises savings per person by more than it does investment. Hence the trajectory crosses the curve $\dot{m} = 0$ and the
model no longer applies. For $k(0) > \hat{k}$ the story is similar only
now the declining capital–labour ratio raises savings per person
by more than it does investment at the point where the trajectory
encounters the curve $\dot{m} = 0$.

Certainly that part of a disequilibrium model which we are considering here behaves 'better' than the equilibrium one. At least there
is a considerable range of initial conditions for which the system
converges. But the shown position of the curves cannot be deduced
from the assumptions given this far – it is not more than a possibility.
If the $\dot{k} = 0$ curve cuts $\dot{m} = 0$ from below we are certainly in as
much trouble as we are in the equilibrium construction.

Suppose, however, that agents regard all price changes as temporary, so that changes in consumption due to value changes in the money stock are small enough to be ignored. Then (a) the term cm disappears from $1/(1 + cm - a)$ in equation (10.23), and (b) the term $Epcm$ drops out from equation (10.25). One then has:

$$\frac{dm}{dk}\bigg|_{\dot{k} = 0} = \frac{sy' - n}{cn}$$

and so certainly the curve $\dot{k} = 0$ has a negative slope at $\hat{k}$. Moreover, from equation (10.24) we see that if $\dot{m} = 0$ has a negative slope at $\hat{k}$ it must be that the picture looks as in Figure 3 — the $\dot{k} = 0$ cuts $\dot{m} = 0$ from above.

Even so, in spite assumption (10.9) it is possible that $\dot{m} = 0$ has a positive slope at k. In that case we are once again in trouble. This possibility can, as equation (10.23) indicates, be avoided if a is sufficiently small.

None of this is in the slightest bit surprising. One has, in the present state of knowledge, great latitude in the construction of disequilibrium models; that is one of the reasons why they are so unattractive, and so a great variety of results can be produced. What the above construction seems to indicate is, that in the situations considered, consumption insensitivity to changes in the rate of return on money and 'slow' adjustments in the desired capital–labour ratio are 'good' for stability. One suspects — nothing stronger can be said — that these are not inappropriate assumptions for small disturbances. In any case, the picture does not look as bleak as it does when continuous equilibrium is a requirement.

On the other hand, it should be emphasised that the case of unemployment has not been considered.

VI SOME CONCLUSIONS

Not very much that is at all firm can be asserted on the basis of the rather simple-minded constructions we have been considering. The following are conclusions the validity of which, of course, depend on the models:

(1) There always exists a policy which will allow a monetary econ-

omy to have a steady state with the Harrod capital—output ratio provided that the demand for money is not purely speculative.

(2) If a planning authority (which does not discount the future) cannot enter the market for goods then it should aim asymptotically either at the golden rule, if that is possible, or if not at the largest possible capital—labour ratio. If it can enter the market for goods then asymptotically the economy will be at the golden rule.

(3) The equilibrium paths of a monetary economy diverge from the steady state except for one singular path.

(4) For certain initial conditions, consistent with an excess demand for goods, a whole class of disequilibrium paths seek the steady state provided changes in consumption induced by changes in the rate of return on money and the response speed of desired capital—labour ratio changes are both small enough.

REFERENCES

Hahn, F. H. 1960. The stability of growth equilibrium, *Quarterly Journal of Economics*, 74

Hahn, F. H. 1966. Equilibrium dynamics with heterogeneous capital goods, *Quarterly Journal of Economics*, 80

Johnson, Harry G. 1966. The neo-classical one-sector growth model: a geometrical exposition and extension to a monetary economy, *Economica*, 33

Johnson, Harry G. 1967. The neutrality of money in growth models: a reply, *Economica*, 34

Shell, K. and Stiglitz, J. E. 1967. The allocation of investment in a dynamic economy, *Quarterly Journal of Economics*, 81

Tobin, James. 1965. Money and economic growth, *Econometrica*, 33

Tobin, James. 1967. The neutrality of money in growth models: a comment, *Economica* 34

Part III

11

The Balance of Payments in a Monetary Economy

This paper will re-examine a number of traditional questions concerning the balance of payments on the assumption that individuals in the countries concerned hold positive stocks of their own currency.[1] Only the 'classical' full employment case will be examined and complete specialisation will not be assumed. The analysis will be carried out in the spirit of well known propositions concerning the stability of general exchange systems and no use will be made of the more usual 'total elasticities'.

The treatment is mathematical rather than geometrical. This is because except in the simplest cases too many variables are involved to be happily analysed by geometry. None of the mathematics is beyond elementary calculus although it is assumed that the reader is familiar with the basic equations of exchange and production. Wherever possible, an intuitive explanation will be given and the more abstruse calculations are relegated to the Appendix.[2]

I TRADITIONAL PROBLEM OF TWO COUNTRIES, TWO GOODS AND NO CURRENCIES

Notation

Let y_{ij} be the output of good i by country j, x_{ij} the demand for good i by country j. Let $y_j = (y_{ij})$ the jth country's output

---

[1] This paper is substantially as published except that the notation has been changed throughout.

[2] I am indebted to H. G. Johnson for considerable stylistic improvements.

vector, $y = \Sigma_j y_j$ and $x_j - (x_{ij})$ the jth country's demand vector and $x = \Sigma_j x_j$. Then $z = y - x$ is the world excess demand vector. Let m_{ij} be the demand for currency i by country j and $\overline{m}_{ij}$ the stock of currency i held by country j. Then $m_j = (m_{ij})$, $\overline{m}_j = (\overline{m}_{ij})$ and $m = \Sigma_j m_j$, $\overline{m} = \Sigma_j \overline{m}_j$, $M = m - \overline{m}$.

I shall write q as the price vector of goods in terms of the nth good ($q_n = 1$) and r as the price vector of currencies in terms of the nth good. On the other hand p is the price vector of goods in terms of country 1's currency and R is the price vector of currencies in terms of country 1's currency.

Lastly $A_j \lessgtr 0$ will denote a transfer to (> 0) or from (< 0) country j measured in terms of the nth good. Transfers are distributed amongst citizens.

Assumptions

(1) There is perfect competition in each country.
(2) There is free trade.
(3) There are no external economies of production and no increasing returns.
(4) There are no transport costs.

Assumptions (1) and (2) imply that:

(a) q is the same in all countries where both the ith and nth good are produced.
(b) p is the same in all countries.

Preliminary: By assumption (1) the following is true for each countr

$$p_i y_j \quad = \max \quad j = 1, 2$$

subject to   (11.1)

$$T_j(v_j) = 0 \qquad j = 1, 2$$

where T_j is the transformation function of country j, given full employment of its resources.

Hence

$$\frac{T_{ji}}{T_{jn}} = q_i \quad j = 1, 2 \tag{11.2}$$

$$T_{ji} = \frac{\partial T_j}{\partial y_{ij}}$$

By assumption (3) elementary calculations show:

$$\frac{\partial y_{ij}}{\partial q_1} > 0 \qquad j = 1, 2 \tag{11.3a}$$

$$\frac{\partial y_{2j}}{\partial q_1} < 0 \qquad j = 1, 2 \tag{11.3b}$$

$$\sum_1^2 q_i \frac{\partial y_{ij}}{\partial q_1} = 0 \qquad j = 1, 2 \tag{11.3c}$$

Equation (11.3) simply states that the production function is assumed concave to the origin. Let an asterisk denote equilibrium values. The $q^*y_j^*$ is the country j's income of terms of numéraire.

Let U_j be the well behaved community utility function of country j. That is all citizens have well behaved utility functions which yield parallel linear Engel curves through the origin. Then x_j^* solves

$$\max U_j(x_j) \tag{11.4a}$$

$$\text{s.t. } q^*(x_j - y_j) \leqslant A_j \tag{11.4b}$$

Using equation (11.4) and elementary theory we find:

$$\frac{\partial x_{ij}^*}{\partial q_k} = (y_{kj} - x_{kj})\mu_{ij} + S_{ik}^j, \quad k = 1, 2 \quad j = 1, 2 \tag{11.5}$$

where $\mu_{ij} = \partial x_{ij}^*/\partial A_j$, country j's marginal propensity to consume good i and S_{ik}^j is the substitution term. We know that $S_{ii}^j < 0$, $\Sigma \, q_i S_{ik}^j = 0$, $S_{ik}^j = S_{ki}^j$ for all (k, i).

By equations (11.2) and (11.4) with $A_j = 0$ for all j, z_1 depends only on q. So

$$z_1(q) = 0 \tag{11.6}$$

determines the equilibrium terms of trade q^*. (Of course $qz_1 + z_2 = 0$ for all q.) Lastly to conclude the preliminaries I define country 1's balance of payment in equilibrium as

$$B_1^* = q^*(x_{12}^* - y_{12}^*) - (x_{21}^* - y_{21}^*) \tag{11.7}$$

where it is assumed that the country exports good 1 and imports good 2.

We will now prove the following Proposition (Johnson, 1956 gives a similar result):

Proposition 1: A sufficient condition for an improvement in the balance of payments of a country, the terms of trade of which have deteriorated, is that the sum of the marginal propensities to spend on imports (in terms of numéraire) should exceed unity).

Proof: Using equation (11.5)

$$\frac{\partial B_1}{\partial q} = \left(q^* S_{11}^2 - S_{21}^1 - q^* \frac{\partial y_{12}}{\partial q} + \frac{\partial y_{12}}{\partial q} \right)$$

$$+ \left(y_{12}^* - x_{12}^* \right) \left(q^* \mu_{12} + \mu_{21} - 1 \right) \tag{11.8}$$

By equations (11.3a) and (11.3b) and the properties of the substitution term, the first expression in parentheses is negative. Since country 1 imports commodity 1, $y_{12}^* - x_{12}^* < 0$. Hence if the condition of proposition 1 holds, then the second part of equation (11.8) is also negative. Hence, say, a fall in q must increase B_1^*.

Remark 1: It is well known that the condition of proposition 1 is also sufficient for the terms of trade to turn in favour of a country making a unilateral payment to another.

Remark 2: The marginal propensities to spend on imports are probably easier to estimate than total elasticities since the latter are made up of both production and demand elasticities.

Remark 3: Proposition 1 has a simple explanation. The substitution effects of demand and production must always be in the 'right' direction. That is, say, a fall in q must always increase the demand and reduce the supply of good 1 and have the reverse effect on good 2. Moreover as long as we are only concerned with substitution effects, the total amount of good 2 offered for 1 must increase. Income effects too are normally in the 'right' direction. If q falls, country 1 is poorer and reduces its imports on that account while country 2 is richer and increases its imports on that account. But country 1 has in fact made an implicit transfer to country 2 by the amount of its exports multiplied by the change in terms of trade. So that unless the change in expenditure (in terms of numéraire) on its exports and its own imports add up to this transfer, the balance of payment must deteriorate on that account. Proposition 1 simply excludes this possibility.

Before coming to the main business of this paper, we will state a slightly weaker alternative to proposition 1.

Proposition 2: A sufficient condition for the balance of payments of a country the terms of trade of which have deteriorated to improve is that the two goods should be gross substitutes in the world market. (Two goods are "gross substitutes" if taking both income and substitution effect, the demand for one changes in the same direction as the price of the other has changed).

Proof: To make things simple, assume production is unchanged. This does no harm since any change in production must be favourable to our proposition. Then

$$\frac{\partial B_1}{\partial q} = q^* \frac{\partial x_{12}}{\partial q} - \frac{\partial x_{21}}{\partial q} + (x_{12}^* - y_{12}^*) \tag{11.9}$$

From equation (11.4b) we find

$$q^* \frac{\partial x_{12}^*}{\partial q} + \frac{\partial x_{22}^*}{\partial q} = - (x_{12}^* - y_{12}^*) \tag{11.10}$$

Substituting equation (11.10) into (11.9) we have

$$\frac{\partial B_1^*}{\partial q} = - \left(\frac{\partial x_{21}^*}{\partial q} + \frac{\partial x_{22}^*}{\partial q} \right) < 0 \tag{11.11}$$

Remark 4: Professor Johnson has suggested to me the simplest intuitive explanation of proposition 2. The trade balance B_1, represents the excess world supply for the second good. Hence if the second good is a gross substitute for the first, a fall in the price of the first (relatively to the second) must diminish the excess demand, increase the excess supply of the second good, and hence make country 1's balance unfavourable.

II TWO COUNTRIES, TWO GOODS AND TWO CURRENCIES

Assumptions

Assumptions 1–4 made in section I above, plus

(5) Each country holds only stocks of its own currency (m_{ij} and $\overline{m}_{ij} = 0$ for $i \neq j$).
(6) For any set of prices, measured in the same currency, the same price index is appropriate to each country (see below).
(7) Producers maximise profits. This means that the supply conditions (11.2) and (11.3) continue to hold.

The Demand for Goods

We shall continue to assume the existence of a community utility function; this is convenient but in no way necessary to the analysis. Using assumption (6), we write

$$U_j = U_j(x_j, R_j m_{jj}^0) \qquad j = 1, 2 \tag{11.12}$$

where $m_{jj}^0 = (1/w)m_{jj}$ and $w = w(p)$ is a price index in terms of currency of country 1. (Recall that $R_1 \equiv 1$.) The assumption that the same price index can be used to arrive at 'real cash balances' in each country is innocuous for present purposes. It reduces the required algebra. Putting real balances in the utility function hides a multitude of sins, in particular lack of attention to a proper intertemporal formulation. But it is a sin which is often committed.
   In each country (11.12) is maximised subject to

$$\Sigma\, p_j(x_{ij} - y_{ij}) + R_j(m_{jj} - \overline{m}_{jj}) \leqslant 0 \tag{11.13}$$

This leads to world excess demand functions for goods

$$Z = Z \left(\frac{1}{w} p, \frac{1}{w} R \bar{m} \right) = 0 \tag{11.14}$$

Hence the world excess demand functions for goods are homogeneous of degree zero in the commodity prices in terms of country 1's currency, the stock of country 1's currency and the price of country 2's currency in terms of the first. The same applies to the excess demand function for the currency of country 1. A world equilibrium relatively to $\bar{m}$ is (p^*, w^*, R^*) which solve

$$Z \left(\frac{1}{w} p, \frac{1}{w} R \bar{m} \right) = 0 \tag{11.15}$$

$$M_1 \left(\frac{1}{w} p, \frac{1}{w} R \bar{m} \right) = 0$$

$$w = w(p)$$

(The Walras Law is $pZ + M_1 + RM_2 = 0$).

The following are rather obvious points.

(a) If Z depends on relative prices only, the equilibrium rate of exchange between currencies would be indeterminate. This is a simple application of Patinkin to the problem of international trade. It is for this reason that diagrams using traditional offer curves are quite unsuitable for an analysis of the effect of changes in the exchange rate on the balance of payments.

(b) If we assume, as is customary, that the goods market is always in equilibrium, then M_1 represents country 1's balance of payments in terms of its own currency. This follows at once from equation (11.13) and the assumption that country 1 exports good 1. It should be noted that this is only so if country 1 does not hold, or wish to hold, any stocks of currency 2.

(c) The assumptions of section I assume that the price of any good in any one currency must be the same in all countries.

Analysis

With these preliminaries out of the way, we can now lay down a number of propositions.

Proposition 3: Assuming the goods market to be in equilibrium both before and after a change in the rate of exchange and the terms of trade unchanged then:

(a) All prices in terms of country 1's currency will change in the same direction as the price of country 2's currency in the same terms has changed.

(b) The proportionate change in the price of currency 2 in terms of currency 1 will be less than the proportionate change in the price of currency 2 in terms of currency 1.

(c) The balance of payments of country 1 will move in the same direction as the price of currency 2 in terms of currency 1 has changed.

Proof: The detailed proof will be found in the Appendix. Here we will only indicate the main lines of the argument:

(a) A glance at equation (11.15) tells us that say a rise in R_2 (i.e. a depreciation of currency 1) must raise the real cash balances of country 2 directly. Hence the demand for some good will be increased without a change in its supply. Since the terms of trade are given by assumption, the only way demand can be reduced again is by a rise in w, i.e. the price level. Since we are assuming the goods market to be in equilibrium, that is what will have happened.

(b) If goods prices rose in the same proportion as R_2 has risen, country 2's real cash balances would be unchanged, whereas country 1's would be lower. Hence there would be excess supply of goods, which we have excluded. It follows that goods prices do not rise in the same proportion as R_2 does.

(c) By the argument of (b) just given, country 1 must be worse off (lower real cash balances) and country 2 better off (higher real cash balances). Hence, there being no change in the terms of trade, the demand of country 1 for imports falls, while that of country 2 for imports rises and the balance of payments must improve.

We have thus isolated the real cash balance effect of a change in the rate of exchange on the balance of payments. Alexander (1951–52) was the first to discuss it, but his treatment is rather different from that proposed here. The following points should be noted:

(a) The effect isolated may be small in practice. This has nothing to do with its logical significance.

(b) The effect may be short lived, but we are here only concerned with the sign of the derivative of the balance of payments and not the dynamics of stability to which we return in the next section.

To get any further we must drop the assumption of constant terms of trade:

Proposition 4: Assuming the goods market to be in equilibrium both before and after a change in the rate of exchange then the terms of trade of country 1 will move in the opposite direction to the change in the price of currency 2, or in the same direction or remain unchanged according as $(\mu_{11}/\mu_{21}) > (\mu_{12}/\mu_{22})$, or $(\mu_{11}/\mu_{21}) < (\mu_{12}/\mu_{22})$ or these two ratios are the same, provided all goods and currencies are gross substitutes.

Proof: Once again the detailed proof will be found in the Appendix and only an outline given here.

The crucial ratios are familiar from Pigou and Samuelson (1952). Since we know that the pure real balance effect is equivalent to a transfer between the two countries, it is not surprising that it is these ratios which determine the direction in which the terms of trade will move when the rates of exchange change. Indeed, we can use a traditional offer curve diagram to illustrate the proposition just as was done by Samuelson. The assumption of gross substitutability assures that the offer curves will be well behaved. But it must be remembered that the intersection of these offer curves does *not* imply balance of payment equilibrium since we have introduced currencies into the picture. What it does imply is that the goods markets are in equilibrium which is an assumption of proposition 4.

It is, I think, reassuring to find that very simply and well known formulae will carry over into the monetary situation. Elasticity formulae would have been both cumbersome and rather meaningless. But let us turn to the balance of payments.

Proposition 5: Assuming the goods market to be in equilibrium both before and after a change in the rate of exchange, the balance of payments of country 1 will change in the same direction as the price of currency 2 in terms of currency 1 changes provided all goods and currencies are gross substitutes.

Proof: Assume first that the price of *both* goods (in terms of currency 1) rise in the same proportion as w rises. Then we know from proposition 3 that $(dB_1/dR_2) > 0$. That is the implied transfer improves country 1's balance of payments. Now if the terms of trade remain the same or turn against country 1, the balance of payments cannot be made less favourable than it has been made by the change in the rate of exchange directly. Hence there only remains the possibility of the terms of trade turning in favour of country 1.

If the terms of trade turn in favour of country 1, it must make country 1's balance less favourable than it would otherwise have been. But it cannot make it unfavourable. For at the improved terms of trade the supply of country 1's exportable cannot be lower than it was before (see equation (11.3)). Hence since the goods markets are in equilibrium, her exports cannot be lower than they were before devaluation. Similarly, the supply of country 1's importables cannot be higher. At the same time, country 1's demand for imports cannot be higher than it was before devaluation for then, there being no inferior goods, the market for country 1's importables could not be in equilibrium. Hence the balance of payment of country 1 must improve if she devalues even if this turns the terms of trade against her.

However, the assumption that the goods markets are in continuous equilibrium is particularly unfortunate. It is extremely unlikely to be so. In that case, the whole question of stability must be tackled in quite a different way which will be outlined in the next section.

The transfer problem

We shall now briefly discuss the transfer problem in a monetary economy. We will assume that the transfer is effected by collecting money taxes and distributing money subsidies. We shall also suppose that the amount to be transferred is fixed in terms of the index of prices which we have already defined. Hence money taxes and subsidies increase *pari passu* with the level of prices. We will assume that country 2 transfers to country 1.

The transfer problem in a monetary economy differs from that of the economy discussed in section I in that it is no longer true that the sum of the marginal propensities to spend on the two goods in any one country is equal to unity. For besides changing their consumption of the goods when their income changes, individuals in each country can, and in general will, also change their money holdings. Let us see what difference this fact makes to the 'classical' discussion.

In a non-monetary economy, when $(\mu_{12} + \mu_{21}) < 1$ it is easily seen that this implies $(\mu_{11} - \mu_{12}) > 0$ and $(\mu_{21} - \mu_{22}) < 0$. (Since in a non-monetary economy, $\mu_{11} + \mu_{21} = \mu_{12} + \mu_{22} = 1$, we find by substitution into $\mu_{12} + \mu_{21} < 1$, that $\mu_{12} + 1 - \mu_{11} < 1$ and $1 - \mu_{22} + \mu_{21} < 1$ which gives $\mu_{11} - \mu_{12} > 0$, $\mu_{21} - \mu_{22} < 0$.) The expression $(\mu_{11} - \mu_{12}) > 0$ means that the direct effect of the transfer will be to increase the excess demand for good 1. For when country 1 receives one unit of transfer, its consumption of good 1 goes up by μ_{11}, whereas country 2 paying the transfer will reduce its consumption of good 1 by μ_{12}. Similarly, $(\mu_{21} - \mu_{22}) < 0$ tells us that the good 2 will be in excess supply. Hence the familiar condition in the marginal propensities to import ensures, (a) that the transfer is underaffected, *and* (b) that the excess demand for country 1's export good increases and that for country 2's export good diminishes, and *hence* the terms of trade will turn in favour of country 1 since all goods are gross substitutes. Lastly, in this economy, the condition on the sum of the marginal propensities to import is equivalent to the Samuelson– Pigou ratio condition $(\mu_{11}/\mu_{21} > \mu_{12}/\mu_{22})$ (since $\mu_{11} > \mu_{12}$, $\mu_{21} < \mu_{22}$).

All this is no longer true in a monetary economy. Let h_1 and h_2 be the marginal propensities of countries 1 and 2 respectively to hoard their currency. Then the condition that the sum of the marginal propensities to import should be less than unity is now equivalent to

$$\mu_{11} + \mu_{12} + h_1 > 0$$
$$\text{(11.16)}$$
$$\mu_{21} + \mu_{22} - h_2 < 0$$

As long as $h_1, h_2 > 0$, it is clear that the condition is quite compatible with a positive *or* negative excess demand in *both* the goods markets. Hence it is not surprising that the 'classical' condition for a transfer to turn the terms of trade against the transferer is no longer adequate. There is no longer the simple link between the excess demand for goods and the balance of payments as there is in the non-monetary case. Moreover, the Samuelson– Pigou ratio condition is no longer equivalent to the condition on the sum of the marginal propensities to import. (Inequality

(11.16) is consistent with $\mu_{11} - \mu_{12} < 0$, $\mu_{21} - \mu_{22} > 0$ and so with $(\mu_{11}/\mu_{21}) < (\mu_{12}/\mu_{22})$.

It has therefore been gratifying to find that none the less, the Samuelson–Pigou ratio condition is still a sufficient condition for the terms of trade to turn against the transferer. The following proposition is proved in more detail in the Appendix.

Proposition 6: In a monetary economy in which the goods markets are in equilibrium both before and after the transfer, fixed in terms of a common price index, the terms of trade will turn against the transferer if $(\mu_{11}/\mu_{21}) > (\mu_{12}/\mu_{22})$ and all goods and currencies are gross substitutes.

The following is an intuitive explanation which is only partially satisfying.

(1) The condition is clearly compatible with an excess demand for good 1 and an excess supply of good 2. There is then nothing further to add to the conclusion that the price of good 1 will rise relatively to good 2.
(2) The condition is *not* compatible with an excess supply of good 1 combined with an excess demand for good 2.
(3) The condition is compatible with an excess supply *or* demand in *both* markets. In the case of excess demand in both markets, it is easily checked that the condition can be written equivalently as

$$\frac{\mu_{11} - \mu_{12}}{\mu_{21} - \mu_{22}} > \frac{\mu_{11} - \mu_{12}}{\mu_{21} + \mu_{22}} \tag{11.17}$$

Suppose then that there is excess demand in both markets as a direct result of the transfer. Since after the transfer the markets are again in equilibrium we can imagine the following experiment. Keep the terms of trade constant and reduce real wealth in *both* countries by raising the prices of both goods. Then the demand for both goods will fall in the same ratio as the righthand side of inequality (11.17). Stop raising prices when *either* of the excess demands disappears. It is clear from inequality (11.17) that the excess demand for good 2 will disappear first, while there is still excess demand for good 1. Hence it is clear that we will now have to allow the price of good 1 to rise relatively to the price of good 2.

Alternatively, think of the experiment of raising the price of good 1 relatively to good 2 until the equality sign holds in in-quality (11.17), keeping the price level constant. Then raise the price level, reducing wealth and both excess demands will dis-appear together. An exactly analogous argument can be employed if there is excess supply in *both* markets, in which case the in-equality sign in (11.17) is reversed.

Before proceeding, I should like to stress again that the condition of proposition 6 is *not* equivalent to the sum of the marginal propensities to import being less than unity. This equivalence is only true in a non-monetary economy.

Transfer, rate of exchange and prices

I have not found it possible to write down a simple and intuitive proposition concerning the effect of a transfer on the rate of exchange and the level of prices. However, if we are willing to regard the differences between certain substitution terms as small it is true that the rate of exchange will turn against the transferer if both the conditions of proposition 6 and the condition that the sum of the marginal propensities to import should be less than unity hold. The point here is that the latter condition ensures that the transfer will be under-affected and so it is reasonable to sup-pose that the rate of exchange should turn against the transferer. The condition of proposition 6 ensures that such changes in the rate of exchanges have the effect of turning the terms of trade against the transferer and so further help to effect the transfer. But it may well be that it is not necessary for the condition of proposition 6 to hold as well. Some further work is needed here. In so far as the rate of exchange moves against the transferer, part of the transfer will be in the form of a once-over cash-balance effect, making the transferer less wealthy, and the transferee more wealthy.

As far as the price level is concerned, a rough guide here are the respective magnitudes of the marginal propensities to consume in the two countries. If the marginal propensity to consume of the transferee exceeds that of the transferer, there will be a tendency for the price level to rise. However, the precise conditions involve other terms, especially substitution terms, between cash and goods, and no simple formula seems possible.

Comparison with existing work

Before concluding this section, it will be useful to put the results into relation with some existing work in this field. This is characterised by two assumptions: (a) that the supply of domestic output is infinitely elastic (the Keynesian case) and (b) that each country is specialised in the production of its export good. Both the assumptions are absent in the above. Even when the transformation functions are the of 'linear programming' type, it is extremely unlikely that *each* country will be specialised. The assumption seems quite needlessly unrealistic. Assumption (a) seems of less relevance today than it used to be. In any case, both assumptions together mean that there is no problem of the effect of change in the exchange rate on the terms of trade. As far as I know it has not been analysed before in a proper monetary setting.

There is a further point to note here. The Laursen–Metzler (1950) and Harberger (1950) analysis of the problem involves the two assumptions above. It has been noted that Harberger implicitly assumes money illusion (Spraos 1955, Pearce 1955). This assumption would make it impossible to analyse the determination of the equilibrium exchange rate (Harberger assumes it fixed by decree). In any case, the assumption moves the whole discussion from the sphere of monetary analysis. Harberger further believed that the Hicksian analysis implies that the substitution effects of a change in the price of imports on the demand for imports and home product would add up to zero even if cash balances are held. Spraos has (kindly) interpreted this belief as an assumption. Its realism and relevance has been discussed. A further logical implication can be noted here. The assumption implies that the substitution effect of a change in the price of home-produced goods on their demand must always exceed (in absolute value) the substitution effect of a change in the price of imports or the demand for imports. That is the compensated demand curve for home-produced goods must always be flatter than that for imports.[3] This has obvious implications for the coefficients employed by Harberger. From our point of view, Harberger's assumption concerning substitution effects would have one advantage: a

---

[3] The proof of this is quite simple. Let h be the home-produced good and let h^h, h^m, h^v stand for the substitution terms for h when its own price, the price of imports and 'the price of savings' changes. Setting all these equilibrium prices equal to unity, we have $h^h + h^m + h^v = 0$, a well know result. Let m be the import good and define m^h, m^m, m^v analogously. It is assumed that $m^v = 0$ and so $m^h + m^m = 0$. But by the well known Slutsky equation $m^h = h^m$ and so substituting we have $h^h - m^m + h^v = 0$. Since $m^v = 0$ it is easily seen $h^v > 0$. Hence since $h^h < 0$, $m^m < 0$, it follows that $|m^m| < |h^h|$.

depreciation, all other things, i.e. price levels and terms of trade, constant, must always improve the balance of payments of the depreciating country (see Appendix). But little is gained, since other things in any case do not remain constant and the assumption seems as doubtful as critics have noted.

III CONCLUSIONS

No-one could deny that we have, by our assumptions, sheltered ourselves from the full impact of the complexities of events as they are likely to be in the real world. It was gratifying to find that opening the floodgates and allowing countries to enjoy the manifest advantages of an exchange, as opposed to barter economy, did not bring the whole edifice tumbling down. Now it must be admitted that this is only so because we have assumed the market for goods to be in continuous and instantaneous equilibrium. This assumption is obviously fantastic. Once it is dropped a great deal of simple theorising goes as well.

It so happens that in the barter economy of two goods and two countries the sign of the derivative of the balance of payments with respect to the terms of trade is all we have to know even for purposes of dynamic analysis. There is only one 'live' excess-demand equation. Once money is introduced, the sign of the balance of payment derivative tells us nothing whatever about stability. We now have three 'live' equations and lots of derivatives. This is a situation well known to economists concerned with the dynamic stability of general equilibrium systems. As is well known the assumption of 'gross substitutability' is very serviceable there and it is so in our case. It can be shown — but to spare the reader, this is only asserted here — that if all goods and currencies are gross substitutions the monetary international trade system analysed in section II will be dynamically stable (in the small). *But*, and this is quite interesting, to prove this we have to assume that the rate at which the price of currency 2 in terms of currency 1 deviates from its equilibrium value is a function of the excess demand for currency 2 and *not* of the balance of payment. As remarked at the outset of section II the excess demand for a currency can only be identified with a balance of payment if all goods markets are in equilibrium. It is here of the essence that this is not so.

What explains this result? The answer is simple. When the goods markets are not in equilibrium, there is no such thing as *the* balance of payments. For the *ex ante* balance of payments of country 1 (her *supply* of exports minus her *demand* for imports) may be quite different from country 2's *ex ante* balance of payments. Thus to argue that changes in the rate of exchange be related to the balance of payments presupposes that supply of goods is always equal to the demand for them. Thus while the various derivatives of the balance of payment (goods markets in equilibrium) are of some interest, they do not tell us anything about the stability of the exchanges or of anything else. For that we must work with the excess demand functions for goods and currencies – in fact in the traditional general equilibrium manner.

APPENDIX

General

Normalise prices so that $P_1^* = P_2^* = w^* = 1$ in equilibrium. Let S_{iw}^j represent the Hicksian substitution term for good i when the price index w changes. Let $\mu_j = \mu_{1j} + \mu_{2j}$. The following partial derivatives are easily calculated (see equations (11.13) and (11.14)) where $x_i^* = \Sigma_j x_{ij}^*$

$$\frac{\partial x_1^*}{\partial P_k} = (y_{1k}^* - x_{1k}^*)(\mu_1 - \mu_{21} + \mu_{12} + \sum_k S_{1k}^i) \qquad k = 1, 2 \qquad (11.18a)$$

$$\frac{\partial x_2^*}{\partial P_k} = (y_{1k}^* - x_{1k}^*)[\mu_{21} + \mu_{12} - \mu_2] + \sum_k S_{2k}^i \qquad k = 1, 2 \qquad (11.18b)$$

$$\frac{\partial x_i^*}{\partial R_2} = \bar{m}_2 \mu_{i2} \qquad\qquad i = 1, 2 \qquad (11.18c)$$

$$\frac{\partial x_i^*}{\partial w} = -\bar{m}_1 \mu_{i1} - R_2 \bar{m}_2 \mu_{i2} + \sum_j S_{iw}^j \qquad (i, k) = 1, 2 \qquad (11.18d)$$

It will be convenient to consider the balance of payments B_1 directly. It is defined as in equation (11.7) but with normalised prices. The partial $\partial B_1 / \partial P_1$ is the same as in equation 11.8. The remaining partial derivatives are:

$$\frac{\partial B_1}{\partial P_2} = \left(S_{11}^2 - \frac{\partial y_{12}}{\partial P_2} - S_{22}^1 + \frac{\partial y_{21}}{\partial P_2} \right) + (y_{21} - x_{21})[1 - (\mu_{21} + \mu_{12})]$$

$$(11.19a)$$

$$\frac{\partial B_1}{\partial R_2} = \overline{m}_2 \mu_{12} \tag{11.19b}$$

$$\frac{\partial B_1}{\partial w} = -P_2 \overline{m}_2 \mu_{22} - \overline{m}_1 \mu_{21} - S_{2w}^1 + S_{1w}^2 \tag{11.19c}$$

Proof of proposition 3

Differentiate M with respect to R and set equal to zero:

$$M_{11} \frac{dP_1}{dR_2} + M_{12} \frac{dP_2}{dR_2} + M_{1w} \frac{dw}{dR_2} + M_{1R_2} = 0 \tag{11.20}$$

By assumption the terms of trade do not change and so on the normalisation

$$\frac{dP_1}{dR_2} = \frac{dP_2}{dR_2} = \frac{d\overline{P}}{dR_2}$$

say. By the definition of w as a price index:

$$\frac{dw}{dR_2} = (w_1 + w_2) \frac{d\overline{P}}{dR_2} = \frac{d\overline{P}}{dR_2}$$

Hence equation (11.20) becomes

$$(M_{11} + M_{12} + M_{1w}) \frac{d\overline{P}}{dR_2} + M_{1R_2} = 0 \tag{11.21}$$

Multiplying equation (11.20) by R_2 and using equations (11.3c) and (11.18a and c) it is verified that equation (11.21) becomes

$$-\frac{d\overline{P}}{dR_2} R_2 (\overline{m}_1 \mu_{11} + R_2 m_2 \mu_{12}) + R_2 \overline{m}_2 \mu_{12} = 0 \tag{11.22}$$

Hence $(d\overline{P}/dR_2) > 0$ and $(d\overline{P}/dR_2)R_2 < 1$.

$$\frac{dB_1}{dR_2} = B_{11} \frac{dP_1}{dR_2} + B_{12} \frac{dP_2}{dR_2} + B_{1w} \frac{dw}{dR_2} + B_{1R_2} \tag{11.23}$$

By the previous argument this can be written as

$$\frac{dB_1}{dR} = (B_{11} + B_{12} + B_{1w}) \frac{d\overline{P}}{dR} + B_{1R_2} \tag{11.24}$$

Using equations (11.3c), (11.9) and (11.19) this expressions reduces to

$$\frac{dB_1}{dR_2} = \frac{d\bar{P}}{dR_2}\bar{m}_1\mu_{21} + \bar{m}_2\mu_{12}\left(1 - R_2\frac{d\bar{P}}{dR_2}\right) \tag{11.25}$$

By our previous result the express in parentheses is positive and so is $d\bar{P}/dR_2$. Hence $(dB_1/dR_2) > 0$.

Proof of proposition 4

Differentiate Z_1, Z_2 and w with respect to R_2 and set equal to zero. Thus

$$\begin{bmatrix} Z_{11} & Z_{12} & Z_{1w} \\ Z_{21} & Z_{22} & Z_{2w} \\ w_1 & w_2 & -1 \end{bmatrix} \begin{bmatrix} \dfrac{dP_1}{dR_2} \\ \dfrac{dP_2}{dR_2} \\ \dfrac{dw}{dR_2} \end{bmatrix} = \begin{bmatrix} -Z_{1R_2} \\ -Z_{2R_2} \\ 0 \end{bmatrix} \tag{11.26}$$

By assumption all goods are gross substitutes: $Z_{ij} > 0$ for $(i \neq 1)$, $Z_{ii} > 0$, since supply is independent of the price level $Z_{iw} < 0$. Lastly, by equation (11.18c), $Z_{iR_2} > 0$. Solving equation (11.26) then yields

$$\frac{dw}{dR_2} > 0$$

Now if $(dP_1/dR_2) < 0$ then since $(dw/dR_2) > 0$ it must be that $(dP_2/dR_2) > 0$ and hence $(dq_1/dR_2) < 0$. (Recall that q represents the terms of trade of country 1). Hence one need only consider the case $(dP_1/dR_2) > 0$. Since $w_1 + w_2 = 1$ we can solve for dq_1/dR_2 by solving equation (11.26) for $(dw/dR_2 - (dP_1/dR_2))$. This yields, using equations (11.18 and 11.3)

$$\frac{dq_1}{dR} = \frac{1}{-\Delta}[\mu_{22}\mu_{11} - \mu_{12}\mu_{21}]\bar{m}_1\bar{m}_2 w_1 \tag{11.27}$$

where Δ is the determinant of the matrix in equation (11.26) and we verify $\Delta < 0$. Hence $(dq_1/dR_2) > 0$, if $(\mu_{11}/\mu_{12} > (\mu_{21}/\mu_{22})$ as was to be proved.

Proof of proposition 6

Let $A > 0$ be the transfer in terms of w from country 2 to country 1. Clearly

$Z_{iA} = (\mu_{i1} - \mu_{i2})$ and $M_{1A} = (-1 + \mu_{12} + \mu_{22})$. So one has to solve

$$
\begin{bmatrix}
Z_{11} & Z_{12} & Z_{1w} & Z_{1R_2} \\
Z_{21} & Z_{22} & Z_{2w} & Z_{2R_2} \\
w_1 & w_2 & -1 & 0 \\
M_{11} & M_{12} & M_{1w} & M_{1R_2}
\end{bmatrix}
\begin{bmatrix}
\dfrac{dP_1}{dA} \\[2mm]
\dfrac{dP_2}{dA} \\[2mm]
\dfrac{dw}{dA} \\[2mm]
\dfrac{dR_2}{dA}
\end{bmatrix}
=
\begin{bmatrix}
-(\mu_{11} - \mu_{12}) \\[2mm]
-(\mu_{21} - \mu_{22}) \\[2mm]
0 \\[2mm]
(1 - \mu_{12} - \mu_{21})
\end{bmatrix}
\tag{11.28}
$$

There is no way out of the tedious business of calculation. On our assumptions Δ, the determinant of the matrix, is positive and

$$
\frac{dP_1}{dA} - \frac{dP_2}{dA} = \frac{N}{\Delta}
\tag{11.29}
$$

where

$$
N = \mu_{22}\mu_{11} - \mu_{12}\mu_{21}
\tag{11.30}
$$

This gives the required result. In finding these expressions one uses equations (11.18) and (11.19) and

$$
Z_{i1} + Z_{i2} + Z_{iw} = -(\mu_{i1} + \mu_{i2}) \qquad i = 1, 2
$$
$$
M_{11} + M_{12} + M_{1w} = -(\mu_{12} + \mu_{21})
\tag{11.31}
$$

where one recalls that units have been chosen so as to make $P_i = 1 (i = 1, 2)$.

REFERENCES

Alexander, Sidney 1951–52 Effects of a devaluation on a trade balance, *International Monetary Fund, Staff Papers*, vol. II

Harberger, A. C. 1950 Currency depreciation, income and the balance of trade, *Journal of Political Economy*, 58

Johnson, H. G. 1956 The transfer problem and exchange stability, *Journal of Political Economy*

Laursen, S. and Metzler, L. A. 1950 Flexible exchange rates and the theory of employment, *Review of Economics and Statistics*, 32

Pearce, I. F. 1955 A note on Mr. Spraos' paper, *Economica*, 22, May

Pigou, A. C. 1932 The effects of reparations on the ratio of international exchange, *Economic Journal*

Samuelson, P. A. 1952 The transfer problem and transport costs: The terms of trade when impediments are absent, *Economic Journal*, 62, June

Spraos, John, 1955 Consumers' behaviour and the conditions for exchange stability, *Economica*, 22, May

12

The Monetary Approach to the Balance of Payments

This is a review of the theoretical papers in *The Monetary Approach to the Balance of Payments*, edited by Jacob A. Frenkel and Harry G. Johnson (1976). The book will be referred to as FJ. Part II of the book contains empirical contributions. They are not discussed here because of the lack of competence of the present author.

I INTRODUCTION

If X_g is the value of the excess demand for goods,

$$X_g \equiv (I - S) + (G - T) + B$$

in simple Keynesian macroeconomics. One may rewrite

$$X_g \equiv E - Y + B$$

where E is total *ex ante* expenditure of all agents. If the economy has only one asset – money – then if X_m is the excess demand for money, the budget constraints of all agents taken together lead to

$$X_g - B + X_m \equiv 0$$

from which

$$X_g = 0 \Rightarrow B = X_m \tag{12.1}$$

'A balance of payments deficit implies *either* dishoarding by residents or credit creation by monetary authorities.' (Johnson, FJ,

p. 51) Notice that relation (12.1) does not say this since Johnson has omitted the condition $X_g = 0$. Notice also that in the 'real' world there are many assets so that the simple accounting does not lead to (12.1). I return to this later.

Now 'the essential assumption of the monetary approach . . . is that there exists an aggregate demand function for money that is a function of a relatively small number of aggregate economic variables.' If so, then given the behaviour of the money stock, $(E-Y)$ must also be such a simple function of a small number of aggregate economic variables. When we come to consider some of the papers in this volume we shall have to bear this firmly in mind to determine whether the 'simple function' which is 'assumed' is plausible.

But as a matter of fact Johnson is not here giving the 'essential' feature of the monetary approach, which is rather more persuasive and which he himself summarises elsewhere. 'Deficits and surpluses represent phases of stock adjustment in the money market and not equilibrium flows and should not be treated within an analytical framework that treats them as equilibrium phenomena.' (Johnson, FJ, p. 153) This passage must again be taken as assuming $X_g = 0$ and only one asset. What is being argued is that since $B \neq 0$ must imply $X_m \neq 0$ (when $X_g = 0$), there will be changes in the money stock implied by the non-zero balance and that these changes in the money stock will change the behaviour of agents. Indeed even with fixed terms of trade and fixed Y and a gold standard these money stock changes will suffice to bring B to zero. Why? Because

$$X_m \equiv kY - \bar{M}$$

where $\bar{M}$ is the money (gold) stock and:

$B > 0 \Rightarrow X_m > 0$ and $\bar{M}$ increasing

$B < 0 \Rightarrow X_m < 0$ and $\bar{M}$ falling

This of course is an old story and Johnson is proud of the venerable ancestry. It leads him to say that the monetary approach attaches relativity little importance to changes in the terms of trade ('the elasticity approach') or changes in the level of income ('the multiplier approach') in studying mechanisms which bring B to zero. Their egges are all in the money stock basket.

Certainly it was high time to reconsider the monetary flows implied by B – a matter which had been much neglected in the possibly mistaken belief that monetary authorities would and could 'sterilise' these effects. But one is bound to note that Johnson's 'stock–flow' remarks apply to other assets as well, notably 'capital goods'. Since Johnson (FJ, p. 155) argues that the monetary approach concentrates on the long run, we cannot neglect such stock changes either. When the authors in this volume note this they largely opt for a study of long run steady state equilibria. This seems a somewhat unsatisfactory device and we shall discuss it in its proper place. We shall also ask whether their 'dynamics' is logically watertight and plausible.

However, by far the strongest impression of reading this book is summed up by Johnson: 'Whereas the Keynesian model assumes that employment and output are variable . . . the monetary models assume that output and employment tend to full employment levels with reaction to changes taking the form of wage and price adjustments.' (Johnson, FJ, p. 155) Now Keynes did not 'assume' but wrote a book to argue his case. What business has the monetary approach to 'assume' what is, after all, a central issue? Is it the case that when the IMF team that recently negotiated terms with Britain was asked 'why should we cut expenditure etc. when we have nearly 1.5 million unemployed?' they answered 'we assume the unemployment will go away on its own'? One hopes not. The contribution of Rodriguez is the only exception in not making the monetary model 'assumption'.

Johnson, I believe correctly, claims that the monetary approach is neither entailed by nor entails monetarism. He does not explain why, with one exception, all the contributions are monetarist or why they are so neo-classical in the old fashioned textbook sense. In any event this circumstance poses a difficulty for the commentator. For one may agree to the importance of studying the balance of payments induced money flows and yet find the actual treatment of this question very unsatisfactory on more general grounds. In particular one is continuously diverted from the main question by naïve monetarism, too much arithmetic and too simple minded and somewhat loose theorising.

In facing these difficulties it seemed best to first dispose of some of the objections which really do not turn on the issue of whether a 'monetary approach' can be useful. This I do by considering the contribution of the hero of the monetary approach – Mundell. I then take these general objections as applying *pari passu* to most of the other contributions and concentrate on what seem to me to be the unsolved problems of the monetary approach itself.

II MUNDELL

Let our country be called 'home' and all other countries taken together 'the world'. Home variables are indicated by the subscript h and world variables by the subscript w. Also y is 'real' income, p is the price of goods, r is the price of one unit of w currency in terms of h currency. Define

$$q(r) \equiv \frac{p_h}{rp_w}$$

where p_i is the price of goods in terms of i currency – the terms of trade.

I start with Mundell I (FJ, pp. 64–91). Take $r \equiv 1$ and fixed, and let

$$\overline{M}_h \equiv \overline{M}_{hh} + \overline{M}_{wh}$$

$$M_h = M_{hh} + M_{wh}$$

where an overbar denotes initial stock, M is 'money', M_{ij} is the amount of i currency demanded by j, $\overline{M}_{ij}$ the stock of i currency held by j. Since $r \equiv 1$ and known with certainty to be constant no one cares about the currency composition of his portfolio. Moreover if p is a price index of h goods and w goods in terms of h currency, one assumes

$$X_{mh} = kpy_h - \overline{M}_h \tag{12.2}$$

It is assumed:

(a) p_w is constant, and so we may as well take $p_w \equiv 1$ and write

$$p = p(p_h), \qquad p' > 0$$

(b) y_h is constant. This (I suppose) means that producers in h are perfect competitors, that the stock of productive capital is given and that since $r \equiv 1$, $p_w \equiv 1$, the money wage is always such as to ensure the same profit maximising output which is 'full employment' output.

With these assumptions we may write

$$X_{gh} = X_{gh}(p(p_h), \overline{M}_h) \tag{12.3}$$

The economy is said to be in equilibrium at $(p_h^0, \overline{M}_h^0)$ if

$$X_{mh}(p(p_h^0), \overline{M}_h^0) = X_{gh}(p(p_h^0), \overline{M}_h^0) = 0$$

Notice that the stock of money is an unknown. Since there is no international lending or borrowing and currency is the only asset, we know that at $(p_h^0, \overline{M}_h^0)$ we also have $B_h = 0$, since

$$X_{gh} + X_{mh} \equiv B_h$$

from the introduction.

That is all there is to the model. I first take it at face value and argue that Mundell treats it in an unsatisfactory way.

Uniqueness of equilibrium

Mundell proceeds by a series of diagrams in the $(\overline{M}_h, p_h)$ plane. He shows a unique equilibrium. His arguments are partly false and partly puzzling. Start in an equilibrium and suppose $\overline{M}_h > \overline{M}_h^0$. On plausible assumptions this gives $B_h(p_h^0, \overline{M}_h) < 0$. Then 'there must be a lower price level at which the balance of trade will again be in equilibrium' (FJ, p. 72). Possibly, but it does not tell us anything about the slope of the curve $B_h = 0$ at $(p_h^0, \overline{M}_h)$. There a lower p_h may further worsen the balance because of 'real cash balance effects'. But Mundell now adds that his postulate must be true 'if the system is stable'. This too is false on his own later assumptions, for a system is stable if it converges to *some* equilibrium. So what he means is 'if the equilibrium is stable'. But if an equilibrium is stable for all initial conditions it must be unique. Now the puzzle: having *assumed* stability of equilibrium in the beginning, why does he devote pages and diagrams to prove this stability?

Why bother with this point? Because it is of importance. If there are several equilibria and the *system* is stable, the monetary approach claim that the authorities cannot control the monetary stock may be false. If the authorities understand the system they can, by giving a locally unstable equilibrium a small kick, get to another, preferred equilibrium, and by giving a locally stable equilibrium a large enough kick do likewise. I return to this later. But the monetary approach and the monetarist approach share a common human failing: they want to have their cake and eat it. That is, they want to use the perfectly competitive equilibrium theory but they don't want to be bound to it where it interferes with simple striking results. I know of no appealing conditions which ensure the uniqueness of a competitive equilibrium.

Stability

Mundell postulates

$$\dot{p}_h = X_{gh}$$

$$\dot{M}_h = B_h$$

Since he has earlier assumed that the Jacobian of this system has a positive determinant and negative trace everywhere, local stability of an equilibrium is assured. Since Mundell draws all curves as linear (I do not know why), one also obtains global stability.

Now something rather odd is going on in this system, for it is not meant to be a tâtonnement yet it seems difficult to give it any other interpretation. Let E_{ij} be the expenditure of j (in j currency) in i. Let

$$B_h = E_{hw} - E_{wh}$$

remembering $r \equiv 1$ — that is, the *ex ante* balance of payments (or trade here). If B_h is also the actual balance then E_{hw} must be satisfied by suppliers in h. This in turn must mean that either h citizens are rationed in h goods or h suppliers are rationed in what they can sell. But how can that be when suppliers can always sell whatever they wish abroad (they act as perfect competitors) and buyers can always buy whatever they wish abroad? Or put more simply: should not the rationing affect the evolution of the economy, for example if h citizens cannot buy as many h goods as they plan would that not affect their desire for w goods? At the very least shouldn't account be taken of unplanned changes in money balances which result from the frustration of purchase or sales by agents in h? Mundell offers neither guidance nor discussion.

Let me briefly discuss a way out of this and, incidentally, illustrate possible stability when there may be many equilibria.

Suppose that $(p_h(0), \bar{M}_h(0))$, the initial conditions, yield $X_{gh} = 0$. Assume that p_h changes instantaneously to keep $X_{gh} = 0$, i.e.

$$(X_{ghp})p'\dot{p}_h + X_{ghm}\dot{\bar{M}}_h \equiv (X_{ghp})p'\dot{p}_h + X_{ghm}B_h = 0$$

so

$$\dot{p}_h = -\left(\frac{X_{ghm}}{(X_{ghp})p'}\right)B_h$$

Choose units so that $ky_h = 1$ and consider $V = \frac{1}{2}(X_{mh})^2$. Then

$$\dot{V} = \left[-\frac{X_{ghm}}{(X_{ghp})p'} - 1\right]X_{mh}^2$$

since by our assumptions $X_{mh} \equiv B_h$. We assume $X_{ghm} > 0$ and $X_{ghp} < 0$. So provided that

$$\left|\frac{X_{ghm}}{(X_{ghp})p'}\right| < 1$$

over a given domain and we can ensure that $(\bar{M}_h(t), p_h(t))$ is bounded, one has $X_{hm} \to 0$ and so $B_h \to 0$. However, these conditions do not preclude multiple equilibria.

Of course this is only an illustration of what might go on. It has the virtue of making economic sense of the dynamics, although it is hardly plausible economic sense.

Devaluation

Mundell argues that r has no effect on equilibrium real magnitudes. Here is the argument. Remove the assumption $r \equiv 1$ so $q(r) = p_h/r$ when $p_w \equiv 1$ and $p = p(p_h, r) = rp(q(r))$. Consider again the equilibrium $(p_h^0, \bar{M}_h^0)$ with $r \equiv 1$. Now let $r' = h$. Then if $p' = hp(q(1))$ and $q(1) = q(r')$, the economy is still in equilibrium with $\bar{M}_h' = h\bar{M}_h^0$. This follows from the absence of money illusion.

But while the argument that every equilibrium real magnitude is independent of r is correct, the assertion that a change in r will leave real magnitudes unaffected does not follow. For as we have already noted, equilibrium in general is not unique. Not only may a particular equilibrium be unstable, but by setting and holding r at some level the authorities may ensure a preferred equilibrium.

Government deficit

Let D_h be the government deficit $(G-T)$. Then, neglecting the tâtonnement difficulty,

$$\dot{M}_h = B_h + D_h$$

In equilibrium, $X_{gh} = X_{mh} = 0$ so $B_h + D_h = 0$. Hence a government deficit simply means that the money pumped in by the government leaks abroad through $B_h < 0$. Once again the view that D_h can be used to guide the economy to a satisfactory equilibrium out of several is not discussed.

These are some of the main technical difficulties. The economic ones seem to me more severe yet.

First, the money wage flexibility – in both directions and instantaneously – which is postulated has no merit. Nor can one, as Johnson so often does, appeal to 'the long run' when one is examining a dynamic process of the kind proposed. Secondly, the absence of a modelling of the demand for physical assets which have been produced in the past, or physical assets such as land, or financial assets like shares and bonds is serious. It just is not true that a shortfall of intended expenditure over income is necessarily equal to intended hoarding. It may reflect a desire to acquire land, buildings, shares or bonds. Granted that Mundell and others are after simple models one must surely ask for a minimal robustness. Thirdly, although it is true that in long run equilibrium all sorts of ratios are constant, it is surely highly implausible to suppose that in the short run the ratio of desired real balances to real income is a constant. Suppose the economy, because of past mistakes, had a high excess capacity of equipment. Would that not be reflected on real balances demanded? Mundell, as we shall see, probably would answer affirmatively. Then what is the point of the whole exercise?

The answer is: to exhibit essentials. What are they? Actual surpluses and deficits in B are associated with changes in the money stock and this affects behaviour. But for *that* we do not need the model. Or perhaps the essential is that the economy will by these money stock changes alone achieve $B = 0$. But that has not been proved theoretically or made plausible empirically.

So on to Mundell II. Here I must warn the reader that my account is hindered by the circumstance that some of what Mundell has to say is to me impenetrable.

There are now three assets: money, claims and capital. If m represents real money balances, then $i(m)$, with $i'(m) < 0$, gives the money rate of interest which at the given m will make agents willing to hold the outstanding stock of securities. I do not know whether this stock is fixed, is growing at a constant rate or, indeed, whether it is government or private debt. Mundell writes: 'When the rate of interest rises people shift out of money into claims raising the price level and lowering the real value of money balances.' (FJ, p. 93) No explanation is offered. I suppose he has in mind that when people want less money (and more debt) the quantity equation drives up prices. But that means he has another equation in the background: demand for goods = supply of goods and that we are to take output as fixed. But who knows?

Next if K is the capital stock and R the marginal product of capital, one would have thought that $R = R(K)$. Not a bit of it. We get $R = R(K, m)$ with 'an increase in the quantity of real monetary balances . . . raises the marginal product of capital' (FJ, p. 94). That again is all. No explanation, no discussion. I have tried hard to make sense of this, even at the cost of some rather odd assumptions, but cannot. In any case, once K is given we can write $R(m)$, with $R'(m) > 0$, as the marginal product of capital at which, given m, the given stock of capital will be held. It is also assumed that R is homogeneous of degree zero in K and m. As I say: I do not understand.

If π is the inflation rate which is also expected, then in asset equilibrium,

$$i(m) - \pi = R(m)$$

But now we concentrate on the quasi-stationary state where growth is at the rate λ and the nominal money stock is growing at the rate μ. In the stationary state m/y = constant, whence on differentiating with respect to time,

$$\pi = \mu - \lambda$$

So in asset equilibrium,

$$i(m) + \lambda - \mu = R(m) \tag{12.4}$$

Since $i'(m) < 0$ and $R'(m) > 0$, a higher λ means that the steady state m satisfying equation (12.4) is higher, and a higher μ means that the steady state m satisfying (12.4) is lower. 'The comparative statics of the system are thus established.' (FJ, p. 96)

The reader must judge for himself whether he thinks this is the way to theorise in economics.

Now to the balance of payments, I reintroduce the subscripts h and w. Let

$$\dot{M}_j = \mu_j \dot{M}_j + \dot{M}_j^*, \qquad j = h, w$$

where $\dot{M}_j^* = B_j$, from which

$$\dot{M}_h^* + \dot{M}_w^* = 0 \tag{12.5}$$

assuming $r \equiv 1$. But m_j / y_j = constant, so on differentiating,

$$\lambda_j \bar{m}_j = (\mu_j - \pi)\bar{m}_j + \frac{\dot{M}_j^*}{p}, \qquad j = h, w$$

where p is the price level (the same everywhere). Using equation (12.5) to eliminate the starred variable, we obtain

$$\frac{\bar{m}_h}{\bar{m}_w} = \frac{\mu_w - \pi - \lambda_w}{\lambda_h + \pi - \mu_h}$$

So that we have an expression for the distribution of real money balances between h and w. Also,

$$\pi = \sum_j (\mu_j - \lambda_j) \frac{\bar{m}_j}{\bar{m}_u} \tag{12.6}$$

where $\bar{m}_u = \bar{m}_h + \bar{m}_w$.

Now $(\lambda_j + \pi - \mu_j)$ evidently has the sign of B_j (since it has the sign of $\dot{M}_j^*$). So suppose, for instance, that $\mu_h = \mu_w = \lambda_w = 0$. Then h has a trade surplus (since $\lambda_h + \pi > 0$) and w a deficit. The world is earning a seignorage by supplying h with money for goods. Also from equation (12.6) $\pi < 0$ so there are capital gains on real balances. Vary the above assumptions by taking $\mu_h > 0$, but $\lambda_h = 0$. Then $\pi > 0$. But also $B_h < 0$ and $B_w > 0$ (since $\pi - \mu_h < 0$). So the money stock of w is growing and h does not suffer the full consequences of inflation; some of them are passed on to w by exporting money which w wants because $\pi > 0$. 'The public determines the quantity of money it wants to hold and the rate at which it is increased, whereas the central bank determines the part of it which is backed by foreign reserves.' (FJ, p. 107)

The system is closed by adding to equation (12.6):

$$i_j(m_j) - \pi = R(m_j), \qquad j = h, w$$

And that is the end of the story.

At this stage I am concerned with objections which apply to this mode of theorising and not to the monetary approach as such:

(a) Once again, the total neglect of money wages, and indeed of the labour market, is deplorable.

(b) Mundell (and other authors) assumes that h can sell to w at the going price whatever it wishes to. This is because h is 'small.' Yet h is large enough to spread inflation to w. Is the world's inflation rate really sensitive to the monetary policy of Haiti?

(c) Growth is exogenous like manna. So Haiti's growth is quite independent of the world's growth. Moreover no distinction is made between the growth in productivity and growth in population. Thus India's B will be the same whether it has a 5 per cent population growth at constant income per head or a 5 per cent growth in income per head and no population growth.

(d) The point in (c) is partly connected with the view of international trade as the exchange of a single good for money – no international division of labour here.

(e) World goods markets are in instantaneous equilibrium and growth is never limited by a lack of demand.

(f) There is a consistent confusion between propositions concerning quasi-stationary equilibria and causal propositions – e.g. '... for any given rate of monetary expansion in A an *increase* in the rate of *credit* expansion is inflationary for the world as a whole' (FJ, p. 103, first italics mine). Not so. He has nothing to say about the consequences of an 'increase'. What he means is that, in comparing two steady states in which the rate of credit expansion in the given country is higher and always has been higher in one state than another, certain propositions follow. No doubt Mundell knows this but the language is an invitation to dangerous mistakes.

As I have already noted, many of these objections apply to most of the papers in this volume, although there are exceptions. In particular, some of the authors, e.g. Frenkel, do consider international capital movements, although none is prepared to consider a speculative or uncertain world. I have dwelled on Mundell's contribution not only because he is one of the leaders of the monetary approach but also because his paper is a good illustration of the difficulty one has of disentangling the fruitful from the naïve, sometimes careless and almost always simplistic monetarist theorising.

III TRUE AND FALSE SCENTS

Mussa writes: 'The balance of payments is an essentially, but not exclusively, monetary phenomenon.' (FJ, p. 189) Why? Because if $B > 0$ the monetary authorities are purchasing foreign exchange, and vice versa for $B < 0$. Hence '. . . analysis of the balance of payments in a theoretical framework where money is not explicitly present is prima facie nonsense' (FJ, p. 189). On similar grounds the market for cheese is an essentially monetary phenomenon. Why? Because if some cheese is sold from stock rather than current production then cheese makers must be purchasing money stocks from households, etc. etc. Here we have a false scent. An economy where money is a medium of exchange and a store of value is best analysed by means of a theory in which money makes an appearance. It does make anything an 'essentially monetary phenomenon' any more than making anything an essentially cheese phenomenon. This sort of language is unhelpful and surely muddling. Mussa no doubt understands this (see FJ, p. 190) but when he feels uncomfortable he translates into 'money plays a vital role' which is not much better. Recent work suggests strongly that a theoretical model with money may yield importantly different results from one without money, and that for every market.

Next Mussa writes that the second basic feature of the monetary approach is 'the use of the money supply process and, particularly, the demand for money function as the central theoretical relationship around which to organise thought concerning the balance of payments' (FJ, p. 190). Later this is supplemented by the well known claim that this function has been empirically shown to be stable. This looks like a neutral scent since one cannot quarrel with the way in which a man organises his thoughts, although the empirical claims are on a different footing. But let us pursue this a little further.

(a) When $E \neq Y$ there is no *logical* entailment of an imbalance in the markets for financial assets. I am of course considering *ex ante* imbalances. For instance when $E < Y$ there may be an excess demand for 'property', e.g. houses, office buildings, etc. A higher price (lower yield) on these may ensure $E = Y$. The money equations may not enter the picture at all.

(b) Suppose that besides money there are government bonds. If X_b is the value of their excess demand, then by the usual arithmetic:

$$X_g - B + X_m + X_b = 0$$

Consider the case $X_m = X_g = 0$. If $B > 0$ then $X_b > 0$. The government 'sterilises' the inflow of money by satisfying the thirst for securities. Suppose $B < 0$ and $X_b < 0$. The government sterilises the outflow of money by selling securities. In either case adjustment proceeds without a change in the money balances in the hands of the public.

(c) Suppose we have $X_g - B \equiv E - Y = 0$. Suppose $B < 0$. Then this means domestic producers cannot sell to foreigners what they have left over after satisfying home producers – a case certainly not unknown. Assume now that money wages are fixed and suppose we are looking for a 'full employment' equilibrium. So let us set the exchange rate lower. That will mean higher home prices of imports and perhaps higher home prices of home produced goods because of the import content in their production. Real cash balances will be lower but so will be real wages. The lower real cash balances will make the excess supply of goods worse. But real profit (of exporters) may be higher and that has to be set against lower real wages in considering the effect on E. It is of course not true that E is independent of the relation of real wages to real profits. But certainly we must consider the possibility that foreigners will now demand more of home produced goods and that home citizens will demand fewer imports and perhaps spend more at home. Our real cash balances do not affect foreigners' demand for our goods, whereas their effect on our demand for foreigners' goods may be dwarfed by the effect of lower real wages.

In fact, suppose the government always keeps E equal to full employment income by means of deficits. Then in looking for a 'full employment exchange rate' the money equation plays no role at all. Of course I am here concerned with the short run. What is important here is the pricing behaviour of producers and of labour and the income and substitution elasticities of demand of citizens and foreigners.

(d) Of course the money wage assumptions of (c) are drastic. They are meant to highlight a general point. Agents in an economy not only experience prices but also situations in which they cannot buy or sell as much as they want. If this 'quantity' experience leads to prices changing, it must be that some agent is changing prices. An equilibrium of the economy is one where (a) all agent's actions which are best for them in the light of price and quantity experience are compatible and (b) no agent wants to change prices. The authors of this volume, by sticking to an auctioneer view of (b), neglect the possibility of non-Walrasian equilibria. In general there may be many of them. The point is of particular relevance in considering the pricing of labour. Concentrating on the mone-tarist X_m is of little help here and is potentially harmful.

(e) It is a characteristic of the monetary approach that it does not split expenditure into investment and consumption. When the stock of productive capital is brought into the picture (Mundell, Frenkel) I fear that it is treated in the neo-classical textbook way, in which capital goods are malleable and transferable. Only in long run equilibrium are we free of this worry. Short run matters, as everyone knows, are rather different. In particular, given the great imperfections in the market for bolted down, second hand capital goods the latter may be held but not planned to be re-placed. Agents may demand more cash balances than exist, not because their cash balances are below their normal long run level, but because their stock of old machines is too high. Moreover even if the price of old capital goods behaved 'perfectly', so as to allow us to assume that all 'own rates of return' are equated, this may mean that their price is now too low to make it profitable to produce new capital goods. To write $X_m = kY - \overline{M}$ and $X_m = Y - E$ is neither logically sound nor plausible in the short run. But that is what Dornbusch does write (FJ, p. 174). But the long run is interesting only if the short runs lead to it. Rodriguez is more careful but he also assumes that the counterpart of $Y - E$ > 0 is an excess of kY, the desired stock of all financial assets over their stock. He writes: 'The desired stock of financial assets is taken to be a constant fraction k of income.' (FJ, p. 226) This in an essay designed 'to analyse some of the dynamic implications of the endogeneity of the money supply implicit in a trading world with fixed exchange rates' (FJ, p. 223). He shares with his co-contributors the absence of a need to justify such assumptions.

I conclude from this that although X_m may be useful in studying B it appears to be rather dangerous.

But let us turn to the next feature of the monetary approach: 'a concentration on the longer run consequences of policy and parametric changes for the behaviour of the balance of payments, coupled with an eclectic view of the processes through which such longer run consequences come about' (Mussa, FJ, p. 193). Having appealed to well known monetarist 'empirical facts' Mussa proceeds: 'Therefore the advocacy of the monetary approach to the balance of payments necessarily involves the assertion that these "longer-run consequences" materialise within a time horizon of two or three years.' (FJ, p. 193) If the reader has judged me as too sour and ungenerous thus far, passages such as this must excuse it. Any economist willing to make the unconditional assertion here proposed is in the wrong profession.

But let us accentuate the positive and consider the scent here offered by looking at the use made of it by Mussa. As usual in this volume, there are many pictures and community indifference curves but we can happily do without them. I ignore Mussa's discussion of the 'real', i.e. non-monetary, economy since here his conclusion is identical with his assumption − namely that because community indifference curves exists and production sets are convex, equilibrium is unique.

Let us now consider an economy, with no capital goods, capable of producing two goods. Labour appears to be in completely inelastic supply, money wages are not fixed (they always are instantaneously 'correct'?) and the long run equilibrium is a stationary state. If good 1 is exported, good 2 imported, then relative world prices $q^* = p_2^*/p_1^*$ are exogenously given and the internal relative prices are

$$q(\tau) = (1 + \tau)q^*$$

where τ is the *ad valorem* tariff. Let $y(\tau)$ be the income in terms of good 1 of our agents − which consists of wages, profits and the proceeds from tariffs. Lastly let r be the rate of interest on securities.

If lower case letters represent nominal variables in terms of good 1, write

$$x_m = x_m (q(\tau), y(\tau), r, \overline{m})$$

$$e - y(\tau) \equiv x_e = x_e(q(\tau), y(\tau), r, \overline{m})$$

where $y(\tau)$ is income, including tariff receipts, in terms of good 1. *Assume*

$$x_{gi} = 0, \qquad i = 1, 2$$

where x_{gi} is the excess demand for good i. Since $q(\tau)$ is known we may use these two goods equations to obtain

$$y(\tau) = y(r, \overline{m}, q(\tau))$$

This allows us to write:

$$x_m = \tilde{x}_m (q(\tau), r, \overline{m})$$

$$x_e = \tilde{x}_e(q(\tau), r, \overline{m})$$

which are two 'reduced form' equations.

Long run equilibrium relative to τ is a pair $(r^0(\tau), \overline{m}^0(\tau))$ such that $\tilde{x}_m = \tilde{x}_e = 0$. In view of $x_{g1} + q(\tau)x_{g2} \equiv p_1(e - y) + B = 0$, we know that $B = 0$ in the long run equilibrium. It follows from the definition that a tariff can do nothing to affect the long run B since it must be zero.

But consider $d\overline{m}^0(\tau)/d\tau$. Since (at fixed exchange rates) the price of good 1 is fixed, this is equivalent to considering the comparative long run equilibrium effect of a change in τ on nominal money balances. If $d\overline{m}^0(\tau)/d\tau > 0$ and if the money stock can only change via B, then the country had better have $B > 0$ for a while in order to accumulate money. But that is fine, for it is assumed that $x_e < 0$ whenever $\overline{m}^0(\tau) > \overline{m}$; and since there is never any excess demand for goods, this means $B > 0$. The 'eclectic mechanism' churns out the answer: the long run effect of a higher tariff is a different stock of cash with a zero balance of payments. It is only by allowing for money that this is possible, i.e. that $y^0(\tau)$

may be different, for when there is no cash we know from the textbooks that a tariff cannot help a country facing perfectly elastic offer curves and having a community indifference curve.

Now I cannot believe that there can be much disagreement with the view that this is a pretty terrible model which is not likely to be robust. For instance, in the world a tariff may affect employment and there must be ways in which cash balances are also changed by other means than $B \neq 0$. Here there is another example of my earlier complaint: it is difficult to detect what might be a promising scent through the odours of the particular model.

We know that tariffs are sometimes proposed as a means of increasing or maintaining employment or as a means of exploiting a country's monopoly power. Since in the present model there is neither unemployment nor monopoly such arguments do not apply. But non-monetary models pay no attention to the real balance effect of tariffs. The result of a tariff is higher import prices and thus lower real cash balances. Provided the impact on $y(\tau)$ is not perverse, agents will attempt to restore their real balances and hence spend less than they earn. By *assumption*, namely that the goods and labour market are in instantaneous equilibrium, this implies $B > 0$ and cash balances increase. The economy moves smoothly to a new long run equilibrium which may be different from the original since money is a non-produced good whose relative price can be changed by τ. I think we ought to agree that this result is of mild interest largely because little theory seems to be available on tariffs in a monetary economy.

But the weakness of this monetary scent is also clear. Suppose that it takes time to shift resources from one use to another. Then the impact of the tariff may be $B < 0$ because home citizens find that they must buy abroad the goods they wish to substitute for imports – that is, one may have $x_{g2} > 0$. Moreover, if we drop the assumption that output is provided by labour alone (and that ploughs can produce shoes) there must be net investment in the transition, as well as capital losses on machines used in the sector which has to contract. Further, the expanding sector must attract labour from the contracting one (peasants into toolmakers in 'three years'?). One could go on. For instance, although there may be a world price for family cars, this does not mean that British Leyland can sell to the Germans whatever they like at that price. It only means that they cannot charge more without losing most of their customers or charge less without strong retaliation. It may be that given long enough the whole converges to a Mussa equilibrium. But of all the forces to be considered the real cash balance effects seem the least, not the most important.

Let me sum up more generally. Johnson is right to claim it an improvement on the absorption approach to take account of changes in the money stock implied by the balance of payments. If nothing else, the logic of the accounting sheet makes this desirable. But beyond this I believe that the monetary approach has its main fruits in the comparison of long run steady state equilibria. In such equilibria all relative quantities remain constant and monetarists can tread safely. But in stories of adjustment the contributors to this volume have assumed away almost every interesting mechanism and then ask us to share their joy at the discovery that only real balance effects remain to do the job. In particular it is vexing to find that a desire to accumulate financial assets must always mean a balance of payments surplus *because* it is assumed that the market for goods is always in equilibrium. When that assumption is occasionally not made one resorts to an auctioneer. The adjustment story is not only 'eclectic', it is downright bad, and is presented as if there were not forty years of economic theorising to be at least considered. At a time when almost everyone concerned with the equilibrium models of Walras is frantically trying to get it into a form where it can account for money, for an uncertain future, for imperfect information and for unemployment, we are given little perfect competition textbook models. At a time when we are increasingly aware that there is no theory of adjustment, i.e. no understanding of it, we are given the assertion that long run equilibrium will be achieved in three years. Why do economists always claim so much more than they can deliver? Would we offer cancer cures with the same certainties as we offer economic cures?

This brings me to my last section.

IV POLICIES

'In a fundamental sense, monetary policy can have no lasting impact on the income level of a small open economy under fixed exchange rates.' (Swoboda, FJ, p. 238) To prove this *only* three assumptions are needed . . . (1) that the economic system is stable (2) that an increase in the money supply from equilibrium tends to create a balance of payments deficit, and (3) that the associated reserve loss tends to reduce the money supply' (Swoboda, FJ, p. 239). The 'proof,' when it comes, turns out to require a little more, in particular the ubiquitous uniqueness of long run equilibrium.

The point of Swoboda's proposition, which is in the monetary approach tradition, is quite simple. Unless home monetary policy affects the world stock of money (home is not small), the home authorities cannot exercise any control over the financial assets held by the home public. Why? Because by definition there is a unique equilibrium in which home citizens spend what they earn. Now money prices are given because the exchange rate and prices are given in the large world. If there is perfect capital mobility, i.e. if the rate of interest is given, and if real output is given, that only leaves real cash balances as an unknown to make $E = Y$. Since this gives a unique answer, say m^0, and since $m > m^0$ has been assumed to give $E > Y$, the balance of payments will see to it that surplus money balances are lost. The monetary authorities cannot hold $m > m^0$ by replacing dwindling reserves, for a point will come when there are no reserves left to dwindle.

This story is not modified if there is less than perfect capital mobility. If (i^0, m^0) are the long run equilibrium interest rate and real money stock, they are unique, and since money prices are given and the system is assumed stable, the same conclusion results. Even if there are non-traded goods so that their money prices can change, the uniqueness of m^0 and the plausible view that non-traded goods price variations cannot fully counteract a variation in the nominal money stock keeps the old result intact.

When our country is large enough that the world money stock is affected by our monetary policy, there is a small variation in the story. We now need to think of a universal long run equilibrium, e.g. a condition of equilibrium is that:

$$x_{gui} \equiv x_{ghi} + x_{gwi} = 0$$

$$x_{mu} \equiv x_{mh} + x_{mw} = 0$$

where x_{gui} is the universal excess demand for good i and x_{mu} is the universal excess demand for real cash balances. These universal excess demands will depend on the universal money stock and on its distribution between h and w. Since we cannot now take prices as known, universal steady state equilibrium cannot determine one's nominal money balances uniquely. But in the perfect competition/unique competition (full employment) equilibrium situation, real magnitudes in long run equilibrium are still independent of home monetary policy. But of course if $\overline{M}_h$ is replaced by $k\overline{M}_h$ we will not have p^0 replaced by kp^0, since the world money stock does not change by the proportion k.

Matters are more interesting in the 'Keynesian' case, which Swoboda does not define. Suppose we take it to mean fixed money prices and wages and the rationing of agents in the amount of work they can do. Hence the excess demand no longer depends on prices and real assets alone but also on Y_h. Let h be small and consider the case of complete capital immobility. We have $X_e - B + X_m + X_b = 0$, and each of these excess demands depends on $(Y, i, \overline{M})$. We solve for their long run equilibrium value by setting $X_e = B = X_m = 0$. Although X_e and X_m are homogenous of degree one in Y and $\overline{M}$, this is not true for B. It is assumed that the equations have a unique solution $(Y^0, i^0, \overline{M}^0)$. If capital mobility is allowed, say perfect mobility, this would give $i^0 = i_w$. Hence a change in the monetary base of h can have no permanent effect on employment, whereas increased government demand for goods could. (Mundell has studied this but his study is not in this volume.) On the other hand if h is large we can take account of the assumption that B is homogeneous of degree one in Y_h, Y_w, $\overline{M}_h$, $\overline{M}_w$. For the universal economy we gain one degree of freedom and h's monetary policy can permanently influence Y_h (as well as Y_w).

We have, I think, finally come to a point where the monetary approach is to be given full credit. For however primitive the models and unrigorous the adjustment analysis, an important conclusion emerges: what has been taken as autonomous — the stock of financial assets in orthodox analysis — may be endogenous. The final money stock may not be controllable by domestic authorities. Anyone concerned with economic policy must take this Humeian insight into consideration. The proposed models will not help much (nor the straight line curves in all the diagrams!), nor do I think the quantity equation of great interest, but the fundamental point on which I quoted Johnson at the beginning — that both stock and flows must be considered — remains valid.

On the other hand, one must be on one's guard. $B < 0$, as I have repeatedly noted, is not of itself evidence, as the IMF believes, that the money stock or 'credit base' is too large. Moreover, a policy of taking the decline in the credit base 'on the chin', i.e. not offsetting $B < 0$ by domestic money creation, may not bring about the desired equilibrium or lead to an undesirable one. For instance, if investment is the carrier of technical progress and if the IMF policy leads to a fall in real demand and thus investment, one can easily construct models in which this policy would be foolish. I must confess that I find the assumption of a perfectly competitive export market far fetched (shipping?) although, as already noted, export prices may indeed have to be taken as given. Lastly, I consider the behaviour of money wages and of labour mobility of much more importance than given here and I do not believe that the long run economic history of a country is well represented by steady state equilibrium. This is especially the case when no attention is paid to the long run forces which determine a country's growth in productivity. So let us take the insight of the monetary approach seriously but let us agree that it is impossible to draw any confidence-inspiring policy conclusions on the basis of the models here given.

That leaves the exchange rate. Johnson kindly refers to a paper of mine (Hahn, 1959), although he found it too mathematical. In that paper I used a Patinkin-like general equilibrium model of the universe with two currencies. I had to make unpalatable assumptions to get uniqueness and stability. But the conclusion was then both clear and obvious: exchange rate changes had to work through the real cash balance effect. I would now like to say that I do not think much of my effort. It was a model without time and without quantity constraints and so it was not a model which could be taken very seriously. Of course it could readily be converted into a quasi-stationary model of growth but that would not help.

The authors of this book do recognise that exchange rates may affect real magnitudes through compositional effects but 'a devaluation is foremost a monetary phenomenon and . . . its effects derive from the reduction in the real value of money attendant upon a devaluation' (Dornbusch, FJ, p. 185). Dornbusch proceeds very much as I proceeded twenty years earlier, although he improves on that by also considering non-traded goods.

Dornbusch (like myself) simply takes full employment for granted and says nothing about money wages. This does not seem very interesting in 1977. One of the most important questions one has to answer now is whether the real wage can be reduced by a devaluation. If it can there will certainly be important compositional effects and real output effects even if the real money stock is kept constant. This transfers interest from the money market to the labour market. For instance, a boost in income may improve the balance of payments on Dornbusch's own assumptions even if the real money stock is constant, for it will raise desired cash balances.

So I can be quite brief on this matter. The monetary approach considers devaluation from the point of view of a Walrasian model à la Patinkin. That model (twenty years on) seems quite incapable of bearing the weight put on it – in particular one would have to have quite singular faith to base policy recommendations on it.

ENVOI

The 'monetary approach to the balance of payments' has surely made a contribution through what I have called its main insight. But there is not a single proposition of importance in the theoretical pieces reviewed here which is clinched or if clinched, robust. This is a great pity. For the insight itself is very simple and, as Johnson notes, old. Surely the intellectual effort should have gone into integrating it into modern, and not old textbook, theory. This opinion I base on the following. Economists, especially those concerned with policy, are always in danger of becoming witch doctors. One of the virtues of careful theorising, even in small models, is that it makes one aware of the very conditional nature of any predictions. It also engenders a healthy scepticism about simple regressions and induction. Above all it should make economists, when they advise, urge that options should be kept open and not all eggs put in one basket. They must realise that their advice is based on slender evidence and incomplete theory.

REFERENCES

Frenkel, J. A. and Johnson, H. C. (eds) 1976. *The Monetary Approach to the Balance of Payments*, Allen and Unwin

Hahn, F. H. 1959. The balance of payments in a monetary economy, *Review of Economic Studies*, 26, February, chapter 11 above.

13

Professor Friedman's Views on Money

> It is a commonplace in economics that one can seldom get something for nothing . . ... As yet, no substitute has been found for the explicit examination of a wide range of evidence, the rigorous excogitation of the links between premises and conclusions, and the thorough testing and amending of tentative findings. (Friedman, 1969, p. 260)

I

The publishers tell us that *The Optimum Quantity of Money* constitutes a 'comprehensive presentation of Professor Friedman's body of monetary thought'. I shall assume that Professor Friedman agrees with this description, and almost all the references in this review[1] will be to this book.[2]

The most obvious point to be made at once is that Friedman neither has nor claims to have a monetary theory. His strong and influential views are not founded on an understanding of 'how money works' but on what his empirical studies have led him to believe to have been the course of monetary history. He himself, at least in this book, claims no more. His celebrated policy recommendations themselves depend on a plea of ignorance.

---

[1] Numerous friends commented on a first draft. In particular I should like to acknowledge the detailed and helpful comments of Charles Goodhart, Nicholas Kaldor, Kurt Klappholz, Robin Matthews, Robert Solow and James Tobin. I have benefited much from their help without always accepting their advice. Responsibility is my own.

[2] I refer to the book as *OQM*. All page references in the text are to *OQM*.

Yet he writes: 'However consistent may be the relation between monetary change and economic change and however strong the evidence for the autonomy of monetary changes, we shall not be persuaded that the monetary changes are the source of the economic changes unless we can specify in some detail the mechanism that connects one with the other.' (p. 229) This, to many, very agreeable statement is however found in a section headed 'A tentative sketch of the mechanism transmitting monetary changes', and he emphasises 'that this sketch is exceedingly tentative and of course not preclusive' (p. 235). Nowhere else is there to be found 'in some detail', let alone with rigour, a theoretical foundation of the sought-for connection between monetary and real changes. In view of this and the quotation there are two puzzles: Friedman's surprise that some economists remain 'unpersuaded', and the high probability which he evidently attaches to the eventuality that his views are the right ones.

It should not be thought that Friedman rejects, as some writers do, highbrow and sophisticated theory. Quite the contrary. He makes repeated but, alas, informal and inadequate appeals to it. Thus he wants to speak of the 'natural' level of unemployment as that level which 'would be ground out by the Walrasian system of general equilibrium equations' (p. 102), which he takes for this purpose to cover market imperfections, stochastic variability in demands and supplies, costs of mobility etc. As far as I know, no one has ever succeeded in writing down such equations nor in 'grinding out' the natural level of unemployment from them. I also doubt that such a task is well formulated. Again, Friedman appeals to a sophisticated theory of household behaviour. But to justify the dependence of the demand for money on 'permanent prices' he is satisfied with the following: 'Holders of money presumably judge the 'real' amount of cash balances in terms of the quantity of goods and services to which the balances are equivalent, not at any given moment of time, but over a sizable and indefinite period.' (p. 121) The force of the word 'presumably' here is obscure and I return to this matter below. Here I simply note the casual theorising. There are many other instances of this lack of seriousness, not least in the title essay which is the most theoretical. Some of these will be taken up later. But the general point is an important one, for we all know the difficulties of statistical inference in the absence of a precisely articulated theory, and it is on the statistics that Friedman in the final analysis rests his case. He and his associates have performed a splendid and difficult task in their studies of monetary history, but they and we are a long way not only from a monetary theory but from a tested monetary theory.

The present book consists of a series of essays written at different times. Besides the title essay and his presidential address to the American Economic Association, Friedman has included his introductory piece to *Studies in the Quantity Theory of Money*, two essays on the demand for money (theoretical and empirical), a historical essay on prices, money and income in wartime periods, studies on money in the business cycle and the lagged effects of monetary policy as well as studies on the supply of money and price and output changes. There are also reflections on Henry Simon and a defence of destablising speculation.

In what follows I propose to concentrate on the theoretical problems raised by Friedman's views. The latter, in a very general way, may be summarised by saying that he finds good correlations between changes in the monetary stock and changes in money income and prices, all appropriately dated and defined, and that he concludes that monetary changes are good explanations of these other changes. But there is a good deal more than that, certainly in this book, and I shall come to deal with this aspect of the story rather later in this article. My plan is as follows. I first discuss Friedman's treatment of the demand for money. Next I take up his theory of the 'optimum quantity of money'. I then turn to his view that a 'long run real equilibrium' cannot be affected by monetary policy. In the last section I discuss the theory of the effect of monetary changes on other variables.

There is one caveat I should like to enter before I start. I shall often be very critical of Firedman's position on grounds both of logic and of economics. This may give the impression that I am in possession of correct answers. I wish to warn against this *non sequitur.* On the contrary, it is a good part of my own position that the formulation of a model of an economy which can account for money is immensely difficult and remains to be accomplished. In particular is this the case when a monetary economy in long run equilibrium is the basis of an argument. Not only do I consider such a description not at present available, but I am not even sure of the appropriate meaning to give to 'equilibrium', or indeed whether this is the right conceptual framework to look for.

II

In his analysis of the demand for money Professor Friedman appeals to 'non-pecuniary' and 'productive services' which money is supposed to yield. The former consist of a 'feeling of security and pride of possession' (p. 24). All assets and not just money yield non-pecuniary services: 'A key point of our analysis is . . . that every form of holding wealth may yield non-pecuniary returns.' (p. 40) Technically, different assets enter as separate arguments of the utility functions. I suppose they all yield the same 'pride of possession', so that this procedure is to be explained by the difference in their yield of 'security services'.

I find this both difficult to understand and unsatisfactory. If we put money into the utility function, we also include money prices because it is believed that the services of money are related to what money can buy. But security services cannot depend solely on the current or indeed on the 'permanent' price level. Friedman does not tell us what parameters to include in the utility function so that their variation can reflect differing security services rendered by a stock of money in different market circumstances. One might for instance put some certainty equivalent price level into the utility function; but this would require some attenton to be paid to the variance etc. in prices, and in any case would be very hard to justify.

In any event Friedman gives no indication of how security services should be represented or on what they depend, and is content with a 'marginal utility of money'. It seems to me that this rather common procedure is as effective a way as any of stopping thought on some of the fundamental issues of monetary theory. When it then leads, as it does Friedman, to calculating consumer surplus triangles it also leads to error. Certainly, when *a fortiori* the marginal utility of money is a variable, and not independent of income, money is a rather difficult measuring rod for changes in the consumer surplus of money. More seriously, since expected prices are evidently involved in the demand curve for money, a consumer surplus calculation cannot be a good welfare measure should expectations be not correct. (When a man insures, believing the distribution of events against which he insures to be different from what it is, the stream of utilities which he receives may be increased by a policy which actually reduces his instantaneous utility at the time of insurance.) Moreover, since expectations are single valued, I do not know what the proper criterion of correctness would be. There are other difficulties also.

On the productive services of money Friedman offers a number of general remarks. For households it seems to be mainly trips to the bank that money balances economise. For business, money balances are substitutes for the additional bookeeping involved in more frequent payments etc. He seems to me entirely right in his view that the real balances used in these ways are the resultant of economic forces. However, he does not study these. This is a serious omission. For instance, to run ahead, the ease with which other things and arrangements can substitute for money balances must be a rather important matter for monetary policy (cf. Radcliffe Committee Report on the Working of the Monetary System, 1959). In any event we finish up with a marginal product for money which is, given a zero non-pecuniary marginal yield, the maximum interest rate an agent would be willing to pay for being able to hold an extra unit of cash balances.

Having made the utility function responsible for all matters connected with uncertainty, Friedman deals with single valued expectations. He also takes magnitudes such as wealth, permanent income etc. as well defined by a single number and as independent variables. There are a good many difficulties here which I pass over. In the background is a rational utility maximising agent. Friedman writes that 'the analysis of the demand of money ... can be made formally identical with that of the demand for a consumption service', but adds that none the less there is a substantive difference because in analysising the demand for money we must take account of 'intertemporal rates of substitution' and cast 'the budget constraint in the form of wealth' (p. 52). This seems to me plainly wrong; one does not have to recast the constraints of a utility maximising agent when one aspect of this agent's plans rather than another is in question; nor can it be true that in studying the consumption plan intertemporal rates of substitution play no part. This seems so clear that I must suppose that I have misunderstood Friedman's purpose. However, it leads me to the first substantive point where there is no question of misunderstanding.

Friedman writes: 'The quantity theorist accepts the empirical hypothesis that the demand for money is highly stable – more stable than functions such as the consumption function. ' (p. 62) He emphasises that it is the functional dependence of money on parameters, and not the demand for money or the money—income ratio, for which this superior stability is claimed. If this claim is correct either it must be taken to mean that the 'empirical hypothesis' refers to a relative lack of success in discovering correct consumption functions or it constitutes a theoretical challenge of great importance, not only for Keynesians but also for Friedman. For his methodology rests firmly on the agent of traditional theory maximising under constraint. This methodology is justifiable if (a) we can specify the variables of the objective function, and if (b) this objective function is relatively stable. But if the objective function is stable and the constraints have been properly specified, then so should be all the optimal policy functions of the agent.[3] If the objective function is volatile, then either one abandons the approach as useless or one argues that it has been wrongly specified. In the latter event, Friedman is of course right in noting the vacuity of a procedure of attempting to find stable functions by incorporating more and more variables. But my point is that in his theoretical guise he proceeds traditionally, i.e. with a stable objective function, and that he must then explain why one policy function should be more volatile than another. The same arguments apply when functions aggregated over individuals are at stake. From the fact that Friedman evidently does not consider these matters pertinent I conclude that the 'empirical hypothesis' in question is nothing more than the claim that empirically established demand functions for money have behaved 'better' than empirically established consumption functions. It is puzzling that· such a claim should be the basis of a school of economic thought. It is also possible that I have misunderstood him when he claims that the analysis of the demand for money is substantively different from the analysis of the demand for consumption and that he has in mind a well founded theoretical framework to explain the different performances of the two functions. If so, it really is rather important that he should produce it. In its absence, the view that 'the proof of this pudding is in the eating' (p. 64) is of course quite worthless.

But there is further trouble since the demand function for money

---

[3] This point should be very acceptable to the Friedman of 'The consumption function', and it may be made again in the following example. Suppose a firm facing stochastic demand conditions chooses an (s, S) stock policy. For a whole set of events stocks will behave like a residual. But the stock policy function is perfectly stable and can in principle be estimated. Friedman might conceivably be thinking of consumption as a residual in this sense. But, odd though this may be, it does not imply an unstable consumption function in the proper variables.

is not well behaved in the natural observable variables:

> Over long periods, *real* income and velocity tend to move in opposite directions; over reference cycles, in the same direction. Over long periods, changes in the nominal stock of money dominate, at least in a statistical sense, the swings in money income, and the inverse movements in velocity are of minor quantitative importance; over reference cycles, changes in velocity are in the same direction as changes in the nominal stock of money and are comparable in quantitative importance in accounting for changes in money income. (pp. 115–6)

To reconcile these findings, permanent income and permanent prices are introduced as arguments of the demand function for money.[4] In a rather obvious way one may then maintain that the 'permanent velocity', unlike the measured velocity, behaves no differently over the cycle than it does in the long run which is taken to give us points on the true demand curve for money. Similarly the behaviour of 'permanent balances', i.e. money balances deflated by permanent prices, can be taken as generated by the 'true' demand curve. The new variables allow one to maintain that the demand function for money is a stable one.

There is here displayed the ingenuity we have come to associate with Friedman; but I do not find the story convincing. First note that there are other common sense ways of reconciling the secular and cyclical behaviour of velocity. For instance, it may well be argued that the variance of the distribution of events for which precautionary balances are held is for obvious reasons smaller in the boom than in the depression. Or, to invoke another methodology, the probability of certain 'disasters' is less in the upswing than it is in the downswing. If Friedman, instead of having adopted his portmanteau utility function approach, had undertaken an an analysis of the agent's actions in the face of uncertainty, his demand function for money would have had to include parameters representing this uncertainty and there might then have been no need for any reconciliation as far as velocity is concerned. (Among

---

[4] No precise definition of these 'permanent' variables is given. When there are many assets, permanent income in the strict sense of the consumption function literature is difficult to define. Permanent prices, I suppose, are the prices expected to rule over the average. For the moment, the important point is that permanent magnitudes change by less then actual ones.

other common sense explanations one may include the sensitivity of velocity to interest rates or simply that the monetary supply is less than perfectly elastic.) However, I do not wish to propound a new theory, but rather note some of the difficulties with the one here offered.

First, permanent income in the strict sense depends, of course, on the portfolio policy (and work policy) of the agent and is not an independent variable. Friedman himself uses the concept more like 'normal income' and we shall do the same. But he considers money 'as a durable consumer good held for the services it renders and yielding a flow of services proportional to the stock' (p. 119), and also argues that among these services the 'precautionary' one is the most important (p. 137). Yet the precautionary services rendered by a unit of money depend on the calculation of abnormal and not normal events. Granted that the demand for these services depends on normal income, it is surely surprising that the quantity of such services yielded by a unit of money should be independent of whether matters are 'normal' or not. (The probability of a disease, say, may be constant, but not the cost of medical services. For business, the events making for precaution must be closely correlated with market phenomena.) Secondly, for the same reasons, it cannot be the case that at any moment of time it is the money stock deflated by permanent or 'normal' prices that is an adequate index for the precautionary services rendered by money at that moment of time. Thirdly, it must be supposed that the agent is concerned with precautionary services and not with the asset which yields them, and it is odd that the relative power to yield such services of different assets should be taken as invariant. Fourthly, what are these precautionary services anyway? One interpretation surely is that the holding of money reduces the variance in consumption. But on this interpretation, transaction costs apart, the portfolio decision is taken myopically[5] (Arrow 1964). Of course, one cannot in general separate the decision of the composition from the decision of the volume of assets, and to that extent all future expected events exert some influence on the current demand for assets. However, it remains

---

[5] The point here is this: the saving decision will in general depend on expected magnitudes of variables over the more or less distant future. In the absence of transaction costs, the composition of assets will depend only on current values and those expected for the more or less immediate future. On these grounds one would not expect 'permanent', i.e. long run, values to be very important, relative to current values and myopic expectations, in explaining the demand for money balances.

true that anything consumed has irrevocably disappeared but a portfolio decision is binding (ignoring transaction costs) for as short a period as it is sensible to take, and to that extent one would expect the present and immediate future to be much more important than the distant or normal future. Fifthly, it is odd that although Friedman makes so much of normal prices and income, he makes nothing of the normal prices of other assets which have played an important role in the Keynesian literature. If in booms the interest rate is higher than the level taken as normal, we should expect the velocity to behave as it does (as Friedman himself notes). (If in the boom, say, interest rates rise, but are expected to fall again, and vice versa in the depression, this will reinforce the expected effect of cyclical variations in interest rates and asset prices on velocity.) But, what is important, we might also expect those other assets to be better carriers of security services than they were hitherto.

Taking a leaf out of Friedman's book, I do not regard these objections as 'decisive'. Rather they are a strong indication that a proper formulation of the theory should be attempted. A model in which the expected utility of consumption over the indefinite future is the objective does not seem capable of generating Friedmanesque results. Of course, he has money in the utility function, but I doubt that that will serve. I do not know whether it is permanent or current prices which are to be included in the utility function, but the indications are that it is the former. Of that I can make no sense. Precautionary services rendered to me by money now can have nothing to do with 'the quantity of goods and services to which these balances are equivalent . . . over an . . . indefinite period'.

But there are also indications that I have been taking the whole business too seriously and that all that is meant is that people notice, and adjust to, current events with a lag. Certainly on this interpretation one could make a good case for the importance of variables which formally look like the 'permanent' ones. Indeed, in the empirical work the 'permanent' variables are simple expected values. Clearly none of the above objections applies to a proposition that at any moment of time agents are adjusted to what they expected the world to look like at that moment of time. In that case we also do not require all the paraphernalia about the services of money etc.; and the empirical results are no test of any such theory.

The empirical work, if not taken as a test of a theory, is certainly interesting and, as Friedman says, suggestive. He finds that the cyclical behaviour of the residual of the demand for money not explained by expected income or prices can be explained by changes in the relative profitability of other assets. However, it is claimed that the behaviour of the total velocity could not be explained in this way. It would be interesting to know whether this would still be the case if 'permanent' as well as 'current' yields of those assets were used in the regressions. Friedman finds the interest elasticity of demand for money to be low, but one is worried by the inclusion of interest-bearing deposits at the bank in the definition of money, which in this connection may be import-ant. However, he is perfectly correct in his assertion that no point of outstanding theoretical importance is at stake here (unless it is claimed that the interest elasticity should be infinite) (p. 150). Some of his critics have been wrong, for instance, in their claim that a zero interest elasticity necessarily implies the 'classical dichotomy'. Of course, policy judgments are indeed affected should the low interest elasticity be a correct finding. (I return to this matter below).

Although I am leaving matters of statistical technique to others more competent, I must take note of the obvious difficulties of identification posed by Friedman's single equation method. I have already quoted his declaration of faith — he calls it an 'empirical hypothesis' — that the demand function for money is stable, so that he has no doubt that his estimates are estimates of demand and not of supply. If one does not share his faith, one should like much more evidence than he gives. It is true that in other connections, for example in the monetary history of wars and gold discoveries, Friedman can argue convincingly that changes in the monetary supply were autonomous, although even here one must suppose it to have had endogenous components. (However, the effect of gold discoveries on income can be given a traditional Keynesian analysis to yield the story which Friedman observes.) As far as I can judge, it is not sufficient to attribute part of a change in the monetary stock to exogenous events to be sure that the single equation estimate is one of the demand, rather than of the supply, function of money. Friedman is aware of the difficulty but has not resolved it, especially as far as cyclical estimates are concerned. To resolve the disputed causal mechanism he appeals, among other things, to a lead in the monetary stock, but agrees that this is not decisive and elsewhere has reiterated a kind of biased agnosticism (Friedman 1970). In any event I cannot at the moment see why the equation of the demand for money could not also be taken as one of supply. Clearly much more sophisticated techniques, and in particular a good many more equations, will be required to settle the matter. As Friedman himself notes, the demand for money is more important than the demand for pins (p. 63); by the same token, a single equation estimate of the demand for pins is much more acceptable than it is of the demand for money. I return to some of these matters below.

To sum up so far. Friedman has a lazy man's theory of the demand for money in that he explains it by unanalysed utility and productive services. A consequence of this is, for instance, that he looks for no indicators of uncertainty or for independent evidence on money as a 'factor of production' in his empirical work. The claim of the superior stability of the demand function for money in the absence of a theoretical explanation seems to me at best to constitute an inducement to engage on more research on the other functions. The theoretical foundations of the permanent income and price hypothesis are not given and its intuitive appeal is not high. The single equation time series estimates may be suggestive, but by Friedman's own standards, hardly persuasive.

III

Before turning to that part of Professor Friedman's work which has important policy implications, I shall consider the academic exercise which gives this volume its title.

An economy is in equilibrium. There is an agent (or agents) prepared to pay a positive interest rate for the services of an extra unit of real cash balances. But real balances can be changed costlessly in an economy. It follows that the equilibrium cannot be Pareto efficient. If the marginal opportunity cost of holding real balances for each agent is zero, this source of Pareto inefficiency will be absent. For a reason which is not at all obvious or explained Friedman calls the real balances which would be held in these circumstances the optimum quantity for money. Friedman does not get beyond the arithmetic of a necessary condition of a Pareto optimum of the textbooks. He pays no attention whatsoever to those features of an economy which make money an important phenomenon, not even to his own view that in 'a world which is purely static and individually repetitive, clearing arrangements could be made once and for all' (p. 3) and there would be no money. He is content to consider stationary or quasi-stationary states in which all returns and prices can be treated as certain, and yet contain money.

First of all let us notice that there is no reason to suppose, money apart even, that economies in which all clearing arrangements are not made once and for all are Pareto efficient.[6] There is the singularly uninteresting possibility that every agent has single valued price expectations held with complete certainty such that the prices expected are also the correct 'shadow' or 'Debreu' prices. When there is uncertainty it is not even clear how Pareto efficiency is to be defined. When there are transaction costs similar difficulties arise, and for an appropriate definition an equilibrium even with announced prices need not be Pareto efficient (Hahn 1971). All these difficulties are intimately connected with money; indeed, without them, it is hard to find a role for money. Even should Friedman's arithmetical conditions turn out to be necessary for Pareto efficiency (where it can be properly defined), it seems heroic to say that the money stocks then held are optimal and to calculate social losses from the violation of these conditions.

It may be helpful to make this important point again, slightly differently. The necessary conditions for Pareto efficiency in a world of uncertainty with intertemporal choice will in general be fulfilled by a market economy only if money plays no role. There are therefore no grounds for supposing that the Friedman rule is either necessary or sufficient for Pareto efficiency since it is of the essence of an explanation for the existence of money that other conventional necessary conditions are violated. Even where money is only held for 'transaction purposes', Pareto efficiency relative to a transaction technology is quite a different animal from the usual textbook one.

Consider a single example. Suppose the future yield from productive capital becomes more uncertain. All agents in the economy react to this by wishing to make greater provision for the future (Levhari and Srinivasan 1969), i.e. they wish to add to their assets. However, because of the relative increase in the riskiness of productive capital, they do this — and it makes no difference to the argument to suppose so — entirely by holding more real balances, which they can always do. This means that although each agent

---

[6] Physically identical goods available at different dates are different goods. Unless at a given date the market for all goods on this definition is in equilibrium, one cannot in general show that the economy is Pareto efficient. But if there are markets for all goods at a given date, all transactions take place at that date and there can be no role for money.

believes himself to have made greater provision for the future, collectively they have not done so at all. That is, should the event occur against which they have desired increased insurance, the insurance will turn out to be illusory. There is here a case where a choice taken collectively would be different from the outcome of individual choices. The proper remedy here would not be to pay interest on money but to reduce the 'marginal utility' of money by making the prospective return on money as uncertain as in fact it is. (Of course, this does not mean that if agents want to become more liquid because they take the wrong view of real prospects, for example in a crisis of confidence, the authorities should do otherwise than supply the necessary wherewhithal.) If the answer to this example is that stationary states with no uncertainty are under discussion, then I will feel that I have made the point.

But quite apart from this chasm which exists between the treatment given and that required for this problem, there is also a variety of holes:

(a) As I have already noted, Friedman represents all rates of return by scalars, and in an 'optimum' the rates of return of all assets including money are equal. What is the 'optimum' when the rates of return are stochastic? When Friedman estimates the welfare losses for the United States, is it supposed that all assets yield the same rate of return, and if so, why?

(b) Consider the asymptotic state of two economies with identical utility measures and production opportunities. In one money earns no return, in the other it earns its marginal opportunity cost. It can be shown by examples that in general the latter economy will have less productive capital per man than does the former. The consequence of the optimum policy, unless it is combined with other policies, is lower consumption per head. What other policies (for example, the monetisation of claims to productive capital) are suggested to enable the economy to enjoy the higher monetary services without sacrificing consumption?[7]

---

[7] It is not suggested that higher real balances can be acquired by the economy as a whole only by forgoing consumption. The proposition is that the 'optimum policy' will have this consequence. Roughly speaking, this is due to agents holding a higher ratio of real balances to productive capital than they would otherwise have done. It is not suggested that therefore Friedman's policy would lower welfare. But if the authorities in addition to this policy were to increase the monetary stock − not by gifts but by buying productive capital − it might be possible to have the greater services of money without sacrificing consumption.

(c) In a Tobin–Baumol analysis of the transaction demand for money, the marginal opportunity cost of holding money is zero in equilibrium when money has no yield and is not a source of utility. If interest were paid on money equal to that which can be earned on debt, the only equilibrium would be one of zero borrowing and lending since these activities involve brokerage fees. It is not clear that one can discourage 'wasteful transactions' without also discouraging beneficial exchange between agents differently placed. Friedman pays no attention to these problems.

(d) How do we calculate the optimum inventories of goods? In a world of certainty the answer may be straightforward, although I suspect that important 'non-convexities' are essentially involved. In a world of uncertainty I do not know of an answer. But this much is clear. The 'precautionary' motive for holding money involves, as Friedman agrees, among other things the calculation that money could in certain circumstances be exchanged against goods. The possibility of actually doing so at given prices must depend on the number of agents wishing to do so at the same time and on the stocks. The 'collective insurance services' of money cannot be independent of the stocks of goods in the economy. This raises obvious externality problems. Since the 'optimum policy' will cause agents to hold higher balances relative to stocks of goods, difficulties arise in the argument that the economy now enjoys more services from money. This rather interesting and, I fancy, important matter is ignored by Friedman.

One could continue in this vein for some time. There is no doubt that Friedman is right when he notes that a private enterprise economy may not have the optimum real balances, whatever these might be. Certainly also it was worth a page to note the arithmetic of marginal benefit and cost. But after that one was entitled to expect a serious study of efficiency in an economy in which money plays an essential role. What is depressing is not only that Friedman does not give it but also that he seems quite unaware of the tasks facing a student of money.

IV

I now turn to the most difficult and most important problem raised by Professor Friedman's work. The good correlation which he finds between changes in the money stock and changes in money income and prices, all variously dated and sometimes represented by new variables such as permanent prices, leads him to claim an important causal role for the actions of the monetary authorities in changing important economic variables. This is to be taken as an 'anti-Keynesian' result (a) because he finds changes in investment expenditures to be a poor explanatory variable, and (b) because Keynesians are supposed to hold the view that money does not matter and are committed to fiscal policy. In addition he asserts that the evidence substantiates a quantity theory in generalised form, and in particular that, since the interest elasticy of demand for money is low, one may do very well in predicting money income by using the money multiplier derived from the stable money—income ratio. Lastly, it is part of the doctrine that the authorities cannot control real balances so that the long run equilibrium of the economy cannot be affected by monetary policy. This is so whether money is, say, dropped by helicopter or increased through open-market operations.

One of the main reasons why all these claims raise the difficulties they do is that Friedman has only the most rudimentary causal stories to support him and, as already argued before both by me and by him, one is not convinced until one is told. There is the further awkward fact that the most casual theorising is combined with such abstraction as the complete and accurate capitalising by all agents of the tax burden of servicing public debt.[8]

I start with the claim that long run equilibrium cannot be affected by monetary policy.[9]

First let me make a pedantic point which would be very awkward none the less for a theorist. Everyone knows that in the general equilibrium models we have been discussing for the past twenty years the real equilibrium values of the volume of monetary assets can be determined, but not their nominal values. Unfortunately, however, the conditions for such an equilibrium to be unique are rather stringent. If there are many equilibria they will not all be stable for any adjustment theory we choose to use.

---

[8] At this point I depart from the book, where this assumption is not explicitly made. However, it seems to be required if money stock changes are to have an effect independent of interest rate changes; and this was once confirmed by Professor Friedman in conversation.

[9] This claim is never precisely made, but I cannot understand chapter 5 without it. Neither Professor Friedman nor I regard the examples of chapter 1, where certain monetary changes affect the long run, as instances of monetary policy. (See e.g. p. 101, where a policy which *could* peg interest rates is dismissed as not relevant.)

It then follows that there is nothing in these models as such to allow one to conclude that the final equilibrium is independent of initial conditions and of monetary policy in particular.

But this is only the most obvious of the difficulties the reader encounters in this connection. Suppose it to have been met. Friedman seems to hold the view that the long run result of a once-over change in the money stock does not depend on whether money has been dropped from a helicopter or whether it has entered the system through open-market operations.[10] The argument is consistent with the assumption that government debt, if taxes to service it are properly capitalised, is always of zero net value to the economy. It is like private debt; your claim to interest is exactly counterbalanced by my tax obligation. Once again let us accept this extreme idealisation and ask whether the conclusions will follow in the context of the Walrasian model which is somewhere in the background of all of Friedman's work.

There is an obvious difficulty in discussing long run equilibrium which is never defined or specified. I return to this almost at once. But we may notice straight away that, if this is Friedman's position, it must be incorrect. It implies that the long run supply of government debt can be anything at all. For instance, it is higher when the nominal stock of money has been increased by helicopter than when it is increased by open-market operations. Suppose the debt to be serviced by lump sum taxation. Of course, for the individual the purchase of a bond yields the usual return since his tax payments are independent of his actions. We now have exactly the situation studied by Lange and Patinkin: the real value of bonds is not an argument of any demand function. They both showed, and their demonstration is perfectly compatible with Friedman's portfolio theory, that the demand function for real bond holdings is homogeneous of degree zero in prices and money. Anyone can look up the simple demonstration. Hence if the long run equilibrium is indeed unique, the required real bonds are uniquely given (and exactly similar point is made in Tobin 1970). Hence an alteration of the ratio in which the two assets are available would make long run equilibrium impossible and the economy would follow a path depending on the manipulation of this ratio. Alternatively

---

[10] Friedman admits that the 'detail' of adjustment may depend upon the source of monetary change (p. 230). but throughout the book the source of monetary change is not a relevant variable. If the view I ascribe to him is not the one he holds, then chapter 5 and much of the empirical work are rather mysterious.

if different long run real bond holdings are compatible with long run equilibrium, then these equilibria will differ from one another.

To be more precise, let me attempt to write down the simplest long run model which fits some of the things Friedman has to say when he speaks of the long run. It is a neo-classical model of steady full employment growth, with capital, money and bonds. Population growth is at the rate n. Prices are steady, r is the real rate of interest on bonds, and $\Phi(k)$ is the real rate of return on capital, where k is the capital–labour ratio. I write m for real balances, and b/r for real bond holdings, per person. y is output per person. Following Friedman and writing a for real assets net of tax obligation per person, the demand function for real balances is written as

$$\mu \equiv m/a = \mu[r, \Phi(k), y/a] \tag{13.1}$$

In portfolio balance,

$$k = (1 - \mu)a$$

The disposable income is $(y + nm)$ and in steady state, y/a is constant. I assume that net asset formation is proportional to disposable income:

$$s(y + nm) = na \tag{13.2}$$

The production functions $y = y(k)$, in asset equilibrium, can be written as $y[(1 - \mu)a]$; Similarly, $\Phi(k) = \Phi[(1 - \mu)a]$. Hence in asset equilibrium, using equation (13.1), equation (13.2) may be written as

$$h(r, a) = 0 \tag{13.3}$$

But from equation (13.3) we conclude that the system has one degree of freedom and that monetary policy can affect long run equilibrium. It does not seem to be the case that monetary policy 'cannot peg interest rates for more than very limited periods' (p. 99). Also this model, if changed in an obvious way to allow price changes and changes in income per head, is very similar to one sketched by Friedman (p. 229).

In the above I have not discussed the demand for government bonds. It will be an equation similar to (13.1). For any (r, a) satisfying equation (13.3) the government simply supplies the bonds demanded at these parameter values. An exceptional case arises if no capital is held when $r > \Phi(k)$, i.e. when $\mu = 1$ for this case. The solution to equation (13.3) must thus satisfy $r \leqslant \Phi(k)$, which on the usual production assumption is not restrictive. But the important point is this: by Friedman's own analysis, portfolio balance does not imply $r = \Phi(k)$, since government debt is not private debt. That is, portfolio balance can be reached for varying values of $[r - \Phi(k)]$ by changing the availability of financial assets; and this explains why monetary policy can affect long run equilibrium.

Let me hasten to add that I do not care much for the above model and that in particular I consider it to be useless for the description of a world in which the uncertainty of future events is fundamental. But it seems to be the best formalisation of Friedman and it shows him to be wrong.

Since it would appear that monetary policy can affect long run equilibrium values, and in my formulation, particularly monetary policy directed towards the control of what I have called r, a good many positions taken up by Friedman can be answered in this simple way. But of course it is his contention that whereas the long run is inviolate to monetary mangement, the short run, and in particular whether we can ever reach the long run, is not. Indeed, monetary changes are among the most powerful autonomous changes working for good or ill. The central contention here is that 'the stock of money is much more closely and systematically related to income over business cycles then is investment or autonomous expenditures' (p. 235), and that history teaches us 'a lesson of the most profound importance . . . that monetary policy can prevent money itself from being a major source of economic disturbance' (p. 106). Let me therefore turn to the short run.

In the context of the kind of long run model which I have been describing consider an unexpected rise in the rate of change in the monetary stock to a permanently higher level by means of a permanently higher rate of open-market purchases by the central bank. Friedman writes that 'although the initial sellers of the securities purchased by the Central Bank were willing sellers, this does not mean they want to hold the proceeds in money indefinitely', and adds that the sale is only a 'temporary step in rearranging their portfolio' (p. 230). The only sense I can make of this in view of Friedman's own portfolio analysis is that to persuade people to sell securities, their price must be raised; and that this price then leads to a rearrangement of the whole portfolio with the consequence that the prices of other assets rise also. This, except for the acknowledged exceptional case of the liquidity trap, is pure Keynes. Should there be a liquidity trap nothing will happen.

But suppose that the demand for non-financial assets, for example investment, is very insensitive to such changes in the rates of return on financial assets and that the saving decision is also insensitive. The story Friedman tells would come to a full stop. The rates of return on financial assets would have adjusted themselves in such a manner as to make people content to hold the larger stock of money. I do not claim that this will happen. What I do claim is that it is the sensitivity of demand for non-financial reproducible assets which is the vital link not only for traditional economics but for Friedman. But then is it not odd that changes in investment demand should be such as a bad explantory variable?

Equally puzzling is the view that nothing essential would have been changed in the 'short period' story had we employed the helicopter instead of open-market operations. Had we indeed used the helicopter, not only would people have found themselves with too much money but they would undoubtedly have been wealthier. Even if real asset demands were interest inelastic, the story would not have stopped there. That is one vital difference. Even if asymptotically the same state is reached, it might take quite different time spans. The helicopter is like Keynesian pump priming; open-market operations are not. The puzzle then is this. The course of events is governed by changes in interest rates and asset prices and by the sensitivity of real decisions to such changes. But the investment and consumption functions are, according to Friedman, very unstable. How does this unstable and vital link between monetary and real changes permit the 'close and systematic' relation between monetary and real changes?

Let me discuss the same problem inaccurately, but perhaps more clearly, in textbook language. For the textbook Keynesian open-market operations may make no difference because LL is perfectly flat. This may be due to a very high interest elasticity of demand for money or, as Kaldor would argue, to a high elasticity of the supply of money (I do not suggest that Kaldor would mean infinite elasticity). For Friedman LL could still be pretty flat in spite of the low interest elasticity of demand for money, if the elasticity of supply is high enough (and in this matter I find both his evidence and remarks ambiguous). But suppose LL to be steep.

It cannot be vertical, else no open-market operations are possible. Also, the steeper it is, the greater is the effect of open-market operations on interest rates. But if IS is moving all over the place, then our predictions from money changes to real changes will also be rather bad, although the steeper LL, the less will be the error in income change forecasts for any given variability of IS. But in any case once a very steep LL is granted, Friedman need not appeal to the instability of the Keynesian expenditure functions: shifts in IS can have little effect on income. The alleged instability of IS is really a red herring; everything follows from a very steep LL, but the latter is by no means a logical consequence of a low interest elasticity of the demand for money even if this much disputed claim is true. Put in yet another way, if LL is as steep as Friedman requires, the instability of the consumption function, say, should be no obstacle to accurate forecasts of the effects of autonomous expenditure changes on income: they will be negligible. On the other hand the steep LL implies very violently fluctuating interest rates. I simply do not believe in it.

Although generally predicting a return to the same steady state in his experiment, Friedman wants the path to be cyclical. He finds the necessary wherewithal in the following consideration. Initially the actions of agents and of banks were geared to the present price level and its present rate of change. However, in the final equilibrium prices will have to be rising at a higher rate (since the money stock is increasing at a higher rate), and 'the amount of money demanded will be less in real terms than it was initially, relative to wealth and hence income' (p. 233). Hence at some stage prices must be rising faster than at their ultimate rate. In addition, there are lags in expectations and the actions of financial institutions to be taken into account.

The first of these explanations, which is the one to which Friedman attaches the most importance, is rather odd for him. If real balances are lower while real wealth is the same, households must be holding more of some other asset. If that is capital, real interest rates will be lower. Monetary prices seem to have been able to affect long run real equilibrium values contrary to the views expressed, for instance, in his presidential address (p. 100). In any case the whole cyclical story requires far deeper analysis than he gives it; and I do not find helpful comments like: 'Presumably, these cyclical adjustments will be damped, though no merely verbal exposition can suffice to assure that the particular mechanism described will have that property.' (p. 233) The 'monetary lead' part of the story is now very much played down (Friedman 1970).

Nor can the famous policy prescription be given much justification in the absence of a well formulated cyclical theory. A steady state is a steady state, and if we are in one we had better increase monetary assets at a steady rate. On Friedman's own views, a departure from this blissful state is ascribable to the 'money side'. But surely this may be just as much due to fluctuations in the demand (not the demand functions) for money as in its supply. Suppose the future becomes more or less uncertain, for instance; then the policy will give violent fluctuations in interest rates and certainly more instability than would be the case if at the prevailing (steady state rates) we gave them as much money as they wished to hold. In any case I have simply not been able to piece together an argument from what Friedman writes which would support his policy recommendations. It should be noted that he himself writes: 'Clearly, the view that monetary change is important does not preclude the existence of other factors that affect the course of business or that account for the quasi-rhythmical character of business fluctuations.' (p. 222) This pretty agnostic and leaves the policy question wide open, especially since it is unlikely that the operation of these other factors is independent of monetary policy.

So far I have not discussed price changes, and Friedman's discussion of the relation between monetary changes and price level changes has some interesting and valuable features. For instance, his distinction between expected and unexpected price change is excellent and he makes good use of it in dealing with money wages. No doubt he is also right in arguing that elementary textbook Keynesians pay far too little attention to prices, although it is hard to maintain that Keynes was guilty of this. But the habit of, say, analysing the effects of a shift in autonomous expenditure by shifting the IS curve to the right and forgetting all about LL is fairly widespread and lamentable. Indeed, one must agree that vulgarised Keynes can be very bad economics.

For Friedman the connection between monetary changes and changes in money income is so direct because he takes velocity to be very interest inelastic. Even when this is granted, rather formidable difficulties remain if this is to be translated into a quantity theory of prices. For instance, when the money stock is lower as a result of open-market operations, the consequent higher interest rate will reduce the demand for goods and services. The extent to which this causes a reduction in prices and a fall in output depends on the conditions of production, the degree of competition, money wage flexibility, etc. Without studying these in their own right nothing of much value can be said.

But we may take this case as a test case. A Keynesian analysis of the rise in interest rates consequent on the monetary operation might go something as follows. The higher monetary rates will cause a fall in productive investment, in the demand, indeed, for all producible durable goods. This will lead to a multiplier contraction. If money wages do not fall in the face of increased unemployment, the new short run equilibrium will be one of lower real income with somewhat higher real wages and possibly higher interest rates. The higher real wage arises from diminishing marginal productivity of labour in the short run, and of course we would not wish to insist on this. The higher interest rate may be required in order to induce agents to hold the stock of money there is. The multiplier itself is not $1/s$, but the resultant solving the two simultaneous relations; the excess demand for goods and excess demand for money. One cannot easily predict what will happen to money wages, and in the long run we are all dead. This I believe would be a 'Keynesian' story with the caveat in the background that, should the contemplated exogenous monetary change cause a significant shift in expectations, the story might be different in detail and possibly even in direction. As far as prices are concerned, the behaviour of money wages is probably the crucial variable, with marginal productivity considerations a poor second.

The Friedman 'short run' story, if I understand him correctly, differs mainly in that he simply speaks of a fall in demand leading to lower prices, and does not distinguish between the price of labour and that of goods. In the present volume no theoretical analysis or empirical evidence is presented on money wages. He is completely specialised to equations in money, money income and money prices. The debate on real wages and profit margins over the cycle is not of interest to him. But there is nothing to lead me to suppose that he disagrees with the above Keynesian sketch, except that he must be taking money wages as much more flexible (whatever that means precisely) than Keynesians do and that he treats 'the long run' as if he, or we, knew what it meant. But then I have already argued repeatedly, it is these relations of wage flexibility, interest elasticity of real demand, production and competitive conditions which must be studied.

Friedman writes continually as if non-Friedmanites are committed to the view that changes in the quantity of money do not matter. The popularity of the IS—LL apparatus is enough to contradict this. Moreover, the inventor of this expository device emphasised that the horizontal piece of LL should be taken as reasonable for deep depressions only. A reading of the *General Theory* will show that Keynes did not build his revolution on the liquidity trap. The 'real balance effect' he neglected; however, this is of academic interest only, and must be particularly unimportant when money balances change through open-market operations and people act on 'permanent prices'. But what Keynesians have argued is that it is the changes in interest rates in the first instance and wage flexibility in the second which are the phenomena of importance. I can see nothing wrong in that. What is more important, there is nothing in this book to persuade one that stability is better served by the possible large fluctuations in interest rates which may accompany Friedman's policy than it would be by a policy designed perhaps not to peg but to reduce fluctuations in interest rates.

V

In reply to a number of criticisms Professor Freidman can no doubt point to some of his famous safeguarding passages. For instance in discussing leads and lags he writes: 'No one of these characteristics alone is a full-description of the money series, any more than one feature in a face is a full portrait. But also the regularities in the series *may* mean that a few such characteristics suffice.' (p. 248, my italics); and later: '*Presumably*, one reason for this consistent relation is because this feature of monetary behaviour is consistently linked with other features, and one reason for variability in the relation is because these links are not rigid.' (p. 249, my italics) Or: 'In a scientific problem, the final verdict is never in.' (p. 277) Or on monetary leads again: 'This is strong though not conclusive evidence for the independent influence of monetary change.' (p. 180) And so on. Moreover, since he has no articulated theory he can always say: 'This is not what I meant at all.'

But it is not easy to take these concessions to academic conventions seriously. All over the world 'finanical experts' have been persuaded of the 'doctrine', and all over the world there is talk of a fundamental change in economic theory. If there had only been talk of 'suggestive' new findings and of theoretical 'presumptions' we would not now be in the position of presenting to the world the impression of rival schools of thought.

In various parts of this book Friedman talks of the failure of Keynesian forecasts (say after the war), and poor Goldenweiser is shown to have made some very injudicious Keynesian-sounding statements. Considering the dates of these occurrences and the relatively unsophisticated techniques, leave alone the paucity of data, then available, one should not have thought that these occurrences constitute anti-Keynesian evidence. But as I have argued in any case, it is hard to see how what Friedman now has to say constitutes such evidence, theoretical or empirical. There is nothing in what he says to make anyone change his view that changes in the monetary stock can exert an influence only if they change people's wealth or interest rates. As far as theory goes, it is only the Pigou effect which had been ignored in the early literature. Friedman may turn out to be right in his judgment of elasticities etc., and certainly these judgments would have policy implications. But he must know that his quasi-reduced-form econometric methods cannot bear the weight he puts on them. And he must know that it is unwise to claim that changes in the monetary stock can be said to 'explain' the other changes we observe when, on his own account, our theory of such changes is so poor.

REFERENCES

Arrow, K. J. 1964. Optimal capital policy, the cost of capital, and myopic decision rules, *Annals of the Institute of Statistical Mathematics*, vol. 16

Friedman, Milton. 1969. The optimum quantity of money, Macmillan

Friedman, Milton. 1970. Comment on Tobin, *Quarterly Journal of Economics*, May

Hahn, F. H. 1971. Equilibrium with transaction costs, *Econometrica*

Levhari, D. and Srinivasan, T. N. 1969. Optimal savings under uncertainty, *Review of Economic Studies*, vol. 36

Tobin J. 1970. Comments for panel on monetary theory, Second World Congress of the Econometric Society, Cambridge

14

Monetarism and Economic Theory

INTRODUCTION

In this paper I want to examine the theoretical foundations of 'monetarism'.

At the outset there is a difficulty. Professor Stein writes: 'Monetarists are policy oriented. Their major propositions are a series of empirical observations . . . rather than a theory in direct opposition to neo-Keynesian analysis." (Stein 1976) And Professor Friedman writes: 'I continue to believe that the fundamental differences between us are empirical not theoretical." (Friedman 1976) Professor Friedman also urges us to paint with a broad Marshallian brush and not to worry too much about the fine detail. All this suggests the claim that there is an accepted theory of the economy and that this theory is capable of yielding both monetarist and other conclusions. For instance, in the IS–LM context the LM curve may be vertical and/or the IS curve could be flat, in which case monetarists' propositions hold. But the shapes of these curves are contingent on time and place, and monetarists do not claim that logically the curves could not have less extreme shapes. Yet it will readily be agreed that this classification of cases by the shapes of the two curves does not exhaust the propositions of either monetarists or non-monetarists. For instance, the former will want to argue that in normal times the intersection of the two curves is at a level of income producible by the economy with a natural rate of unemployment. Moreover, it is by no means the case that we are agreed that the IS–LM cross is a generally accepted theory of the economy. So for the moment at least let us suspend judgment on this matter.

There is also another difficulty: how are we to define monetarism? Professor Friedman himself has drawn our attention to the necessarily coarse division of opinions any definition is bound to imply (Friedman 1976). I think he is right and accordingly do not attempt a formal definition. It should be realised that nothing of substance hinges on a definition. I shall, as the story unfolds, label certain views as monetarist, and I shall naturally not be wilfully perverse in this. But it will be of no importance whether there exists an individual who assents to all the propositions thus labelled. I am not here interested in the history of thought.

I THE WALRASIAN FOUNDATIONS

I start by considering the simplest Walrasian economy in which agents hold money and treat prices parametrically.

Let time be divided into the present and the future. Do not assume that there is a market in the present for all future contingent goods. The present plans of agents depend on present and expected prices. The latter are contingent on the state of nature. I shall be interested in rational expectations. At its simplest this means that the prices expected to rule in the future given any state s are in fact the prices that will clear markets if state s occurs. If there is noise then we assume the probability distribution of prices contingent on any state assigned by the agent is in fact the distribution that will be generated by the economy. In either case the actual distribution of prices or the actual price given any state will be generated by the requirement that markets clear. This means that price expectations must be conditioned not only by the state of nature but also by the value of any exogenous variable that helps to determine prices in any state. One of the variables may be the stock of money.

I shall take it that money is intrinsically worthless but that it is needed in exchange. Indeed in order to avoid complications I shall follow Clower (1965), and Grandmont and Laroque (1976), in assuming that money receipts from sales cannot all be used instantaneously for purchases. However, I do not want to assume that money is the only asset. There is also internal debt as well as public debt, both denominated in money, and there are also physical assets like machines and houses. For brevity I refer to the constellation of assets at any date as the stock of that date. If agents know the stock at any date and state s then they would also know market-clearing prices, and the real variables of the economy will be affected by the noise. By a long run rational expectation equilibrium we mean a set of future and present prices such that markets clear at all dates and such that no agent can improve his forecast of the probability distribution of prices given the information provided by the market.

One of the claims that I label 'monetarist' is that actual economies are only for short periods out of rational expectation equilibrium. This does not mean that real variables like output and employment are constant through time. They may change because states change or because of noise in the environment. But for most of the time agents are not systematically disappointed in their plans, and in particular for most of the time there is no involuntary unemployment.

It is now also claimed that the equilibria of the economy are homogeneous of degree zero in money stock and in current and expected prices. It follows that if agents can predict the money stock it will be a rational expectation equilibrium to predict prices proportional to that stock. At least, this is so if rational expectation equilibrium is unique. But homogeneity itself cannot be deduced from first principles of rational behaviour in an economy with internal debt denominated in money. Equiproportional price changes lead to redistributions between debtors and creditors. The effects of this can be ignored if debtors and creditors are 'sufficiently' alike. I have no evidence on this matter but would be surprised to find these distributional effects to be negligible. Certainly there are historical accounts of inflation where the plight of creditors did not seem to be offset in its effects by the bonanza to debtors, and there are accounts of deflation where the bankruptcy of debtors seems to have been of real significance. In any case, the decision to abstract from distributional effects is now also of help in arguing that rational expectation equilibrium is unique. Only some further relatively mild postulates are needed to make this rigorous.

When there is government debt the homogeneity postulate must be false unless one can legitimately leave out the real value of bonds from the aggregate excess demand funtions. This could be so if agents correctly calculate the present value of the real tax burden of financing the debt and if once again all agents are alike in the Gorman (1953) sense. In addition, it should further be noted that if the real tax system is progressive a k-fold change in the money prices will also have real effects.

There is also another, somewhat more technical, point drawn to my attention by Professor Stiglitz. Let the money supply depend

in a regular manner on the state of nature. Even if perfectly foreseen, this will mean that the prices in that state that clear markets
depend on the money supply. But now the mere fact that the
money stock varies over states of nature may give some opportunity of re-arranging portfolios over states, an opportunity that
earlier, in the absence of contingent futures markets, was not
available. The monetary policy may thus have real effect since it
affects the rates of return of holding money until the future with
different states.

But let us agree that the values of real variables should, in a
rational expectation equilibrium, be independent of the stock of
money if the latter can be perfectly predicted. If it cannot be thus
predicted then agents may find it impossible to learn the true state
of the economy from market signals. For behind the rational expectation hypothesis is the Bayesian econometrician who updates
conditional priors from observation as long as the latter contain
new information. Thus ideally agents can deduce from prices what
the true state of the economy is. But if prices depend on a random
monetary component as well as the state of the economy this may
not be possible. Thus money can have real effects when its stock
cannot be predicted, or, as Professor Lucas would say, if relative
price movements owing to the state of the economy cannot be
disentangled from movements in absolute prices.

Let us now call the values of real variables in rational expectation equilibrium their *natural* values. Let us further suppose that
at any date and state market prices clear markets. Thus the actual
values of real variables are those derived at that date in that state
at these prices. For instance, the actual level of unemployment is
always the desired level at the given market signals. A difference
between the actual and natural values of a real variable must then
be due to the circumstances that actual market signals were not
what they were expected to be; for if they were the economy
would, by the uniqueness hypothesis, be in rational expectation
equilibrium. Thus real variables can diverge from their natural
values only if agents make mistakes. Since any systematic monetary policy will be discovered by intelligent agents either directly
or indirectly, a policy can move real variables from their natural
values only if it has a random component. But that is not much
comfort for those who look to monetary policy to affect real variables. In particular, the time profile of the response of real variables
to an unexpected shock will be hard to predict and may, with
enough lags, be cyclical (Lucas 1975). Certainly there is unlikely

to exist an unpredictable policy that will keep a real variable permanently above or below its natural level.

This rather condensed account suffices to show that modern monetarists have at least one important point to make which everyone can agree to. It is this: monetary policy, or indeed any government policy, is part of the economic environment of agents who can learn or deduce what this policy is. But then, in evaluating the policy we must not model the actions of agents as if they were independent of the government's policy. For instance, the behaviour of money wages and employment, given any level of unemployment, will be affected by the knowledge that it is government policy to make the growth of the money stock proportional to the deviation of unemployment from this level. These effects do impose considerable constraints on what government policy can achieve, and in any case it would be wrong to ignore them in analysis.

On the other hand, there are some observations on the theory that I have outlined, which I now make in a preliminary way.

In the model that I have sketched real variables can deviate from their natural values because expected market signals, including the stock of money, deviate from their rationally expected value. But even so, real variables take on the values they would have in short period Walrasian equilibrium. Thus current prices always clear current markets. In particular, then, there is no Keynesian unemployment, nor in the long run are there any of the expectational disturbances that Keynes considered. There simply is no scope for Keynesian macropolicy with Keynesian aims. In a sense, then, not only is monetary policy ineffective, but happily there is no Keynesian need for it. This suggests that in the arguments about policy monetarists have loaded the dice by proposing a model where no *raison d'etre* for macropolicy of the Keynesian type exists. It is true that governments might still seek, unsuccessfully, to reduce the variance of real variables. But the motive here is not involuntary unemployment or indeed anticyclical in the usual sense. All this suggests that Keynesian interventionists must have a different model of the economy. If the difference of opinion is really empirical it is so on a grand scale concerned with what is the most appropriate model of the whole economy.

But even with the existing model monetarists sometimes overstate their case. The government is an agent, a large agent, in the economy with a set of possible actions and a budget constraint. It is more than a device for distributing and sucking up money by helicopter. It may, for instance, use newly printed money to bid for resources to build a new trunk road. If the road is built, even at the cost of crowding out private casino building, the real description of the economy will have changed. In the very long run the road may be allowed to decay and casinos will reappear. But that is not a long run that counts for economic policy. More generally, if we agree that monetary policy can affect the asset composition of an economy, then we must also agree that it can have real effects. I shall return to this matter in another context later, but the present point is one monetarists can probably agree to.

Lastly, let me underline that the theory I have just discussed demonstrates the ineffectiveness of a systematic monetary policy and not the ineffectiveness of any other government policy. A great deal in the argument depends on the homogeneity postulate and thus on the invariance of the natural values of real variables to the stock of money. Government taxes and government demand for goods and services will, even if foreseen, have real effects. But these are not expressible in terms of real income and employment simply because every rational expectation equilibrium relative to a government policy is one of zero involuntary unemployment, and government policy will largely affect the composition of output and perhaps the leisure-to-work margin. These observations now lead me to the next stage of the argument.

II DEPARTURE FROM WALRAS

It is one of the paradoxes of the debates in recent years that both sides have often been willing to use the IS–LM apparatus. For instance, Blinder and Solow (1973) study the question of whether fiscal policy matters in the context of fixed prices and involuntary unemployment and continue with the fixed price assumption to the long run. One would have thought that monetarists would be unwilling to proceed on this basis were it not for writings by Friedman and other monetarists who assume the IS–LM story with fixed prices. This is of course to be explained by the desire of both sides to arrive at macroeconomic propositions concerning the level of output and the level of employment. They thus use excess demand functions like IS and LM which have income as one of their arguments. But this is not true of any of the excess demand functions that make up a Walrasian equilibrium, and it certainly is not true of the theory that I have outlined. Behind the IS–LM story there must be a non-Walrasian story of thwarted transactions. The question then is whether it is a logically coherent story that does not violate the twin axioms of private greed and private rationality on which economic theory is based.

Consider first the rather secure fact that British Steel cannot sell all it would like to sell at prevailing prices. These prices thus do not clear the Walrasian market for steel, and British Steel is rationed. How can this be made consistent with rational market theory? One needs to argue that British Steel calculates correctly that it cannot improve itself by offering to trade at a different price. One must also argue that somehow it is too difficult for steel customers to attempt to lower the price at which they trade. In all of this one must leave the realm of perfectly competitive markets, and one should not do this by fixing prices arbitrarily except in the very short run.

In general, then, the question is this: do there exist prices and quantity constraints on the trading of agents such that all constrained trades balance and no agent can improve himself by change in price? Notice that in this definition agents are taken to be correct in their *conjecture* that they cannot improve themselves by changing price. The existence of such a *rational conjectural–rational expectation* equilibrium has not been established for the general case. But there are examples that show that the concept in a restricted sense is not vacuous (Hahn 1978).

If one can give a coherent account of an economy in rational conjectural and rational expectation equilibrium, then the story I have told so far will have to be fairly radically altered. The signals are now prices and quantities, and the simplest rational expectations equilibrium is one in which prices and quantities as functions of date and state are known and markets clear in the constrained excess demand functions. In general there will be many such equilibria. They may still all possess the homogeneity property. But even if all distributional matters are ignored, the step from 'all equilibria have the homogeneity property' to 'a k-fold increase in the money stock will leave all real variables unchanged' is now very insecure. The first reaction to the k-fold change will be in the demands for goods, services and assets. Thus the first impact will be on the quantity signals of the economy. Selling agents, when k is greater than one, who were quantity constrained will now wish to sell more. Prices may change if the consequences of such changes are now different. But we can all think of constant return economies with rationed supplies including labour. Here all that happens is that production increases until the extra money stock is the desired stock.

I should now like to make the same point in a slightly different way. In the Walrasian economy that I have discussed one may as a first approximation abstract from distributional affects and argue that it has a unique rational expectation equilibrium. This allows one to speak of *the* natural value of real variables. In the rational conjecture—rational expectation Walrasian equilibrium the non-uniqueness may be not only endemic but of great relevance to the discussion. When Keynesians claim, for instance, that government action can permanently reduce involuntary unemployment they often implicitly suppose that there are a number of different equilibria. For instance, a government deficit may lead to changes in output until the deficit is again abolished through increased tax receipts. But if so then there are at least two equilibria with zero deficit. This is not possible in a model that yields unique natural values for the real variables.

Before I proceed I must insert a word of caution. The model of a rational conjecture—expectations equilibrium is in its infancy. I cannot be certain that it too may not yield unique equilibrium values of the real variables. At the moment I think that this is unlikely, and indeed believe that there is likely to be a continuum of equilibria. This belief is based partly on examples and the fact that these models seem to have a number of degrees of freedom. If this belief were to prove wrong, then the monetarist case would be greatly strengthened.

In any case, the proposition that monetary policy that is systematic cannot affect the natural values of real variables is essentially related to the Walrasian model. In that context it can sometimes be made to be logically entailed. But the Walrasian model does not capture any of the market failures macroeconomists have been concerned with for forty-five years. The argument must thus be (as already noted) about appropriate models of the whole economy, and that strikes me as largely a theoretical problem. Now the difficulty is that one can describe a non-Walrasian economy in rational conjectural—rational expectations equilibrium, but there are still large problems with a rigorous proof that it exists. But monetarists have not been much concerned with 'existence' problems (see Friedman 1976), and so perhaps we can use such a model at least provisionally. If we do then some monetarist propositions will not hold in this economy.

The single most important departure from the Walrasian and

hence monetarist view is the proposition that an economy can be in long run equilibrium with involuntary unemployment. By this I mean a state where some agents are effectively rationed on the labour market, so that this ration has a positive shadow price. It thus follows that these agents would be willing to supply labour at a lower real wage, which is exactly the definition of involuntary unemployment proposed by Keynes. One must therefore describe a situation where labour is willing to work at a lower real wage, if work is offered at that wage, but is unwilling to reduce their wage in the hope of finding employment. Moreover, that unwillingness must be rational. For instance, Negishi (1976) has recently described an equilibrium model where the increase in the probability of finding a job at a lower wage is small enough to be outweighed by the lower wage received when employed. These expectations in this model are rational.

One would, in this matter, probably wish to appeal to some extent to certain instituitional arrangements. For instance, an unemployed worker may have to make a discrete reduction in the wage at which he is willing to work if he is to induce an employer to substitute him for an existing worker. This can be rationalised by, for instance, an appeal to training costs. There are also a number of embryonic 'implicit contracts' theories that can be called to aid here. The point of course is to establish that wages may not fall at every   level of involuntary unemployment, and not that wages never fall.

In this matter much of search theory has loaded the dice against Keynes. For it mostly assumes that agents search for the best wage but not for a job. Thus every employer contacted by the worker makes a wage offer, i.e. an offer of employment at that wage. The uncertainty concerns the wage and not the job. But if employers cannot reduce the wage of their existing workers without large scale quits or perhaps a strike, the story becomes much modified, since it is not unreasonable to stipulate that all workers in the same job must be paid the same by the employer. A good deal of the search literature employs a model that makes sense only if the whole workforce is hired and rehired at each round. When employers are rationed in their sales their willingness to hire labour will depend on their expectations of sales as well as their expectation of prices. If the sales expectations are pessimistic and there is only limited possibility of substitution in favour of labour in the production process, then a lower wage will benefit the unemployed only if he can induce the employer to hire him at the expense of someone who is already in the job. But this for instituitional reasons may not be possible. If the wages are not reduced and employment is not increased, the pessimistic sales expectation will be substantiated. Notice that none of this makes sense in a Walrasian context, where the actions of agents are exclusively guided by prices.

In the first instance the question is a theoretical one: can one describe an economy in non-Walrasian equilibrium without violating the fundamental rationality postulate of economic theory? Up to the degree of rigour employed by monetarists the answer is pretty clearly that one can. The theory will not be one of large economies where every agent rationally has competitive conjectures. For instance, it must not be the case that either the unemployed or British Steel conjecture that an arbitrarily small reduction in their price will remove all quantity constraints. Some feature of imperfect competition is required for a coherent non-Walrasian model. But this causes me very little concern. I want also to re-emphasise that in such an equilibrium prices are not fixed by fiat but are the outcome of the decisions of rational calulating agents.

In the second instance one must look at the facts. Harry Johnson, in a related but different context, wrote: 'The assumption of normally full employment reflects the passage of time and the accumulation of experience of reasonably full-employment as the historical norm rather than the historical rarity that Keynes' theory and left wing Keynesian mythology make it out to be .' (Johnson 1976)

I do not know what Johnson's evidence is, and I do not know how broadly he has interpreted 'reasonably full employment'. But if true one might conclude that the Walrasian theory is here not grossly falsified and the non-Walrasian theory is at risk. In particular, if the latter always has multiple equilibria it would be surprising if it generated the observations that Johnson claims. I am not really competent to judge the facts, but I view these claims with a certain amount of suspicion. The reason is that monetarists are apt to label any given unemployment level as 'natural' or perhaps as 'reasonable'. Thus for instance there is some evidence that the higher UK and US level of unemployment of recent years is being diagnosed as a (largely unexplained) shift in the natural level. Since my main concern today is theoretical I leave the matter there.

The point I have now reached is this. Fundamentally, the dispute between monetarists and Keynesians does not turn on the role assigned to money. For instance, both sides would digest the fact, if fact it is, that the desired money stock is proportional to money income. What is at stake is the underlying description of the economy. The Walrasian description adopted by the monetarists essentially removes the need for systematic government policy even if in some sense such a policy has real effects. The non-Walrasian model that should underpin the Keynesian position is not one of perfect competition, and it does give considerable scope to government policy, a matter that I shall take up almost at once. Of the two models the Walrasian is theoretically more securely based because a great deal of very good work has gone into its making. But the non-Walrasian construction is sufficiently coherent to warrant the belief that it can in due course be as polished and as tightly knit as its Walrasian competitor. It seems very doubtful that empirical evidence will at present be decisive in deciding between the usefulness of the two theories. But I am prepared to chance my arm and argue that there must be few firms in the United Kingdom who sell as much at the going price as they would want to.

III THEORY AND POLICY

Good insights are gained into the nature of the fundamental disagreements if one considers the policy proposals that they give rise to. It is to this that I now turn.

One of the propositions considered to be monetarist is that pure fiscal policy does not matter. Tobin and Buiter write: 'a characteristic monetarist proposition is that pure fiscal policy does not matter for aggregate real demand, nominal income and the price level.' (Tobin and Buiter 1976) In particular, it seems to be maintained that the ultimate journey of the price level depends only on the journey of the monetary stock Opponents of this view, in particular Blinder and Solow (1973) and Tobin and Buiter (1976), have constructed IS–LM models, both long run and short run, to show that this monetarist view is mistaken. However, much of the story, particularly that of Blinder and Solow, is, as already noted, based on a world of fixed prices and involuntary unemployment. This is not, as I have also argued, the world of the monetarist.

Let me therefore first consider an economy in rational expectations Walrasian long run equilibrium. Matters are much simplified if one assumes, as the authors I have quoted assume, that the equilibrium is the classical stationary state. It follows that the government budget is balanced, else there would be changes in the stock of money and/or the stock of government debt. One supposes that taxes are proportional to income, so in the equilibrium real income must be such as to generate real tax receipts to finance real government expenditure. Now compare two economies A and B, which are exactly alike except that in A real government expenditure is greater than in B. Tobin and Buiter argue as follows. The A economy must have higher real income than does B, otherwise the budget would not balance. Since the money stock is the same in both A and B but by the usual assumptions the demand for real balances is higher in A than it is in B, the price level must be lower in A. This is reinforced by the consideration that A's higher real income must come from more work and/or more capital per person. If work is in inelastic supply, neo-classical assumptions ensure that the higher capital—labour ratio will entail a lower rate of interest. But a lower rate of interest also implies a higher demand for real balances, and so once again a lower price level in A. Tobin and Buiter are of course aware that their result does not logically entail the proposition that *raising* government expenditure will *raise* real income and *lower* prices and the interest rate. Indeed, they rather sadly conclude that the question of stability seems to hinge on fine differences in parameter values.

What in fact the Tobin—Buiter example amounts to is a case where the Walrasian stationary rational expectations equilibrium is not unique. For given the tax rate, we can set government expenditure always equal to tax receipts and search among prices and the real variables for an equilibrium. According to Tobin and Buiter there are many such equilibria, whereas the monetarist position entails the claim that there is only one. This claim in general however is simply incorrect, although there may be special examples where it is valid. For instance, the Tobin—Buiter result would not work for a fixed-proportion economy. It also would be in some difficulty if the aggregated production function in terms of a capital aggregate were not 'well behaved'. But in general one can always find nonpathological examples where the uniqueness hypothesis of the monetarists fail. The habit of thinking in terms of *the* natural rate of employment and *the* natural level of income serves the monetarists badly simply because the model that they favour, the Walrasian one, does not allow such thinking to go unpunished.

The importance of the Tobin—Buiter result is this: it shows that even in full rational expectation Walrasian equilibrium the price level is not known once the money stock is known. For even if one adheres strictly to the quantity equation, and even if one considers only cases with no involuntary unemployment, the behaviour of the government sector has implications for equilibrium velocity and for equilibrium level of real output that is produced by a given labour force. There are thus a number of equilibrium values P and T. Of course, none of this conflicts with any homogeneity postulate one may wish to impose: a higher money stock may be sufficient for higher equilibrium prices; it is not necessary.

These anti-monetarist points seem well taken, but they remain somewhat academic in the absence of a convincing dynamic. Much of the analysis here that is on offer is both *ad hoc* and very sensitive to the lag structure. But even so it may be instructive to consider a process informally at least, as far as that can be done.

We start again in stationary Walrasian equilibrium and consider an increase in government expenditure net of interest payments. This is to be financed by government borrowing. Many years ago Robertson saw the main problem with the first step: could the increased government demand be translated into a higher aggregate demand for goods and services? In the absence of money creation he saw that the answer depended on the interest elasticity of the demand for money. If a small fall in the price of bonds consequent upon the increase in their supply led to a large decumulation of idle balances in favour of bonds, there would be a net increase in the demand for goods and services. The decumulation of idle balances plays a crucial role. For some time monetarists claimed that the empirical evidence supported an almost zero interest elasticity of demand for money balances, but this claim has now been withdrawn. The first step can therefore stand.

Since there is no involuntary unemployment and we continue to take labour supply as inelastic over the relevant range, the output of goods and services cannot be increased over the short run. Hence the short run effect will be a rise in prices as well as in the interest rate, since we are to suppose that markets clear in the short run as well as the long run. With real income as yet unchanged the government receives no new tax receipts and must go on issuing bonds. But the higher prices and so lower real balances cause private agents to 'make room' for the government demand. To clear the labour market real wages must rise since the higher interest rate would otherwise cause an excess demand for labour. If we are lucky with the elasticity it will now be profitable to produce output more capital intensively, and so to produce more. As this happens the market-clearing prices begin to decline again. On the other hand, if we are unlucky the economy will move further and further away from its equilibrium which we know to be one of lower prices and interest rates.

During an adjustment path, even if it seeks the new long run equilibrium, the initial deficit may be converted into a surplus and that part of government expenditure not used to service the debt may decline. In any case one cannot be certain that after a full adjustment the outstanding debt will be greater than it was before the story started. No simple 'crowding out' argument will be generally valid. Indeed, the government by its actions, if the system is stable, will have caused capital deepening which would not have taken place without it. On the other hand, should the economy be unstable then a pure fiscal policy a *posteriori* has real effects.

It is now fair to notice that Friedman believes that pure fiscal policy can have real effects. But he thinks that they are more of the kind to be expected, say, from a change of the price of oil (Friedman 1976). In other words, he does not expect any systematic macro effects.

So far I have confined myself to a Walrasian economy in full equilibrium, although I have given reasons why I think one should also consider non-Walrasian equilibria, which I shall now proceed to do.

The first point to be made is this. In the monetarist Walrasian economy differences in the money stock, if expected, can affect no real variable. The reason, as already noted, is the homogeneity postulate. In the non-Walrasian economy the homogeneity postulate may be true, but it is now insufficient to rule out a dependence of natural values on the money stock. For one theory the agents may hold is this: if the money stock is higher, then demand for goods will be higher. Suppose that there are constant returns to scale and that we are starting from a position of involuntary unemployment. Then there may well be a rational expectations equilibrium with higher real income, higher employment, higher cash balances and possibly slightly lower interest rates. This may all happen when agents correctly anticipate government policy. The latter may well be to finance a government deficit by printing money. More money will be held at higher income, although it may be necessary to have a lower interest rate. What then the contrary monetarist view depends on is not just the homogeneity, nor yet the perfect learning on the part of the public about what monetary policy is, but on a unique Walrasian equilibrium and the denial of the possibility of rational expectations conjectural non-Walrasian equilibria.

It seems to me that I have now made the case for the view that quite fundamental theoretical matters are at stake. If further study should show that the notion of rational non-Walrasian equilibrium is not viable, then there would be a great strengthening of the view that systematic monetary policy is ineffective. If on the other hand the non-Walrasian equilibrium survives the detailed study it is now rather widely receiving, rather more old fashioned Keynesian views will survive without violating the axiom of rationality and greed. But since homogeneity will not go away, outcomes will crucially depend on which of two equally rational, i.e. self-verifying, theories of the economy agents hold. For instance, in the United Kingdom the public seems to be in the grip of the homogeneity postulate, which may be due to *The Times* having been more widely read than can be thought of as prudent.

Let me now also sketch the arguments concerning pure fiscal policy in the context of a non-Walrasian economy.

The following is an analysis from a more or less *ad hoc* macro model. It is agreed that if there are more bonds to finance more government spending interest rates will be higher; put traditionally, the LM curve will shift up. It should have been agreed straight away that much Keynesian textbook writing has ignored the shift. The IS curve will shift outwards because the government spends more. Also, ignoring the increase in the present value of taxes to service the higher debt, wealth will be higher. The net result of these two shifts may be a higher, lower or no change real output. We are thus back in arguments about slopes as the main bone of contention between monetarists and Keynesians. Professor Stein certainly believes these slopes to be the crux of the whole matter (Stein 1976). His model is rather macroeconomic, and I cannot decide whether it is Walrasian or not.

But certainly Professor Stein's model allows only expected prices and not at all expected quantities to influence present actions. It therefore follows that the decision of the government to increase its demand for goods has no effect on the expectations of future sales and thus on current investment. The only effect on investment demand is the higher interest rate, not the changed expectation of sales. When quantity constraints are noticed there is also a more subtle point to be made. In any given rational expectation quantity constrained equilibrium, a firm's liquidity may depend on the prospects of sales. Indeed, in the United Kingdom the rise in firms' liquidity in the 1974—75 recession was marked. The reason is the rationing of current sales and the uncertainty of future sales. Government action to demand more goods may thus lead to dishoarding simply because sale prospects of all kinds improve. This would in general mean that interest rates would not rise by as much.

Of course, even when a properly formulated non-Walrasian model is used one cannot be certain of the direction of the effect of pure fiscal policy. For one thing, a good deal will depend on the set of self-verifying theories agents can hold. But my point is that we are not purely, or perhaps not mainly, concerned with slopes but also with how they should be calculated. The disagreement is about the arguments that should enter the functions that constitute the model.

As an example, consider transaction uncertainty that appears quite naturally in a non-Walrasian setting. It is however entirely absent from a Walrasian world, where every agent assigns unit probability to being able to buy or sell what he likes at the going prices. When agents encounter quantity constraints this type of uncertainty is closely linked to liquidity preference. For instance, there are some traditional micromodels where one can show that the fraction of income held in cash is an increasing function of transaction uncertainty measured in a simple way. If now this transaction uncertainty is inversely related to government anti-cyclical policy, it may become possible to finance part of increased government debt from the decumulation of precautionary balances. This in turn would mean that there is less "crowding out" than would otherwise be the case. It is not my claim that this is bound to happen. What I do claim is that this matter cannot even be discussed in the Walrasian context.

The real points at issue thus seem to me to be about the kind of economic world that we inhabit, and here we are quite far from a definitive theory. One way in which one may think of oneself as 'Keynesian' is simply by the view that the invisible hand may cease to move before its task is done. In other words, one considers a failure of the decentralised signalling system to be logically and, probably, practically possible. In this it does not help to appeal to arbitrarily given prices, but one may appeal to prices that no self-interested agent wants to change. In the world of the monetarists macropolicy is at best of limited importance even if it could work. For it is supposed that there is never any involuntary unemployment and certainly no meaning can be given to, say, a shortage of demand. If there are quantity-constrained states, then monetarists call them disequilibria, thereby hinting at their impermanence. But they should really be called non-Walrasian states, and some of them may be non-Walrasian equilibria.

It should now be recalled that Friedman claims that the effects of fiscal policy financed by borrowing are 'temporary and minor' when compared with the effects of a change in money stock (Friedman 1976). Since natural values of real variables do not depend on the money stock, this is slightly puzzling way of putting things, but I assume that Friedman has nominal values in mind. On the other hand, Brunner and Meltzer (1976) have announced that the long run effect of increased government spending is to depress output and to raise prices. So the government's action has either hardly any effects or else only bad effects.

Unfortunately, I have found the Brunner–Meltzer analysis impenetrable in spite of the labours of Dornbusch (1976). The two authors *assume* that the private sector when not disturbed by government policy is stable. By this, I think they mean that the undisturbed long run Walrasian equilibrium is stable. Since that is precisely a proposition denied by Keynes and his followers, who give reasons why they do not believe the invisible hand to be performing so well, it is difficult to see where the Brunner–Meltzer story gets us. As far as I can see, with totally non-perverse derivatives on their somewhat *ad hoc* functions we can obtain almost any answer.

But though I find it hard to enjoy or even to understand some of the more recent macroliterature on this topic, one can discern that there are two elements in it that Keynesians have for long ignored. The first of these is giving importance to the government budget. As long as it is not balanced, the stock of financial assets will be changing and the economy cannot settle down to its long run stationary equilibrium. Government expenditure on goods and services plus their debt servicing must thus equal tax receipts. That, for a given tax system, does constrain the equilibria that can be reached, and we have already seen in the Tobin–Buiter case that there are real consequences.

The second element of the story is the importance given to wealth effects. These effects see to it that IS and LM curves are not independent. For instance, a change in the stock of government debt will shift both curves. The effects of government policy are thus transmitted not only via differences in interest rates but also directly, through changes in wealth and in portfolio composition.

There can be little doubt that the macroliterature for too long ignored these ingredients of a satisfactory model. This may be due to the special attention that was focused on the short run. In any event, matters must now be rectified. To do so will require going further back in the analysis to the decisions of agents. At present much of the macroliterature proceeds in a purely *ad hoc* way. In any case, in models with three assets and the most elementary intertemporal structure the full effects of fiscal policy are ambiguous as long as the Walrasian equilibrium is taken as a point of departure. A good deal will simply depend on the elasticities of substitution between different assets and between assets as a whole and consumption. One can see with the naked eye that pure fiscal policy will have a real long run effect, but one cannot be at all sure of the directions.

Stability is even more dubious, especially when the story allows more than two assets and when once again disequilibrium quantity signals are allowed to exert an influence. Although Brunner and Meltzer, for instance, distinguish between the short, the intermediate and the long run, they present no true dynamics. The economy moves from a more or less Keynesian short run response through an intermediate stage to finish up somewhat triumphantly in Walrasian long run equilibrium. I have not been able to decide what it is that makes this a credible story to the authors. We simply have no soundly based dynamics at the moment, and we had best admit to that.

At the end of all these special models the main question is unanswered: are there durable non-Walrasian equilibria? By durable I do not mean lasting for twenty years but, say, five to ten years. If there are, wealth and government budget effects will get modelled almost as a matter of course for an analysis that starts with economic agents. None of these effects however need be of vital qualitative importance for a Keynesian theory firmly grounded in quantity constraints and price setting agents.

IV BALANCE OF PAYMENTS: STOCKS AND FLOWS

I now want to extend the analysis very briefly to an open economy and to problems connected with the balance of payments. This will also give me the opportunity of praising the monetarists for having kept their heads in the stock—flow distinction.

Suppose that we are in Walrasian equilibrium and that exchange rates are fixed. Now let the domestic money stock be higher. Agents will be richer and will demand more goods. The balance of payments goes into deficit and foreign reserves are reduced. This will reduce the stock of monetary assets in our economy.

If the country is very small relative to the world economy and there are no non-tradeables, the new equilibrium will be one where the stock of domestic money plus the domestic value of foreign money is what it was before. Without involving homogeneity or rational expectations, we deduce the impossibility of monetary policy by the impossible of changing the stock of money of both kinds together in this economy. By paying proper attention to stock disequilibrium monetarists have made a fairly obvious, but much neglected point.

Now remove the assumption of a fixed exchange rate. Then certainly the homogeneity postulate and the assumption of a unique rational expectations equilibrium will mean that once again all natural values of real variables are invariant to the domestic money stock. The exchange rate will be inversely related to that stock in such a way as to make the real stock of financial assets invariant to the stock of domestic currency.

But now consider the non–Walrasian case with involuntary unemployment. This, it should be noted, entails that exporters cannot, at the going prices, sell as much as they would like. This seems pretty realistic. Suppose the domestic money stock is higher. We might not be tempted to argue that output will be higher to the extent required to make the higher monetary stock the desired stock. If so, then since there is no excess supply of money one might follow the monetary approach and deduce that the balance of payments is in equilibrium at this higher level of output. But that cannot be right if exporters are quantity constrained. So in order to be in equilibrium again the terms of trade must be different. But it may not be possible to attain world equilibrium at different terms of trade. It would then be the case that we have followed the wrong track and that the Walrasian answer will also be the right one for the non-Walrasian case.

This of course is only a sketch, and detailed study may reveal a different answer. But it suggests that there may be cases where the apparently extra degrees of freedom given by a non-Walrasian world do not suffice to escape Walrasian conclusions. The question is whether the non-Walrasian case can generate a number of different equilibria – really a continuum of them. For special cases the answer is positive. But the example from international trade suggests that there will be difficulties with generalisations.

International trade theory also suggests that the old Keynesian analysis stopped too soon. The Keynesian flow equilibrium is consistent with a non-zero balance of payments and hence with

a changing stock of financial assets. Of course, positive investment has similar implications for the stock of physical assets. The
practical question then is how long the economy takes to reach
a quasi-stationary equilibrium, assuming that there is one and that
the economy seeks it. Purely theoretical analysis seems to show
that the adjustment process may be very long. Monetarists assume
that everywhere along this process all markets clear including
of course that for labour. In particular, they suppose that any
desired quantity can, at the going price, be sold abroad. Thus, for
instance, assume that starting in equilibrium the demand for
money balances is higher because the future is more uncertain.
For the monetarist the consequences are these. Domestic producers
will find that they are selling more abroad and less at home. There
will be a balance of payment surplus and more money will flow in.
At fixed exchange rates this is all that will happen, and it will
continue until money stocks have risen to meet the higher demand.
I am assuming in this that our country is very small relative to
the world and that there are no non-traded goods.

To Keynesian ears this story is wholly unconvincing because
the assumption that domestic producers can sell as much at the
going price as they want to is wholly unconvincing. The Keynesian
story goes something as follows. The higher demand for cash
balances will be accompanied by a lower demand for goods and
services at home as well as a lower demand for imports. Output
and employment will be lower. There just might also be a reduction in domestic prices, but this is ignored on the grounds that
unemployment does not lead to lower money wages. The reduction in output will lower the demand for money and the positive
payments balance will increase the stock, so that a new equilibrium
is reached with lower output and higher unemployment.

Further, this story has some very strong *ad hoc* assumptions,
especially as far as the behaviour of prices is concerned. It also
suffers from a fatal flaw. If the country we are considering is
really small in the proper sense, then it will indeed be true that
the demand curves facing them will be nearly perfectly elastic.
If then we are looking at rational conjectural equilibria it will
not be true that producers are quantity constrained. Once again,
considering international trade leads to a strengthening of the
Walrasian case.

There is here a very interesting problem requiring further
investigation. In general, the goods of one country are not perfect
substitutes for those of another country even if we ignore trans-

portation costs. We ought to distinguish English tweed from tweed. This might help with the present dilemma, which is this: if the world economy is a large economy, then rational conjectures are nearly competitive and the Walrasian model gains in strength. In particular, there is then no meaning to a shortage of aggregate demand. By increasing the variety of goods by labelling them also by their country of origin we may be able to argue that the world economy is not large enough to force us to conclude that all rational conjectures are competitive. This is an area requiring a good deal more work.

The case illustrates very well the present theoretical uncertainty. It seems a fairly firm fact that firms cannot sell abroad as much as they want to at the going prices: they are quantity constrained. This fact causes problems for the monetarist purely Walrasian approach. But it is also the case that the fact is not easy to rationalise by rational conjectures in a large world. The question then is whether the facts have been interpreted correctly or alternatively, whether we are right to insist on rational conjectures. The difficulties are almost all theoretical.

V SUMMING UP

I now want to look back over the road we have travelled.

I started by quoting the monetarists as believing that it was fact not theory that divided economists. I believe this view to be quite false even though it is also sometimes held by Keynesians. I therefore do not think that you can be Keynesian on the basis of a Walrasian world, and I do not think that you can be monetarist, with one exception, on the basis of a non-Walrasian world. The exception is this: the homogeneity postulate can be true in both worlds.

I have argued that the homogeneity postulate cannot, without further assumptions, be deduced from first principles. I now want to emphasise that there is still a large gap between that postulate and the proposition that the doubling of the money stock at each date and in each state will lead to a doubling of all prices in each state at each date. This gap I think is wider in non-Walrasian economies than it is in Walrasian ones. In the latter if there are many equilibria they none the less have it in common that there is no involuntary unemployment in any of them. In the non-Walrasian case one equilibrium may have less involuntary unemployment than another. In both cases however the stability question is quite unsettled. We do not even have many plausible adjustment mechanisms, and we have none that can be deduced from the first principles of rational actions.

In this connection I want to re-emphasise the work of Tobin—Buiter which I have discussed. It shows that it is not a necessary condition of a different price level to have different stocks of money. As I noted at the time, their result is really a demonstration that there are many (long run) equilibria in which government expenditure is equal to tax receipts. This result is true for a Walrasian economy with no involuntary unemployment. It will *a fortiori* be true of a non-Walrasian economy where examples of multiple equilibria are easy to construct.

But in any event, if the world is in continuous Walrasian equilibrium then the monetarist case is strong, although perhaps not quite as strong as some monetarists claim. In such an economy there is no involuntary unemployment at any date, and therefore the main Keynesian macro-objective is absent. The monetarists in some sense do not just object to Keynesian remedies: they argue that there are no Keynesian ills to remedy. There is here a fundamental theoretical question: can a coherent theory with involuntary unemployment be produced? If so, we will at least have a Keynesian theory. As everyone now knows, one can build such a theory on the basis of given prices or of prices that are allowed to vary only in narrow limits. If one can give this strong assumption a short period interpretation, as has recently been done by Malinvaud (1976), one will have gone part of the way to a Keynesian theory; but only part, since we cannot insist on fixed prices forever. This then leads to the notion of a rational conjectural equilibrium. Here one of the many unsolved problems is how to model the labour market. Certain formal results are available, but there is a good way to go. If the task can be accomplished we would have a theory of the economy in which prices are not rigid but are rationally chosen.

The main questions then are not about the slopes of IS—LM curves. Professor Stein, who holds the contrary view, has arrived at a somewhat paradoxical result. In the context of a macro-model he claims that, depending on the sign of a certain derivative, macroeconomic predictions that pure fiscal policy lowers real income are correct. He does not continue to the conclusion that in that case the government should borrow less and spend less if it wants to raise income. This would indeed be an interesting conclusion. But his model is not derived from any particular theoretical base, so any conclusions must be tentative. To give just one example, Professor Stein makes consumption independent of income but dependent only on wealth. This can be justified provided we also include the probability of not finding a job when we come to formulating human wealth. But this is not done.

The overwhelmingly most important postulate of the monetarists is that the invisible hand works and that it works pretty swiftly, although not instantaneously. In such a world with rational expectations monetary policy may be quite without real effects, but if there are any they will be bad. The main conclusion is not only that money does not matter unless its stock is changed randomly, but also that inflation resulting from a systematic monetary policy does not matter. This, paradoxical as it may sound, is the strict monetarist view. For Keynesians, on the other hand, money always mattered to the extent that different money stocks went with different equilibrium interest rates. The Keynesians had no price theory to speak of and it is to remedy this that one wants to study rational conjectural equilibria.

If this account is correct it is surprising that the editor of *The Times* and other monetarists are forever feverishly monitoring the money supply figures in their various incarnations. If the government made the rate of change in the money stock proportional to, say, the difference between actual unemployment and half a million unemployed, then this would be a pretty systematic policy, which is not one recommended by Friedman. According to the monetarists it will make no difference. According to the non-Walrasian view it will. Let the government try it!

REFERENCES

Blinder, A. S. and Solow, R. M. 1973. Does fiscal policy matter? *Journal of Public Economics*, 2, pp. 319—337

Brunner, K, and Meltzer, A. H. 1976. An aggregate theory for a closed economy. In *Monetarism* (Stein, J. ed.), 69—103

Clower, R. W. 1965. The Keynesian counterrevolution: a theoretical appraisal. In *The Theory of Interest Rates* (Hahn, F. H. and Brechling, F. P. eds.), 103—125

Dornbusch, R. 1976. Comments on Brunner and Meltzer. In *Monetarism* (Stein, J. ed.), 104—125

Friedman, M. 1976. Comments on Tobin and Buiter. In *Monetarism* (Stein, J. ed.), 310–317

Gorman, W. M. 1953. Community preference fields. *Econometrica*, **21**, 63–80

Grandmont, J. M. and Laroque, G. 1976. On Keynesian temporary equilibria. *Review of Economic Studies*, **43**, 53–67

Hahn, F. H. 1978. On Non-Walrasian equilibria. *Review of Economic Studies*, **45**, 1–17

Johnson, H. G. 1976. Towards a general theory of the balance of payments. In *The Monetary Approach to the Balance of Payments* (Frenkel, S. H. and Johnson, H. G., eds.), 46–63

Lucas, R. 1975. An equilibrium model of the business cycle. *Journal of Political Economy*, **81**, 1113–1144

Malinvaud, E. 1976. *The Theory of Unemployment Reconsidered* (Yrjo Johnson Lecture). Oxford: Blackwell

Negishi, T. 1976. Unemployment, inflation and the micro-foundations of macroeconomics. In *Essays in Economic Analysis* (Artis, M. and Nobay, A. R., eds.), 33–41

Stein, J. 1976. Inside the monetarist black box. In *Monetarism* (Stein, J. ed.), 183–232

Tobin, J. and Buiter, K. 1976. Long-run effects of fiscal and monetary policy on aggregate demand. In *Monetarism* (Stein, J. ed.), 273–319

15

Why I am not a Monetarist

I INTRODUCTION

The title of my talk is adapted from Bertrand Russell, who wrote a book *Why I am not a Christian*. In it he tried to convince his readers that neither reasoning nor serious moral thought could support Christianity. I am not in a position to affirm or to deny that he succeeded in his task but I conceive that mine is of the same kind. Russell's dagger came at a time when his foe seemed already in retreat. My small stiletto is to be pointed at a monster which is very much alive.

Monetarism I take to be the doctrine that the perfectly competitive economy in Walrasian equilibrium is adequately descriptive of the world we live in and that the model itself can be treated roughly enough to survive the coarse-grained hands of econometricians. This characterisation may be found surprising since it makes no mention of money. But almost everything monetarists have said about money is trivial, not to say banal, once one has jumped through the Walrasian hoop. My characterisation may also be found to be surprising since it seems to embrace upright economists who do not regard themselves as monetarist. That really cannot be helped when one is using any kind of simple categorisation. The important aspect for me is that monetarism can have no truck with Keynes and indeed must regard him as some sort of crank. For Keynes not only considered it possible that people could be involuntarily unemployed but even talked of equilibrium with such unemployment. He thought that these unsatisfactory states could be rendered more agreeable by rather simple actions on the part of the Government. None of this is wrong in the Walrasian equilibrium context — it simply does not make sense. It is, if you like, so ungrammatical as to be incomprehensible. This really is the centre of my concern today.

Is it the case that if we accept a world of self-seeking rational
agents we will by simple logic be driven to renounce Keynes and
all his works as mumbo-jumbo?

But first I want to concentrate on simpler prey, which is the
actual way in which monetarists reach their conclusions. As
Macaulay used to say, 'every schoolboy knows' that an agent's
best choice of action will remain unaffected if all money prices
(including of course money wage and expected prices) are different
in the same proportion as his money wealth is different. From
this we conclude that when any Walrasian equilibrium is taken,
if every agent's money wealth were different in the same proportion and if prices including expected prices were all different in
the same proportion from their previous value, the economy
would still be in equilibrium. This elementary result is then
translated by monetarists into 'a k-fold change in the money
stock of an economy will bring about a k-fold change in all money
prices'. It is hard to live in a world in which such sloppiness
goes unpunished. In any case the correct *homogeneity* property
of agent's choices will have to be just as much a part of a Keynesian
theory based on rational actions as of any other such theory. The
difference for Keynesian theory among other differences will be the
recognition of multiple equilibria. To this I return at length later.

But let me start at the beginning. As far as I am concerned
that is the beautiful theory which we call the Arrow–Debreu
model. It showed that it is logically possible to describe a world
where greedy and rational people responding only to price signals
take actions which are mutually compatible. The theory does
not describe the invisible hand in motion but displays it with its
task accomplished. The importance of this intellectual achievement is that it provides a benchmark. By this I mean that it serves
a function similar to that which an ideal and perfectly healthy
body might serve a clinical diagnostician when he looks at an
actual body.

Now one of the mysteries which future historians of thought
will surely wish to unravel is how it came about that the Arrow–
Debreu model came to be taken descriptively; that is, as sufficient
in itself for the study and perhaps control of actual economies.
Having spent most of my life as an economist on this theory I
confess that such an interpretation never occurred to me. Indeed
it was clear from the beginning that we only had half a theory
anyway since there was (and is) no rigorous account, derived
from first principles, of how the Arrow–Debreu equilibrium

comes to be established. But even the half which we had was quickly seen to have serious gaps: it could not account for money or a stock exchange; there were, more importantly, no increasing returns possible; there was no theory of actual exchange; the number of firms was taken as exogenous, and one would require set-up costs to make sense of firms anyway; information was symmetric and complete; labour was sold like peanuts are sold; unborn generations implausibly made themselves felt on current markets, and there were far too many markets anyway. If ever a theory was straightforwardly falsified it is the theory of the American economy in Arrow–Debreu equilibrium. But it was never meant to be so obviously falsified; it was designed as both a reference point and a starting point.

However it will now be argued that these remarks are beside the point for my present concern, since few monetarists do not care to use Arrow–Debreu theory. The models which for the most part *are* in use are founded on simple microeconomic text-books and use very special functional forms and are in any case 'macroeconomic'. It is true that in these models prices and wages are at all times clearing the Walrasian markets which the construc-tion contains, but the models themselves have been given a sequen-tial structure which is not the case in the Arrow–Debreu world.

All of this is indeed correct. But it is my contention that it is precisely this having one foot in the tranquil Arrow–Debreu waters and the other in seemingly plausible *ad hoc* models that makes the work of these economists so unsatisfactory. For instance they often claim that they can apply the fundamental theorem of welfare economics, which is firmly based on Arrow–Debreu theory, to their world of implicitly missing markets and of transaction costs. Recently a book published by one of them, for instance, claimed that rational expectations equilibria were Pareto efficient. The history of the 'optimum quantity of money' shows that it was only when it was examined by general equilibrium theorists that sense could be made of it. Similarly monetarists either construct miniature models in which equilibrium is unique or when the multiplicity stares them in the face they arbitrarily pick one of them.

It is at this point that I must pause, with some reluctance, to face a number of methodological questions. I must do so because they keep coming up in discussions even with the wise and good and because if I don't get them out of the way now some of you will go away unenlightened by the substantive points to come.

II METHODOLOGY

To be as brief as possible I shall be schematic.

(a) 'Simple models are what we should aim for.' This always strikes me like the parson's urging that virtue is better than vice. It is also without content or, as no doubt many of you would prefer to say, it is not operational. Like virtue, simplicity has its own reward if it works. It works if it provides robust insights. For instance amalgamating investment and consumption into something called total expenditure, instead of treating them separately, no doubt reduces equation numbers and allows monetarists to ignore variables like productive capacity. However, not only does it give wrong insights but also the model is not robust when the distinction between the two kinds of expenditures is reintroduced. This really given the clue: successful simplification is so by virtue of the robustness of its qualitative message to complication. If you are a true simplifier and not just sloppy and lazy then you must be able to claim to arrive at essentials which are also to be found in what you regard as complicated. Current monetarist writing does not survive this test.

(b) 'Economics is not a game of chess and our theories must be of a kind where they can be used.' Keynes after all urged us to be like dentists. The message here is that general equilibrium theory which is not specialised and simplified is so general that 'anything could happen'. To this my first answer is that although this is too sweeping it is true that many things could happen and that this may not only be a reflection of our ignorance but also of the world. Here is one example: President Reagan announces that he has seen the error of his ways and that he will now proceed to some old fashioned pump priming. One possible outcome is purely monetarist: prices and interest rates will rise to nullify the effects otherwise to be expected. That is because many people have come to believe Chicago. Another outcome is that observing all the slack in the economy and seeing a converted president, people will expect higher demand and output, prices will not change much and the Keynesian results ensue. All of this is really an aspect of multiple equilibria. But if I do not know which of these two and of the many intermediate outcomes will occur, what is the point of enshrining a guess in some highly special model in which one or the other is bound to occur? It is true that I can then say something but it seems to me better to have kept quiet. The circumstance that we must always make public choices does not seem to me to lead to the conclusion that we must always cook the books. On the contrary. The economist's main contribution at present is precisely to urge that many things can happen. This might stop politicians putting all their eggs into one basket.

(c) 'Macroeconomics is different from microeconomics.' If it is then I for one do not know what it is. It can hardly be the case that models which look on the world as if there were a single firm, a single household, and a single good thereby create some new kind of economic theory. Of course, like in physics and perhaps in Marxian economics it could be otherwise. There could be theories — holistic theories — in which aggregates do not behave as simply added microentities. Indeed, general equilibrium theory itself shows that the interaction of many individuals needs a special theory. In our present state of knowledge, macroeconomics is simply the project of deducing something about the behaviour of such aggregates as income and employment from the micro-theory which we have. The whole enterprise of giving micro-economic foundations to macroeconomics is therefore misnamed. If macroeconomics before this enterprise was innocent of micro-economics it is not easy to see that it was anything at all. But of course Keynes never went on such a hare-brained path and he can claim to have founded the subject. Almost two thirds of *The General Theory* is in fact devoted to microeconomics.

If one looks more closely one finds, as usual, that this corrupt use of language, this sloppiness in making sentences, is sinister in intent. For what many people who set out to look for foundations meant was that the Walrasian equilibrium economy cannot ac-commodate the Keynesian insights. They then drew the conclusion that there were no such insights. It did not seem necessary to enquire whether the Walrasian equilibrium model was itself adequate or logically robust. The true question then is whether there are rigorous models of the economy whose premises are no less acceptable at least than those of the Walrasian model, which can in fact support Keynesian contentions. That question cannot be answered if we start *by fiat* as the Lucasians do, with a world in which Walrasian markets always clear. (I ought here to add that Keynes himself is much to blame for the muddle. He had a poets' intuition and a practical man's grasp but he did not begin to know how to theorise rigorously.)

(d) The last methological point which I wish to make is this: the answer which one receives over and over again to one's criticisms is that the model 'works' and that the theorist's concerns are therefore of no relevance. Just so might an ancient Roman have spoken about the oracles or the method of finding a propitious time for battle by consulting the entrails of animals. This certainly worked as well as does most econometrics. The view I am here considering can be traced back to Friedman and to old fashioned and discredited positivism. But a fact not confirmed by theory is a fact we do not understand. It cannot be brought into proper relation with what we know or think we know. That does not mean that we should reject the fact if such it is. It means that all our work still remains to be done. If a monetarist model is logically flawed then I for one do not give a fig for its predicative power. I chose to be an economist – not a witch doctor.

Here is an example. Everyone knows by now that Walrasian sequence economies have many – mostly a continuum of – rational expectation equilibria. Among these there may be just one which seeks the steady state or there may also be a continuum of these. Some others may become infeasible in a thousand years time. Monetarist econometricians have chosen to work with models in which there is only one path that converges to the steady state. They then declare that this is the path which an actual economy follows. Since there is nothing in the theory which suggests that this is so or how it could be so they add that their latest three stage econometric estimate based on this sort of assumption 'works'. If they are also trying to placate you they will mumble something about transversality conditions. This however gives the game away. For these conditions are only relevant in an optimising context. Thus their 'explanation' is implicitly that the economy must behave as if someone performed an infinite optimisation exercise on it. But *that* is precisely the issue at hand – indeed, it is at the heart of Keynes. His description of an actual capitalist economy makes it very clear that it would not be Pareto efficient, leave along Ramsey optimal. From an epistemological point of view the whole sequence of arguments is illiterate. It may be that tomorrow someone will turn up who forecasts the economy by scanning tea leaves and who has great success in this as econometricians understand success. He might be a very useful person to President Reagan or to someone playing the stock exchange. But it is hard to see how anything he does has any bearing on the enterprise which is economics. Let us recall that

Ptolemy can be made to 'work' even now but that we reject it because there is no way of understanding his construction.

III THE ARGUMENT

I now leave methodology behind me and come to the centre of my argument. This I fear will be a little more technical. It will be in two parts. The first will repeat at a rather more general level what I have already touched on before, namely that monetarists' doctrines are not logically entailed by their theory. The second will argue that there are very strong grounds for looking for another theory anyway.

If we are going to have theories which can encompass some of the important world phenomena which I have ennumerated as being beyond Arrow—Debreu theory, then we shall, it is I think universally agreed, have to modify this theory to give it a sequential structure. By this I mean that there will have to be trading at every date. This for a careful theorist then entails the necessity of forging an endogenous theory of markets. But this I shall not now discuss, and I shall take 'missing' markets as given. Even so an agent's plans and current action will now depend on expectations. We know next to nothing about expectations, and that is why we take the step of demanding that they be rational. In the present Walrasian context a rational expectation equilibrium occurs when each agent knows the prices which will clear markets in each date—event pair when all agents are equally clever.

So let us stop right here. The theory as such says nothing about the underlying stochastic process and so the definition which I have just given is not the same as that used by macroeconomists of the RE type when they ask expected prices to be unbiased estimators of actual price. Much less do they say that agent's activities depend only on their actuarial expectations. Every schoolboy knows — to go back to Macaulay — that this is a very special and not very plausible case. But there are also several logical problems of which I wish to pick only one. There is nothing in the world as God amd Mammon have created it that guarantees, or indeed makes it likely in any precise sense, that for each date—event pair market clearing prices are unique. When that is so national expectations equilibrium requires expectations concerning the expectations of other agents. But as I have already stressed, non-uniqueness of equilibria is what Keynesian policy prescriptions must be about. The problem does not arise for those macroeconomists who are filling the journals with three or four log-linear equations. Not only are there no relative prices (in fact many do not distinguish between wages and prices) but in the nature of such models multiple solutions cannot arise.

This is worth a moment's pause. When these equations are written down they almost always include an error term with zero mean and with no serial correlation. If one thinks about this one comes to realise that the underlying economy of many agents and goods is assumed to be exposed to lots of uncorrellated shocks which are idiosyncratic to different agents and that, as it were, steps are taken instantaneously to 'cancel' these shocks. Lucas has recently realised that these are tall assumptions and by abandoning them has got himself a trade cycle model with always clearing markets.

But let us now accept a unique Walrasian rational expectations equilibrium as describing the American economy as it would be if it were not continuously surprised by the quite inexplicable actions of government or the Fed. I want you on the way to notice one quite startling implication. In such an economy, although there would be trading at every date, there would, as in the Arrow–Debreu economy, be decisions only at one date – the first. The economy unfolds as dates and states unfold. But 'all things and all manner of things' have already been provided for. In this world firms need a high powered executive only once to make all the plans for all contingencies and dates. Thereafter it is all routine. At least this is the way the world would look in the absence of a random government. Such a government would be the only occasion for decision making. This seems to me pretty close to nonsense for someone engaged in fashioning a theory to his econometric purposes. It also is an extraordinarily difficult way to analyse the Schumpeterian circumstance of the world.

But let us close our eyes and proceed. The economy in the equilibrium which I have described is by no means at rest. As states unfold the allocation of labour will change, some firms contract and others expand. Indeed total employment will vary from state to state as the appropriate real wage varies. So what exactly is the 'natural rate hypothesis' in this world? The latter is supposed to have something to do with search, a phenomenon I have no seen formally incorporated since Phelps studied it and Diamond's splendid recent paper which is not in this mould anyway. Is the amount of search independent of state and independent of the number of people seeking work? If there is a wage distribution, why is it not given and what are the conditions under which it is invariant under the unfolding of state?

However, let us shut our eyes to this difficulty. Also, no doubt some stochastic definition of the natural rate can be cooked up. The problem which I do not think we can shut our eyes to is the central confusion between the sentence starting 'there exists' and one starting with 'it is the case'. It is a confusion which I regret to say is much in evidence among students which must be their teacher's fault. In suitable conditions a rational expectations equilibrium exists of the type here discussed. But no one has shown that it is the case that an economy always seeks that equilibrium. I do not mean that no one has shown 'empirically'. I mean that no one has shown it theoretically and by that in turn I mean that no one has done this at the level of serious theory. So the answer one gets is 'that it works' and that, as I have already argued, is not our answer at all. Half the story is simply missing — the invisible hand is superinvisible.

Now I have already remarked that Lucas, by far and away the most accomplished in this group, has noticed the difficulty and has in fact shown that, even though markets clear at any date, mistakes rationally made may never wash out. But he has not considered what this discovery entails for his rather famous monetarist ineffectiveness proposition. For it is by no means the case that on these errant cyclical paths monetary policy fully anticipated must be ineffective. To show that he would need to show that the errors people make must have the homogeneity property. But that must be wrong, at least in general if for no other reason than that there is no precise account of how the errors are formed. Thus if I cannot disentangle a monetary from a real shock the manner in which I resolve the ambiguity is quite open to the extent that it depends on my priors; and who is to say that they are independent of monetary policy?

Let us consider an example. Firms, wrongly for whatever reason, expect that investment in fixed capital goods has become more profitable when the monetary policy is a constant stock of money. The economy will now follow a certain path in which the initial error will not quickly go away because it is embodied in the extra fixed capital which firms have installed. Indeed one can readily see how cycles may arise. Now let the monetary policy be one in which the money stock rises in proportion to the difference between actual and some target income. If we accept monetarist doctrine then this will leave the path unaffected in real terms but the price level will behave differently. But firms who invest borrow money or do not pay out money, and the holding of money depends on the nominal and not on the real interest rate. So here at once is a source of real effectiveness and non-homogeneity of the error. But there is a much more serious argument: if all firms were to believe that under the second monetary policy the future would be different than under the first then it would be different and there is nothing to gainsay that, since we are *not* in rational expectations equilibrium. That is agents may know a model of the economy but there is no 'the' model since there is no way in which they can model each others mistakes. Keynesian agents will make different mistakes from monetarist agents.

So even in this rarefied model there does not seem much joy for monetarists. But perhaps this is too rarefied. I was recently taken to task by a high ranking economist at the Bank of England for just this failing. He told me that sensible people were monetarist in a 'pragmatic and Friedmanite way' which I took to mean that sensible people had no good reason to believe what they do believe. But let me try to be sensible.

If there is one thing that distinguishes the 'sensible' monetarist it is his view that (a) a firm control on monetary aggregates is essential for economic health and (b) that inflation is the greatest evil to which we can be exposed. I shall not discuss (b) since it is inconsistent with any monetarist theory and makes inflation a 'bad' in itself — a primitive bad as it were.

Now to (a). We know that except for 'shoe-leather' effects the monetary aggregates are, on any monetarist theory, irrelevant if they are foreseen. This is they have no 'real' consequences. If however in our simple, sensible and pragmatic mood we believe that they do have real effects then we have to be persuaded that some particular formula dreamed up by a central banker by which the money supply is to be governed yields the best real effects. Since no such argument has been offered I conclude that after all nothing more is at stake then the provision of a simple formula — any formula — which will permit agents to forecast prices. So it must after all be the case that monetarists believe monetary policy which is not random to have no real effects. But that is so plainly false that we had better extend a helping hand and consider the proposition that monetary policy properly foreseen can have no lasting real effects.

Indeed there is a pragmatic monetarist view that a change in monetary policy, in particular a change to a more restrictive policy, is bound to be 'painful' in the short run. In puritanical Britain this promised joy through pain is much admired. Suppose then that it is true that we must first be punished before we can enjoy the benefits of what Mrs Thatcher calls 'honest' money. Then for less masochistically inclined economists a simple cost—benefit question arises: how many billions of pounds of GNP is 'honest' money worth? In fact: what precisely is the benefit of such money and how long will it be delayed? I cannot myself answer this question since for monetarists, as I have already argued, 'honest' money should have no benefits, long run or short run. If you think that you can control the rate of change in money prices by controlling the money supply, then you can set it at zero or 12 per cent and it should make very little difference — certainly not several percentage points of GNP. But of course the model may be wrong. It is simply that on their own grounds, pragmatic or otherwise, they seem at sea. The arguments do not cohere at the crudest level and there really is an end on it.

So I now turn to the view that there are the strongest grounds for breaking out of the Walrasian straightjacket, and indeed that some of the breaking out which has already been achieved is impressive and rather favourable to a roughly Keynesian view. Before I do this I reiterate once more my warning: the circumstances that I consider it crucial that we look beyond the Walrasian horizons does *not* mean that I believe this to be possible without a thorough knowledge of where these horizons are. Progress in a subject is rarely made by the throwing out hook, line and sinker, what went before. Mostly it comes as a natural and inevitable development.

Since on this occasion I have to attempt to hit the nail on the head with one blow I shall concentrate on the single proposition that the Walrasian model seriously understates the scope of externalities and as a consequence is too sanguine in its belief that capitalist outcomes cannot be improved by explicit co-operation. To put it somewhat more theoretically, it seems to be the case that rather slight departures from the economy's description lead to rather large changes in our judgement of its performance and the role of policy. There are very many ways in which this can be argued, but I shall concentrate on only one.

Of course even in orthodox economies there may be externalities: smoke and laundries, and beekeepers and apple farmers, are familiar to the undergraduate. It can be argued that such externalities can be eliminated by appropriate allocations of property rights. For the externalities which concern me, that is not the case. They arise from the nature of the economic game and from the manner in which the players in such a game can communicate. Some of the most prominent monetarists – the name of Barro comes to mind – are quite unaware of these and consequently have become advocates of a Panglossian view of the world, that no state can be in equilibrium unless it is Pareto efficient. We are asked to share their naïve glee at this confusion.

Let me start then with what appears an old fashioned Keynesian argument. Assume, provisionally of course, that there are people who at the going real wage would prefer to work but cannot find anyone to employ them. However in the market for goods tranquillity reigns: firms employ just as many as they regard most profitable and manage to sell what at the going price they wish to sell. Households on the markets for goods buy at the going prices what they consider best. Keynes' proposition now went as follows. At the going wage no firm would wish to have more labour given the output and hiring decision of all other firms. However if all firms together co-operatively hired more labour the demand of the newly employed would shift the demand curves facing firms to the right. If they are producing under diminishing returns the real wage would be somewhat lower, but under our provisional postulate that would not lower the supply of labour. There would then be a new state of the economy in which again except possibly still on the labour supply side, all agents were in equilibrium. This new state would have more employment and under mild assumptions would Pareto dominate the old state. All of this can be made precise and ship-shape. The Nash-like externalities here are clear to the naked eye.

Since this story as such is perfectly correct, everything turns on what I have called the provisional hypothesis that there are states in which there are people willing to work at the going wage who cannot find jobs. In the first instance that may be taken to mean that the price mechanism does not work infinitely fast to clear Walrasian markets and only a madman would deny that. This then leads to the next stage in the Keynesian argument which has been most neglected. This is that if in the situation which I have outlined we leave it all to the game in which agents can only communicate by price signals, the outcome is slow and indeed uncertain. Money wages will not fall in a co-ordinated way and the process will involve changes in relative prices and relative wages and so in allocations. Expectations enter the story in an important but uncertain way. As the price level falls, people with debt commitments in terms of money are made worse off or even bankrupt. The nominal interest rate will also take time to adjust and may not do so monotonically. A prevailing expectation of falling prices may, for a time, discourage investment. In short, there is a complex and not well understood dynamic process to be examined. But suppose that it succeeds after trials and tribulations and with considerable real cost, in guiding us into the Walrasian haven. It will do so largely by the twin forces of lower real wages and higher real cash balances. But then Keynes very reasonably thought it not sensible to reach the good co-operative outcome in this absurdly costly uncertain and round-about way. For exactly the same outcome can be achieved by a direct route. Let the government give everyone a gift of money. Agree with the monetarists that prices will rise, but do not agree that money wages will rise since labour is 'off its supply curve'. Employment will increase on impeccable monetarist grounds. Since output will be higher once again on impeccable monetarist grounds, real cash balances will be higher. There will be no bankruptcies and we do not have to rely on the slow and uncertain process of money wage declines. Of course here too there is an appeal to a dynamic which none of us can vouch for. But it seems no worse, indeed a great deal more persuasive, than that of the monetarist.

It has not escaped my attention that if under the government policy all money wages had risen as well, the state of the economy would have been unchanged except for distribution effects through debt. I often think that monetarists are bewitched by such homogeneity theorems. Of course they are correct but they are also irrelevant here. Since by hypothesis there are more people willing to work than there are jobs at the going wage, the monetarists' own arguments predict a declining real wage. So let us not be held up by such observations.

In any case in the first instance Keynes' argument is not that markets cannot deliver (much less that money wages are rigid downwards) but quite simply that the route the economy must take when workers must signal their willingness to work by lower money wages is more costly and more uncertain than is the alternative which he proposed. It will be clear that such arguments do not apply to uncorrelated price adjustments which take place when, say, there is a change in preferences between bananas and fish.

But matters are really more Keynesian than Keynes proposed because he rather unwisely retained a Marshallian foundation. What needs to be recognised is that price signals in themselves are sufficient for co-ordinating agents' actions only in perfectly competitive, that is in general in 'large' economies. Even then constant returns cause a problem since at competitive prices producers do not know how much to produce until they know how much is demanded. I think that there is in any case no good ground for doubting a commonplace observation that firms in investing and producing not only attempt to calculate the price at which they will be able to sell but consider how much can be sold. No car manufacturer, no steel producer, no shop owner, no gas station manager believes that he can sell any quantity at the going price. So at the root of a good deal of Keynesian analysis there is that other upheaval of the 1930s, the imperfect competition revolution. But imperfect competition is intrinsically a situation with externalities, because what Ostroy has called the 'no surplus condition' is in general not satisfied. That is for instance removing one firm and redistributing its inputs among remaining firms may lead to a reduction in output less than is represented by the profits of the departing firm.

When firms have to consider demand functions rather than prices in making their decisions, it is elementary to see that these functions will depend on employment (or income) as long as the labour market is not in perfectly competitive equilibrium. This is just another way of making the familiar Clower point. At this stage of the argument Keynes considered another source of externality. He argued that workers cared not only about their real wage but also about their position in the wage distribution. In particular he maintained that if all real wages were lowered together an unemployed worker would be willing to work even though, given all other wages, he had been unwilling to reduce his own because of the worsening of his relative position such a lowering would imply. Hence there may be many equilibria with different levels of employment and different real wages. Again Keynes seems to me to be here appealing to a phenomenon we both observe in others and in ourselves. You will notice that it does not entail any assumptions that real wages are downwardly rigid. What it does do is to pay some attention to the otherwise totally mysterious manner in which real wages might be changed.

There are of course many other features of the labour market which merit attention – unions and training and selection and contracts to name a few. But the most important one is simply that this market is not at all like a fish market. This is so because the relation between employer and worker is of some duration and because workers are capable of calculating and following strategies. The axiom that wages must change as long as the Walrasian excess demand for labour differs from zero lacks merit on these grounds alone.

But my argument started with involuntary unemployment and has finished with some partial arguments that this could be consistent with equilibrium if we do not ask for a Walrasian auctioneer but allow agents to set prices. Let me now be as Lucasian as I can be and simply deny the possibility of involuntary unemployment not just in equilibrium but ever. Does that, admittedly slightly bizarre, resolve deliver me into the hands of the monetarists?

I am glad to report that even this putting of my head into the devil's mouth keeps me perfectly safe.

It will be agreed that production in a firm is rarely the outcome of labour alone. Since I am far away from the 'true' Cambridge, let us say that it also requires capital. So the marginal product of labour will depend on the amount of both labour and capital employed. Now either the economy is in a steady state or it is not. Suppose the latter. Then its future is of interest. Since we are now Lucasians let us consider only rational expectation futures. Let us further suppose that all paths of the economy will eventually get arbitrarily close to a unique steady state. Then as I have noted before it will still be the case that there is not a unique path of this kind. Indeed in many cases there is a continuum. Which one (if any) the economy will choose depends on the expectations of agents. There is no reason to suppose that all these paths are equally desirable. But more importantly, until the steady state is reached there are many different evolutions of what has been so tendentiously called the natural employment level, and there is, as far as I can see, no way at all of deciding which path the economy will take or of telling a story of how it comes to take any of them at all.

I must break off here to return to a technical point which I have already mentioned once, and which is of practical relevance simply because it is so poorly understood by many who conceive themselves engaged in providing econometric evidence for monetarism. If one could think of an economy as behaving though time as if it were guided by a Ramsey maximiser, then indeed it would often be the case that there is a unique path that an infintely lived economy would follow from any given initial condition. But there is not the slightest reason to suppose that the economy behaves in this way or indeed could behave in this way. Certainly expectations may be rational for a thousand years and yet the economy could then have many possible futures. To require rational expectations over infinite time is just nonsense. But even when there are such expectations, provided there is no social maximand which guides the economy, there can be a whole manifold of rational expectation paths. This is a logical canker at the heart of national expectations theory and until someone resolves this indeterminacy we had better remain quiet. In particular it is something of a scandal that so much macroeconometrics appeals to transversality conditions to resolve this fundamental indeterminacy. It is a scandal because such conditions belong to optimisation theory and only foolishness can turn it into a descriptive theory.

The outcome of all this is that there seems to be no such thing as *the* natural level of employment and output. But there is worse to come.

Let us once again be as forthcoming as possible and drop the objection I have just raised. However let·us now insist that the world is uncertain, so that we are thinking of a stochastic equilibrium through time. Then as the economy unfolds the appropriate level and distribution of employment will differ from one moment to the next. It is true that we can, under our self-denying ordinance, say exactly what values these variables as well as all prices should have in an equilibrium. But what makes them so? Just think of an example. In equilibrium at date 1 and state 1 wages are the same in A and B. At date 2 and state 2 wages for equilibrium must again be the same in both industries but half the labour force which worked in A must now work in B. What brings this about if relative wages never differ? It cannot be part of rational expectation as formulated that you have to forecast in which industry you will work in any state. The invisible hand has here become a metaphysical hand. In fact of course the required inducements to reallocation as well as the process itself will be a potent cause of disturbances. But to the theorists there is an even more troubling matter. Agents will have to forecast adjustment processes and I cannot see how that is to be done.

I have recently argued elsewhere that considerations such as these may lead to the view that there is something which one might call the *natural rate of inflation*. It is a commonplace enough idea: essentially it says that the reallocations required for different states will be accomplished at lower utility cost if we bring it about by letting some prices and wages rise while none fall than would be the case if some prices and wages also had to fall. I cannot claim that this conclusion has the status of a general theorem although it is true in plausible enough examples. However it shows how much work the monetarists have to do before they begin to deserve serious attention.

So even on purely Walrasian grounds one can see that we are being invited to board a leaking ship. But it is also a ship of folly. For instance to take just one example a passenger is asked to believe that three and a half million unemployed, give or take half a million searchers, are to be explained by their desire to substitute present for future leisure.

My conclusion then is this. If one takes Walrasian theory seriously then one cannot take seriously the use monetarists make of it. Moreover, and far more important, if one takes Walrasian theory seriously then one understands the many lacunae which it has and the need for quite large scale modifications and amplifications. I have argued that from the point of view of macrotheory the Walrasian model greatly underestimates what may be important externalities and indeed cannot even discuss the existence of a certain kind of these. In this view I have been anticipated by Diamond and Weitzman. Weitzman makes the simple but much neglected point that without set-up costs there would be no firms and indeed there would be no meaning to unemployment. There are thus increasing returns and one can show benefits of co-operation over non-co-operation in finite economies. Diamond's work is very close to my own thinking. He has presented several models, but essentially what is happening is that there are externalities working through demand. Thus for instance in a search situation my decision to search more for an exchange partner will increase the probabilities of someone else finding a partner.

In my own work I have taken as one case the situation which arises with implicit labour contracts. I have modified the usual model by including an incentive problem which has the consequences that workers cannot get full insurance. Hence layoffs are accompanied by utility losses to the laid off. Putting this in a general equilibrium context, it will be the case that the demand for goods will depend not just on prices but also on layoffs. One can then show in certain economies that there are multiple rational expectation equilibria which can be Pareto ranked. Understanding comes from remarking that layoffs in one industry adversely affect profitability in other industries and lead to higher layoffs in these.

But of course we were all anticipated by Keynes. Macroeconomic writings in the last ten years have highlighted his claim to the title of great economist. His theoretical sloppiness is rendered trivial by his remarkable insight and by his directness. He saw the unemployed of the Great Depression. He saw them marching, protesting, and queueing up at labour exchanges. He concluded that they would prefer to work. It is hard to see how any scientifically minded investigator could have reached any other conclusion. He then realised that there was something to be explained which contemporary theory claimed to be impossible. There were Lucasians before Lucas. He hit on a most interesting answer which the vulgarisation of subsequent textbooks has rendered as rigid money wages. The answer turned as I have argued on the kind of game a labour market is. There were under its rules grave difficulties in any one worker changing his wage or any one player doing so, and there was no way in which they could do it all together. However the government could act in such a way as if all workers had changed their wage simultaneously. He did not, to repeat myself, argue that money wages would never fall. If anything he argued that if they did the consequences might be undesirable since unlike modern monetarists he did not ignore the long run of the past represented by debts denominated in money. It did not occur to his sane mind that everyone would accurately forecast the price level of each date when contracting a debt. He gave an account of expectation with due attention to contagions and the difficulty of disentangling the 'real' from the spurious occasioned by other agent's expectations. It is difficult to believe that future historians of thought will not come to recognise his analysis here as vastly superior as a guide to understanding than current practice.

Once the possibility of involuntary unemployment is recognised, ordinary theory requires us to put quantities like income as well as prices as arguments of the excess demand functions and as variables subject to expectations. It is this move which conspicuously allows for co-operation to dominate competition.

If there are involuntary unemployment states, transitory or

not, there is a possible role for government policies, fully anti-cipated or not. It is at this point that the monetarists have done most harm, and a strong argument can be made on the grounds of welfare economics that monetarist writings should be taxed and Keynesian ones subsidised. For once one admits that in-voluntary unemployment states are possible, government pump priming can have one of two effects. To reiterate what I have already argued before: if citizens have been reared on the current mumbo-jumbo, especially if bankers and businessmen (who are amongst the most credulous of people) have been thus indoc-trinated, them all that may result is a rise in prices. On the other hand if those citizens had been raised on Keynes they would come to expect that people will buy more cars and washing machines and even hamburgers. Since there is absolutely no evidence of diminishing return when there is excess capacity and labour the economy could deliver these goods at more or less constant prices. More importantly no one could have any induce-ment to raise prices if others don't. Wages would on good orthodox lines not rise because we have involuntary unemployment. A benificent scenario is possible. Moreover if sane people like that expected such policy whenever such bad states occur, the carrying out of it may not even be necessary. We have here a classic instance of a proposition first made, I believe, by Max Weber: what social scientists say and write affects the material which they study. That does not mean that they can never be right; there is, as it were, at least one fixed point in this mapping. In the present case there are at least two: a monetarist and a Keynesian. It just so happens that the latter is vastly to be preferred on grounds of welfare to the former.

One should now ask how the present mess came into being. For macroeconomics today is in the state in which astronomy would be if Ptolemaic theory once again came to dominate the field. There can in fact be few instances in other disciplines of such a determined turning back of the clock. A great deal of what is written today as well as the policy recommendations which have been made would be thoroughly at home in the 1920s. So something needs explaining. But I shall not attempt to do so. For it is time to draw this to a close, although there is much left to say.

You may recall that when Miss Prism commanded Cicily in *The Importance of Being Earnest* to study her chapter on political economy she urged her to omit the section on the Indian rupee 'since it was altogether too sensational'. I am more liberal than Miss Prism but I urge you to recognise that monetarism or what passes for modern macroeconomics is also 'altogether too sensational'. It represents the triumph of artifact over plain and direct thinking. It is sensational in its conclusion that the market always yields the best of all possible worlds. It is sensational in its contention that there are no social phenomena relevant to economic life which are not captured by prices. It is sensational in the sheer bravado of reducing the beautiful structure of general equilibrium theory to one or two log-linear equations and in its neglect of every subtlety. It is sensational in its ignorance of both the scope and limit of economic theory. Above all it is sensational in its confidence in conclusions which are neither proven nor plausible. For all these reasons I am not a monetarist.

16

Economic Theory and Policy

INTRODUCTION

The importance of theory for economic policy is this: without
theory there could be no policy discussions and no reasons could
be given for adopting one policy rather than another. However,
importantly, it is not the case that the significance of theory lies in
its ability to deliver the 'best' policy. Nor is it crucial for its importance and relevance that it should, with more or less error, be able
to predict the future. These observations seem plainly true to me
but they are not uncontroversial. I shall therefore defend them in
the sequel.

If my first claim is provisionally accepted, then a seeming paradox
arises. Politicians decide on policy and presumably discuss them
with their experts. Politicians, however, are noted neither for their
grasp of such economic principles as there are, nor for analytical
habits of thought. It is not at all plausible to suppose that they
could follow an economic argument of any complexity. Moreover,
they normally carry a large load of commitments and beliefs. So it
would appear that in fact policy does get made and discussed
without the benefit of theory.

But I do not think that this is in fact what happens, and I am
much persuaded by Keynes' remarks concerning 'practical men' and
their enslavement by theory. Indeed, politicians seem madly addicted to theory. It just so happens that their theory will normally
not withstand logical, and rarely, empirical scrutiny. The importance
of what I will now call 'serious' theory is then much enhanced
since with the optimism of the Enlightenment we may hope that
eventually, even if it cannot reveal truth, it can nail error. Of course
the politicians get much of their theory at second and third hand
and in that they are aided by many economists. The temptations

of the economist are many, and very rarely do they reap the whirl-wind of poor John Law. These worldly temptations are obvious and need not detain us. But there is also a more insidious temp-tation: the temptation of faith.

I think it is entirely plausible that the purveyor of miracle cures in cancer firmly believes in the efficacy of what he is purveying. I would not for a moment deny that Professor Friedman genuinely believes what he has been advising or that Mr Benn's economic advisers are firmly convinced that they have seen the light. What, however, remains indisputable, and I intend to argue, is that there are no reasonable grounds for these certainties. Indeed I shall want to try and establish that one of the virtues of serious economic theory is that it shows why such certainties are not to be had, and equally importantly it is able to pinpoint rather precisely the source of the uncertainties which we must live with. But doubt — especialiy intellectual doubt — that the DNA molecule seems in general to have programmed against. It is, in short, against human nature That is why serious thinking is in every sense a discipline and contrary to deep inclinations. That is why two economists can proclaim diametrically opposed propositions on the economy, each claiming to derive his view from economic principles. What has happened is not necessarily that either proposition must be false, but rather that they could both be true. However, in the absence of faith we cannot decide which, if either, is true.

This propensity to believe, this addiction to the intuitive leaps of faith, has not only done much harm to the reputation of econo-mics as a discipline, it has done a good deal of harm all round. Witch doctors may not always kill their patients but I suspect that they rarely cure them. In the present case, however, what is alarm-ing is not so much the pursuit of policies whose consequences turn out to be rather strikingly different from those predicted with the eye of faith. After all, if I am right we shall often embark on undesirable policies. What is sad and deplorable is that the faith-healers have delayed the time when economic policy is discussed in the light of serious theory — that is, in the light of reason. How-ever, at this point I must issue a warning — I cannot prove that a hundred years in which reason is the mistress will on average deliver more desirable economic outcomes than a hundred years of faith-healers. At the very best I might be able to demonstrate a proba-bility of this. This is the measure of what economic theory can in sober fact deliver and also the occasion for my own leap of faith.

What I must now do is to pass from these generalities to argument and to concrete illustrations. However, before I do that I shall still need a brief interlude to allow me to give an account of what I mean by serious economic theory.

SERIOUS THEORY

Every theory in whatever discipline is formulated on the basis of assumptions. In some subjects some of these assumptions are beyond reasonable doubt although ritually one always says that they may yet turn out to be false. Others, however, are quite doubtful. For instance, cosmology has typically a good many assumptions which one understands would not cause great surprise if shown to be false. Economics has many such assumptions. An obvious first requirement of serious theory is to state these clearly and precisely. For instance, I know of no monetarist theorist who has stated, leave alone precisely investigated, the assumptions required to render his equilibrium unique – a necessary requirement for the conclusions that are offered. It is a virtue of the kind of theory most disliked by practical economists – I mean theory which is formulated mathematically – that it habitually avoids such sloppiness. It happens that the assumptions they have to write down in order that propositions be logically implied are often seen to be 'unrealistic'. But they are doing no more than making explicit what the man of faith and the man of affairs must reasonably be taken to be implicitly supposing. In doing so they surely perform the important service of allowing an honest assessment of the realism and relevance of any particular proposition.

The next important outward and visible sign of serious theory is a certain economy of assumptions and a certain fastidiousness in their selection. In the first instance I mean by this that as far as possible the theory relies on first principles which for the moment I shall call axioms. An example of such an axiom is that if a feasible action is to someone's advantage then that someone will, or more exactly is likely, to take it. Axioms of course can be false. Their role at any one time is to embody hypotheses which either are very widely agreed as likely to be true or make reasoning possible at all. So what I am doing for serious theory is at least distinguishing between those assumptions that are deducible from first principles and those that are not. Rather imprecisely I shall call the latter contingent.

I have now reached a point where I find myself at variance both with some of my respected theoretical colleagues and with those who are keen to bring theory quickly to the point where it has bearing on policy. So I must put my cards on the table.

One argument against the advice to afford priority to first principles is that theories become so general as to be useless. Thus, for instance, it is often said that general equilibrium theory is so unspecific in its postulates that anything is possible. Apart from the fact that this is not so, my first reply is that indeed it may be true that a large number of outcomes are possible and that the theory, by not claiming more than we know, simply does the best it can in the light of what we do know. Not long ago an advocate of the opposite view told me the following parable in order to get me to mend my ways. A man has lost his keys in a dark corner of a street but is found searching for them under a street light. When asked to explain himself, he pointed out that he could only search where there was light. The moral of the story is that it is better to make pronouncements on the basis of specific contingent assumptions than to say nothing at all. I confess that I was not convinced since it seemed to me certain that the man would not find his keys.

But of course that is altogether the wrong argument, since it is implausible to suppose that it is always better to make some pronouncement than to admit to a 'don't know'. A much more convincing line is to notice that we live in a contingent world. For instance, there is no necessity for preferences to be of a certain sort – the axioms only specify that there are preferences. But as a matter of fact and historical circumstance they may indeed be of a particular sort. Few English people would have a positive shadow price for sheep's eyes. So indeed once the theory has been seriously formulated there is every reason to make it specific for particular application. But the point here is that this is not a theoretical but an empirical step. Thus there is a theory of the behaviour of gases under pressure, but the behaviour of a particular gas in a particular container will depend on the parameters. Just so we may know how to formulate the general principles of tax incidence but its actual incidence in a particular economy at a particular time will depend on contingent particulars. A function of axiomatic theory is to provide the logical framework deduced from agreed general first principles in which contingent knowledge can be shown to have its particular consequences.

In this light models based on very particular assumptions are either empirical applications or theoretical exercises. But obvious though this must be it is of some importance to understand. Thus, for instance, there is no proposition deducible from first principles, to the effect that the demand for money must be proportional to money income. Indeed there is no such deduction possible in favour of the proposition that this demand is a given invariant function of income, current prices and current interest rates. A model and its attendant deducible propositions based on some such assumption concerning money demand is thus in the first instance an empirical and not a theoretical construct. That of course is just as it should be. Any application of economic theory must be of this kind. But its empirical basis must be sufficient to rule out, up to a margin of error, other possible premises admissible by the axioms. It is the case that this is possible only extremely rarely. Moreover even when it is possible the theory will in general contain many operations whose mode we have not been able to tie down empirically to something particular. Hence it is even rarer that an agreed specific assumption can be shown to entail unique consequences. The function of serious theory is to make this clear, a task which it can only perform if it does not start with singular assumptions. That, as the Americans say, is how the cookie crumbles, and no desire to be 'able to say something', in particular to say something unqualified, will make it crumble any differently.

Closely associated with these matters is the question of 'simple' models. Many of my most respected economist friends favour them. The simplicity of course does not turn on anything so commonplace as, say, the number of commodities you include, although there are good grounds for saying that you had better allow for at least three. Rather it turns on something that is best called 'insight' or getting to the 'essentials'. Simplicity consists in ignoring all matters which are not directly germane to the qualitative result which you wish to establish. For example, simple partial analysis suffices to demonstrate the possibility of a backward sloping supply curve of labour. Or there is the virtuoso performance of Samuelson which demonstrated the problems of infinite time horizons by means of a model of overlapping generations with a single good.

How could one object to such simplifications? Indeed it may be argued that it is only simple models which we can bring to the point of empirical application. But there are two caveats. In order to know, indeed even to have a feel, that the simple model has yielded an essential insight, the more general theoretical possibilities must be understood. In other words one must be sure that the simplification was not essential to the insight one claims to have gained. Secondly, it must be understood that in its empirical applications the insight derived from the simple model may be far from simple. Thus one only needs a single industry theory to establish that there may be divergences between private and social cost. One needs a good deal more than that before one could advocate taxes or subsidies to eliminate these divergencies. However, I agree that simple theory can be serious theory; I doubt that it can be sufficient theory. I shall illustrate these remarks later.

So far I have not yet come to the fundamental reason why theory deducible as far as possible from first principles is so important not only intrinsically but in thinking about policy. Propositions in economics deducible only from contingent assumptions are more contingent or differently contingent than are propositions thus derived in other disciplines. Empirical knowledge in physics is simply different from empirical knowledge in economics. Of the former a philosopher may argue that it is not necessary but would agree that this is not a circumstance which should greatly influence praxis. In economics the empirical knowledge we have is not just contingent, but we suspect, ephemeral. Which loglinear equation of the econometrician is a suitable 'rock of ages'? Which lag structure, which mark-up coefficient, which test of significance has the force of the rising and setting sun?

The point is somewhat subtler than the rhetorical question might indicate. For I do not wish to deny that there are empirical regularities of human economic behaviour awaiting discovery. But I claim that these will be, as it were, much deeper down, more elementary and closer to the form in which axioms are postulated than are the complex, institution and history dependent 'facts' of the econometrician. We have very few of such facts, and it is for this reason that it is important that policy take explicit note of the contingency of the arguments adducible in its favour. It is for this reason also that serious theory has a vital role to perform.

An example will make this clear. The proposition that a k-fold change in the stock of money appropriately defined will lead to a k-fold change in money prices and money wages and no change in any real magnitude is not a proposition deducible from serious theory. It can be deduced from the following simplified theory. There is a unique long run competitive equilibrium and the economy always seeks that equilibrium. This simplified theory requires a rather large number of specific, or what I have called contingent, assumptions. The empirical foundation for these is non-existent. However, Professor Friedman claims that the basic proposition is itself an empirical one which has been confirmed by records going back to the dawn of commerce. The fact that Hume held a similar theory is often quoted as supporting evidence.

A quite crucial role of serious theory here is to provide the means of assessing the quality of the evidence and to show what else must be true if the evidence is to be believed. But equally important is its role in deducing the logical implications of the evidence if true. For instance, one of the implications will be that it should not matter much what the increase in the money stock is, provided the increase is predictable and not indefinitely accelerating. Such 'costs' as there are could not only be estimated but avoided, for example, by paying interest on current deposits. But above all, serious theory will alert us to other interpretations of the evidence. For instance, the causal chain from money to prices is, as Kaldor notes, in doubt. Equally important, the evidence may be what it is because it is believed. In the golden days before money supply figures were printed daily in the newspapers, the report of an increase, when unemployment was high, might well have been correctly interpreted as a signal that output and sales will increase. Now, again correctly, the same news may be taken to predict a rise in prices. The extraordinary reaction of the stock exchange at present to the money supply statistics, suggests, very strongly, a Keynesian bootstrap. In any case it is only by means of serious theory that the possibilities are seen and the importance of that for policy is rather obvious.

But there is another important characteristic of serious theory which, alas, does not mean that it is a very notable characteristic of many theoretical writings — that is, that it provides quite clearly the documentation of its own inadequacies and incompleteness. There are many examples, but I take only one. It becomes quite clear to the serious theorist that he has no serious theory even of equilibrium prices in the presence of significant increasing returns. That is simply so because he cannot deduce propositons about competitive prices in such conditions and he has no serious theory of non-competitive prices. Of course work, in the nature of pilot studies and special models, is going on at a brisk pace. But it is still in the realm of the very special and indeed the anecdotal. No one has yet managed to construct a theory based on what I have called agreed first principles and designated as serious. But serious theory knows what is missing.

Now, consider what is the most popular account of the Phillips curve — at least it is popular in America and, I suspect, in Downing

Street. Ask whether that account would survive significant increasing returns? Would it be still true that there is a unique natural rate of unemployment to which the economy always tends? Indeed, would the whole account not be at considerable risk? I know of no evidence which rules out increasing returns, and of some which suggests it. But how many textbooks of the new macroeconomists even discuss this matter?

This is only one example. Serious theorists know that there is literally no meaning to the assumption that profits are maximised in the absence of all possible contingent futures markets and no reason deducible in general from the self-interest of shareholders that expected profits be maximised. They know that missing markets and asymmetric information play havoc with efficiency properties of equilibria and that therefore claims that this or that policy 'distorts' an allocation are often just a sign that a bad textbook has been consulted. They also know that there is no theory worthy of the epithet 'serious' to tell us how prices and quantities adjust in response to market signals.

This self-knowledge of serious theory, of its large gaps, far from making the whole enterprise useless is essential to policy, especially to what I shall call *grand policy*. Moreover, as I shall now argue, in many applications these lacunae — although casting a shadow — do not block out all light.

SMALL SCALE POLICY

I now want to look at a number of examples which illustrate the role of theory in policy formation. I shall here concentrate on cases which do not turn on grand issues such as the case for or against a market or planned economy. On these matters I shall say something later. What I hope will emerge from the few cases I can look at is that economic theory of the serious variety provides what I elsewhere called a grammar of argument. This is, it enables orderly argument to the point at which judgement has to be used. Without it there is simply chaos. It will also emerge that contrary to hopes, aspirations and pronouncements, neither theory nor evidence will often suffice to establish uniquely what is to be done to achieve what is desired. Moreover, very often there will be the additional difficulty that what is desired is not known by the policy maker either precisely or usably. However, here too theory will be of help.

As my first example, let me take the present policy of some nationalised industries of raising prices in order to obtain finance for investment projects, which in turn is connected with the government's restrictions on their borrowing on the capital market. The first move of theory here will be clear to the first year student. The policy, without additional evidence, will impose a deadweight loss on the economy by preventing prices from signalling resource use in producing the good in question. The second move is to check on the first. Although not adduced in support of their action by the nationalised concerns, is it the case that, if all but one are doing what they are doing, the deadweight loss is smallest if the one does it as well? Are there deviations from sensible prices elsewhere in the economy which make this particular deviation reduce deadweight loss as a whole? Notice that *none* of these considerations ostensibly appears in the government's arguments. Notice also that it should if the government is interested in the welfare of its citizens.

That distributional effects must next be considered and brought into the discussion is obvious and requires no further comment. But there are other important matters. If, for instance, railways price in this way, there will not only be obvious effects on road transport and the pressure for new roads, but there may also be long term locational effects. For instance, city centres may further decline as work moves to the commuter centres. Much, although not all, of this is almost the level of 'common sense' and none of it is exactly 'high theory'.

But since none of these considerations has in fact been brought forward in arguing for the higher prices, we must look at those which have been given. They are, apparently, that the borrowing of nationalised industries would raise the PSBR and so interest rates, and that is taken as undesirable in a self-explanatory way. But theory will now say that this is no ground for the policy at all, even if the prediction on interest rates is correct. For, suppose, as the government does, that there is a fixed 'investment fund' in the economy. (I note parenthetically that there is no sound reason for supposing that.) Then unless they themselves believe that a market economy is so flawed as to give no solid meaning to its allocative role, the rising interest rate is the appropriate means of allocating competing claims on this fixed fund.

So now the argument must shift yet again. The goverment may argue that the claims of the nationalised industries are socially bad claims. But then why allow them to be met by raising prices? Or they may claim that those in charge of the industry cannot be relied upon to provide for the repayment and servicing of debt since in the last resort they can always fall back on government. But this is an argument for choosing the managers better, controlling them better and for devising appropriate incentive (and punishment) schemes. For instance, even the Russians have found a way of giving managers and workers an equity interest in their concern.

But of course the interest rate argument is itself open to objection. If the companies get hold of their extra investment funds by raising prices, it does not follow that they can force extra savings to be made. This is, people may simple refuse to save more and so reduce the investment fund which the government regards as fixed. But this too may lead to higher interest rates, so nothing will have been accomplished by the policy. Lastly, the effects of the policy on nominal magnitudes, such as money wages, to which the government attaches great importance, will not be exactly favourable. One can continue for a long time.

To economists these will appear as quite elementary and self-evident arguments. That they do not appear to be so to ministers and indeed to many businessmen suggests that indeed there is something to economics and to habits of mind which its study engenders. But I want to claim more. I want to claim that as the argument proceeds more and more serious theory is brought into play. For instance, one way in which the government seeks to control the nationalised industries is by setting target rates of return. The question then is, not what is 'the' right rate to set, but what are good arguments for setting it at the level at which we do set them? In such a discussion the lack of our theoretical and empirical knowledge will have to play an important role.

I should like to emphasise this point before I proceed. Imagine that you are in a twin seater plane piloted by Professor Friedman. You are discussing economics, he gets exasperated and jumps out. Of course he has a parachute. You do not. What do you do, not having learned to pilot a plane? Do you say that you do not understand the machine, so anything goes? Do you at random yank first this lever than that? Or do you think a great deal harder about what to do and its likely consequences than you would do if you knew the machine perfectly? The answer seems obvious. Yet many people adduce the uncertainty of our knowledge as a justification for not thinking carefully when it should be the occasion of thinking particularly precisely and rigorously. If in the above example we can do no more than make a guess at the odds that interest rates will rise when prices of nationalised industries are raised, then the guess should figure in our deliberations. Moreover, even if only a guess, there is nothing harmful in putting numerical bounds on it. Indeed it is the civilised and useful thing to do.

My second example is altogether more contentious. There are three million or so registered unemployed. What exactly and precisely are the arguments against a straightforward Keynesian policy of pump priming? Are these arguments, if not conclusive, at least sufficiently convincing to lead a prudentially inclined government not to pursue this policy? My illustration will be conducted in a number of schematic steps. Even so, of course, I shall only scrape the surface.

Step 1

We must decide whether a significant fraction of the unemployed are so by choice: that is, they find unemployment pay preferable to working at the current wage, or (the somewhat bizarre suggestion that has been made) they are substituting present for future leisure in the expectation of a rise in the real wage. In addition, unemployment pay generosity may have increased the job fastidiousness of the unemployed and they may be taking their time searching. I do not believe that any of these things go far to account for the high unemployment. But fortunately I do not have to give grounds for my belief since it is shared by the government. It will, for instance, be common ground between us that teenagers and others are willing to work at the going wages but that they cannot find jobs.

Step 2

Granted the diagnosis that some of the unemployment is of this kind, what is its explanation? The government answers: the real wage is too high; workers have, as they say, 'priced themselves out of jobs', and minimum wage legislation has had similar effects. But looking at a firm, we may ask: is an extra worker at the going wage not profitable only because the extra output to be gained yields too little extra revenue at the going prices? Or is there the further element that, to sell the extra output, the firm would have to lower prices a good deal? Indeed must that not be the case if, as so much evidence suggests, much production at unused capacity as at present is under falling or constant prime cost? But then in the latter case, if demand were higher, i.e. the typical demand curve had shifted to the right, and its elasticity was more or less constant, the profitability of employing people at the going real wage would also be higher. So there are strong grounds for supposing that the state of demand has a good deal to do with whether workers have priced themselves out of employment.

Step 3

Workers are rarely hired by the hour and indeed present legislation makes them share some features with durable capital. Hence the expectations of firms become important in deciding whether it is worthwhile to hire more labour. The degree of certainty of these expectations also becomes highly relevant. For most reasonable, not to say rational, firms the expectation for the past few years must have been of falling demand for their products. But expected layoffs are costly. So once again it is clear that the price of a job is not simply a matter of technology.

Step 4

Suppose the above points are taken as likely to be correct – there are of course no certainties. Then the next view one must consider is that, even so, the government can do nothing about it. In particular Keynesian policies will have inflationary consequences and will if anything make unemployment worse. Indeed Mrs Thatcher announced the other day that such Keynesian money is for this reason 'dishonest' money.

At this stage we must proceed carefully and use some serious theory. Suppose that we are actually considering using the dreaded printing press to finance our pump priming. Suppose further that everyone knows this. Then it is conceivable that having been fed on monetarist doctrine all money prices and wages will be marked up in the proportion in which the stock of money has increased. If we ignore the implied redistribution between debtors and creditors which will occur if the events were not foreseen in the past, then indeed the real situation is what it was before the pump priming. Of course the exchange rate will be lower.

But although this is a logically possible scenario it is not the only logically possible one. Moreover, we notice that all the proponents of this view agree that it will take time – eighteen months is often mentioned – for Keynesian money to turn dishonest. In any case, the serious theorist knows that there exists no convincing account, either empirical or theoretical, of how money wages and prices are set. But consider once again the typical firm. The first impact of the policy will be to increase demand. Even if that firm expects this to be transitory and expects prices in general to rise, why should that make it profitable for it to raise its own prices now? From what little we know about oligopolistic competition one would on the contrary conclude that the firm will be reluctant to be the first to raise its price. On the other hand, since there is excess capacity it can expand its output without giving hostage to fortune in the form of capital investment. If it has laid off or short time workers it need not enter into any long run commitments. In fact output and incomes will certainly in the first instance rise, and since falling marginal productivity of labour in our present situation is hardly the case for moderate expansion, this need not be a source of rising prices. At higher incomes the authorities tell us that agents want to hold more money. So the initial excess of money stock over what is desired is now reduced.

However, these are conjectural dynamics which, although a good deal better, at least in being more explicit than any on offer by the government's advisers, cannot be relied on as in any way certain. What can be done is to demonstrate that if as a first approximation marginal costs are constant and if, for a moment longer, we ignore the balance of payments, there will indeed be a state – a pseudo-equilibrium – in which output is higher and employment is higher and prices and wages are what they were before. So in fact both a monetarist and a Keynesian outcome are possible. In view of my conjectural dynamics I would place a higher bet on the latter than on the former.

Step 5

But that leaves the exchange rate and money wages. In step 1 we agreed that it is highly unlikely that at present 'labour is on its supply curve'. But then of course on strict textbook lines there is no reason for wages to rise with a moderate increase in the demand for it. For a theorist the possibility of labour being off its supply curve requires explanation, for he has been indoctrinated to believe that in these circumstances money wages must fall. A great deal of recent work from bargaining theory to implicit contract theory has gone a long way towards showing our indoctrination to have been premature. I elsewhere give an account of my own analysis. Here I am afraid I must simply assert that there is a route strictly based on the first principles of rational, greedy men and women which is consistent with what Keynes called involuntary unemployment.

However, the textbook line is itself suspect. For even if labour is off its supply curve, money wages may yet rise since, for instance, unions may be more interested in the employed than they are in the unemployed. But if this is so, to any extent, unions may frustrate not only pump priming but any endogenously generated expansionary forces. For instance, an increase in productivity may simply be swallowed by a rising real wage of those already in employment. However, if the situation is that bad the market economy is in real trouble and does not work as assumed so far. Then indeed we had better turn from pump priming to something altogether more drastic.

I think one must have grave doubts that matters are like that. For instance, at present we are observing lower real wages and lower money wage settlements. To surface theory this is evidence that the unemployed have a higher marginal utility of being idle than of earning the wage. To serious theory it may be the consequence of involuntary unemployment – an excess of the market over the short run wage. Indeed it may be evidence for the textbook line. In any event, it is difficult to see how reasonable policy decisions can put all their eggs in the basket labelled 'money wages must rise', or rise significantly, if employment rises.

But that leaves out of account the likelihood that the exchange rate will decline, for obvious reasons, and this becomes a cause of higher domestic prices and *that* surely will lead to higher money wages. I want to answer that on two levels. First, on the theory espoused by the government, this cannot be what will happen. For on that theory what prevents involuntary unemployment from persisting is that it causes real wages to fall. Hence, if we are starting with involuntary unemployment, and even if left to itself it would cure itself, the pump priming will do no more than hasten the process – that is. money wages will not rise because of the exchange-induced rise in domestic prices.

Second, however, the theory espoused by the government is not the only account of what happens when there is involuntary unemployment which is derivable from accepted first principles. Indeed there are accounts based on models of rational bilateral bargaining where the fall in the exchange rate would, if nothing is done, raise money wages. But why should nothing be done? Why, for instance, should VAT not be used to counteract this effect? Of course this must be taken into account when setting the initial stimulus. There will, however, be no 'absorption' problems in present circumstances.

Evidently the argument can continue, and if it is serious it will be accompanied by evidence. But without serious theory we are in fact where we are now – that is, in the power of slogans. Without serious theory we swallow the proposition that increasing the money stock causes *only* inflation *and* also the proposition that inflation causes unemployment. Or we accept that unemployment brings about lower real wages without drawing the inference that we might have kept the same employment level at the same real wage. Or we accept, as true, propositions only deducible on the hypothesis that the currently unemployed would turn down any job offered to them at the going wage. I can think of nothing of more practical relevance to economic policy, than a requirement on those concerned to clinch a policy argument in the sense in which serious theory takes an argument as clinched.

This, as I have been at pains to argue, does not mean that we attain certainty – rather the reverse. It is precisely what I believe to be intrinsically present uncertainties which are important and which will, when recognised, perhaps induce the reasonable procedures we would expect from the passenger in Professor Friedman's biplane. In the present instance what I think we can assert is that the dishonesty of Keynesian money is in reasonable doubt. So, therefore, is its contrary. Prudential considerations would then stop us from putting everything into either the Keynesian or the monetarist basket. Moreover, some of our arguments have suggested ways in which we can reduce the uncertainty of the outcome.

Of course this comes down to saying that economics will not yield or forecast accurately the effects of policy. Indeed it will not forecast accurately. It is only servitude to a naïve and out-of-date positivism which will lead to the view that this is a crippling admission to make. In the first case the set of possible outcomes is a good deal larger than the set arrived at by economic theory. Secondly, as I have been continuously emphasising, the fact that one cannot seriously exclude a variety of outcomes is of prime significance to economic policy. If a doctor prescribing certain pills tells me that there is a chance that they will cure me and also a chance that they will not, but that I shall become addicted to them, this is plainly a great deal more valuable than if he asserts that one or the other outcomes is certain when he has no grounds for doing so. If in the light of theory and such empirical evidence as we have, one for instance concludes that a particular policy could either raise or lower interest rates in the medium run and that there seem no grounds for making one a more likely outcome than the other, then that is a description of our state of knowledge. It seems preferable to act on the basis of that, than on some fudged plausible pseudomodel which assets definite outcomes. The modesty of serious theory, that is its canon of not asserting more than can be demonstrated, also makes it important.

But now of course it will be argued that I am naïve, academic in the worst sense, and that I have no understanding of how policy is actually made. A good many economists, who although not corrupted by power have been much impressed by what is called the art of the possible, will be among my critics. They will also argue that only quite elementary economics is ever useful in policy discussions, partly because that is all the politicians understand, partly because that is all the economists themselves remember, and partly because decisions must be made and because there is never time to think. For all I know these are all valid points. But so much the worse for the actual process of policy formation. We would not like our hospitals to be run on these lines, we would not care to have a safety policy for aircrafts thus arrived at, and we even expect better from those who run large firms or the police. In any case I have not set out to describe how policy is actually made and I am willing to believe the worst. I have set out to show how economic theory can be an aid to reasoning about policy.

But I will allow myself one remark on the present situation. I have been much impressed by the number of people of affairs who claim to act on 'judgement' rather than on analysis and detailed knowledge. From what I have already said it will be clear that I agree that in our present state of knowledge, judgement – if no more than in assessing likelihoods – will sooner or later have to be exercised in policy matters. What I find alarming is that it always seems to be sooner – much sooner. Of course there are rare individuals who, as Virginia Woolf had it, can go from A to Z in a flash. Unfortunately in economic affairs we rarely know who these individuals are since many who could hardly get to B are also claiming to have arrived at Z. In any case in a civilised society actions should be accounted for by reasons and not by private intuition. The stockbroker claiming judgement which he does not possess will go out of business – the politician and his advisers need only fear the House of Lords!

Before I leave these particular issues I want briefly to take a last example and draw a moral from it.

Suppose that we think of a quite old fashioned Keynesian model to give a good enough descriptive account of an economy. Of course we should not think that, but this is not relevant to my present concern. If the economy is like that then we know that there is much scope for public finance to do macroeconomic good. A procedure followed after the war, so I understand, was to estimate the gap between 'full employment' and actual GNP and, after taking full account of multiplier effects, to set the budget deficit accordingly. There are of course all sorts of things wrong with this, but I want to concentrate on one particular wrong.

This was pointed out by Phillips many years ago. A policy as just described may, on their own description of the economy, lead policy makers to destabilise the economy. Phillips, who knew a good deal of control engineering, realised that switch-on—switch-off mechanisms of this kind had not been found helpful in engineering. If one only thinks of the simple mechanics of a water closet one will at once see what he was after. What Phillips showed was that a stabilising policy would have to be a feedback rule from a number of different error magnitudes and, moreover, that it would have to be based on rather precise knowledge of the system. Particularly, the lag structure would have to be known. He did not consider the further important complication which arises when the policy itself changes the structural description of the economy.

One obvious moral is of course this: if you judge Keynes to have been proved wrong by the history of Keynesian policies, you had better think again. Keynes' theory of the economy did not demand bang-bang policies.

The more important moral is that such stabilising policies may be impossible even if Keynes was right. They may be impossible because we know too little to implement them usefully, because parliamentary democracy is incompatible with the devising of the required feedback rules, and lastly because the reaction of agents to such a policy commitment would nullify its effects. All these are arguments of the first importance and they need to be very carefully taken into account. I believe there is some way one can get by using what is known about the control of systems whose operation is only uncertainly known. I cannot attempt to do that now. But there is one *non sequitur* which should not be drawn. There is nothing in these arguments to lead to the conclusion that, say, the government should always balance its budget, whatever the conjuncture. This seems obvious. There may be other arguments for this but they cannot be deduced from the unavailability of satisfactory feedback policies.

But the most important moral of the story is this. There is no way in which the government can do 'nothing'. There is no argument deducible that, in the light of ignorance, we should choose an invariant action. The only possible course for reason is to get as good a measure of the likely errors, to be as sophisticated in this as we now know how, and then, and only then, to arrive at a judgement.

GRAND POLICIES

I have left to the last what I shall call 'grand policies', or what others might wish to call the projects of ideology. It is here that the beneficent potential of serious theory is at its highest and the likelihood of it being realised is at its lowest. But the payoffs are high so that even a low probability of success is worth the effort.

I can, however, at this late stage do no more than offer a few remarks on certain aspects which seem to me important. I certainly do not myself propose to reach any grand policy conclusion.

As my main example I shall consider the advocates of socialism and for their foil the advocates of a market economy. I shall be quite parochial and think of Mr Benn and of Mrs Thatcher. The intention of course is not to adjudicate, much less to reach comprehensive conclusions. It is rather to consider, by example, the manner in which economic theory can increase the fraction of the argument which is accessible to reasoning about the world. That is, the intention is to take a small step in distilling what are genuinely questions of values. Of course I do not hold the view that questions of values are not subject to reasonable argument. Quite the contrary. But values are not as such the concern of economic theorists.

I begin with a famous remark of Wicksell's, that as far as economic theory is concerned it makes no difference whether labour hires capital or the other way round. Taken at face value this is a striking proposition which may suggest that Mr Benn's New Jerusalem is no different from Mrs Thatcher's. Of course both of them will want to argue that Wicksell is wrong. I shall want to maintain that, although he claims too much, he directs attention to something of essential importance.

The argument is quite simple: if a group of workers own a firm they will want to do as well for themselves as they can. This of course as Meade and Vanek (1970, 1972) remind us is not straight-forward to define, especially when it comes to letting new workers join or considering the terms at which existing ones can leave. But the central point is clear without refinement — that is, that there is no reason to suppose that the group would forgo what it regards as gains. If new groups of workers can, by borrowing, set up new firms and compete, the outcome for the economy can be just the same as it would have been in the traditional competitive economy. That is what Wicksell had in mind. But one can be less exacting. For instance, if there are monopolistic rents to be made in both the worker-run and the capitalist economy, then it will now be the workers who receive these rents. But these rents will, from the point of view of society, be just as undesirable as ever they were. They would not constitute a good argument in favour.

But now Mr Benn, or someone not too different, will object on two grounds: the above argument does not account for ex-ploitation of workers by capitalists and it pays no attention to the alienating process of capitalist modes of production. Mrs Thatcher will object on the grounds that the story pays no attention to one of the central features of capitalism, namely its dynamism and potential for desirable change and improvements.

In Marxist theory a positive rate of profit is a necessary and sufficient condition for exploitation. But the group of workers, unless they are simply rationed by the state with obvious un-desirable consequences, will have to pay for their capital. If new groups can form then the state had better set a rate of interest close to the Wicksellian rate. Moreover, is borrowing of one group of workers from another to be prohibited? The case for that is obscure. If not then of course the Wicksellian line is strengthened. In the final outcome workers will be exploited just as they were before. To which the reply will be that in paying interest to the state they are really paying interest to themselves. That, however, I think even Mr Benn might agree leaves a perilous distance be-tween the lip and the cup.

Alienation is something else again and I must simply hand on the argument, not to those who know the doctrine but to those who know such facts as there are. There is something called the iron law of oligarchy and I must admit that after long experience of a self-governing college, I cannot report that alienation has been eradicated.

Mrs Thatcher on the other hand might have more of an argument only because it is less precise and less understood. There is, on the face of it, no compelling reason why a worker co-operative should be less innovative or for that matter less greedy, less willing to form cartels, advocate protection etc. than its capitalist counterpart. The evidence of the nineteenth century can only support her on the starkest historicist lines. Of course if it is a question of handing the firms over to ministries, her side of the argument would be much stronger. But that is not what Wicksell or, as I understand, Mr Benn has in mind.

At the end of this superficial look, I think Wicksell comes out pretty well. The essentials, as opposed to the precise particulars, of his case seem to me to be this. Neither side of the argument has given any grounds for departing from the first principle that individuals and groups of individuals are likely to take actions when they are to their advantage. Unless the set of the actions which can be taken is much reduced by the state this in itself suggests that distributional changes will have small long run effects on the disposition of resources. That is, there are no compelling arguments to suggest that when workers own the means of production their disposition will be vastly different from what it is when capitalists own them. Monopoly apart, the distribution of income between interest or profit receipts and labour receipts will not be much affected either. But workers as a whole could get both and indeed some of them may turn into capitalists. There are also no compelling reasons to lead one to conclude that economic progress would be much different between the two systems. In fact it is an important circumstance that the ownership of the means of production has no independent role in bourgeois economic theory and it has no worked-out role in the corresponding part of Marxian theory. On the other hand if the question turns from worker-run and -owned to state-run and -owned firms the answers will be quite different.

This then leaves one with the questions about the kind of society one regards as good. For I cannot claim that Yugoslavia is just like the United States. But that is precisely the point of the argument I was aiming for.

Economists in the 1930s laid the groundwork for the economics of socialism which was Wicksellian in spirit. That is, they designed a system which would make good the claims of the textbooks describing an ideal capitalist economy. To that extent they certainly expected no difference between either ideal system except of course that the distribution of income was to differ between them. It is in fact useful to remind ourselves of what is known as 'the fundamental theorem of welfare economics'. It is a jewel in the crown of orthodox economics. Paraphrased, it states that anything the ideal economy can do the state can also do, but not vice versa since there may be externalities and public goods. So the Wicksell tradition goes deep.

Hayek, however, was the odd man out and interestingly so. He pointed out that neither idealised picture paid any attention not only to the asymmetry of information but also to the essentially particularised aspect of some of the information possessed by private individuals. He saw no way in which this information could be aggregated other than by the market. To this we can add that the economists of the 1930s paid no attention to what we now call incentive compatibility – that is, the devising of incentives which ensure that your agent's best choice is the choice which you want him to make.

A great deal of fascinating theoretical work has been going on in connection with both these problems in recent years and I cannot now rehearse it. But one can say that Hayek was not quite right about the market's role in information aggregation and he certainly did not clinch the case that only the market can aggregate it. Yet something must be devised and that something *will* have to have decentralised decision features if the information is to be gained and used. Many socialists do not understand that. However, once again the ownership of the means of production is entirely peripheral to the issue.

Incentives, however, are not peripheral and of course they place an obstacle in the way of egalitarian intentions. The arguments here are so well known that I need not dwell on them in any detail. However, I think that there is a duty for economic theorists to bring their insights directly into the debate. Many people now dislike the competitive aspect – the rat race – of capitalism more than almost any other aspect. We all have our inner picture of the tranquil and harmonious life. What needs to be more widely understood is that this has a cost – not just a cost in terms of motor cars or lipstick or other things the middle class socialist regards as frivolous, but a cost in hospitals, schools, opera and above all in the discovery and application of new knowledge. These costs will arise as long as our first principle of human action remains generally valid. Of course there are saints, but generally speaking there are not many Mother Theresas.

If the first principle is denied then a great deal of evidence will have to be faced, not least evidence from every socialist country so far known. More likely the answer will be that socialism in itself will transform human nature or at least its operation under new modes of production. I do not see how this possibility can be denied. But what must be admitted is that it will be uncertain and that it will take time. But then this uncertainty and the intervening costs must be weighed and taken into account. It is not clear that one is willing to sacrifice everything for one's grandchildren. However, that is not my point. My point is that these problems should be lucidly and clearly discussed by both proponents and opponents. I have always found it surprisingly strange and awful that these matters are ignored in the spirit of what is called ideology — that is, religion.

I now want to emphasise that the marketeers have to face quite analogous questions. For instance, incentives are also costly in terms of the inequality which they generate and the coarsening of human motivation which they reinforce. Moreover, it is not at all clear how the incentives operate in the age of large corporations and worker coalitions. A capitalist economy can, as we know only too well, also stagnate and turn sour. Evidently the marketeers have a lot to do to put their side of the argument in order. In this, much attention will have to be paid to the departures from textbook economics which serious theory tells us are required. For instance, it will not do, as is Professor Friedman's wont, to appeal to Adam Smith. He certainly had important insights and I am all in favour of regarding him reverently. But since his day, we have asked questions and given answers which never did or could occur to him. Unlike philosophy, for instance, ours is not a subject for great men and their thoughts — it is, with fits and starts, one where knowledge does grow.

What I have said so far has all the hallmarks of 'on the one hand and on the other'. In short, I seem to be lending support to what nowadays is called 'the moderate' approach to these grand matters. And that leads me to my last point.

I have already repeatedly argued that uncertainties should not be faced by throwing up the sponge but by the methods of making them discussable. Large, or as some like to say, radical changes in economic institutions must carry correspondingly large uncertainties. It is bogus and dishonest to maintain otherwise. This large uncertainty many — say Burke — regarded as a strong argument against large changes. Now if for a moment I may revert to my biplane. When Professor Friedman jumps out the plane may be heading for a mountain. In that case the slow step-by-step manipulations which would otherwise be appropriate will surely not recommend themselves. Large, and thus also, highly uncertain action seems the right one. Just so, if the evils of capitalism can be shown to be very large or perhaps getting disastrously worse, an argument for a large change is possible. But it must be given. For my own part I must confess that I find the plane wobbly and slightly sick-making but I do not see the mountain.

ENVOI

Inevitably what I have had to say on both grand and small policy has been on the surface of things. More seriously, it has had a programmatic air: how much better we could justify policy if we used serious theory. But this is an area where the doing is everything. I have tried some examples but the treatment of these had to be quite incomplete.

Nonetheless I hope that I have at least given grounds to suppose that there is an argument here − that policy formation by 'common sense' and 'hunch' guided by economically ignorant politicians could be improved. I also, I hope, have persuaded you that this by no means implies handing policy over to expert economists and denying the democratic process. As I have argued, economics cannot say what the unique consequences of policy will be, leave alone what is best to be done. What it can do is to replace the mixture of *non sequiturs*, contradictions and pious hopes which now seem so frequently the basis of economic policy by the use of reason.

REFERENCES

J. Meade (1972) The theory of labour-managed firms and profit sharing, *Economic Journal*

J. Vanek (1970) *The General Theory of Labour-Managed Market Economics*, Cornell University Press

Part IV

17

The neo-Ricardians

I

I want to consider the claim that neo-classical economics is logically faulty, which has been advanced by the followers of Sraffa (1960). I shall first have to give an exposition of Sraffa's own construction and I shall then discuss what his followers have made of it. I shall then wish to show that there is no correct neo-Ricardian proposition which is not contained in the set of propositions which can be generated by orthodoxy. I shall therefore conclude that the neo-Ricardian attack via logic is easily beaten off.

Before I start, it is important to emphasise the distinction between Sraffa and his followers. Sraffa's (1960) book contains no formal propositions which I consider to be wrong although here and there it contains remarks which I think to be false. The book was called *Production of Commodities by Means of Commodities* and had the important subtitle *Prelude to a Critique of Economic Theory*. With one exception, Sraffa does not claim to have got beyond the prelude. The exception arises from his view that marginal productivity theory requires a wellbehaved aggregate measure of capital. Since he shows such a measure in general not to be available (Sraffa 1960, p. 38) he concludes that the marginal productivity theory is logically false. It will be rather easy for orthodoxy to stand up to this criticism. But his followers have gone very much further. They claim that Sraffa's work shows that orthodoxy cannot logically provide a closed model which treats relative prices and the rate of profit as endogenous variables determined within the system (see, for example, Garegnani 1970, Pasinetti 1966, 1969). They claim that Sraffa has established the irrelevance of the psychological theories of demand and indeed of demand to the determination of relative prices. They assert that Sraffa shows that distribution has to be determined of by considerations outside the economic model, that it is 'logically prior' to the determination of relative prices, and above all that it is independent of the circumstances of production. I have of course here lumped several followers together. (Representative statements of some of these views can be found in the writings of Eatwell 1974, 1975, 1977, Garegnani 1966, 1970, Robinson 1960–80 and other followers, such as Dobb 1973, chapters 6, 7, 9, Harcourt 1975, Roncaglia 1978. For an earlier critique by the present author see Hahn 1975.) But the preliminary point I wish to make is simply this: these claims are not found in Sraffa's book.

One further matter merits consideration before we get down to business. I often refer to neo-classical theory and I had better make clear what I do and do not mean by this designation. For present purposes I shall call a theory neo-classical if (a) an economy is fully described by the preferences and endowments of agents and by the production sets of firms; (b) all agents treat prices parametrically (perfect competition); and (c) all agents are rational and given prices will take that action (or set of actions) from among those available to them which is best for them given their preferences. (Firms prefer more profit to less.)

Now there are many writers whom we regard as neo-classical who have either made mistakes of reasoning or based themselves on special assumptions which have themselves nothing to do with neo-classical theory. For instance Levhari (1965) was simply wrong in the reswitching debate. Equally it seems to me impossible (as a matter of intellectual history) to maintain that the possibility of perfect capital (or labour) aggregation is a neo-classical doctrine. For instance it was soon realised that Böhm-Bowerk's attempt at capital aggregation was logically flawed. In any event I shall stick to my definition and will not care at all about authors regarded as neo-classical, who have proposed conclusions which cannot be deduced from the basic axioms.

Of course neo-Ricardians and Sraffa followers pose the same sort of problem. I base myself here on Sraffa's book and on over twenty years of argument in Cambridge. After all they call themselves 'the Cambridge school'. But should it be the case that some of those who regard themselves as carrying on 'the Sraffa revolution' repudiate the views which I report then I shall be delighted.

II

I shall now give an account of one part of what Sraffa has to say, I will choose the simplest case where there is no joint production and all goods enter directly or indirectly into the production of every other (all goods are 'basics'). In particular, I shall concentrate on what are essential features rather than technical detail (e.g. the possibilities of non-basics). To make life as simple as possible we will consider a world of two goods and labour.

Suppose that in this world we can observe all inputs and outputs. We find that good j uses a_{ij} units of good i and a_{oj} units of labour per unit of output. We do not ask and we are not encouraged to ask why this is the case. If we observe gross output x_j of good j then

$$\sum_j a_{ij} x_j, i = 1, 2 \quad a_{ij} > 0, i, j = 1, 2$$

is the amount of good i used to produce goods and

$$\sum_j a_{oj} x_j, \quad a_{oj} > 0, j = 1, 2$$

is the amount of labour used.

So far all of this is description and the hypothesis is that the economy described has no joint production and no non-basics. Sraffa now proposes to process this description by defining a composite good to be called the *standard commodity*. This is done as follows.

Let us ask what outputs of the two goods we would have to observe if the ratio of the gross output of any good to the amount of it used in production were to be the same for all goods. If the hypothetical gross outputs are distinguished by an asterisk we want to solve

$$\frac{x_1^*}{\sum_j a_{1j} x_j^*} = \frac{x_2^*}{\sum_j a_{2j} x_j^*} = G^* \text{ say} \tag{17.1}$$

where we would like $x_i^* > 0$, i = 1, 2. One can alternatively say that we are looking for (x_1^*, x_2^*) and G^* such that

$$x_i^* = G^* \sum_j a_{ij} x_j^*, \quad i = 1, 2$$

or in matrix notation

$$x^* = G^* A x^* \tag{17.2}$$

where x^* is the vector (x_1^*, x_2^*) and A is the 2 x 2 matrix of elements a_{ij} ($i, j = 1, 2$). We now have a purely mathematical problem for which there is a standard mathematical result (see e.g. Arrow and Hahn, 1971, appendix 2).

Theorem 1: If all elements of A are positive and

$$1 - \sum_i a_{ij} > 0, \quad j = 1, 2$$

then there is (a) a positive vector $(\lambda_1^*, \lambda_2^*)$ unique except for scale and (b) a unique real number $G^* > 1$ which solves equation (17.2).

Since we are taking all elements of A to be positive and since we shall be concerned with the case of 'production with a surplus', (that is, A satisfies the so-called Hawkins—Simon conditions), the conditions of the theorem are satisfied. We may therefore write

$$G^* = 1 + g^* \text{ where } g^* > 0$$

and we may write

$$x_i^* = k\lambda_i^*, \quad i = 1, 2, k > 0$$

where we fix k by:[1]

$$k\sum_j a_{oj}\lambda_j^* = \text{available labour} = 1, \text{ say}$$

The composite good consisting of x_1^* units of good 1 and x_2^* units of good 2 is then defined as one unit of standard commodity.

It is to be emphasised that Sraffa does not claim that the world yields the observation x^*. The latter vector is a pure construct as of course is equation (17.2) used in its derivation. The system (17.2) is called the *standard system*.

So far then, nothing has occurred other than the manipulation of data given by A and (a_{01}, a_{02}). To get any further, and in particular to get somewhere where these manipulations are fruitful,

---

[1] We here depart a little from Sraffa in an inessential way. He normalises on the labour used rather than the labour available.

the following assumptions are made about the actual world:

(a) The price of every good as output is the same as its price as input.
(b) The rate of profit in the production of every good is the same.

I shall discuss these assumptions later but accept them now in order to continue with the story.

Before writing the price equations, we note that Sraffa thinks of wages as paid at the end of the production process so that no rate of profit is charged on the outlays on labour. (Throughout I use rate of profit to stand for the interest rate which producers use to discount future receipts.) We also think of wages as payment over and above subsistence. If the latter is thought of as a given basket of the two goods per unit of labour we may take subsistence requirements as already embodied in the coefficients a_{ij}. So now let P_j ($j = 1, 2$) be the price of a unit of good j. The assumption that the profit rate r is the same in all lines and assumption (a) can be formally stated as

$$P_j = R\Sigma_i a_{ij}P_i + a_{oj}w, \qquad j = 1, 2 \qquad (17.3)$$

where $R = 1 + r$ and w is the wage of one unit of labour. To see that equation (17.3) is just a restatement of the assumption notice the identity: price per unit of output = cost of goods per unit of output plus wages cost per unit of output plus profits per unit of output.

Express profit per unit of output as a fraction of the cost of goods used per unit of output. Add the assumption that this fraction is the same whichever good is produced and you get equation (17.3). It will be convenient to define the two row vectors: $P = (P_1, P_2)$, $a_o = (a_{o1}, a_{o2})$, and to write equation (17.3) as

$$P = RPA + a_o w \qquad (17.4)$$

Suppose R is given. What would it mean to have a solution P, w to equation (17.4)? It would tell us what the prices of outputs and the wage would have to be in order that the assumption of a particular uniform profit rate be correct. The uniform profit rate 'determines' P and w only in this sense. We also notice that if for given r (i.e. R) P^o, w^o solve equation (17.4) then so will kP^o, kw^o for any $k > 0$. So there can be no harm in restricting solutions to those values of P and w for which

$$P_1 + P_2 + w = 1 \tag{17.5}$$

So equation (17.4) and (17.5) constitute three equations, and if R is given we also have three unknowns. But we want a solution for which $P_i \geqslant 0$, $i = 1, 2$ and $w \geqslant 0$.

For this we have

Theorem 2: Under the hypothesis of theorem 1, the system (17.4, (17.5) has a unique solution $P_i > 0$, $i = 1, 2$ and $w > 0$ for all R such that

$$1 \leqslant R < G^* \text{ (or } 0 \leqslant r < g^*)$$

If we look at (17.4) and (17.5) again we notice that we have one more unknown than equations. It is for this reason that we have prefaced the remarks about solutions with 'given R'. That is, we have arbitrarily fixed one of the unknowns. But as far as the formal story goes we could have arbitrarily fixed *any one* of the four unknowns and looked for a solution of the remaining three. (For instance, the government could control the price of some good in terms of numéraire or in an open economy this price could be given from abroad.) There is no sense in the sentence: 'Equations (17.4), (17.5) still leave R to be determined.' However, the neo-Ricardians like to think of R (or w) as the 'free' variable and that is where we return to the standard commodity.

The first thing to do is to replace the normalisation (17.5) by

$$rPAx^* + w = 1 \tag{17.5'}$$

This makes the length of the vector (P, w) depend on r. But that does not matter since the length of that vector is of no significance. What is the interpretation of this normalisation? It is that we have arbitrarily decided to consider only those prices and wage rates which make the values added in the production of one unit of standard commodity equal to one. I re-emphasise that there is absolutely nothing wrong or limiting in this since the length of price vectors cannot matter to anything. I call the value added ($rPAx^* + w$), just defined, the *standard net product*. Professor Steedman has pointed out to me that Sraffa uses the term *standard national income*.

Now with this new normalisation let $P(r)$, $w(r)$ solve equations (17.4), (17.5) for given r. From equation (17.2)

$$P(r)x^* = G^*P(r)Ax^* = P(r)Ax^* + g^*P(r)Ax^*$$

or

$$\frac{P(r)x^* - P(r)Ax^*}{P(r)Ax^*} = g^* \tag{17.6}$$

The left hand side of equation (17.6) Sraffa calls the *standard ratio*. Since g^* depends only on A, the standard ratio is independent of all market happenings such as P, w or r. Moreover, the reader will quickly verify from equation (17.4) that the numerator of the standard ratio is just another way of writing the standard net product. Since the solution satisfies equation (17.5′) it is equal to one. Hence we can write equation (17.6) as:

$$P(r)Ax^* = \frac{1}{g^*} \tag{17.6′}$$

Substitute equation (17.6′) into (17.5′) to obtain

$$r = g^*(1 - w) \tag{17.7}$$

Equation (17.7) is simply the consequence of the normalisation (17.5′). Since net product = 1 we can interpret w as the wage in terms of net product or simply the share of one unit of labour in standard net product. Then equation (17.7) tells us that this share is inversely and linearly related to whatever the rate of profit happens to be. It is an example of a *factor price frontier*. It has caused a good deal of excitement among some economists.

Before I consider this, let us make clear what has been achieved by the standard commodity. To see this, let us return to the system (17.4), (17.5) and for any given r let $\hat{P}(r)$, $\hat{w}(r)$ be the solution. Then from equation (17.4)

$$\hat{P}(r) = a_0[I - RA]^{-1}\hat{w}(r) \tag{17.8}$$

By theorem 2 for $r < g^*$ the inverse matrix has only positive elements. Let $e = (1, 1)$ a column vector. Then since the solution satisfies equation (17.5)

$$\hat{P}(r)e + \hat{w}(r) = 1$$

or using equation (17.8)

$$[a_0 [I - RA]^{-1} e + 1] \hat{w}(r) = 1 \qquad (17.9)$$

This is the factor price frontier we get from the normalisation (17.5). Since it is easy to verify that the square bracket term is increasing in r we also have that $\hat{w}(r)$ and r are inversely related. But equation (17.9) is not linear. The merit of using the standard commodity is then to enable us to express our solution in normalised form which yields a linear factor price frontier. Although, as we shall see, the standard commodity, if it describes an *actual* and not a hypothetical basket of goods, has further interest, this is not the case in Sraffa's work. Its task is to rearrange data so as to yield linearity and that exhausts its merit.

Readers of Sraffa may be surprised at this since they know that he is much concerned with an *invariant standard of value*. This has something to do with Ricardian theory but to a modern theorist it is almost incomprehensible. The normalisation (17.5) also yields an invariant standard of value as does any such normalisation. In (17.5) our 'standard' is the value obtained from one unit of each good plus one unit of labour. Here w is then the rate at which one unit of labour exchanges against *that* basket. A numéraire is a numéraire. The price of the numéraire can be set equal to one. Sraffa has chosen standard net product as numéraire and there's an end to it.

Lastly to complete this part, notice that for $R < G^*$, equation (17.8) may be written

$$\hat{P}(r) = a_0 [I + RA + R^2 A^2 + \ldots] \hat{w}(r) \qquad (17.8')$$

This is the well known reduction of prices to dated labour. Sraffa correctly notes that there is nothing in the mathematics which tells us how $\hat{P}_1(r)$ will be affected relative to $\hat{P}_2(r)$ by stipulating a different value of r. But

$$\Sigma \hat{P}_i(r) \Sigma_j a_{ij} x_j^*$$

is the value (in numéraire) of the means of production (capital) used in the production of one unit of standard commodity. This value depends, in general in a complicated way, on r. Therefore it cannot be used to determine r without circular reasoning. A generation of Cambridge students have been taught that this argument is logically fatal to neo-classical economics. This matter will be discussed later.

III

Sraffa writes:

> It is, however, a peculiar feature of the set of propositions now published that, although they do not enter into any discussion of the marginal theory of value and distribution, they have nevertheless been designed to serve as the basis for a critique of that theory. If the foundation holds, the critique may be attempted later. (Sraffa 1960, p. vi)

I shall not give a preliminary consideration to that claim. It must be preliminary since the summary so far has not discussed Sraffa's chapter XII, 'Switch in methods of production'. On the other hand, the summary will do for the rest which elaborates the story to decomposable matrices (basics and non-basics) and constructs the standard commodity for a von Neumann model with fixed coefficients. These further complications need not concern us since Sraffa's 'foundations' are all there in the simplest case.

Imagine that Sraffa and I, a representative of 'the marginal theory of value and distribution', arrive on an island. Sraffa suggests that we should look at the very elaborate statistics of inputs and outputs for a given year which the islanders have collected and that we should each construct the input–output matrix (A, a_0). Our arithmetical skills are the same and we produce the same answer. Next, Sraffa suggests that we find what the composition of output would have had to be in order that the ratio of output of every good to the amount of it used in production be the same for all goods. No sooner asked than the computer churns out the answer. Sraffa now performs some more calculations and announces: 'if in this island the rate of profit in every line is 5 per cent then these are the relative prices that would rule'. I go into my corner, calculate, and come out with the same answer. Next we calculate the wage in standard net value and then we calculate the linear factor price frontier. Every answer, since we make no mistake, is *necessarily true*. All we are doing is to provide descriptions of the island and descriptions of hypothetical states.

I conclude that the only falsifiable entailment of the Sraffa equations is the postulate of a uniform rate of profit. His followers often interpret this as the state to which the system tends and they think of Sraffa prices as 'normal' or long run prices. As will become clear in the sequel this entailment of Sraffa's theory is also an entailment of the neo-classical theory of balanced growth. Therefore the two theories cannot be distinguished by that particular entailment.

We have already seen that Sraffa does not offer a theory of the rate of profit which he takes as given (but see Sraffa 1960, p. 33). His followers have seen great merit in this. For they argue (a) that technology cannot determine the rate of profit since many different rates are consistent with Sraffian prices, and (b) that Sraffa's system shows quite clearly that, in the factor price frontier, the working of class struggle for the profit rate and the real wage are inversely related.

These arguments are false on several grounds. First, if on our island the input—output table had been (B, b_0) rather than (A, a_0) then a given r would in general have yielded a different real wage. Thus, it cannot be true that technology has no role in determining equilibrium shares. Indeed, the standard commodity for (B, b_0) is not the same for (A, a_0) and if we used one of these to compare shares we would no longer have the linearity of the factor price relations for each of the technologies.

So what Sraffa followers can reasonably be taken to mean is this: if we know technology and nothing else we do not have enough information to say what prices and what rate of profit will prevail. We are one equation short. As I argue below, exactly the same is true of neo-classical theory, so that on this score we cannot decide between them.

The same applies to the factor price frontier. This frontier can be derived from neo-classical theory with a choice of techniques. If the inverse relationship between the rate of profit and the real wage suggests conflict to Sraffa followers then such conflict will also be present in neo-classical theory. This will become clearer in the sequel.

Exactly the same is true of the fact that Sraffa prices can be found once the rate of profit is known without any appeal to the preferences of households between goods. This of course is also true for a special neo-classical mo'del which is discussed below. This special model ensures constant returns to scale which Sraffa claims not to posit. I have been at a loss to understand him here. For the claim reduces everything we have discussed so far to just a fancy way of presenting accounts *ex post*. If there is enough time for equal rates of profit to be established then there is also enough time for producers to decide which technique to use.

Let me break off here to give the neo-classical theory which justifies these claims.

IV

When the neo-classical economist arrives on the island, he is told all the alternative ways known to islanders in which each good can be produced by means of goods and labour. This information is summed up by

$$1 = f_j(a_{1j}, a_{2j}, a_{oj}), \qquad j = 1, 2 \tag{17.10}$$

So there are constant returns to scale and no joint production. Each function $f_i(\cdot)$ shows all the combination of inputs capable of producing one unit of output good j. Besides equation (17.10) the neo-classical visitor is given the following information (1) relative input and relative output prices are the same and the common rate of profit is r and (2) both goods are produced. He is told nothing about tastes. On the basis of this information and of *a theory* of action by economic agents, the visitor now undertakes to calculate (a) the actual input—output table, and (b) all relative prices.

The well known theory to be used is that·island producers of good j maximise their pure profits. (By pure profits I understand the difference between receipts and costs where the latter include the opportunity cost of investment exemplified by r times the value of investment.) Since there are constant returns to scale this implies that pure profits per unit of output are maximised. The fundamental hypothesis is that each agent treats (R, P, w) parametrically.

Let $a_j = (a_{ij}, a_{2j}, a_{oj})$ and A_j the set of all a_j which satisfy (17.10) (A_j is taken to be convex). Then the theory predicts the choice $a_j(R, P, w)$ at the market signals (R, P, w) where

$$a_j(R, P, w) \text{ solves: } \max_{A_j} [P_j - R\Sigma_i a_{ij}P_i - a_{oj}w]$$

Define: (17.11)

$$\pi_j(R, P, w) = \max_{A_j} [P_j - R\Sigma_i a_{ij}P_i - a_{oj}w]$$

One calls $\pi_j(\cdot)$ the unit profit function. It gives the maximum pure profit per unit of output given the technological possibilities A_j and the market signals (R, P, w). If $\pi_j(\cdot) < 0$, producer of good j will not produce, so $\pi_j(\cdot) \geq 0$. If $\pi_j(\cdot) > 0$, the rate of profit is not r. Hence

$$\pi_j(R, P, w) = 0, \qquad j = 1, 2 \qquad (17.12)$$

But as one easily verifies

$$k\pi_j(R, P, w) = \pi_j(R, kP, kw), \text{ any } k > 0$$

so once again the length of the vector does not matter. So we arbitrarily add

$$P_1 + P_2 + w = 1 \qquad (17.13)$$

The system (17.12), (17.13) gives three equations in three unknowns (P, w) since R is fixed. This is not quite satisfactory yet because one would like the solution to be non-negative and unique. This is purely technical matter. If there are no non-basics so that every pair (a_1, a_2) with $a_1 \in A_1$ and $a_2 \in A_2$ forms an indecomposable input–output system one has available a theorem very much like theorem 2. Only now G^* *is* defined as the largest of the numbers (1 + standard ratio) which we can find by going through all the input–output systems which can be constructed from A_1 and A_2. One wants $G^* > 1$. But under assumptions no more stringent than Sraffa's, we can solve (17.12), (17.13) satisfactorily and uniquely when R is the appropriate range.

It will be clear that we have solved for our unknowns (P, W) and $a_1(R, P, W)$, $a_2(R, P, W)$ jointly. It will also be clear that equations (17.11), (17.12) could be written differently. Let $f_j(\cdot)$ be differentiable (i.e. a continuum of techniques) and write

$$f_{ji} = \frac{\partial f_j}{\partial a_{ij}}, \qquad i = 1, 2, \text{o}$$

Then f_{ji} depends on a_j and we could have written down necessary conditions for maximum profit when all inputs are used

$$P_j f_{ji}(a_j) = RP_i, \qquad i = 1, 2, \quad j = 1, 2$$

$$P_j f_{jo}(a_j) = w, \qquad j = 1, 2 \tag{17.14}$$

Together with equation (17.13) this gives seven equations. Because of constant returns to scale

$$\sum_i f_{ji}(a_j)a_{ij} = 1, \qquad j = 1, 2 \tag{17.15}$$

which adds two equations so we have nine equations for the nine unknowns (a_1, a_2, P, w). (Equation (17.15) is the famous adding-up equation. It says that under constant returns to scale when each input receives its marginal product, input payments exhaust the total product.) I emphasise that equations (17.13), (17.14) and (17.15) are only a rewriting of what we had already.

But we have now reached the first of our conclusions. It will be agreed that you cannot get more neo-classical than differentiable $f_j(\cdot)$, and it will have been recognised that f_{ji} is the marginal product of i in the production of j. In equations (17.14) and (17.15) *every* possible marginal product has been used. It follows that if you ask the neo-classical economist: but what 'determines' r? he cannot find yet another marginal product to do it for him. He is in *exactly* the same boat as the Sraffians, i.e. he needs one more equation which cannot be derived from the production relations which he has given. Moreover, notice the meaninglessness of a sentence like: 'the marginal product of labour determines the real wage'. You need to solve all nine equations to find either labour's marginal product or the real wage. This was patiently explained by Robertson (1931) and it is rather odd that neo-Ricardians continue to assert that in neo-classical theory the rate of profit or anything else is 'determined' by marginal productivity.

Before we go on the hunt for the missing equation, I shall get another stumbling block out of the way and sum up so far.

If $f_j(\cdot)$ is not differentiable (a spectrum of techniques) we must distinguish between a 'right hand' and a 'left hand' marginal product. For instance, $f_{jo}^+(a_j)$ is the change in output of j for a small *increase* in the labour employed and $f_{jo}^-(a_j)$ the change in output of j for a small decrease in the labour employed. The reader will check that when profits are maximised

$$P_j f_{jo}^+(a_j) \leqq w \leqq P_j f_{jo}^-(a_j) \tag{17.16}$$

and analogously for other inputs. The inequalities (17.16) replace (17.14) and

$$(RP, w)a_j = P_j, \qquad j = 1, 2$$

replace (17.15). Mathematical economists know how to solve this system too, and in it also all 'marginal productivity relations' available have been used up. I know of no neo-classical economist who insists on the equality of some price ratio to the first differential of a non-differentiable function.

Sraffa can be interpreted — he does not do so — as dealing with an economy in which inequality (7.16) simply says that the wage must be non-negative and not infinitely large. For the neo-classical economist that is the singular case of fixed coefficients, i.e. where A_j has only a single member. But this is not what Sraffa asserts. Rather he takes the actual techniques of production as unexplained. That being so, they may well be the outcome of the kind of choice which we have described. Sraffa landing on the island will never discover whether this is so or not. For he does not ask and of course he can calculate standard ratios and commodities on the basis of technological observation which are what they are because of a rational choice of technique. Moreover, for the inquisitive neo-classical economist who wants to explain the choice of techniques as well as for the easily satisfied Sraffa, it will be the case that equilibrium prices are independent of preferences.

This argument then shows that nothing, with one exception, that Sraffa says or does as far as we have discussed it, can conflict with the deepest neo-classical theory, Indeed, it is irrelevant to it. The exception is the linear factor price frontier. In neo-classical theory different specified values of R will give rise to different input—output tables and so to different standard commodities. However, it is well known and easily verified that the neo-classical factor price frontier, on any normalisation, is downward sloping, so that we can still have class conflict. But again, since Sraffa simply takes the input—output table as given and unexplained, this can hardly be a point at issue. The neo-classical economist, if asked to draw the factor price frontier on Sraffa's normalisation for a given technique, will draw the same one. He will note that he would not expect the technique to be the same at different R but until chapter XII he can only expect a shrug of the shoulder in reply. For until that chapter, we are not told whether there is or is not any choice.

Lastly, note the following obvious point. The neo-classical theory may be wrong. Agents may not treat prices parametrically nor need they maximise profits. That is a virtue not shared by an accounting system.

V

So far we have been in familiar waters. But now we set out in search of the 'missing equation'. Sraffa himself never set out on this voyage and confined himself to the remark that the equation cannot be one which demands the equality of the marginal product of 'capital' and the rate of profit. We have already seen that the neo-classical economist has the same view but his reasons are not those given by Sraffa. This matter will be taken up again later. At the moment I am only concerned to show how neo-classical theory deals with the missing equation. It is the Sraffa followers who are most at risk here, although Sraffa himself will be found to have been too reticent on certain crucial matters.

Sraffa writes: 'We retain however the supposition of an annual cycle of production with an annual market' (p. 3) So let us consider an economy which, at the beginning of 1976, has available to it $\bar{W}_{76}$ units of wheat and $\bar{B}_{76}$ units of barley. They are simply the outcome of past production decisions. The economy has one unit of labour at the start of 1976. The agents in the economy can consume some wheat and barley in 1976 and sow some to produce wheat and barley for 1977. I assume that the world ends in 1977 not because the theory requires such a disaster but because it makes for simple exposition.

Now wheat and barley available in 1977 are not the same goods as wheat and barley available in 1976. So in obvious notation, we have four prices seen in 1976

$$P_W^{76}, P_B^{76}, P_W^{77}, P_B^{77}$$

In addition, we write w as the wage of one unit of 1976 labour which gets paid in 1977. As usual the length of the price vector is without significance and we normalise by:

$$P_W^{76} + P_B^{76} + P_W^{77} + P_B^{77} + w = 1 \qquad (17.17)$$

Producers of wheat and barley 1977 face the technological possibilities discussed in the previous section which include fixed coefficients as a special case. But explicit attention is now given to dates: inputs are dated 1976 and outputs are dated 1977. If we put

$$Q = (P_W^{76}, P_B^{76}, P_W^{77}, P_B^{77}, w)$$

a five-vector, then the unit profit function for wheat and barley is

$$\pi_i(Q), \qquad i = W_{77}, B_{77}$$

The choice of technique, if there is one, will depend on Q. The equilibrium condition for producers is:

$$P_j^{77} = \Sigma a_{ij}P_i^{76} + a_{oj}w, \qquad i, j = W, B \qquad (17.18)$$

where the a_{ij} are the most profitable input coefficients from among those available. This equation does not look like a Sraffa equation and before we proceed this rather crucial matter must be investigated.

Consider the two numbers $R_i \equiv 1 + r_i$, defined by

$$R_i = \frac{P_i^{76}}{P_i^{77}}, \qquad i = W, B$$

Then R_W, for instance, is the number of units of 1977 wheat which can be obtained for one unit of 1976 wheat. Keynes (1936, chapter 17, p. 223, but he obtained the idea from Sraffa 1932, p. 50) called r_W ($\equiv R_w - 1$) the wheat own rate of return on wheat since a man will not exchange 1976 wheat for 1977 wheat indirectly through storage or production unless he does as well as the direct exchange. Arithmetic gives

$$(P_W^{76}/P_B^{76})(P_B^{77}/P_W^{77})R_B = R_W \qquad (17.19)$$

where

$$(P_W^{76}/P_B^{76})(P_B^{77}/P_W^{77}) - 1 \qquad (17.20)$$

is the proportional difference in the relative prices of wheat and barley at the two dates. This relation (17.19) can be interpreted as follows. Suppose you have one unit of 1976 wheat. You can exchange it indirectly for 1977 wheat as follows. Buy P_W^{76}/P_W^{76} units of 1976 barley and exchange it for $R_B(P_W^{76}/P_B^{76})$ units of 1977 barley. This can be exchanged for $(P_B^{77}/P_B^{77})R_B(P_W^{76}/P_B^{76})$ units of 1977 wheat. So equation (1919) says that the indirect exchange of 1976 wheat for 1977 wheat yields the same return as does the direct exchange. The left hand side of (17.19) minus one is called wheat own rate of return on barley.

It will now be clear that Sraffa is considering a very special state of the economy where factor (17.20) = 0, that is, where the relative prices of 1976 wheat and barley are the same as those of 1977 wheat and barley. The neo-classical economist is quite happy with more general situations.

Sraffa then postulates that on his island

$$R_W = R_B = R, \text{ say} \qquad (17.21)$$

so that the wheat own rate of return of wheat is equal to the barley own rate of return of barley. From the definitions, we now can write equation (17.17) as

$$RP_W + RP_B + P_W + P_B + w = 1 \qquad (17.17')$$

where the superscript '77' has been omitted since it is now otiose. One sees at once that the decision to consider only states for which equation (17.21) holds reduces the number of unknowns from five $[P_W^{77}, P_B^{77}, P_W^{76}, P_B^{76}, w]$ to four $[P_W, P_B, w, R]$. This, as we shall see in a moment, is of some importance. The reader can check that if (17.21) then (17.18) has the usual Sraffa form (except that I here take wages to be paid in advance).

Before we consider the very special Sraffa island, let us look at the neo-classical general case. We arrive on the island and find that history has given it an endowment $\overline{W}_{76}, \overline{B}_{76}$. We do not worry what history the island has had. On the island all agents treat prices parametrically and all agents are greedy. We are asked to calculate that value of Q at which agents who have done as well for themselves as they could take actions which are mutually compatible, i.e. an equilibrium Q.

I now list the familiar steps:

(a) We only consider values of Q which satisfy equation (17.17).

(b) If Q^0 is an equilibrium where both goods are produced, then it must satisfy

$$\pi_i(Q^0) = 0, \qquad i = W_{77}, B_{77} \tag{17.22}$$

For if $\pi_i(Q^0) < 0$ good i will not be produced, and if $\pi_i(Q^0) > 0$ producers who treat prices parametrically will wish to produce an unbounded amount. Since available inputs are finite this could not be consistent with the actions of agents being compatible.

(c) Let X_i^{76} ($i = W, B, L$) be the difference between the demand for 1976 wheat, barley and labour and the amount of these three goods available. From elementary theory we know that this difference depends on prices and on endowments, i.e.

$$X_i^{76} = X_i^{76}(Q, \overline{W}_{76}, \overline{B}_{76}), \qquad i = W, B, L$$

Let $\overline{Q}^0$ be the set of vectors Q for which equations (17.17) and (17.22) hold. We already know that any candidate for equilibrium must belong to that set. But if Q^0 is a member of $\overline{Q}^0$ then, whatever the amounts of 1977 wheat and barley demanded, producers are willing to supply them, i.e. Q^0 is compatible with equilibrium on these markets. This of course is a consequence of our postulate that there are constant returns to scale. Hence

$$X_i^{77}(Q, \overline{W}_{76}, \overline{B}_{76}) = 0 \text{ all } Q \text{ in } \overline{Q}^0 \qquad i = W, B \tag{17.23}$$

where X_W^{77} for instance is the excess demand for 1977 wheat.

By accounting, no one can spend more than they get from sales. So one has, in view of equation (17.23),

$$P_W^{76} X_W^{76} + P_B^{76} X_B^{76} + W X_L^{76} \equiv 0 \text{ for all } Q^0 \text{ in } \overline{Q}^0 \tag{17.24}$$

If Q^0 is an equilibrium we need $X_i^{76} = 0$, $i = W, B, L$. In view of relation (17.24) it suffices to search for Q^0 in $\overline{Q}^0$ such that

$$X_i^{76}(Q, \overline{W}_{76}, \overline{B}_{76}) = 0 \qquad i = W, B \tag{17.25}$$

(d) Now (17.17), (17.22) and (17.25) give five equations in the five unknowns in Q. If we assume that at all Q there is a positive demand for 1977 wheat and 1977 barley, then one can prove under the usual neo-classical conditions on preferences that there exists Q^0 with strictly positive components which satisfies all the equations. This solution need not be unique.

(e) When we have calculated an equilibrium Q^0 we know everything we want to know. We know the technique of production which will be used, we know the composition of output of 1977 goods, and if we choose wheat as numéraire we can calculate the common wheat own rates of return of wheat and barley. Sraffa can calculate standard commodities. However, our solution, and so the rate of return in terms of wheat, will not in general be independent of the amount of 1976 wheat or barley history has provided.

The last observation serves as a useful transition to the special Sraffa case. We now stipulate equation (17.17). As I have already noticed, this means that we lose one unknown and so it looks as if we have too many (*not too few*) equations. The model is over-determined. This is exactly what common sense tells us. For suppose that a single element of $\bar{Q}^0$ (i.e. Q_1^0) solves the equations which we have just discussed for given $\bar{W}_{76}, \bar{B}_{76}$. Suppose Q_1^0 does not satisfy equation (17.21). The imposing of (17.21) makes it impossible to find an equilibrium. So we must turn the question upside down and ask: is there a set of histories $(\bar{W}_{76}, \bar{B}_{76})$ such that if Q^0 is calculated for any one of them (17.21) also holds? I want to emphasise that this question must be faced whether you are a neo-Ricardian or not. For it cannot be part of the doctrine that you are uninterested whether there is enough 1976 wheat and barley to meet demand. Yet Sraffa does not consider this matter.

So the neo-classical economist who is always happy to consider interesting special cases sets to work to find a proper equilibrium for Sraffa:

(a) If (17.21) then we now confine attention to (17.17′). Let

$$Q(R) = (RP_W, RP_B, P_W, P_B, W)$$

so that conditions (17.22) now become (17.12), which we write as

$$\pi_i(Q(R)) = 0, \qquad i = W_{77}, B_{77} \tag{17.22′}$$

For given R we have (17.17′) and (17.22′), i.e. three equations. If R is properly chosen they suffice to give us the equilibrium values: $(P_W(R), P_B(R), W(R))$.

(b) From what has just been said we can write

$$X_i^{76} = \tilde{X}_i^{76}(R, \overline{W}_{76}, \overline{B}_{76}) \qquad i = W, B$$

whenever $Q(R)$ satisfies (17.17′) and (17.22′). For then, given R, all relative prices are known. So now condition (17.25) becomes

$$\tilde{X}_i^{76}(R, \overline{W}_{76}, \overline{B}_{76}) = 0, \qquad i = W, B \qquad (17.25')$$

and as we expected, this is two equations in one unknown when the availability of 1976 wheat and barley are arbitrarily given by the past.

(c) In general, then, we must make one of $\overline{W}_{76}$ and $\overline{B}_{76}$ into an unknown. Say we fix $\overline{B}_{76}$ and now search by means of (17.25′) for the two unknowns $\overline{W}^{76}$ and R. If a solution can be found write it $W_{76}(\overline{B}_{76})$, $R(\overline{B}_{76})$ to indicate that it depends on B_{76}. Notice that $R(\overline{B}_{76})$ will have to fall into the range for which (17.17′) and (17.22′) give positive prices. By varying $\overline{B}_{76}$ the neo-classical economist can generate all histories which are compatible with Sraffa's demands. If Sraffa lands on an island whose history does not belong to this set, he will be out of luck.

But the neo-Ricardian followers will not yet be satisfied. For the equilibrium R is still not independent of endowments. So if we are to help them, we will have to be more special still.

Let

$$Z = P_W(R)X_W^{76} + P_B(R)X_B^{76}$$

The reader will verify that Z is the difference (in value) between investment and savings when we regard the expenditure of producers on 1976 wheat and barley as investment. Next let all households be alike in preferences and let their total endowment of leisure be equal to one. Then

$$V = P_W(R)W_{76} + P_B(R)B_{76} + w(R)$$

is the total 'wealth of households'. Textbook economics tells us that given Sraffa's equation (17.17') and (17.22') we can write[2]

$$Z = Z(R, V) \tag{17.26}$$

Now let us replace equation (17.25) by the two equations (17.26) = 0 and $X_W^{76} = 0$. Clearly if they are satisfied, then $X_B^{76} = 0$ and $X_L^{76} = 0$ also.

Now to the specialisation. If householders have preferences such that the proportion of their wealth spent on any good is independent of wealth (their preferences are homothetic) then (17.26) may be written as

$$Z = g(R)V \tag{17.26'}$$

For, recall that there are constant returns to scale. But now (17.26) = 0 and $V \neq 0$ implies

$$g(R) = 0 \tag{17.27}$$

so that we have at last found one equation in one unknown. History does not enter into the determination of equilibrium R. But history still matters since we must still satisfy $X_W^{76} = 0$ and we have already 'determined' R^0.

This new specialisation of assumptions has been fully incorporated into the neo-classical framework. Notice, in particular, that at the R^0 which solves equation (17.27) all the deep neo-classical marginal productivity relations of equation (17.14) hold. Not only do they hold but we need them since we know that they are only a rewriting of the Sraffa price equations when there is a choice of technique. This is hardly surprising. It was a neo-classical simplification (which Keynes disliked) to propose that R was 'determined by savings and investment'.

But even now the followers are restless and unhappy. For the function $g(\cdot)$ depends on technology since the producer's demand for input is not independent of technology. So let us see whether the neo-classical economist can find an island where that is not true.

Begin by looking for islands in which the past is like the present.

---

[2] Excess demand depends on prices, R and on wealth. But prices are known once R is, i.e. they are determined by R so that Z depends only on R or V, if producers are always in equilibrium.

That is if R etc. are today's (1976) equilibrium solutions then they were also yesterday's equilibrium solutions. Next, we distinguish between households that in 1976 are repaid the wheat and barley 1975 which they lent to producers and households who are paid the wages for their 1975 labour. The former group is called the capitalist group and the latter the workers. Capitalists receive

$$R[P_W(R)(a_{WW}\overline{W}_{76} + a_{WB}\overline{B}_{76}) + P_B(R)(a_{BW}\overline{W}_{76} + a_{BB}\overline{B}^{76})]$$

(17.28)

of which they spend nothing on 1976 wheat or barley, i.e. they reinvest the lot. Workers receive their wages and they spend all of them on 1976 wheat and barley. So Z may be written as

$$P_W(R)(a_{WW}W_{77} + a_{WB}B_{77}) + P_B(R)(a_{BW}W_{77} + a_{BB}B_{77}) - (17.28)$$

(17.29)

where W_{77}, B_{77} are the outputs of wheat and barley for 1977.

Now we have the next restriction on the kind of island which we are prepared to visit. Not only should the past be like the present but the future is also restricted. In particular, we shall only admit solutions to be equilibrium solutions if for a predetermined number G we have

$$\frac{W_{77}}{\overline{W}_{76}} = \frac{B_{77}}{\overline{B}_{76}} = G$$

(17.30)

Notice that equation (17.30) together with $Z = 0$, $X_W^{76} = 0$ are now three equations in three unknowns (R, $\overline{W}_{76}$, $\overline{B}_{76}$) so that we may be able to tie down a unique history which the island must have had in order to have Sraffa's (17.21) and the stipulated future. Moreover, in view of what has been said we now have

$$Z = (G - R)K$$

where K is the term in square brackets in (17.28). Hence for $Z = 0$ and $K > 0$, one needs $G = R$ for an equilibrium. Hence in islands of the kind we have described, R in equilibrium must have the value G whatever the technological possibilities are.

Now there is an interpretation of G connected with 'animal spirits' which would cause difficulties to the neo-classical theory.

But interpretation here is of no importance. What has been shown is this. The fundamental neo-classical approach of rational choice and market clearing prices is quite unaffected by the successive specialisations which we have discussed. At no stage do the variations impinge on the marginal productivity conditions. Moreover, the last variation which we have discussed does not lead to the conclusion: the equilibrium R is independent of endowments or technology. On the contrary, the dependence on endowments (history) is admitted and one has to search for just that combination of endowments for which a consistent story can be told. This 'right' combination of course depends on technology. I find it hard to believe that there is anyone who has followed this section who can claim that the last story is not a very special case of the first story or who can continue to believe that there are unknowns for which the neo-classical model cannot provide an equilibrium account.

Before leaving this part of the argument, let me briefly dispose of some wrong-headed objections:

(a) I have admitted that the special Sraffa island must have a special history. But then is it not true that we cannot talk of the marginal product of some input? For if there were a little more of one input, history would be different and equilibrium price would be different and so there would be no neo-classical marginal product. This argument (see, for example, Robinson 1974) is false. In the neo-classical model producers treat prices parametrically and the consequences of their actions are calculated by them at prevailing prices. If that is so, then for their actions to be equilibrium actions requires that there are no other actions available which on the hypothesis of given prices are more profitable. This calculation does not require an actual increase in factors but simply a hypothetical one. Of course producers may be wrong when they conjecture that prices are independent of their own actions. This would not invalidate the importance of marginal products in their calculations and in our theory of their actions. If producers are not to be wrong in their conjecture, they must be small relatively to the economy (see Hahn 1978). In both cases, producers calculate the marginal worth of inputs at given prices.

(b) Sraffa does not require a marginal productivity theory as far as chapter XII. This is correct but only because he treats technology as given. It should be noted that there is a paradox here. For the equalisation of the profit rate, stipulated by Sraffa, can only be sensible for a world of rational and greedy producers. But rational and greedy producers will compare gains and losses and will not be satisfied with a given technique if a better one is available.

(c) In the very special case we looked at, the equilibrium R was independent of technology. Is it not true, therefore, of this very special case at best that the distribution of income has nothing to do with technology? Answer, no. For even here to calculate relative shares we need to know prices and the composition of output and both of these, as we know, depend on technology. Nor does the fact that in the special case R is known once G is known remove the importance of the marginal productivity conditions. For now we must find the technique which is compatible with the given R and in doing so we shall find equilibrium relative prices.

(d) It is true that in the very special case the equilibrium R is known once G is. But in less specialised stories, e.g. that leading to equation (17.27), that is not the case. There relative prices, the composition of output and R must be found simultaneously. But in any case, as I have shown, there is no difficulty for neoclassical economies with the special case.

(e) Sraffa does not discuss how the composition of output is to be explained. Neo-classical theory does. But in my account I have treated endowments as unknown. This is required for the Sraffa price equations to make sense in a world where inputs precede output. But neo-classical economics can study the economy for an arbitrary history, Sraffa cannot.

(f) The neo-Ricardians attach significance to the fact that for any arbitrary R in a given range one can find Sraffa prices and so R cannot have anything to do with technology or marginal productivity. This is perfectly correct for a fixed coefficient technology where marginal products do not exist in any case. But with a variable technology, the given R will affect the technique of production precisely in such a way as to lead to the marginal productivity conditions (17.14) to be satisfied.

(g) Let me now return to equation (17.8') which I reproduce below

$$\hat{P}(r) = a_0 [I + RA + R^2 A^2 + \dots] \hat{w}(r) \tag{17.8'}$$

from which we deduce that no price is simply related to r. Now let us quote Sraffa more fully. 'The reversals in the direction of the movements of relative prices (when r changes) in the face of unchanged methods of production cannot be reconciled with any notion of capital as a measurable quantity independent of distribution and prices.' Hence there is no 'independent measure of the quantity of capital which could be used, without arguing in a circle, for the determination of prices and of shares in distribution' (Sraffa 1960, p. 38). Let me couple with this a quotation from Frank Knight (1921): 'If we speak of "factors" at all there will thus not be three but a quite indefinitely large number of them.'

Now, in a properly formulated neo-classical theory the vector $(\overline{W}_{76}, \overline{B}_{76})$ helps to determine equilibrium prices and distribution. Suppose that instead of the vector we were given a number K where

$$K = K(\overline{W}_{76}, \overline{B}_{76})$$

(so K may be thought of as a measure of capital stock). Then there may be all sorts of values of $\overline{W}_{76}, \overline{B}_{76}$ which give the same K. But we already know that different values of $(\overline{W}_{76}, \overline{B}_{76})$ in general generate different equilibria. So even if for each $(\overline{W}_{76}, \overline{B}_{76})$ there is a unique equilibrium, knowing K would not allow us to 'determine' equilibrium. This argument, the reader will notice, is quite damaging enough even when K, as here, is independent of R. Moreover, notice that the argument is entirely neo-classical.

On the other hand, suppose that in fact there is a number C (a measure of capital) defined by

$$C = C(R, \overline{W}_{76}, \overline{B}_{76})$$

For instance, C may be the value of the endowment calculated at the Sraffa prices for a given R. If now we treat as given C and W_{76}, B_{76} then we shall have one equation too many, since the information is equivalent to being told R. But that of course is not 'arguing in a circle'.

Lastly, suppose that we are given C and nothing else. Then the investment savings equation (17.26) can be written as

$$Z(R, C) = 0$$

which now, since C is fixed, is one equation in one unknown. The condition that the wheat market also clears and the definition

$$C = P_W(R)\overline{W}_{76} + P_B(R)\overline{B}_{76}$$

then give us what the amount of 1976 wheat and barley would have to be in order to have a consistent story. Once again 'arguing in a circle' is not the problem. The problem is the sense to be made of C being given from outside.

All of this has nothing to do with Sraffa's rather special equation (17.8′) or indeed with the circumstance that the relative prices are complicated functions of R. The point is much simpler. In general, there does not exist a function from the vector of endowments to the scalars such that knowledge of the scalar (and of preferences and of technology) is sufficient to allow one to determine a neo-classical equilibrium. If you put it the other way round, it is even more obvious. In general, the neo-classical equilibrium can be found given the vector of endowments which may have, say, 10^8 components. It would be surprising if there were a single number which gives the same information as the 10^8 dimensional vector. In fact, sometimes and in very special cases, this surprising property holds. But neo-classical economists have shown these special cases to be without interest.

So why the fuss? The answer is partly that Sraffa and his followers are much concerned with the history of thought and with economists long since deceased. After all, there have been many attempts to find a scalar representation of the endowment vector, e.g. the period of production. These earlier economists had no rigorously formulated model to help them and they got into trouble. But neo-classical economics is alive and kicking and has not got stuck in Böhm-Bowerkian arithmetic or even in Wicksellian puzzles. Another part of the answer is to be found in the simple neo-classical model, in particular the postwar growth models. Even if some authors regarded these as parables, textbooks testify that they can be misused. Sraffa and his followers deserve the credit for making such misuse less likely in the future. On the other hand, I doubt that they are correct in their view that the simple (essentially one capital good) models are useless. It is perfectly true, as we have seen, that one can always construct examples where the answer of the simple model is false. But we use simple models (e.g. macroeconomics) to gain insights of a certain kind. Simplification is never without cost and the cost is sometimes loss of rigour. It remains to be shown that the cost is too high in this instance, i.e. that in actual problem application the chance of large mistakes is great. I know no Sraffian who has shown this. Lastly, the fuss is to be understood by a persistent misunderstanding by Sraffians of what a 'marginal productivity theory of distribution' is. In particular, they have not been content with enunciating paradoxes of aggregation but have proceeded to use essentially neo-classical procedures to tilt at some fictitious neo-classical windmills.

The Sraffian picture of neo-classical theory is this. At any moment of time we can observe something physical called the stock of capital (K) as well as the amount of labour (L). There is a concave production function

$$Y = F(K, L)$$

where Y is output. In a neo-classical equilibrium all inputs are used and must be paid their marginal products. The latter are known once (K, L) are known. Hence the rate of profit of capital, the real wage and the distribution of income are all known once $F(\ )$, K and L are known. The concavity of F further implies that the rate of return on capital is non-increasing (generally decreasing) in K. This construction, to be called the parable, Sraffians claim to be not logically watertight except in the single good economy. In this they are generally correct.

But first let us notice a difficulty with the parable which has nothing to do with aggregation. So consider a genuine single good economy — say a wheat economy. Knowing the endowment of wheat (here K) is not enough for the claimed results of the parable. For we must know how much of it will be used in production and how much of it will be consumed. Without a saving–investment equation, the equilibrium rate of profit cannot be found. Hence as already noted, even the most primitive neo-classical model claims to be short of equations when only the endowment and the production functions are known. There is no way that one could here claim that an independently given K determines the equilibrium rate of return etc.

This is a point on which Sraffians seem sometimes to be in a muddle, so I make the point again. Even when an aggregate like K logically exists, one would have to know how much of it is used in production before being able to claim that one can determine the equilibrium payments to inputs. If K is a substance which can only be used in production (and not consumed) then K is not the same 'good' as is output Y and we gain a new unknown price, namely that of K, which can now differ from the price of Y. Once again we need one more equation. Not many people have read Solow's famous paper (1956) as far as its dual formulation to see this. One concludes that there exists no neo-classical formulation whether in parable or single good form which claims to determine equilibrium distribution from a knowledge of endowments and production conditions alone.

If that is understood, then the question naturally arises as to what neo-classical propositions are at risk when it is granted that Professor Gorman's necessary conditions for capital aggregation are extremely unlikely (Gorman 1959, 1968). For instance, from what we already know every neo-classical economist can agree that the 'equilibrium rate of profit' could be determined outside the sphere of production and that whether he uses a parable or not. For there is nothing in neoclassical theory which excludes the possibility that workers consume and do not save which together with the postulate of steady state equilibrium is enough to give an example of such a theory. Indeed, at first sight, no neo-classical proposition seems at risk.

But something called 'the marginal productivity theory of distribution' is said by neo-Ricardians to be at risk. As far as I have been able to gather this is claimed to be so because one cannot arrive at a measure of 'capital' which is uncontaminated by market happenings. A fair amount has already been said in this paper on this matter and Bliss (1975, chapters 5, 8) has lucidly made the case again. So I can be brief and fairly dogmatic.

A crucial and beautiful theorem in neo-classical economics goes as follows. (I am considering a world with a long but finite future). Consider the set of all goods which an economy could feasibly consume. In the definition of goods, proper attention is paid to the date of their availability. In the definition of feasibility, proper attention is paid to technological knowhow and the initial endowment of goods. If this set is convex, bounded and closed then every feasible efficient consumption plan can be 'supported' by a set of prices. A consumption plan is efficient when no other feasible plan gives more of one good without giving less of another. A plan is 'supported' by prices if at these prices profit maximising producers treating prices parametrically would choose productions which result in the goods of the given consumption plan. It is a mathematical truth that if the feasible set has a differentiable boundary, then every efficient consumption plan is supported by prices unique up to scalar multiplication. It is now a fact that when we introduce the given preferences of agents and take them to be convex and stipulate non-satiation then every Pareto-efficient consumption plan, i.e. a plan such that no other feasible plan is higher in one agent's preferences without being lower in some agent's preferences, is also an efficient consumption plan. Moreover, there are again prices such that if they rule there would exist a distribution of wealth between agents which would ensure that those prices were in fact the neo-classical equilibrium prices. Lastly, under the given assumptions every competitive equilibrium is Pareto efficient.

These results are theorems and they are not at risk. They are not based on any aggregation hypothesis. They contain all valid neo-classical sentences using the words marginal productivity. Under the differentiability assumption the support prices are the gradient vector of the feasible set at the given point. Elementary calculus will explain why it makes no sense to argue that undertaking the (infinitesimal) changes which give us the gradient vector will change the support prices.

Suppose, for the sake of exposition, that there is a single consumption good at each date. Choose the consumption good at a date 0 as numéraire. Then the price of consumption good date 1 in terms of numéraire is the (marginal) rate of transformation of consumption date 0 into consumption date 1 at the given point. Subtracting unity gives us also the rate of return in terms of numéraire. At the support price profits are maximised at the given production plans and the economy is in equilibrium. The rate of return in terms of numéraire on any asset which is used or held must be the same. Then the same must be true of any composite bundle of assets bought at the going prices. Hence, the defined rate of return (minus one) measures the marginal rate at which consumption at date 0 can be transformed into consumption at date 1. Putting it this way does not add anything to what we already know from the theorem. Pasinetti (1969, pp. 525–526) however, is wrong to think it a tautology, because

(a) There would be no sense in the claim that the rates of return in terms of numéraire are *determined* by marginal productivity (marginal transformation rates). To know the latter, we must know where on the feasible set we are.

(b) The fundamental theorem is not in conflict with special classical saving hypothesis.

(c) Strictly the latter is embodied in preferences and we need to know these to get rates of return.

If the frontier is not differentiable, then it is not differentiable and support prices are not unique after normalisation. But left and right hand gradient vectors have already been discussed and the reader can check that the neo-classical can continue happily and safely.

There is thus no joy for the neo-Ricardians along this route. But what of reswitching?

Towards the end of his book Sraffa writes:

> We have been assuming that in a system of single product industries only one way of producing each commodity is available with the result that changes in distribution can have no effect on the method of production employed. (Sraffa 1960, p. 81)

What could be clearer than that? Sraffa says that he has been postulating a world of fixed coefficients and he is about to drop the postulate. That is of course why I have repeatedly referred to this chapter. It is the only one which can conceivably be relevant to a critique of neo-classical economics.

Sraffa proceeds in an impeccable neo-classical manner. That is, he studies an economy where there is a choice of technique and where the choice is made by greedy (i.e. profit maximising) agents. This suggests at the outset that switching paradoxes are unlikely to invalidate any properly formulated neo-classical propositions which invoke marginal productivity.

If at R the Sraffa prices for technique (A, a_0) are the same as those for technique (B, b_0) and if all other techniques make it impossible to earn R times the value of non-labour inputs, then that R and the associated Sraffa price vector is terms of labour is called a switch point. That is, every agent is there indifferent between the two techniques. From this definition one sees that

$$P = a_0 [I + RA + R^2 A^2 + \ldots .]$$

$$P = b_0 [I + RB + R^2 B^2 + \ldots .]$$

and subtracting one of these equations from the other we have the polynomial

$$0 = (a_0 - b_0) + R(a_0 A - b_0 B) + R^2 (a_0 A^2 - b_0 B^2) + \ldots$$

which plainly can have a number of real roots R. So there may be many values of R at which rational producers are indifferent between the two techniques. Suppose they are R' and R'' with $R' < R''$. Then when $R' < R''$, suppose technique (A, a_0) is more profitable than (B, b_0). Then at $R' = R''$ there is a switch to technique (B, b_0) and for R such that $R' < R < R''$, (B, b_0) is more profitable. But when $R = R''$ the two techniques are again equally profitable. Then plainly we cannot say that one technique is more capital intensive than another *and* that capital intensity is inversely related to R. So the parable can get into difficulties since it stipulates a concave production function in (K, L).

It is worth noting that reswitching cannot arise in the case where the production frontier is differentiable (see Garegnani 1970, pp. 412–14). On the other hand, differentiability does not ensure a well behaved parable production function. In particular, it does not ensure that we can order techniques by their capital intensity and that the latter is inversely related to R.

What could be simpler or more neo-classical? What is at risk is a simplified neo-classical comparative equilibrium analysis and a simplified neo-classical dynamics. Sraffa's point was a fine technical insight into neo-classical economics but the Sraffians and possibly Sraffa himself have not exploited it. Matters were further confused by a straightforward mistake by an eminent neo-classical economist even though he quickly made amends (see Samuelson 1962; Levhari 1965; Levhari and Samuelson 1966; Samuelson 1966).

There is no doubt that in neo-classical economics as in macroeconomics simple models are used in order to obtain definite answers and that these simple models will not survive logical scrutiny. Whether they can be useful none the less is a hard question which I cannot answer. But just as the multiplier collapses when fixed prices are not assumed so does the neo-classical parable claim that of two economies in Sraffian equilibrium, the one with the higher rate of interest (profit) will have the lower 'capital'–labour ratio. Nor can one argue that the economy with the higher interest rate will have lower consumption per head. All of this is simply a reiteration of the proposition that there is no valid aggregation of wheat and barley into something called capital. But unless one wishes to claim that aggregation is essential if a theory is to be called neo-classical, so that Arrow—Debreu for instance are not neo-classical, none of this has any bearing on the main issue of this lecture. Sraffa performed a service in showing how neo-classical arguments can be used to show neo-classical aggregation parables to be in logical difficulties. But that cannot help with a critique of marginal theory.

I have said that neither Sraffa nor his followers have made anything of reswitching. By this I mean that they have continued to believe that it is damaging to neo-classical equilibrium theory which it is not and have neglected various neo-classical adjustment theories which are certainly at risk. Certainly the famous Solow parable (Solow 1956) in which all equilibrium paths seek the steady state depends on just those possibilities of aggregation which reswitching examples show not to be available. Indeed, the circumstance that 'capital' consists of a number of hetero- geneous objects and that only in very special cases can their relative prices to be taken as constant causes considerable difficulties to the 'invisible hand'. Professor Robinson was right in arguing that capital aggregation in the parable where there is only one asset (money is not modelled) has had the consequence that no agent needs to have expectations concerning the future, especially future relative prices, when he takes decisions today. This is a very limiting consequence of the simplified model and suggests that something essential has been missed out. But it was left to neo- classical economists to attempt to study the precise pathology of the price mechanism which may result when heterogeneous inputs are modelled explicitly.

The relevant conclusion is straightforward. Reswitching and the general impossibility of capital aggregation have no bearing on anything which can be called marginal productivity theory. Such a theory concerns an economy in full neo-classical equilibrium which, I have repeatedly argued, has nothing to fear from anything in Sraffa's or in his followers' work. But on the manner in which such an equilibrium is supposed to come about, neo-classical theory is highly unsatisfactory. Sraffa's work shows that certain simplified routes are very risky and not free from logical difficulties. The remarkable fact is that neither he nor the Sraffians have made anything of this.

REFERENCES

Arrow, K. J. and Hahn, F. H. 1971. *General Competitive Analysis*, San Francisco, Holden-Day; Edinburgh, Oliver and Boyd

Bliss, C. J. 1975. *Capital Theory and the Distribution of Income*, Amsterdam, North-Holland; New York, American Elsevier

Dobb, M. H. 1973. *Theories of Value and Distribution since Adam Smith: Ideology and Economic Theory*, Cambridge, Cambridge University Press

Eatwell, J. L. 1974. Controversies in the theory of surplus value: old and new, *Science and Society*, Autumn

Eatwell, J. L. 1975. Mr Sraffa's standard commodity and the rate of exploitation, *Quarterly Journal of Economics*, November

Eatwell, J. L. 1977. The irrelevance of returns to scale in Sraffa's analysis, *Journal of Economic Literature*, March

Garegnani, P. 1960. *Il Capitale Nelle Teorie della Distribuzione*, Milan, Guiffrè

Garegnani, P. 1966. Switching of techniques, *Quarterly Journal of Economics*, November

Garegnani, P. 1970. Heterogeneous capital, the production function and the theory of distribution, *Review of Economic Studies*, October

Gorman, W. M. 1959. Separable utility and aggregation, *Econometrica*, July

Gorman, W. M. 1968. Measuring the quantities of fixed factors in Wolfe, J. N. (ed.), *Value, Capital and Growth*, Edinburgh, Edinburgh University Press

Hahn, F. H. 1975. Revival of political economy: the wrong issues and the wrong argument, *Economic Record*, September

Hahn, F. H. 1978. On non-Walrasian equilibria, *Review of Economic Studies*, January

Harcourt, G. C. 1975a. Decline and rise: The revival of (classical) political economy, *Economic Record*, September

Harcourt, G. C. 1975b. Revival of political economy: a further comment, *Economic Record*, September

Keynes, J. M. 1936. *The General Theory of Employment, Interest and Money*, London, Macmillan

Knight, F. H. 1921. *Risk, Uncertainty and Profit*, Boston, Houghton Mifflin

Levhari, D. 1965. A nonsubstitution theorem and switching of techniques, *Quarterly Journal of Economics*, February

Levhari, D. and Samuelson, P. A. 1966. The nonswitching theorem is false, *Quarterly Journal of Economics*, November

Pasinetti, L. L. 1966. Changes in the rate of profit and switches of techniques, *Quarterly Journal of Economics*, November

Pasinetti, L. L. 1969. Switches of technique and the 'rate of return' in capital theory, *Economic Journal*, September

Robertson, D. H. 1931. Wage-grumbles, in *Economic Fragments*, London, P. H. King

Robinson, J. V. 1960–80. *Collected Economic Papers, Vols II–V*, Oxford, Basil Blackwell

Robinson, J. V. 1974. *History versus Equilibrium*, London, Thames Polytechnic

Roncaglia, A. 1978. *Sraffa and the Theory of Prices*, Chichester, Wiley

Samuelson, P. A. 1962. Parable and realism in capital theory: the surrogate production function, *Review and Economic Studies*, June

Samuelson, P. A. 1966. A summing up, *Quarterly Journal of Economics*, November

Solow, R. M. 1956. A contribution to the theory of economic growth, *Quarterly Journal of Economics*, February

Sraffa, P. 1932. Dr Hayek on money and capital, *Economic Journal*, March

Sraffa, P. 1960. *Production of Commodities by means of Commodities: Prelude to a Critique of Economic Theory*, Cambridge, Cambridge University Press

Index